NUMBER TWO HUN

MW00713079

The Old Far

CALCULATED ON A NEW AND IMPROVED PLAN FOR THE YEAR OF OUR LORD

2005

BEING 1ST AFTER LEAP YEAR AND (UNTIL JULY 4) 229TH YEAR OF AMERICAN INDEPENDENCE

Fitted for Boston and the New England states, with special corrections and calculations to answer for all the United States.

Containing, besides the large number of Astronomical Calculations and the Farmer's Calendar for every month in the year, a variety of

NEW, USEFUL, & ENTERTAINING MATTER.

Established in 1792 by Robert B. Thomas

The most completely lost of all days is that on which one has not laughed.

–Sébastien-Roch Nicolas de Chamfort, French writer (1741–1794)

Cover T.M. registered in U.S. Patent Office

Copyright 2004 by Yankee Publishing Incorporated
ISSN 0078-4516

Library of Congress
Card No. 56-29681

Original wood engraving by Randy Miller

Address all editorial correspondence to: THE OLD FARMER'S ALMANAC, DUBLIN, NH 03444

Create the perfect ambiance with Yankee Candle® Housewarmer® scents for holidays and every day.

Scents for the Seasons

MacIntosh™

You can almost hear it crunch—the true scent of crisp, fresh apples—Uplifting.

> *An old weather proverb states, "If autumn leaves are slow to fall, prepare for a cold winter."*

Harvest®

A cozy blend of warm sweetness and crisp spices—Comforting.

> *The Harvest Moon is the full Moon closest to the autumnal equinox (when day and night are of equal length).*

YANKEE CANDLE

yankeecandle.com

Pumpkin Pie

Warm pumpkin filling with cinnamon and nutmeg, baked to perfection in a flaky crust.

Months that start on a Sunday always have a Friday the 13th.

Cranberry Chutney

Savour the sweet yet tangy aroma of this cranberry treat.

Native Americans brewed cranberry mixtures to draw poison from arrow wounds. They also pounded cranberries into a paste and mixed the paste with dried meat to extend the life of the meat.

Holiday Bayberry™

A scent to celebrate—the traditional evergreen aroma is infused with the glow of seasonal spices.

Tradition says that you can expect good fortune throughout the coming year if you burn a bayberry candle all the way down on New Year's Eve.

Home for the Holidays™

A zesty potpourri of the season's best: balsam fir and cinnamon spices—Uplifting.

The top-selling Christmas trees, as reported by U.S. growers, are Scotch pine, Douglas fir, white pine, and balsam fir, in that order.

Visit Almanac.com through December for sensational seasonal offers from YANKEE CANDLE®

Contents

The Old Farmer's Almanac • 2005

continued on page 6

Endless Summer

Still have a passion for all that's good about summer? Succulent peaches. Juicy pears and plums. Tangy fresh cherries and all the fruity favorites of the sunny season. The flavors of summertime are yours to enjoy any time of year with Ball® Home Canning Products. Sprinkle on a little Fruit-Fresh® Produce Protector and you'll capture the color and flavor of fruits and vegetables just as nature intended. It's a delicious and nutritious way to indulge your passion. Make it an endless summer.

Ball®

Home Canning

Bring Out Your Best™

Available where Home Canning supplies are sold.
Need advice? Ask the Home Canning experts. Call 1-800-240-3340.

www.homecanning.com   www.fruit-fresh.com

"It's so easy, I just open the door and step in..."

...I really used to enjoy having a bath

but I realized as I got older that the fear of slipping, or the effort of pulling myself up after I had finished bathing was becoming a real problem...

Premier Bathrooms has the largest range of walk-in bath tubs in the country, and buying one helped me regain my independence."

Premier BATHROOMS™

For further details or to receive your FREE brochure
CALL NOW TOLL FREE
1-800-578-2899

To Patrons

Who Reads This Almanac?

Have you ever wondered who reads this Almanac (that is, other than you)? We did. Of course, we had some general ideas about the estimated 18 million of you who peruse these pages every year. But we wondered, for example, how many of you are farmers. How did you come to know about the Almanac? What do you like most about it? And what, if anything, would you like to see us do differently?

In 2003, we put these and other questions to several thousand readers in a survey. Here is some of what we learned:

■ 56 percent of you are between the ages of 25 and 54. (Just as we suspected, you're *not* all seniors.)

■ You live in all 50 states and all 10 Canadian provinces. 26 percent of U.S. readers use our Southern edition, 17 percent use our Western one, and the rest use our National version. Canadians make up 7 percent of our total readership (they use the special Canadian edition).

■ 57 percent of you are women.

■ 58 percent of you own no more than an acre of land (which suggests that you live in a small town or suburb).

■ About 11 percent of you are small farmers or ranchers, with more than one but fewer than 50 acres, living in southern or western states.

■ Your favorite pastimes are gardening, cooking, reading, caring for pet(s), collecting antiques, being outdoors (fishing, hunting, hiking, camping), and exploring the Internet.

■ 45 percent of you discovered this Almanac in the home of a friend or relative (that's what friends are for!), and 36 percent of you found it on a newsstand (further proof that the content herein *is* news).

■ Weather forecasts and features are your favorite parts of this Almanac, followed by gardening tips, amusing stories and folklore, and little-known facts. (Marketing researchers call you "information seekers.")

–Gil Martinez

Janice Stillman
(13th Editor since 1792)

■ 58 percent of you want us to keep on being a general-interest publication addressing a variety of topics.

■ 60 percent of you refer to this Almanac at least ten times per year (as we say, this is a book to be read all year long), and 53 percent of you spend at least four hours with each issue.

■ 64 percent of you share your copy with at least one other person. (Thanks, and please remember to tell them where you bought it.)

■ 68 percent of you have discussed an Almanac article with a friend. (Thanks again, and keep talking!)

continued

The __affordable__ way to keep insects from spoiling your time outdoors!

Shown with our optional Patio Lights

Cool Shade and UV Protection, too!

Corner Zippers Offer Easy Entry

Factory-Direct Prices Save You Hundreds of Dollars!

Now Enjoy Your Deck or Patio __BUG-FREE!__
... with the SunSetter Screen Room!

Forget annoying "bug zappers" and smelly citronella candles. Now get the __best protection__ from flies, mosquitoes, and other insects — day or night — with a SunSetter Screen Room. Mounted on a SunSetter Awning, this great Screen Room creates a beautiful **"outdoor room"** that guards you from insects, showers, UV rays, and scorching hot sun. (**It can be as much as 20 degrees cooler under a SunSetter!**) You'll get far more use and enjoyment out of your deck or patio,

because you control the weather — and the bugs! With sizes and colors to fit every home and decor, a SunSetter Screen Room will give you years of trouble-free service. It's backed by a full **5-Year Warranty**, and a **90-Day No-Risk Money-Back Guarantee of Satisfaction**. Best of all, you'll save hundreds of dollars on your Screen Room. Let us send you a complete **FREE Information Kit and Video,** without any obligation.

Good Housekeeping Promises

Awning available separately... add a Screen Room anytime! Complete protection from hot sun, showers, and insects!

- ● __Low__ Factory-Direct Prices
- ● Easy Payment Plans
- ● No-Risk, Money-Back Home Trial
- ● Superb Quality, 5-Year Limited Warranty

Call Today for a __FREE__ Catalog & Video:
Toll Free: 1-800-876-8060, ext. 2927
24 hours a day, 7 days a week

☑ **Yes, please send me your FREE catalog and video on SunSetter Screen Rooms and Retractable Awnings.**

Name _____

Address _____

City _____ State _____ Zip _____

E-mail address _____

Important: Be sure to include your e-mail to learn about specials and sales!

SunSetter, Dept. 2927, 184 Charles St., Malden, MA 02148

SunSetter®
RETRACTABLE AWNINGS

Or visit us at www.screen-room.com

© 2004 SunSetter® Products

■ 85 percent of you with Internet access have visited www.almanac.com, our Web site. (Come again—and bring your friends.)

Our goal in tabulating this data is to use it to make this Almanac as much in tune with your 21st-century interests as we possibly can. (After all, we're "old" in name only.) In this issue, we've done that by providing you . . .

■ More weather information: winter and summer weather maps (page 64) and revised U.S. weather regions (page 68).

■ More navigation aids, including black tabs on the Weather and Calendar pages.

■ More suggestions on how to make better use of this Almanac through www.almanac.com. (See the "footers" that often appear on left-hand pages.)

When Robert B. Thomas founded this Almanac, he knew exactly who his readers were. (They were farmers, as was he.) That knowledge enabled him to tailor the contents of each issue to his readers' needs.

Two hundred and thirteen years later, our aim is the same. So, send us your comments—by regular mail or through the Feedback option at www.almanac.com—and let us know what you enjoy most about your Almanac. J.S., June 2004

However, it is by our works and not our words that we would be judged. These, we hope, will sustain us in the humble though proud station we have so long held in the name of

Your obedient servant,

Versatile <u>New</u> DR® FIELD and BRUSH MOWER...

cuts down and chops up tall, wiry field grasses — even 2-1/2"-thick hardwood saplings!

6-MONTH RISK-FREE TRIAL!

- **PERFECT FOR RECLAIMING** overgrown pastures, meadows, ditches, roadsides, fencelines, trails, pond edges, and woodlots of overgrown vegetation... <u>any</u> area too rough for ordinary mowers!

- **PIVOTING MOWER DECK** follows the ground without scalping. **MULCHING CHAMBER** shreds most vegetation into small pieces — so there's nothing to trip over or pick up like you get with hand-held brush cutters and sicklebar mowers.

  - **4-SPEEDS, POWER-REVERSE!** Your choice of engines up to 17 HP with electric-start!
    - **LIMITED-SLIP DIFFERENTIAL** for positive traction and easy turning.
      - **PLUS!** New SCOUT™ Model for smaller properties is HALF THE PRICE of our larger models!

The DR® CONVERTS in seconds without tools to a —

Pro-Style LAWN MOWER...

Powerful SNOW THROWER...

SNOW BLADE and more!

MADE IN USA
GSA Approved

For Full Details of the New Multi-Purpose DR® FIELD and BRUSH MOWER

CALL TOLL-FREE
1-800-736-1166

THE 2005 EDITION OF

The Old Farmer's Almanac

Established in 1792 and published every year thereafter

ROBERT B. THOMAS (1766–1846), *Founder*

YANKEE PUBLISHING INC.

EDITORIAL AND PUBLISHING OFFICES

P.O. Box 520, 1121 Main Street, Dublin, NH 03444
Phone: 603-563-8111 • Fax: 603-563-8252

EDITOR IN CHIEF: Judson D. Hale Sr.
EDITOR *(13th since 1792)*: Janice Stillman
ART DIRECTOR: Margo Letourneau
SENIOR EDITOR: Mare-Anne Jarvela
COPY EDITOR: Jack Burnett
SENIOR ASSOCIATE EDITOR: Heidi Stonehill
RESEARCH EDITOR: Martie Majoros
ASSISTANT EDITOR: Sarah Perreault
WEATHER GRAPHICS AND CONSULTATION:
AccuWeather, Inc.

PRODUCTION DIRECTOR: Susan Gross
PRODUCTION MANAGER: David Ziarnowski
SENIOR PRODUCTION ARTISTS: Lucille Rines,
Rachel Kipka, Nathaniel Stout

WEB SITE: WWW.ALMANAC.COM

CREATIVE DIRECTOR: Stephen O. Muskie
DESIGN COORDINATOR: Lisa Traffie
PROGRAMMER: Peter Rukavina

CONTACT US

We welcome your questions and comments about articles in and topics for this Almanac. Mail all editorial correspondence to Editor, The Old Farmer's Almanac, P.O. Box 520, Dublin, NH 03444-0520; fax us at 603-563-8252; or send e-mail to us at almanac@yankeepub.com. *The Old Farmer's Almanac* can not accept responsibility for unsolicited manuscripts and will not acknowledge any hardcopy queries or manuscripts that do not include a stamped and addressed return envelope.

The newsprint in this edition of *The Old Farmer's Almanac* consists of 23 percent recycled content. All printing inks used are soy-based. This product is recyclable. Consult local recycling regulations for the right way to do it.

Thank you for buying this Almanac!
We hope you find it new, useful, and entertaining.
Thanks, too, to everyone who had a hand in its creation, including advertisers, distributors, printers, and sales and delivery people.

OUR CONTRIBUTORS

Bob Berman, our astronomy editor, is the director of Overlook Observatory in Woodstock and Storm King Observatory in Cornwall, both in New York. In 1976, he founded the Catskill Astronomical Society. Bob will go a long way for a good look at the sky: He has led many aurora and eclipse expeditions, venturing as far as the Arctic and Antarctic.

Castle Freeman Jr., who lives in southern Vermont, has been writing the Almanac's "Farmer's Calendar" essays for more than 20 years. The essays come out of his longtime interest in wildlife and the outdoors, gardening, history, and the life of rural New England. His latest book is *My Life and Adventures* (St. Martin's Press, 2002).

George Greenstein, Ph.D., who has been the Almanac's astronomer for more than 25 years, is the Sidney Dillon Professor of Astronomy at Amherst College in Amherst, Massachusetts. His research has centered on cosmology, pulsars, and other areas of theoretical astrophysics, and on the mysteries of quantum mechanics. He has written three books and many magazine articles on science for the general public.

Celeste Longacre, our astrologer, often refers to astrology as "the world's second-oldest profession." A New Hampshire native, she has been a practicing astrologer for more than 25 years: "It is a study of timing, and timing is everything." Her book, *Love Signs* (Sweet Fern Publications, 1999), is available on her Web site, www.yourlovesigns.com.

Michael Steinberg, our meteorologist, has been forecasting weather for the Almanac since 1996. In addition to having college degrees in atmospheric science and meteorology, he brings a lifetime of experience to the task: He began making weather predictions when he attended the only high school in the world with weather Teletypes and radar.

No springs.
No air. No water.
No kidding!

You'll enjoy the miracle of **Weightless Sleep**™

Furniture components not included

No better bed than Tempur-Pedic.

Our Weightless Sleep bed embodies an *entirely new* sleep technology. It's recognized by NASA. And widely acclaimed by the media. It's the _only_ one recommended worldwide by more than 25,000 medical professionals. Moreover, our high-tech bed is preferred by countless stars and celebrities, people who demand the best.

Our scientists invented an amazing viscoelastic sleep surface: TEMPUR® pressure-relieving material. It _reacts_ to bodyshape, bodyweight, *bodyheat*. Nothing mechanical or electrical. Yet, it molds precisely to your every curve and angle.

Tempur-Pedic brings you a relaxing, energizing quality of sleep you've never experienced before. That's why 91% of our enthusiastic owners recommend us to friends and family.

Please call us toll-free, without the slightest obligation, for a FREE DEMONSTRATION KIT!

THE _ONLY_ MATTRESS RECOGNIZED BY NASA AND CERTIFIED BY THE SPACE FOUNDATION ✦

Free Sample/Free Video/Free Info
FREE IN-HOME TRYOUT CERTIFICATE

YOURS FOR THE ASKING!

BEST BUY

Tempur-Pedic Swedish Mattress
"This is the mattress that set the industry ahead."
—Consumers Digest

888-702-8557
Call toll-free or fax 866-795-9367

TEMPUR·PEDIC®
PRESSURE RELIEVING
SWEDISH MATTRESSES AND PILLOWS

Archeology proves the Bible

As a result of man's continual search for truth...

...archeological discoveries have unearthed many artifacts which establish Biblical records as both reliable and accurate.

The booklet "Archeology Proves the Bible," unveils these findings and confirms the validity of Bible truths—historic and prophetic.

The spade and pick of the archeologist have uncovered city ruins in the very locations in which the Bible places them!

Your confidence in God's Word will be confirmed and strengthened as you read this little booklet.

Send today for your FREE copy to:
"Archeology Proves the Bible"
Dawn Publications, Dept. F
East Rutherford, NJ 07073

1-800-234-DAWN
www.dawnbible.com

Tastes & Trends 2005

What's new, what's novel, and what's on people's minds in 2005? We've spent months researching and talking to experts about the fads, fashions, and farsighted ideas that define our life and times. Here is some of what we found.   *by Christine Schultz*

ON THE HOME FRONT

"In 50 years, I think the world is going to be full of robots."

–Rodney Brooks, cofounder, iRobot Corporation

A FACT OF LIFE

Family members now often communicate by sending electronic messages to each other in different rooms of the same house.

THE OUTSIDE STORY

With alfresco entertaining all the rage, the open-air living room has become one of the hottest trends in home design. U.S. and Canadian homeowners also are installing patios, decks, and courtyards in record numbers. The new spaces feature elaborate gardens, indoor/outdoor lounge furniture, sculptures, fountains, and fireplaces.

THE NEW HOME DECORATORS

Instead of hiring decorators to buy all-new furniture and art for their homes, people are enlisting "interior arrangers" to come in and move around what they already own. The craze, made popular by such TV shows as *Trading Spaces,* has found interest among newly moved families, downsizing divorcé(e)s, empty nesters, spring-cleaners, and home-owners looking for a change.

HOUSEHOLD HAUTE COUTURE

U.S. and Canadian consumers are demanding finer designs for their kitchen gadgets, furnishings, electronics, and appliances. Now in vogue are . . .

■ **Shapes:** super-slim silhouettes, and those with perforated or crisp edges

■ **Textures:** traditional materials (such as houndstooth, twill, and tweed) with handcrafted accents. Think hand-hooked rugs and embroidered linens.

■ **Scents:** fig, orange flower, pine-scented amber

■ **Colors:** chocolate, caramel, and mocha browns mix-matched with shades of cream; black, white, sepia, and flannel gray accented by electric blue or sunshine yellow; mauve; soft rose

FURNITURE FASHIONS

The rich can afford to buy 18th- and 19th-century original furniture, but everybody else is going for 1930s knockoffs. An example: a curved-front chest painted white with flowers and distressed.

We're also seeing mix-matched furniture give way to more sets, matched woods, and chairs reupholstered to match.

THE GREAT KITCHEN UPHEAVAL

More than half of U.S. residents who remodel their kitchens this year will do it themselves, spending an average of $17,700. They'll be hiding kitchen appliances behind paintings and paneling, creating a library effect, and disguising kitchen computers as breadboxes, toasters, and biscuit tins.

New kitchen or not, the latest rage is a private culinary class conducted by a star chef, followed by a divine dinner party—all in the host's home.

TECHNO-HELPERS

Available now . . .

■ **Appliances** that reset their own digital clocks when the power blinks

■ **Traffic clocks** that keep you updated on how many minutes your commute will be as traffic flow changes

Coming soon . . .

■ **Washing machines** that automatically call the repairman when they need to be serviced

■ **Laptop computers** that project 3-D images by pointing pixels at each of your eyes

■ **Electronic newspapers** and magazines

on flat, vinyl, roll-up sheets that act as portable computer screens

■ **Solid-state lighting:** luminous wallpaper, illuminated shower stalls, color-changing kitchen counters, ceilings that glow with the shifting spectrum of a sunrise or sunset

HELLO, GREEN FRONTIER

■ "Neo-organicism" is a growing trend among designers to use nature's forms—spiraling nautiluses, unfolding flower petals—in architecture.

■ Twenty percent of new U.S. homes are being built with environmentally friendly features, such as double-pane windows, air filtration systems, and non-toxic paints.

■ Residents of Calgary, Alberta, can receive a $50 government rebate for installing a low-flow toilet.

■ Residents of Ottawa, Ontario, can receive a rebate of up to $1,000 for making their homes more energy efficient. It's part of Canada's commitment to a 240-megaton reduction in greenhouse gas emissions by 2010.

GOOD-BYE, LOST KEYS

■ **A good idea:** a GPS (global positioning system) locator inside your keys so that you can track them anywhere

■ **Better yet:** a new door lock with a sensor that can recognize your fingerprints as well as those of 50 friends—no keys needed

■ **Best of all:** a high-tech caretaker that e-mails you a photo when a guest or service person rings the doorbell, so that you can unlock the door from afar—even out of state

CONTINUED

HOT COLLECTIBLES

"The grungy, peeling-paint look is going away, and we're seeing more very elaborate, Italian-looking, painted furniture coming back."

–Terry Kovel, coauthor of
Kovels' Antiques & Collectibles Price List 2004

A FACT OF LIFE

Because the supply of available antiques has dwindled, minor flaws on items valued at more than a couple hundred dollars are not affecting prices the way they once did. (A chipped Roseville vase that used to bring 10 percent of value now brings 90 percent.)

HAVE IT YOUR WAY

A trend toward self-expression has taken hold. "A lot of people are collecting their own strange things in quantity that not everybody else is collecting," notes collectibles expert Terry Kovel. Such as . . .

- **Nut dishes**
- **Apron clothespin bags** from the 1930s and '40s
- **Photographs and illustrations** of people reading books
- **Tin bandage boxes**
- **Hand-carved wood or cork fishing bobbers** from the 1800s—especially painted ones

TRADING ON SENTIMENT

With old toys so rare and expensive, more middle-age collectors are buying back their 1950s and '60s childhood memories based on old TV shows and movies. Must-have memorabilia include toys, props, and costumes from the *Mickey Mouse Club, Mr. Rogers' Neighborhood, Captain Kangaroo,* and *Ding Dong School* for under $1,000.

Meanwhile, teens are going crazy for the "Hello Kitty" line.

RISING IN VALUE:

- **Antique cuff links,** especially the older, chain-joined type
- **Patriotic costume jewelry,** such as a flag pin
- **Silver dinner or tea service pieces.** A 1915 Georg Jensen sterling-silver coffee service can be worth $4,600.
- **Italian free-form plastic items:** vases, ashtrays, waste bins, bowls, pencil holders from the 1960s and '70s (think drippy candles molded into plastic)
- **Out-of-production figurines** from the 1950s (such as Royal Doulton)

PAST THEIR PEAK:

- **Industrial goods:** electric fans, irons, manual typewriters, old toasters
- **Limited-edition figurines** (such as Precious Moments, Hummel)

CONTINUED

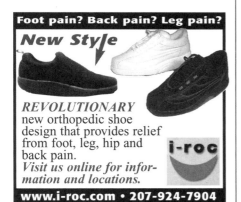

"We are overstressed and don't want the same pressure in our gardens. There's a strong interest in low-demand gardening that meets low-maintenance lifestyles."

—Susan McCoy, president, Garden Media Group

Tastes Trends 2005

A FACT OF LIFE

An attractive landscape increases the value of a home by 15 percent and reduces its selling time by five to six weeks.

ALL ABOARD!

Combining two of the hottest hobbies in North America—gardening and model trains—railroad gardening has become a favorite pastime enjoyed by men and women of all ages. The railroads run on low-voltage electricity and chug through elaborate villages peopled with miniature figures in over 70,000 private gardens and botanical exhibits.

WHAT "OFF-SEASON"?

Two or three seasons are no longer enough for some gardeners. Here's how they're making do:

■ **Growing mushrooms** with kits indoors during winter

■ **Bringing outdoor furniture** into family and living rooms. It's called "outside-in" design.

■ **Planting hardy flowers** that bloom through three seasons. 'Knock Out' shrub roses, 'Endless Summer' hydrangeas, and 'Wave' petunias are favorites.

URBAN FLOWER POWER

In a throwback to Frederick Olmsted's 19th-century City Beautiful movement, some urban leaders now recognize that greenery draws visitors and relieves residents' stress. They've fueled the trend by . . .

■ **Planting flowers in median strips** of highways to slow (admiring) traffic

■ **Offering tax deductions** to U.S. residents who grow "green" garden roofs

■ **Piloting a country lanes program,** combining paved and grass surfaces, in Vancouver, British Columbia

■ **Sponsoring America in Bloom and Communities in Bloom competitions** to recognize U.S. and Canadian cities with the best urban gardens

GROWING THE SPIRIT

Gardening is becoming more social than solitary, with programs like Unity Gardens, which encourages people to share their gardens with others (www.garden.org), and Plant a Row for the Hungry, which encourages sharing homegrown produce with local food banks and soup kitchens (www.gwaa.org).

CONTINUED

ON THE FARM

"People have grown food in urban centers from the earliest of times, and I now see that kind of movement spreading in Canada."

–Michael Levenston, executive director, City Farmer, Office of Urban Agriculture, Canada

A FACT OF LIFE

Forty-four percent of people in Greater Vancouver and 40 percent in Toronto grow some of their own food—vegetables, fruit, nuts, or herbs—in their yard, balcony, or community garden.

HERITAGE BREEDS THRIVE

The movement to bring back the rare heritage breeds of livestock, poultry, and crops that are threatened with extinction is growing. Groups such as the American Livestock Breeds Conservancy, the Society for the Preservation of Poultry Antiquities, Slow Food U.S.A., and hundreds of heritage-breed farmers are offering the often tastier varieties—such as Bourbon Red turkeys descended from the Pilgrim era and the ancient heirloom Tuscarora White Corn grown by the Iroquois.

FROM THE FARM TO YOU

■ **Flavored food-wrap:** The new food-wraps not only preserve our produce, but they're edible, too—in tomato, broccoli, pear, and peach flavors.

■ **Ready-to-eat indicators:** Pears inside plastic clamshell packages bear sensor labels that respond to subtle chemical changes by turning from red to orange to yellow, indicating ripeness. Watch for smart sensors to appear next on kiwis, avocados, mangoes, and melons.

THE MASCOT CARROT

Wanting to breed a hybrid carrot that matched one of the school colors of Texas A&M University, Dr. Leonard M. Pike, research leader at the school's Vegetable Improvement Center, came up with a maroon-on-the-outside, orange-on-the-inside carrot that's also sweeter and higher in vitamin A and beta-carotene than other strains.

WHAT'S NEXT?

■ **Manure power:** Watch for more farmers to convert waste to energy by adding water and heat to tanks of manure. The methane that results can power a generator to produce electricity.

■ **Robot pollenizer:** Expect insectlike robots to be pollinating crops by 2012.

■ **Designer eggs:** Chickens fed sea kelp, flaxseed, canola oil, and other nutritional ingredients lay low-fat eggs rich in omega-3 fatty acid, iodine, and vitamin E. Health-conscious consumers are gobbling them up, even at higher prices.

CONTINUED

FLORIDA'S BEST®

ALL-NATURAL PAIN RELIEF & SKIN CARE PRODUCTS

Back Pain RELIEF!

Made with all-natural oils imported from all over the world and used for centuries for their beneficial properties.

Florida's Best was founded by Florida naturalist James Toler in 1978. His award winning pain relief and skin care products were developed based on his extensive study of the healing and moisturizing properties of essential oils. Mr. Toler's family-run business is headquartered in Orlando, Florida.

APR (Pain Relief)
All time best seller.

Developed by Jim Toler and based on a centuries old herbal formula handed down from generation to generation by his great Grandmother who was a midwife in the hills of southern Italy, many years ago…

APR is made from 16 different oils, imported from all over the world. This safe and gentle formula contains all-natural ingredients.

There are many uses for APR. One of the most common is to help relieve pain. The formula helps the body to heal itself by helping to increase circulation, and it helps to activate endorphins which reduce swelling and promote healing.

APR's deep penetrating action helps soothe and give relief from arthritis pain, leg cramps, and back and neck pain.

Other uses for APR include: Headache relief, helps heal bug bites, cuts and scratches, hemorrhoids, snoring relief, sunburn, sinus & hay fever, and is an effective stimulant for diabetic feet, and relief of cramps.

APR is like aspirin, we don't understand completely how it works, all we know is that it does. It's often called "First Aid in a Bottle."

This good old fashioned pain relief remedy is not sold in stores.

(available in 8oz....$24.95 and 16oz....$39.95 bottles) add $4.95 postage and handling.

Florida's Best, P.O. Box 616945 Dept. 70, Orlando, FL 32861-6945

FOR FASTEST SERVICE CALL TOLL-FREE
1-800-735-8912

Visit us on the web! www.jltindustries.com
Send for our FREE product catalog
100% Satisfaction Guaranteed or Your Money Back.

MAKE EXTRA $ INCOME $
Exclusive distributorships now available! Sell our products at shows and fairs. Home Party program starting in Fall 2004.
Call Greg
1-800-981-7071

Thousands of happy customers

Free APR Sample—
Just For Calling Toll-Free!

Plus with order Free APR Mini Brochure tells you how to get fast relief from dozens of common ailments with just a few capfuls of APR— Some might even surprise you!

All orders shipped within 24 hours via UPS.

FOOD FADS

"I really believe that we have turned the tide on obesity when it comes to food, health, and diet."

–Supermarket guru Phil Lempert

A FACT OF LIFE

More families—79 percent—are "sharing" five or more meals together each week, but mealtime has become a choose-your-own, sit-and-eat-anywhere, mad-dash event.

HEALTHY FOOD AS A HABIT

The trend that started as the Atkins diet will continue. Watch for . . .

■ **Take-out restaurants to downsize** gargantuan portions and diversify high-fat menus

■ **A new breed of fast-food eateries** serving healthy seafood dishes such as Maryland crab

■ **Organic "Peanut Better"** in flavors like Deep Chocolate and Spicy Southwestern, plus baked goods and confectionery products minus the high fats and carbohydrates

■ **On-campus vegetarian cafes** serving low-calorie food to help incoming college students beat the classic "freshman 15" weight gain

THE BAD-FOOD BACKLASH

In the face of so much healthy food, watch for a countertrend of even greater high-caloric indulgence. Expect a run on . . .

■ **Twinkies, Oreos, and Snickers bars** dipped in batter and fried in lard

■ **Grilled chocolate sandwiches** (like cheese, only chocolate)

■ **Cupcakes** in exotic flavors like mojito lime or rum

THE NEW ALTA COCINA (HAUTE CUISINE)

The new Latino/Hispanic fare that's redefining North American tastes has become increasingly regionalized. Look for more unusual food from Oaxaca, Mexico, and the Catalonia region of Spain. This culinary trend is showing up in restaurants and on supermarket shelves, which now feature foods from Brazil, Puerto Rico, and Cuba. Expect to see more . . .

■ **Tapas bars,** where appetizers are the main course

■ **Whole-pig roasts.** In the Cuban-American tradition, a whole pig is roasted inside a box called La Caja China and served over garlicky black beans and rice.

■ **Exotic foods** like specialty limes, fried pomegranate seeds, and paletas—Mexican frozen-fruit bars in flavors such as cucumber-chile, mango-chile, and papaya

CONTINUED

HOW WE HAVE FUN

"Soon, going to the mall to pick up the latest compact disc by the newest and hottest boy band or pop star will be a thing of the past."

–World Future Society

A FACT OF LIFE

As luxury cruises entice more people to the Arctic and Antarctic, the Arctic polar bear population is declining—to zero by 2100, predicts the World Future Society, if warming trends continue.

MAD ABOUT ME (AND YOU)

Self-tailored entertainment is big:

■ People are hiring professionals to document their loved ones' life stories with personal video biographies.

■ For about $50, a photo of you or your loved one can appear on the cover of a coffee-table book.

THE NEW TOYS

■ **Foldable bikes and collapsible kayaks** that fit into your luggage

■ **Self-heating hiking and ski boots** powered by piezoelectric materials in the heel that turn pressure into electricity

■ **Self-powered fishing lures** that attract fish by making the sound of their mate

WHAT WOMEN ARE DOING

■ **Heading for the woods:** More urban wives in their late 20s to mid-40s are joining their husbands on hunting trips.

■ **Heading for the water:** Since 2000, the number of females riding the waves has risen 280 percent. Surfing companies now design boards and surfing shorts for women (25 percent

of the estimated 1.6 million surfers).

GAMES PEOPLE ARE PLAYING

■ **Cashflow.** Players use this board game to learn how to manage their money (cost: $195).

■ **Quickball.** Leagues of four-person teams have sprung up to play two-out games on a field one-quarter the size of a regulation baseball diamond.

ON THE RIDE . . .

The world's tallest (420 feet) and fastest roller coaster, the Top Thrill Dragster at Cedar Point Amusement Park in Sandusky, Ohio, propels riders at 120 mph, taking as little time (four seconds) to go uphill at its highest point as it does to go down at its lowest. Total trip time: 2,800 feet in 30 seconds.

ON THE SIDE . . .

Cedar Point Amusement Park has 16 roller coasters—the most in the world. So many people would rather watch than ride the Top Thrill Dragster that bleachers were built for the first time in the park's history.

CONTINUED

"We're tired of seeing everyone's belly button. Now we're dressing more grown-up."

–Sharon Graubard, creative director, ESP Trendlab/ Ellen Sideri Partnership

Tastes & Trends 2005

A FACT OF LIFE

The metrosexual man is paying closer attention to his grooming habits and using bronzers, lip gels, eyeliner, concealers, and mascara—makeup once reserved for women.

MENSWEAR MUSTS

▢ A mix of plaids, checks, and stripes in the British style, but less serious

▢ The polished look: tailored jackets, cardigans, stylish neckties

▢ Suits and coats in postman-blue, olive drab, and bold red, occasionally even with gold epaulets

■ Skins: shearling, leather, fur

▢ Elegant accessories: diamonds, bold rings, bracelets, pendants

▢ Wing-tip shoes and vintage slippers (at work!)

GUYS HAVE GOT TO GET . . .

▢ **Lively-color T-shirts:** blazing reds and oranges or electric blue

▢ **Jeans,** especially gray denims

■ **Snowboard graphics,** neo-hip-hop layering, soccer and rugby influences

WOMENSWEAR WISH LIST

▢ Ladylike prim looks, echoing the 1950s, but with Bohemian flair: a vintage shirt hanging out of a jacket

▢ Blouses with dressmaker collars

▢ Pretty, fitted jackets with three-quarter sleeves

▢ Pumps

■ Colored and suede gloves

■ Rich textures: satin, velvet, fur

▢ Colors: wine, purple, teal, brown

▢ Giant prints on shoes, handbags, and hosiery

WHAT WOMEN WANT . . .

▢ **Personalized purses:** Decorate-a-purse parties are the hottest ladies' night out.

■ **Spray-on "hosiery,"** invented for Tokyo women required to wear stockings even in the heat. A week's worth costs $15.

FINISHING TOUCHES

▢ Gin as a fragrance for men and women

■ Waxing of the hair on men's backs, arms, and legs

CONTINUED

DEMOGRAPHICA

"There used to be a societal expectation that people in their early 20s would have finished their schooling, set up a household, gotten married, and started their careers. Now, that's the exception rather than the norm." –Frank Furstenberg Jr., sociology professor, University of Pennsylvania

A FACT OF LIFE

The average middle-class married couple can expect to spend $250,000 to raise a child to age 17, with an additional $40,000 per year tacked on (at today's rates) for tuition, room, and board at a private college.

THE MODERN AMERICAN HOUSEHOLD HAS . . .

■ **More vehicles than drivers,** with commuter cars, family vans, and fun cars as options

■ **A grandparent at its head** (over 4.5 million homes, at last count)

■ **An adult child back in the nest:** The number of 24- to 34-year-olds living with parents rose 50 percent from 1970 to 2000, and is trending upward.

MIGRATION PATTERNS

Futurists foresee a reversal of the urbanization trend, with megacities being replaced by telecities. Data from the U.S. Census Bureau already indicates a higher outbound migration from the northeastern and midwestern states to points south and west, with popular destinations including Oregon, Montana, and Alaska.

MORE WOMEN FARMING

The number of women who farm full-time in the United States has increased by 37 percent since 1997.

COMING: MORE ELBOWROOM

The United Nations forecasts a drop in fertility trends in developing countries and has lowered its long-range prediction for the world's population in 2300: Instead of 12 billion people on the planet, there'll be only 9 billion.

U.S. MARRIAGE, THEN AND NOW

Median age of . . .	1975	2005
■ Women, first marriage	21	25
■ Men, first marriage	23	27
Percentage of . . .		
■ Married adults	75	56
■ Married-with-children households	45	26

CONTINUED

Having trouble losing weight?

Now you can
LOSE 5-7 LBS
in just *5 DAYS!*
(and there's more good news)

With Puranol™ you'll lose weight fast and restore your body back to health so the weight doesn't come back!!

Are you having a hard time losing weight? Just can't seem to lose those last 5-10 lbs? Chances are your body is toxic! What does that have to do with weight loss? EVERYTHING! A toxic body can't function properly. You may not know it, but your body is exposed to harmful, unhealthy toxins at any given time. These nearly invisible toxins can slow down your metabolism, depress your immune system, drain your energy or even worse!

If you're serious about losing weight and getting healthy... Puranol™ is for you. This specially formulated 2-step system will jump start your weight loss and cleanse your toxic cells back to health! Remember, healthy cells are the building blocks of a healthy body. In addition, this probiotic formula helps to promote prolonged weight management and helps to support the essential building blocks of your body's immune system. So not only will you lose weight, you'll feel great!

Call now and try Puranol™ absolutely risk-free! If you're ready to lose weight and feel great it's time you tried Puranol™. Give your body the *"internal shower"* it needs and shed those excess pounds! Call now and you can try Puranol™ absolutely risk-free for 30 days. We guarantee you'll lose weight and feel great! Call now, get Puranol™ and <u>get healthy!</u>

"I lost 6 lbs in one week! Puranol™ is amazing. I can't believe how good I feel, it's like I'm a whole new person!"
-B. Douglas

"Thanks to Puranol™ I finally reached my weight loss goals! Not only did I lose the weight, I now have a whole new level of energy AND a clear complexion."
-S. Sawyer

<u>See results in just 5 days!</u>
Jump start your weight loss

Speed up your metabolism

Support your immune system

Promote better overall health

Look & feel younger

Even have clearer skin!

Call now for your risk-free trial!
Lose weight and feel great!
1-800-450-3851

(articulus integritas) tablets

Promotion #901

THE NEXT GENERATION

"For mothers who thought spiked hair and tongue bolts were bad, just wait: Soon, kids will be able to make the ultimate statement by altering their skin pigment to be both black and white."

–Frank Ogden, Canada's "Mr. Tomorrow"

A FACT OF LIFE
The current generation views surveillance as cool—not controlling.

THUMBS UP

Parents who want to better understand their babies and allow them to express themselves are teaching sign language to their infants.

ON-TARGET MARKET

Many retailers are wooing 'tweens and teens with goods and services previously offered only to adults:

■ **Spas have become a cool place for teenage boys** to get acne facials, haircuts, and highlights (plus, spot girls).

■ **YogaKids is spreading** among children ages 4 and up. They learn breathing exercises and stretches, and get music, storytelling, and creative arts.

■ **The first diet pill** (Xenical) specifically for teenagers has been approved by the Food and Drug Administration.

TOYS 'Я' SMARTER

With more than 70 percent of new toys using microchips, playthings are getting smarter. Here's how:

■ **InteracTV invites kids to shout out questions** and get responses from their favorite characters on DVDs.

■ **Interactive dolls talk back to kids,** the more the kids talk to them. Dolls from Bandai America know over 60 words.

THEY KEEP GOING AND GOING AND GOING . . .

A "playful energy" converter uses compressed air produced by the natural action of kids playing on a seesaw, merry-go-round, or swings to make electricity. Look for kid-powered equipment in museums and schoolyards in a year or two.

LOOK WHO'S CHEATING

With calculators and text-messaging features built into the cell phones carried by nearly a third of American teenagers, students have plenty of new ways to get "extra help."

■ **40 percent admit to plagiarizing** from the Internet.

■ **43 percent say that lying or cheating is necessary** for success.

THAT'S ENTERTAINMENT

More than twice as many young adults apply to MTV's *Real World* show as apply to Harvard University.

CONTINUED

32

TO OUR HEALTH

"If we don't start selling public health with the same level of effectiveness and sophistication as McDonald's, we're going nowhere."

–Health advocate Bill Reger

A FACT OF LIFE

Canadians living in cities have fewer health problems than those living in the country or small towns.

NO SIZE FITS ALL

With over 20 percent of Americans overweight, some things are getting bigger:
- **Scales** (registering up to 400 pounds)
- **Seat belts** (extended for greater girth)
- **Caskets** (wider)

And some are getting smaller:
- **Dress and pants sizes** (to make us feel skinnier)

TRENDING TOWARD IMMORTALITY

- **Move over, Botox.** Doctors are already clucking about the next big wrinkle treatment, which comes from a compound (hyaluronan) extracted from the red combs of roosters and hens.

- **"Face-lifts" below the chin.** Baby boomers are also getting necks, chests, and hands surgically "rejuvenated."

OUR MOOD

"It's a noisy world now, and people want to take a break from all that."

–Paul Rebhan, cofounder, Quiet Parties, social gatherings where people write notes to each other instead of talking

A FACT OF LIFE

Trend-watching has become a hot occupation, with an industry of spotters.

SIGNS OF THE TIMES

Virtual reality therapy: 3-D software and vibrating platforms that enable therapists to simulate anxiety-inducing experiences and help their patients work through them

"Masstige" retail: prestigious products (from hot dogs to "director's hall" seating in theaters) marketed to the masses at affordable prices

WHERE'D EVERYONE GO?

Individual culture rules, as people download their own music, tune in to diverse cable shows, and create their own Internet experiences. The 21st-century "love-in" is a hodgepodge of ages and demographics joined up only fleetingly for Internet-arranged "flash mob" events, before going their own way. □□

SO, WHAT ELSE IS NEW?

For more statistics, data, and other colorful details of our life and times, go to WWW.ALMANAC.COM and click on ARTICLE LINKS 2005.

Do you have high cholesterol?

Now there's an all-natural way to reduce your cholesterol and promote better overall cardiovascular health.

If costly prescriptions, added exercise, or change of diet have failed, you MUST try LESSterol™, the all-natural way to reduce cholesterol levels and support better cardiovascular health!

LESSterol™ is an all-natural dietary supplement thats active ingredients are proven to reduce cholesterol levels and help support better overall cardiovascular health. Unlike costly prescriptions, LESSterol™ is all-natural, so there are no negative side effects and it is conveniently available to you without a visit to your doctor.

What are you waiting for?

Millions of Americans are living with unhealthy cholesterol levels, and you don't have to be one of them. Call now and get your risk-free trial of LESSterol™ rushed right out to you. Get LESSterol™ and get heart healthy. Call now, **1-800-573-8167**, be sure to mention offer# **901** and get your risk-free trial sent out to you today!

Call Today For Your Risk-Free Trial:
1-800-573-8167 Offer# 901

LESSterol™
Consanesco XDL Tablets

Tailor Your
TOMATOES

–John Burwell/FoodPix

Tips for

having

luscious,

vine-

ripened

tomatoes

all

season

long.

BY JOHN C. FISHER

Homegrown tomatoes are just about everyone's favorite garden delight. But often they don't ripen as early as we would like, or they are finished producing in midseason. By assessing your tomato needs and uses, whether cooking, canning, juicing, or just plain eating, you can tailor your crop to meet those needs.

The key to having a season-long harvest is to select varieties based on when you want your tomatoes and what you plan to do with them. Then, pay attention to the growth habits and maturity dates of the varieties you select.

PICK YOUR PLEASURE

■ Do you want to harvest tomatoes all at once or throughout the season?

Determinate tomatoes, which are usually bush varieties, tend to provide a large number of ripe tomatoes at one time, which is helpful if you want to can them or make juice or salsa. They can be grown without staking or caging. The plants' growing points terminate in a flower cluster, and they put on only a small amount of growth after setting fruit. If you want to have a heavy mid-season crop for canning, plant a good determinate variety. 'Celebrity', 'Floramerica', 'Mountain Pride', and 'Pik-Red' are good choices.

Indeterminate varieties will continue to grow, flower, and set fruit, and will provide your main supply of large slicing tomatoes from midseason until frost. Your success will depend somewhat on your care. These tall, sprawling plants should be properly supported with stakes or cages. Some well-known varieties in this group are 'Better Boy', 'Big Beef', 'Big Boy', 'Goliath', and 'Supersteak'.

(c o n t i n u e d)

Right: '**Beefmaster**', for slicing.

Left, top to bottom: '**Big Beef**', for slicing; '**Brandywine**', for flavor; '**Super Sweet 100**', for snacking.

With a little

planning, you can

be harvesting

tomatoes throughout

the season.

COUNT THE DAYS

■ Pay attention to maturity date, the number of days from transplanting until ripe fruit. Maturities range from 50 to 80 days, but because of local growing conditions, the actual time may vary from that given for a particular variety in a catalog or seed packet description. The earliest varieties generally do not produce tomatoes as large as mid- and late-maturing types, but planting a few of these can help ensure that you will have the first ripe tomato in the neighborhood. 'Early Girl', a top yielder in this group, produces four- to six-ounce fruits. 'Quick Pick' is another good early variety.

To provide a continuous supply of tomatoes for canning and slicing, divide the remainder of your planting between the midseason determinate varieties and the midseason to late-maturing indeterminate ones. The late-maturing varieties can provide not only late-season slicing tomatoes but also abundant small green ones for making relishes. Try 'Better Boy', 'Big Beef', 'Big Boy', and 'Goliath'.

PLAN THE HARVEST

■ If you want to make tomato sauce, paste-type or plum tomatoes such as 'Roma' and 'Viva Italia' are good choices. These varieties are meatier and have a lower water content, allowing for a thick, rich sauce.

Cherry and grape tomatoes make great snacks or toppers for salads. 'Super Sweet 100' and 'Sweet Million' are two of the better cherry tomato varieties. 'Sweet Olive' and 'Juliet' are two good grape tomato varieties.

Beefsteak types like 'Beefmaster' and 'Supersteak' can produce tomatoes weighing over a pound. They make large slices that are nice not just for sandwiches and hamburgers, but also for serving attractively as a side dish on the table.

Want to add interest to salads or table slices? Put out a few plants of a yellow variety such as 'Lemon Boy'. You'll also enjoy their sweet flavor.

Speaking of flavor, many gardeners prefer heirloom varieties, such as 'Brandywine', over hybrids. (In addition, heirloom tomato seeds can be saved and will produce plants that are true to the variety the following year.) However, heirloom varieties tend to be less productive and more susceptible to disease, particularly in warm climate areas, than newer varieties, so don't depend on them for your main crop.

With a little planning, you can be harvesting delicious tomatoes throughout the season.

TOMATO-BASIL JAM

This is a wonderfully tasty condiment that can be enjoyed in countless ways.

6 large ripe tomatoes, peeled, seeded, and finely chopped
1/4 cup lemon juice
4 tablespoons coarsely chopped fresh basil
1 package (1 3/4 ounces) powdered fruit pectin for lower-sugar recipes
3 cups sugar, divided

■ Place tomatoes in a kettle. Bring to a boil, reduce heat, cover, and simmer for 10 minutes. Add the lemon juice and basil. In a small bowl, combine pectin and ¼ cup of the sugar; add to tomatoes. Heat to a full rolling boil, stirring constantly. Add the remaining 2¾ cups sugar. Return to a rolling boil and cook for 1 minute, stirring constantly. Remove from heat and skim off the foam. Ladle the jam into hot, sterilized, canning jars, leaving ¼ inch of headspace. Seal with lids and process in a boiling-water bath for 5 minutes. **Makes about 2 1/2 pints.**

–from *The Old Farmer's Almanac Blue Ribbon Recipes*

'Juliet', for snacking.

(c o n t i n u e d)

· · · · · · · · · · · · · ·

TOMATO JUICE

Here's a delicious way to use midseason determinate tomatoes.

20 pounds fully ripe tomatoes, washed and quartered
14 tablespoons bottled lemon juice
7 teaspoons salt (optional)

■ Place tomatoes in a large pot on medium heat. Simmer for 30 minutes, stirring frequently, until thoroughly cooked. Remove from heat and press tomatoes through a colander or sieve to remove seeds and skin, collecting the juice in the pot. Return pot to the stove and keep hot over low heat. Fill hot, sterilized, 1-quart canning jars with juice, leaving ½ inch of headspace. Add 2 tablespoons of bottled lemon juice (to increase acidity) to each quart, and 1 teaspoon of salt, if desired. Seal with canning lids, but do not overtighten. Place jars in a pressure canner according to manufacturer's directions and process for 15 minutes at 10 pounds of pressure. **Makes 7 quarts.**

Green tomatoes can be as useful as ripe red ones. Any of the varieties producing medium- to large-size tomatoes will work well for frying. Delicious relishes and pickles can be made from green tomatoes. Reserve this task for late fall, when there is an abundance of one- to two-inch green tomatoes that will not ripen before the first frost.

· · · · · · · · · · · · · ·

FRIED GREEN TOMATOES

Use end-of-season indeterminate varieties and serve them hot.

1 cup flour
1 cup cornmeal
salt and pepper, to taste
4 to 6 green tomatoes, sliced into 1/4- to 1/2-inch-thick rounds
2 eggs, beaten
oil for frying

■ Mix flour and cornmeal together and season with salt and pepper. Dip tomato slices into eggs, then into flour mixture. Heat oil in a large skillet to 350°F. Fry tomatoes until golden, then turn over and fry other side. Remove from oil and drain on paper towels. **Makes 4 to 6 servings.**

Left to right: 'Viva Italia', for sauce; 'Lemon Boy', for slicing; 'Celebrity', for canning.

–left, W. Atlee Burpee & Co.; center, Seminis Vegetable Seeds; right, Johnny's Selected Seeds

(c o n t i n u e d)
· · · · · · · · · · · ·

Gardening's
Most Wanted
Catalogue
is Yours Free

BURPEE®

www.burpee.com

☑ **YES! Send my FREE 2005 Burpee Catalogue**

Name _____

Address _____

City _____ State _____ Zip _____

E-Mail _____

Please mail to:
Burpee, 51152 Burpee Building, Warminster, PA 18974
or Call TOLL FREE 1-800-888-1447

© 2004 W. Atlee Burpee & Co.

GREEN TOMATO RELISH

When the cold winds blow, a batch of relish will always remind you of summer.

4 cups chopped onions
1 medium cabbage, quartered
10 green tomatoes, quartered
12 sweet green peppers, quartered and seeded
6 sweet red peppers, quartered and seeded
3 pods hot peppers, halved and seeded
1/2 cup pickling salt
6 cups sugar
1 tablespoon celery seed
2 tablespoons mustard seed
1 1/2 teaspoons turmeric
4 cups cider vinegar
1 cup water

■ Grind the vegetables in a food processor, using a coarse blade. Put in a large bowl, sprinkle with the salt, cover, and let set overnight. Drain. Rinse with cold water and drain again. Put vegetables in a large pot. Combine remaining ingredients in a bowl; pour over the vegetables. Heat to boiling. Simmer for 3 minutes. Pack in hot, sterilized, 1-pint canning jars and seal. Process in a boiling-water canner for 5 minutes or according to manufacturer's directions. **Makes about 8 pints.**

Note: To convert these recipes to metric, see the Table of Measures on page 226.

WHAT'S GROWING?

■ In an e-mail survey, Almanac readers voted the following as their favorite backyard tomato varieties:

1. **'Brandywine'** (superb flavor, thin skin, wonderful on bread with a skim of mayo)

2. **'Beefsteak'** (eat 'em just like apples)

3. **'Better Boy'** (God's perfect fruit, great taste)

4. **'Early Girl'** (loads of tomatoes)

5. **'Roma'** (a paste variety, not soggy on bread, great flavor)

6. **'Celebrity'** (sweet and juicy, loves hot weather)

7 **'Rutgers'** (never splits, very good taste)

8. **'Sweet 100'** (cherry type, perfect for snacking, really sweet)

9. **'Hillbilly'** (heirloom, great taste)

10. **'Black Prince'** (heirloom, extraordinary taste, great for slicing)

Other favorites included 'Abe Lincoln', 'Avalanche', 'Big Beef', 'Creole', 'First Lady', 'Gurney Girl', 'Jetsetter', 'Mr. Stripey', 'Sun Gold', and 'Wisconsin 55'. One reader uses the 'Sweet 100' variety for canning juice, Amish paste tomatoes for canning sauce and for drying, and 'Aunt Molly's' ground cherries for making preserves. Another grows 75 varieties and uses many of them in her tomato sauce. □□

John C. Fisher farms 250 acres near Kennett, Missouri. In his 40x40-foot tomato plot, he grows the 'Beefsteak', 'Better Boy', 'Celebrity', 'Goliath', and 'Show-Me' varieties.

SEEING RED. For tips on growing tomatoes and more recipes for your harvest, go to **www.almanac.com** and click on **Article Links 2005.**

What
GROWS
There:
FRIEND
or FOE?

Plant companions

ensure a happy garden

—and gardener.

by George and Becky
Lohmiller

–illustrated by Margo Letourneau and David Ziarnowski

■ **It takes more than good soil, sun, and** nutrients to ensure success in a garden. Plants have to grow well with one another, and those that do are known as companions.

In nature, companion plants are the norm. For example, blueberries, mountain laurel, azaleas, and other ericaceous (heath family) plants thrive in the acidic soils created by pines and oaks, while shade-loving plants seek the shelter provided by a wooded grove. The shade-lovers in return protect the forest floor from erosion with their thick tangle of shallow roots. Legumes and some trees, such as alders, have symbiotic relationships with bacteria in the soil that help them to capture nitrogen from the air and convert it to fertilizer, enriching the soil so plants can prosper in their presence.

Today, we recognize many plant companions. Some plants, especially herbs, act as repellents, confusing insects with their strong odors that mask the scent of the intended host plants. Dill and basil planted among tomatoes protect the tomatoes from hornworms, and sage scattered about the cabbage patch reduces injury from cabbage moths. Marigolds are as good as gold when grown with just ·about any garden plant, repelling beetles, nematodes, and even animal pests.

Some companions act as trap plants, luring insects to themselves. Nasturtiums, for example, are so favored by aphids that the devastating insects will flock to them instead of other plants.

Carrots, dill, parsley, and parsnip attract garden heroes—praying mantises, ladybugs, and spiders—that dine on insect pests.

Much of companion planting is common sense: Lettuce, radishes, and other quick-growing plants sown between hills of melons or winter squash will mature and be harvested long before these vines need more legroom. Leafy greens like spinach and Swiss chard grown in the shadow of corn or sunflowers appreciate the dapple shade they cast and, since their roots occupy different levels in the soil, don't compete for water and nutrients.

Just as some people seem to rub each other the wrong way, so are many plants incompatible with one another. These plants are known as combatants or antagonists. While white garlic and onions repel a plethora of pests and make excellent neighbors for most garden plants, the growth of beans and peas is stunted in their presence. Potatoes and beans grow poorly in the company of sunflowers, and although cabbage and cauliflower are closely related, they don't like each other at all.

Sometimes plants may be helpful to one another only at a certain stage of their growth. The number and ratio of different plants growing together is often a factor in their compatibility, and sometimes plants make good companions for no apparent reason. You would assume that keeping a garden weed-free would be a good thing, but this is not always the case. Certain weeds pull nutrients from deep in the soil and bring them close to the surface. When the weeds die and decompose, nutrients become available in the surface soil and are more easily accessed by shallow-rooted plants. Perhaps one of the most intriguing examples of strange garden bedfellows is the relationship between the weed stinging nettle and several vegetable varieties. For reasons that are unclear, plants grown in the presence of stinging nettle display exceptional vigor and resist spoiling.

One of the keys to successful companion planting is observation. Record your plant combinations and the results from year to year, and share this information with other gardening friends. Companionship is just as important for gardeners as it is for gardens.

continued

The THREE SISTERS:
They'll Grow on You

■ **Vegetable gardeners have long ob-**served that many plants grow better when planted with companions than each individual plant would do if grown alone. The classic example of this is the legendary "three sisters"— corn, pole beans, and either pumpkins or squash. This trio is one of the easiest and most satisfying to grow.

To try them in your garden, in spring, prepare the soil by adding fish scraps or wood ash to increase fertility, if desired. When the danger of frost has passed, plant six kernels of corn an inch deep and about ten inches apart in a circle about two feet in diameter. As the corn grows, mound up the soil around the base of the stalks until a hill about a foot high and three feet wide is formed. When the corn is about five inches tall, plant four bean seeds, evenly spaced, around each stalk. About a week later, plant six squash seeds, evenly spaced, around the perimeter of the mound.

Each of the sisters contributes something to the planting. As older sisters often do, the corn offers the beans needed support. The beans, the giving sister, pull nitrogen from the air and bring it to the soil for the benefit of all three. As the beans grow through the tangle of squash vines and wind their way up the cornstalks into the sunlight, they hold the sisters close together. The large leaves of the sprawling squash protect the threesome by creating living mulch that shades the soil, keeping it cool and moist and preventing weeds. The prickly squash leaves also keep away raccoons, which don't like to step on them. Together, the sisters provide a balanced diet from a single planting.

■ **By the time European settlers arrived in America in the early 1600s, the Iroquois had been growing the "three sisters" for over three centuries. The vegetable trio sustained the Native Americans both physically and spiritually. In legend, the plants were a gift from the gods, always to be grown together, eaten together, and celebrated together.**

George and Becky Lohmiller, who write the essays in *The Old Farmer's Almanac Gardening Calendar*, run a garden center and landscaping business in Hancock, New Hampshire.

GET GROWING!

For advice on planting and growing vegetables and more on herb companions, go to **www.almanac.com** and click on **Article Links 2005.**

A VEGETABLE GARDEN'S BEST FRIENDS
(and Worst Enemies)

Here is a list of friends and foes for ten common vegetables.

FRIEND	FOE	FRIEND	FOE	FRIEND	FOE
BEANS		**CORN**		**ONIONS**	
Beets	Garlic	Beans	Tomatoes	Beets	Beans
Broccoli	Onions	Cucumbers		Broccoli	Peas
Cabbage	Peppers	Lettuce		Cabbage	Sage
Carrots	Sunflowers	Melons		Carrots	
Cauliflower		Peas		Lettuce	
Celery		Potatoes		Peppers	
Corn		Squash		Potatoes	
Cucumbers		Sunflowers		Spinach	
Eggplant				Tomatoes	
Peas		**CUCUMBERS**			
Potatoes		Beans	Aromatic	**PEPPERS**	
Radishes		Cabbage	herbs	Basil	Beans
Squash		Cauliflower	Melons	Coriander	Kohlrabi
Strawberries		Corn	Potatoes	Onions	
Summer		Lettuce		Spinach	
savory		Peas		Tomatoes	
Tomatoes		Radishes			
		Sunflowers		**RADISHES**	
CABBAGE				Beans	Hyssop
Beans	Broccoli	**LETTUCE**		Carrots	
Celery	Cauliflower	Asparagus	Broccoli	Cucumbers	
Cucumbers	Strawberries	Beets		Lettuce	
Dill	Tomatoes	Brussels		Tomatoes	
Kale		sprouts			
Lettuce		Cabbage		**TOMATOES**	
Onions		Carrots		Asparagus	Broccoli
Potatoes		Corn		Basil	Brussels
Sage		Cucumbers		Beans	sprouts
Spinach		Eggplant		Borage	Cabbage
Thyme		Onions		Carrots	Cauliflower
		Peas		Celery	Corn
CARROTS		Potatoes		Dill	Kale
Beans	Anise	Radishes		Lettuce	Potatoes
Lettuce	Dill	Spinach		Melons	
Onions	Parsley	Strawberries		Onions	
Peas		Sunflowers		Parsley	
Radishes		Tomatoes		Peppers	
Rosemary				Radishes	
Sage				Spinach	
Tomatoes				Thyme	

47

Frosts and Growing Seasons

■ Dates given are normal averages for a light freeze; local weather and topography may cause considerable variations. The possibility of frost occurring after the spring dates and before the fall dates is 50 percent. The classification of freeze temperatures is usually based on their effect on plants. **Light freeze:** 29° to 32°F—tender plants killed. **Moderate freeze:** 25° to 28°F—widely destructive effect on most vegetation. **Severe freeze:** 24°F and colder—heavy damage to most plants.

–courtesy of National Climatic Data Center

City	State	Growing Season (days)	Last Spring Frost	First Fall Frost	City	State	Growing Season (days)	Last Spring Frost	First Fall Frost
Mobile	AL	272	Feb. 27	Nov. 26	North Platte	NE	136	May 11	Sept. 24
Juneau	AK	133	May 16	Sept. 26	Las Vegas	NV	259	Mar. 7	Nov. 21
Phoenix	AZ	308	Feb. 5	Dec. 15	Concord	NH	121	May 23	Sept. 22
Tucson	AZ	273	Feb. 28	Nov. 29	Newark	NJ	219	Apr. 4	Nov. 10
Pine Bluff	AR	234	Mar. 19	Nov. 8	Carlsbad	NM	223	Mar. 29	Nov. 7
Eureka	CA	324	Jan. 30	Dec. 15	Los Alamos	NM	157	May 8	Oct. 13
Sacramento	CA	289	Feb. 14	Dec. 1	Albany	NY	144	May 7	Sept. 29
San Francisco	CA	*	*	*	Syracuse	NY	170	Apr. 28	Oct. 16
Denver	CO	157	May 3	Oct. 8	Fayetteville	NC	212	Apr. 2	Oct. 31
Hartford	CT	167	Apr. 25	Oct. 10	Bismarck	ND	129	May 14	Sept. 20
Wilmington	DE	198	Apr. 13	Oct. 29	Akron	OH	168	May 3	Oct. 18
Miami	FL	*	*	*	Cincinnati	OH	195	Apr. 14	Oct. 27
Tampa	FL	338	Jan. 28	Jan. 3	Lawton	OK	217	Apr. 1	Nov. 5
Athens	GA	224	Mar. 28	Nov. 8	Tulsa	OK	218	Mar. 30	Nov. 4
Savannah	GA	250	Mar. 10	Nov. 15	Pendleton	OR	188	Apr. 15	Oct. 21
Boise	ID	153	May 8	Oct. 9	Portland	OR	217	Apr. 3	Nov. 7
Chicago	IL	187	Apr. 22	Oct. 26	Carlisle	PA	182	Apr. 20	Oct. 20
Springfield	IL	185	Apr. 17	Oct. 19	Williamsport	PA	168	Apr. 29	Oct. 15
Indianapolis	IN	180	Apr. 22	Oct. 20	Kingston	RI	144	May 8	Sept. 30
South Bend	IN	169	May 1	Oct. 18	Charleston	SC	253	Mar. 11	Nov. 20
Atlantic	IA	141	May 9	Sept. 28	Columbia	SC	211	Apr. 4	Nov. 2
Cedar Rapids	IA	161	Apr. 29	Oct. 7	Rapid City	SD	145	May 7	Sept. 29
Topeka	KS	175	Apr. 21	Oct. 14	Memphis	TN	228	Mar. 23	Nov. 7
Lexington	KY	190	Apr. 17	Oct. 25	Nashville	TN	207	Apr. 5	Oct. 29
Monroe	LA	242	Mar. 9	Nov. 7	Amarillo	TX	197	Apr. 14	Oct. 29
New Orleans	LA	288	Feb. 20	Dec. 5	Denton	TX	231	Mar. 25	Nov. 12
Portland	ME	143	May 10	Sept. 30	San Antonio	TX	265	Mar. 3	Nov. 24
Baltimore	MD	231	Mar. 26	Nov. 13	Cedar City	UT	134	May 20	Oct. 2
Worcester	MA	172	Apr. 27	Oct. 17	Spanish Fork	UT	156	May 8	Oct. 12
Lansing	MI	140	May 13	Sept. 30	Burlington	VT	142	May 11	Oct. 1
Marquette	MI	159	May 12	Oct. 19	Norfolk	VA	239	Mar. 23	Nov. 17
Duluth	MN	122	May 21	Sept. 21	Richmond	VA	198	Apr. 10	Oct. 26
Willmar	MN	152	May 4	Oct. 4	Seattle	WA	232	Mar. 24	Nov. 11
Columbus	MS	215	Mar. 27	Oct. 29	Spokane	WA	153	May 4	Oct. 5
Vicksburg	MS	250	Mar. 13	Nov. 18	Parkersburg	WV	175	Apr. 25	Oct. 18
Jefferson City	MO	173	Apr. 26	Oct. 16	Green Bay	WI	143	May 12	Oct. 2
Fort Peck	MT	146	May 5	Sept. 28	Janesville	WI	164	Apr. 28	Oct. 10
Helena	MT	122	May 18	Sept. 18	Casper	WY	123	May 22	Sept. 22
Blair	NE	165	Apr. 27	Oct. 10					

Frosts do not occur every year.

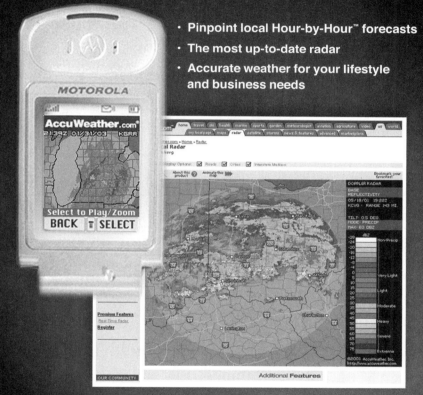

AccuWeather.com®

Now the Best Weather on the Web™ is also on your cell phone

- Pinpoint local Hour-by-Hour™ forecasts
- The most up-to-date radar
- Accurate weather for your lifestyle and business needs

Bookmark *accuweather.com* for your home or office PC

Visit *wireless.accuweather.com* to begin your wireless weather delivery

Calling All
BIRDS!

Create a bird-friendly habitat

with plants that invite birds to

your garden. *by Kris Wetherbee*

IMAGINE THE SWEET SONG OF A WAR-
bler as it greets morning's first light, or
the amusing acrobatics of a swallow
while catching bugs on the wing. Now,
stop dreaming and start enjoying a
front-row view of nature's winged
wonders right in your own backyard.

Creating a bird-friendly environment is simply a matter of providing
the creature comforts we all crave:
food, protective cover, and a cozy spot
for raising a family. A diversity of
trees, shrubs, and other plants, as well
as ground covers and vines, offers a
complete package for backyard bird
habitation. What's more, most experts
agree that an assortment of plants at-
tracts the widest variety of birds.

Understanding a bird's preferences
will help you determine which plants
to grow. Different plants will provide
for different needs, whether that
bounty is in the form of seeds, fruits,
nuts, or nectar, as well as for a host of
plant-munching caterpillars and in-

-Lynda Richardson/CORBIS

An American robin eating a mulberry.

sects. A garden filled with a mixture of plants producing flowers, seeds, berries, and nuts will always attract the largest number and variety of birds. For example, seed-eating birds, including goldfinches, chickadees, and towhees, will seek out seed heads from an assortment of flowering plants and ornamental grasses. Any daisylike flowers such as sunflowers, asters, and black-eyed Susans, in addition to rudbeckias, zinnias, and echinaceas, would be good choices. Finches, sparrows, and nuthatches are a few of the birds that will flock to marigolds, cosmos, coreopsis, goldenrod, phlox, and

51

a wide selection of salvias. Hummingbirds are happy with nectar from bee balm, geraniums, veronicas, delphiniums, and penstemons.

Remember, too, that birds are attracted to seasonal food. They will stay longer in your garden if it contains plants that flower or fruit at different times of the year. For example, hollies and roses provide winter fruit; serviceberries and chokecherries offer late-spring berries; blueberries and mulberries bear summer fruit; and honeysuckle and pyracantha round out the fruit season in the fall.

Plants that provide shelter—a safe haven from predators, protective cover from harsh weather, or a cozy spot, whether to nest or just settle in for the night—appeal to just about any bird, regardless of food preference. But a plant that provides food and shelter says, "Come on in." For example, pine trees provide evergreen shelter enjoyed by many birds as well as nourishing pine seeds favored by chickadees. Low-growing junipers not only hide birds from imminent danger, but also offer an insect buffet for ground-insect feeders such as wrens, towhees, and juncos, in addition to providing a bevy of berries for titmice and waxwings. Some vines and shrubs (like Virginia creeper, clematis, serviceberry, and privet) are also multifunctional plants. Towhees, larks, and sparrows enjoy the seed heads of their spent flowers, while fruit-eating birds such as robins, thrushes, and tanagers gorge on their berries. These vines and shrubs also provide a safe haven. On

BUG BITES

Depending on the time of year, most birds eat bugs in addition to seeds, fruits, and nuts. Some birds eat nothing but bugs. Swallows, swifts, flycatchers, goatsuckers, brown creepers, warblers, wrens, and vireos are among the birds that have a voracious appetite for insects and non-insect creatures like slugs, snails, centipedes, pill bugs, and worms.

page 55, you'll find a list of shrubs and trees that provide food and shelter, as well as the birds they attract.

As you develop your garden, consider grouping your plants in layers. You'll be creating a multilevel habitat of food and shelter for a variety of birds, whether they feed on the ground, in trees and bushes, or in the air. Include fruit-bearing shrubs, deciduous trees, and evergreens of all heights in your upper layers. At ground level, consider planting ground covers as well as petite perennials and annuals. Fill the layers in between with perennials, annuals, ornamental grasses, and low-growing shrubs.

When it all comes together, your garden just may become a bird's favorite place to be!

(continued)

Catalog Emporium

−Index Stock

FEATHER YOUR NESTING AREA

To catch a bird's eye, your garden area should include

■ a continual source of water for drinking and bathing, whether in a pond, stream, fountain, or birdbath

■ a few brush piles and untidy corners to provide areas where birds can nest and rest

■ less lawn grass, more weeds—which provide additional sources of food and shelter (for example, thistles provide seeds and nesting materials for goldfinches).

DON'T FORGET A FEEDER!

When a bird's natural plant food has waned or withered away, a few well-placed feeders can entice it to stay. There are four basic types of feeders, but the type of feeder and food it's filled with will determine which birds will visit.

■ A tray or platform feeder placed one to three feet above the ground will lure ground-feeding birds like juncos, towhees, and mourning doves.

■ Hung from a tree or mounted on a pole, "house"-style feeders with seed hoppers and perches on the side will usually entice grosbeaks, cardinals, and jays.

■ Long, cylindrical tube feeders suspended in air will bring in an array of small birds, including grosbeaks, finches, titmice, nuthatches, siskins, and chickadees.

■ A fruit feeder stocked with fresh fruit will tempt colorful birds like tanagers, orioles, bluebirds, and waxwings.

Birds will seldom drop or pick out unwanted seeds if you fill your feeder with only one type of seed rather than a generic mix. Black-oil sunflower seeds are the most widely preferred, though white millet is popular among ground-feeding birds. A tube feeder containing thistle seeds will whet the appetite of buntings, goldfinches, siskins, or redpolls. Jays, chickadees, and juncos love shelled peanuts or cracked corn as a treat in a tray feeder.

Kris Wetherbee, who lives in Oregon, is the author of a new book tentatively titled *Backyard Birds, Butterflies, & Other Winged Wonders* (Lark Books).

OFFER A BIRD BUFFET
To get recipes for Woodpecker Pudding, Junco Cornbread, and Suet Cake, go to **www.almanac.com** and click on **Article Links 2005**.

SHRUBS AND TREES
TO PLANT FOR THE BIRDS

F = Food
S = Shelter

Bird	Ash	Birch	Blackberry/raspberry	Blueberry	Cedar (red)/juniper	Cherry/plum	Crab apple	Dogwood	Elderberry	Hawthorn	Holly	Honeysuckle	Mulberry	Oak	Pine	Rose	Spruce	Sumac
Blue jay	F/S	F	F/S	F/S		F	F	F/S	F/S	F	F/S	F/S	F	F/S	F/S		S	F
Cardinal	F		F/S			F		F		S		S	F	F	F	F/S		F
Catbird			F			F	F/S	F/S	F/S	S	F/S	F/S	F			F/S	F	
Cedar waxwing	F/S	F	F/S	F/S		F	F/S		F	F/S	F/S	F/S	F	F	F/S	F	F	F/S
Chickadee	F/S	F		F/S					F/S		F/S	F		F	F	F	F/S	F
Crossbill		F/S			F/S												F	F/S
Finch	F/S	F	F/S		F/S	F	F/S		F/S	F	F/S	F	F	F/S	S		S	
Flicker				F/S		F	F/S	F/S	F/S		F/S			F	F			F
Goldfinch		F/S				F	F	S		S						F	F/S	
Grackle			F		F/S								F					S
Grosbeak	F/S		F/S			F	F/S	F/S	F/S	S		F	F	F/S	F	F	F/S	
Junco		F						F/S				F/S			F			
Mockingbird			F/S		F/S	F	F/S		F/S	F	F/S	F/S	F	S		F	F/S	F
Mourning dove		F	F/S					F/S	F	F/S				F	F		F/S	
Nuthatch								F/S		F/S				F	F		F/S	
Oriole	F	S	F	F		F	F	F/S				F	F			F/S		
Pine siskin	F/S	F											F/S				F/S	
Redpoll		S	F/S		F/S													F
Robin	F		F	F	F	F	F/S	F	F	S	F	F	F			S	F	S
Sparrow			F/S	F/S		F		F/S	F/S	F		F/S		F/S	S	S	F/S	
Tanager						F		F			F/S		F	S	S		F/S	F
Thrasher			F/S			F		F/S	F/S	F/S	F	F			F	S		F
Thrush			F/S		F/S	F		F/S	F/S	F/S	F			F/S	F	F		F
Titmouse		F	F/S				F			F/S				F	F			F
Towhee		F	F/S			F	F		F/S		F/S	F			F	S		F
Warbler			F/S		F/S		F		F/S	S	F/S			F/S		S		F
Woodpecker						F	F/S	F/S	F/S		F/S		F	F	F		F/S	F

FATAL ATTRACTIONS

THESE FLOWERING

BEAUTIES WILL TAKE

YOUR BREATH AWAY—

IF YOU'RE NOT CAREFUL.

I n the garden as in the real world, beauty and desirability sometimes veil an inherent danger. In a strange masquerade of nature, the petals, leaves, stems, and even seeds of sought-after plants act as factories for some of the most potent poisons known to man. Gardeners who are smitten with these beauties must realize the risks as well as the rewards.

BY HILDA J. BRUCKER

THE FEMME FATALE OF
FLOWERS

OLEANDER

■ Where winters are mild, gardeners have long had a love affair with oleander. Easily naturalized in subtropical and desert areas (Zone 8 and above), this shrub blooms its toxic little heart out 8 to 12 months out of the year. So bewitching is its beauty to northern gardeners that some hybridizers are devoting themselves to creating hardier varieties. Others are focusing on breeding dwarf cultivars more suitable for container culture in areas where oleander must overwinter indoors. From the original single-white and double-magenta flower forms, an array of salmons, pinks, reds, and yellows have sprung.

An evergreen shrub, *Nerium oleander* requires only a site in full sun. Dig a hole twice as wide and deep as the root ball. Break up the clods in the soil you've removed, and shovel half of it back into the hole (this loosened soil will encourage roots to grow deeply). Place the shrub into the hole and fill it in so that the top layer of roots is level with the surrounding soil. Water well until established; further care is optional. According to Elizabeth Head, president of the International Oleander Society, the streets of her hometown of Galveston, Texas, are lined with oleanders that get no supplemental water or nutrients. She adds that pruning can encourage heavier flowering, improve the shape of the shrub, and limit size (untended, shrubs can reach 15 feet). Container culture is similar. You can keep dwarf varieties to four feet with pruning but will have to irrigate and protect them from hard freezes.

Oleander thrives in sandy soil or sticky clay; tolerates the salty air and soil of the seaside; is drought- and heat-tolerant enough for Xeriscaping; and can even withstand a light frost. Plus, most pests aren't the least bit interested in it. The milky, sticky sap that courses through oleander twigs and leaves is highly lethal when ingested.

The BEASTLY SIDE OF THIS BEAUTY

Oleander may be the most lethal plant known to medical science. All parts contain a toxic cardenolide glycoside that adversely affects the heart: Consuming just one leaf can kill a person. Symptoms show up within hours and include severe abdominal pain, vomiting, racing heartbeat, and breathlessness. Eventually, death results.

−David Cavagnaro

One species of moth, Syntomeida epilais jucundissima, *feeds exclusively on oleander leaves during its larval stage— and is impervious to the poison. Unfortunately, any birds that snack on the well-fed caterpillars are doomed.*

(c o n t i n u e d)

ANGEL'S TRUMPET

■ From its divine scent to its startlingly large, cornet-shape blooms, angel's trumpet is an aptly named flower. Once of interest only to botanists, this group of plants is now lending bright color and bold form to terraces and flower beds in summer. There are currently ten species of angel's trumpet belonging to two different genera. Until the 1970s, all were classified as *Datura*. These days, however, the treelike forms and some of those with dangling, pendulous blooms have been reclassified as *Brugmansia* (although the taxonomy of the various types is hopelessly confused). Generally, the nursery trade offers only four species as ornamentals.

Brugmansia arborea and *B. suaveolens* are the largest of the angel's trumpets, reaching ten

The easiest way to tell Brugmansia *from* Datura *is that* Brugmansia *has dangling, pendulous blooms, and* Datura *sports upright trumpets. They are equally toxic.*

Psoriasis?

Restore your skin to a healthier, clearer state fast!

The
ORIGINAL

A product by

BEFORE

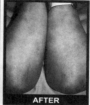
AFTER

**FDA-approved active ingredients • Won't stain clothing • No steroids
No burning • Easy application • Non-prescription
No oily or chalky mess • Spray goes on like water**

Feel like you have brand-new skin.

The revolutionary SkinZinc™ system is specially formulated to treat psoriasis and its painful, stubborn symptoms. The odorless, colorless formula goes on easily, like water, and thoroughly penetrates to deliver medicated strength relief. As your skin becomes clearer and smoother, the SkinZinc™ system promotes healing and helps manage future flare-ups.

SkinZinc™ is the most effective product I've seen for the treatment of skin disorders such as psoriasis, dermatitis and dandruff."
- Dr. S. Ravitz

The SkinZinc™ system is the choice of psoriasis sufferers because it contains FDA-approved and doctor-recommended active ingredients. And, SkinZinc™ is gentle thanks to all-natural tea tree oil and alfalfa extract which soothe on contact without the irritation, burning or drying associated with other treatments.

feet in a single growing season. Though treelike, they are actually herbaceous perennials in warm climates (Zones 7 to 10) and grown as annuals farther north. Whether grown in a patio tub or in the ground, they are truly spectacular, with bluish-green, toothy foliage and six-inch white trumpets. Flowers tend to close during the hottest parts of the day and open in the evening. At twilight, fragrance is at its most intense, as the plant seeks to seduce lunar moths and other nocturnal pollinators.

Datura is the original genus of the angel's trumpets; the following species have been hybridized widely. *D. metel* is a smaller, shrubby ornamental, reaching three to six feet. Hybrids are available in a rainbow of colors: lavender, blue, dark purple, yellow, pink, and coral. The closely related *D. meteloides* is perhaps the showiest of all, often sporting ruffly looking double and triple flower forms. Like most annuals, the daturas can either be started from seed indoors or be bought in pots from a nursery. They require full sun and are extremely drought tolerant, blooming profusely until frost. They also make excellent winter greenhouse plants.

The BEASTLY SIDE OF THIS BEAUTY

All the ornamental daturas are closely related to *D. stramonium*, the infamous jimsonweed of the Jamestown, Virginia, colony. Reportedly, settlers observed the Native Americans' religious use of the plant and decided to harvest it for their own use. Lacking any knowledge of *Datura*'s pharmacology, they "went mad" for several days, as the legend goes. Today, *Datura*'s effects on the central nervous system are well known. All parts of the plant are toxic, containing the alkaloids atropine, hyoscyamine, and scopolamine. Most toxic of all are the seeds: When ingested, they can cause delirium, disorientation, and even hallucinations, possibly resulting in reckless behavior. (You can become a danger to yourself.) In parts of the Northeast, angel's trumpets are still referred to as jimsonweed, locoweed, or thorn apple (for the spiked seedpod they produce).

Gardeners should be most aware of the plant's sap. It contains large amounts of atropine, the substance used by ophthalmologists to dilate the pupil and relax the optic muscles during eye exams. There are numerous reports of people who have rubbed their eyes after working with angel's trumpet and suffered from dilated pupils for days. Because you can also absorb the alkaloids through an abrasion or open wound, it's best to wear gloves and wash your hands frequently if you're cultivating angel's trumpet.

(c o n t i n u e d)

DELICATE BUT DECEPTIVE

MONKSHOOD

■ Along about August, when most other perennials have petered out, monkshood is putting up tall spires of flowers in shades of azure. This relatively late flowering period makes monkshood precious to gardeners. The species itself, *Aconitum napellus,* is scarcely seen anymore because a host of new cultivars has appeared. 'Bicolor' is a favorite, sporting blue flowers tinged with white. It grows to three or four feet. 'Newry Blue', with deep indigo blooms, is the tallest of the monkshoods, topping out at five feet. More compact is violet-blue flowering 'Bressingham Spire'. At just 30 inches, it's not as likely as the others to require staking. (Tall varieties require full sun; partial shade leads to weak-stemmed plants that need support.)

With its love for cool summers, monkshood was a mainstay of traditional cottage gardens—but it is finicky: It sulks in high heat and humidity and puts on the best show in Zones 3 to 6. Give it a moist loam rich in organic material, and choose a spot where you won't be tempted to move it.

–David Cavagnaro

As far back as the days of the Roman Empire, monkshood root was added to meat for use as bait to poison predators, earning it the moniker of "wolf's bane."

𝒯𝒽𝑒 BEASTLY SIDE

OF THIS BEAUTY

Toxicologists warn against planting any species of *Aconitum* where you might dig it up and mistake the fleshy root for an underground crop (turnip, radish, ginger, etc.). Beware: The toxin aconitine, present in all parts of all species of monkshood, is most concentrated in the root. Eating it either raw or cooked can bring on heart failure and death within six hours.

Once established, monkshood resents transplanting—not entirely a bad thing, since toxins can enter your body if the rootstock makes direct contact with your skin. Aconitine numbs the skin and causes a tingling sensation. It's best to wear gloves when planting monkshood, as prolonged exposure to it sometimes can affect both the nervous and cardiac systems.

□□

Hilda J. Brucker is a frequent contributor to gardening magazines.

A TRIPLE THREAT

Elderberry, pokeweed, and fool's parsley are tempting—and potentially toxic—wild plants. To learn more about them, go to **www.almanac.com** and click on **Article Links 2005**.

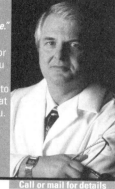

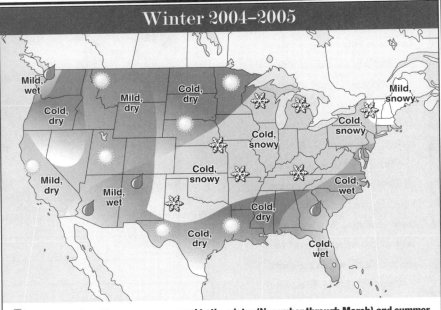

Winter 2004–2005

These seasonal weather maps correspond to the winter (November through March) and summer (June through August) forecasts on page 66. A map of our 16 weather regions is on page 68; the detailed forecasts for those regions begin on page 70. For an explanation of our forecast methodology, see "How We Predict the Weather" on page 67.

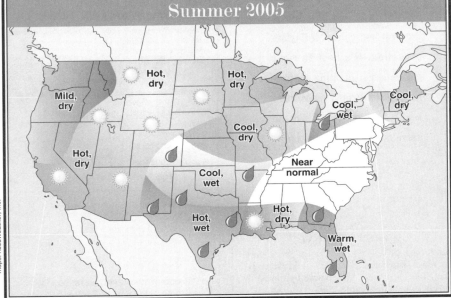

Summer 2005

Why wait ten months?

Now you can have rich, dark compost _in just 14 days!_

With the amazing ComposTumbler, you'll have bushels of crumbly, ready-to-use compost — _in just 14 days!_ (And, in the ten months it takes to make compost the old way, your ComposTumbler can produce _hundreds of pounds_ of rich food for your garden!)

Say good-bye to that messy, open compost pile (and to the flies, pests, and odors that come along with it!) Bid a happy farewell to the strain of trying to turn over heavy, wet piles with a pitchfork.

Compost the Better Way

Compost-making with the ComposTumbler is neat, quick and easy!

Gather up leaves, old weeds, kitchen scraps, lawn clippings, etc. and toss them into the roomy 18-bushel drum. Then, once each day, give the ComposTumbler's _gear-driven_ handle a few easy spins.

The ComposTumbler's Magic

Inside the ComposTumbler, carefully positioned mixing fins blend materials, pushing fresh mixture to the core where the temperatures are the hottest (up to 160°) and the composting bacteria most active.

After just 14 days, open the door, and you'll find an abundance of dark, sweet-smelling "garden gold" — ready to enrich and feed your garden!

NEW SMALLER SIZE!

Now there are 2 sizes. The 18-bushel original ComposTumbler and the NEW 9.5-bushel Compact ComposTumbler. Try either size risk-free for 30 days!

See for yourself! Try the ComposTumbler risk-free with our 30-Day Home Trial!

Call Toll-Free 1-800-880-2345

NOW ON SALE— SAVE UP TO $115!

ComposTumbler®

The choice of more than 250,000 gardeners

☐ YES! Please rush FREE information on the ComposTumbler, including special savings and 30-Day Home Trial.

Name _____

Address _____

City _____

State _____ ZIP _____

MAIL TO: **ComposTumbler**
30 Wright Ave., **Dept. 42015C**
Lititz (Lancaster Co.), PA 17543

© 2003 PBM Group

General U.S. Weather Forecast

For detailed regional forecasts, see pages 70–87.

Nearly all of the country will have above-normal snowfall or colder-than-normal temperatures—or both—this winter. The summer will be moderate in much of the country, but hot weather and drought may spark an intense fire season in the Pacific Southwest and Intermountain regions. The hurricane season will be active, with the threat of a severe hurricane along the Atlantic Coast.

November through March will be colder than normal from the Atlantic Corridor south- and westward through the High Plains. Temperatures in the Southeast, Florida, Deep South, Ohio Valley, Heartland, and Texas–Oklahoma will be especially harsh—much below normal, on average. In the West, the only area that will be colder than normal will be the interior Pacific Northwest. The Pacific Southwest will have much-above-normal temperatures. Above-normal temperatures will occur along the Pacific Northwest coast, in the Desert Southwest, and in much of the Intermountain region.

Precipitation will be much greater than normal from central Florida northward through the Southeast, Atlantic Corridor, and Northeast and above normal in south Florida and the Appalachians, from the Desert Southwest northeastward into Iowa, and in coastal Washington state. Precipitation will be much below normal in California and south Texas. Elsewhere, precipitation will be below normal.

Snowfall will be greater than normal from the Great Lakes eastward through the New England states and from eastern New Mexico eastward to the mid-Atlantic states. Snowfall will be below normal in most other areas that receive snow.

April and May will be cooler than normal in Florida and the Deep South, the Pacific Northwest, interior California, the Intermountain region, and much of the northern High Plains and Upper Midwest. Temperatures will be much above normal in the Northeast and above normal in the Atlantic Corridor, Southeast, Lower Lakes, Ohio Valley, Heartland, southern High Plains, Desert Southwest, and coastal sections of the Pacific Southwest.

Precipitation will be above normal in the Pacific Northwest, south Florida, and northern New England states, and near normal in the eastern Lower Lakes, Atlantic Corridor, and Heartland. Elsewhere, precipitation will be below normal.

June through August will be cooler than normal from the Northeast southwestward to northern Texas–Oklahoma. Temperatures will be above normal in the Pacific Southwest, Desert Southwest, much of the Intermountain region, northern High Plains, Upper Midwest, and near the Gulf Coast. Elsewhere, temperatures will be near normal.

Rainfall will be above normal in all of Florida except the western panhandle, south Georgia, Texas–Oklahoma, and the eastern Desert Southwest, southern High Plains, southwest Heartland, and eastern Lower Lakes. Rainfall will be below normal in the Northeast and southern Deep South, and from the Pacific Southwest and western Desert Southwest north- and eastward through much of the Intermountain region, northern High Plains, Heartland, Upper Midwest, and western Lower Lakes. Elsewhere, rainfall will be near normal.

September and October will be cooler than normal in the Atlantic Corridor, Appalachians, Lower Lakes, Upper Midwest, Heartland, and western Deep South, and near normal in the Intermountain region. Elsewhere, temperatures will be above normal.

Rainfall will be much above normal in Florida and much of the Northeast; above normal in the Atlantic Corridor, Appalachians, Deep South, Pacific Southwest, and Desert Southwest; and near normal in the Pacific Northwest. Elsewhere, rainfall will be below normal.

How We Predict the Weather

■ **We derive our weather forecasts from** a secret formula that was devised by the founder of this Almanac, Robert B. Thomas, in 1792. Thomas believed that weather on Earth was influenced by sunspots, which are magnetic storms on the surface of the Sun.

−Beth Krommes

Over the years, we have refined and enhanced that formula with state-of-the-art technology and modern scientific calculations. We employ three scientific disciplines to make our long-range predictions: solar science, the study of sunspots and other solar activity; climatology, the study of prevailing weather patterns; and meteorology, the study of the atmosphere. We predict weather trends and events by comparing solar patterns and historical weather conditions with current solar activity.

Our forecasts emphasize temperature and precipitation deviations from averages, or normals. These are based on 30-year statistical averages prepared by government meteorological agencies and updated every ten years. The most recent tabulations span the period 1971 through 2000.

We believe that nothing in the universe happens haphazardly, that there is a cause-and-effect pattern to all phenomena. However, although neither we nor any other forecasters have as yet gained sufficient insight into the mysteries of the universe to predict the weather with *total* accuracy, our results are almost always *very* close to our traditional claim of 80 percent.

U.S. Weather Regions

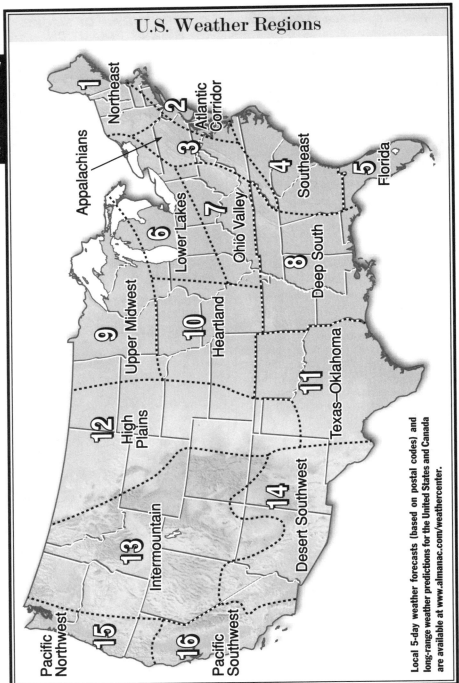

1 Northeast
2 Atlantic Corridor
3 Appalachians
4 Southeast
5 Florida
6 Lower Lakes
7 Ohio Valley
8 Deep South
9 Upper Midwest
10 Heartland
11 Texas–Oklahoma
12 High Plains
13 Intermountain
14 Desert Southwest
15 Pacific Northwest
16 Pacific Southwest

Local 5-day weather forecasts (based on postal codes) and long-range weather predictions for the United States and Canada are available at www.almanac.com/weathercenter.

Northeast

REGION 1 SUMMARY: Don't be fooled by mild periods in late January and February. Although the first part of winter will be mild, on average, cold weather will return, and March will be chilly. The coldest temperatures will occur in early January, with other cold periods in mid-December, mid- to late January, and late February. Snowfall will be near or above normal, with the heaviest snow in mid-November, early to mid-December, mid-January, mid- and late February, and early to mid-March.

After a chilly start, April and May will be mild, with near-normal rainfall. Late April to early May will be warm. Summer will be pleasant, with temperatures and rainfall below normal. The hottest temperatures will occur in mid- to late July and mid- to late August.

Heavy rain from a tropical storm will occur in early September. Otherwise, September and October will bring near-normal temperatures and precipitation.

NOV. 2004: Temp. 38° (avg.); precip. 4.5" (1" above avg.). 1-5 Sunny, cool. 6-11 Rainy. 12-16 Cold; snow showers. 17-23 Heavy rain and snow. 24-30 Sunny, mild.

DEC. 2004: Temp. 28.5° (2.5° above avg.); precip. 4" (1" above avg.). 1-4 Rain and snow showers. 5-7 Heavy rain and snow. 8-11 Mild. 12-18 Cold, flurries. 19-24 Heavy snow. 25-27 Sunny. 28-31 Rain, then snow.

JAN. 2005: Temp. 20.5° (0.5° above avg.); precip. 2.5" (0.5" below avg.). 1-6 Very cold, flurries. 7-16 Seasonable, snowy. 17-19 Sunny, cold. 20-23 Snow. 24-31 Flurries; cold, then mild.

FEB. 2005: Temp. 26° (5° above avg.); precip. 3.5" (1" above avg.). 1-5 Mild; snow, then rain. 6-8 Cold, snow. 9-12 Sunny, mild. 13-20 Seasonable, snowy. 21-24 Sunny, cold. 25-28 Cold; heavy snow south.

MAR. 2005: Temp. 29° (4° below avg.); precip. 4" (1" above avg.). 1-5 Sunny, cold. 6-12 Chilly, snowy. 13-15 Sunny. 16-22 Snow showers, cold. 23-31 Rain, some heavy.

APR. 2005: Temp. 48° (3° above avg.); precip. 2.5" (0.5" below avg.). 1-6 Chilly, showers and flurries. 7-11 Sunny, warm. 12-21 Warm, showers. 22-26 Sunny, then rain. 27-30 Sunny, very warm.

MAY 2005: Temp. 61° (5° above avg.); precip. 4.5" (1" above avg.). 1-2 Sunny, warm. 3-10 Showers, seasonable. 11-15 Sunny, warm. 16-20 Rain. 21-24 Sunny, warm. 25-31 Warm, t-storms.

JUNE 2005: Temp. 64° (1° below avg.); precip. 3" (0.5" below avg.). 1-7 Sunny, cool. 8-12 T-storms, seasonable. 13-19 Sunny, then t-storms. 20-23 Sunny, warm. 24-30 Cool, showers.

JULY 2005: Temp. 68° (2° below avg.); precip. 4.5" (0.5" above avg.). 1-7 Warm, showers. 8-11 Sunny, comfortable. 12-16 Cool, t-storms. 17-22 Sunny, comfortable. 23-25 Hot, then t-storms. 26-31 Sunny, cool.

AUG. 2005: Temp. 67° (avg.); precip. 3" (1" below avg.). 1-4 Cool, t-storms. 5-9 Sunny, then t-storms. 10-13 Sunny, warm. 14-17 T-storms. 18-22 Sunny; cool, then warm. 23-26 Showers, warm. 27-31 Sunny; chilly nights.

SEPT. 2005: Temp. 60° (1° above avg.); precip. 5" (avg. north; 3" above south). 1-2 Sunny, warm. 3-7 Tropical storm. 8-14 Sunny, then rain. 15-22 Sunny, mild. 23-26 Rain, chilly. 27-30 Sunny, cool.

OCT. 2005: Temp. 48° (avg.); precip. 4" (0.5" above avg.). 1-4 Sunny, cool. 5-10 Showers, mild. 11-15 Cool, rain and snow showers. 16-19 Rain. 20-25 Sunny, pleasant. 26-31 Rain, then flurries.

Caribou

Augusta

Burlington

Concord

Albany

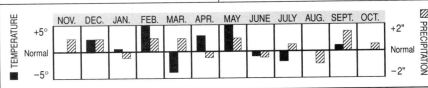

Atlantic Corridor

REGION 2 SUMMARY: November through mid-February will not be too severe, but cold temperatures and heavy snow in late winter will mean a colder- and snowier-than-normal season. The coldest temperatures will be in mid-December, with other cold periods in mid-November, early and mid-January, and from late February until the first day of spring. Significant snowfalls will occur in mid-December, early and late February, and early March.

April will be pleasant, with well-above-normal temperatures and well-below-normal rainfall. Expect summerlike warmth in the month's second week. May will be near normal.

Summer temperatures and rainfall will be near normal. The hottest temperatures will occur in mid- to late August. Watch for a tropical storm in mid- to late July.

A hurricane will threaten or strike the coast in early September. Otherwise, September and October will be close to normal in temperatures and rainfall.

NOV. 2004: Temp. 47° (0.5° above avg. north; 2° below south); precip. 4.5" (1" above avg.). 1-6 Rain, then sunny, cool. 7-11 Showers. 12-14 Sunny, cold. 15-22 Heavy rain, mild. 23-29 Sunny; cold, then mild. 30 Rain.

DEC. 2004: Temp. 40.5° (2.5° above avg.); precip. 4.5" (1.5" above avg.). 1-5 Rain and snow, then sunny. 6-11 Mild; rain, then sunny. 12-17 Rain to snow, then sunny, cold. 18-23 Snow north; mild, rain south. 24-26 Sunny, cold. 27-31 Rain, then snow.

JAN. 2005: Temp. 35° (2° above avg.); precip. 2.5" (1" below avg.). 1-4 Sunny. 5-13 Seasonable; snow north, rain south. 14-20 Sunny, cold. 21-25 Rain, mild. 26-31 Sunny, then rain.

FEB. 2005: Temp. 32° (3° above avg. north; 5° below south); precip. 5" (2" above avg.). 1-5 Warm; sunny, then rain. 6-8 Snow, heavy south. 9-11 Sunny. 12-18 Rain, then sunny. 19-22 Rain and snow, then sunny. 23-28 Northeaster.

MAR. 2005: Temp. 37° (4° below avg. north; 8° below south); precip. 4.5" (0.5" above avg.). 1-4 Snowstorm, cold. 5-9 Sunny, cold. 10-15 Snow, then sunny, cold. 16-20 Cold, flurries. 21-31 Heavy rain, mild.

APR. 2005: Temp. 56° (4° above avg.); precip. 1.5" (2" below avg.). 1-5 Chilly; showers north. 6-11 Sunny, very warm. 12-14 Seasonable,

showers. 15-19 Very warm, t-storms. 20-30 Showers, then sunny, seasonable.

MAY 2005: Temp. 62° (1° above avg. north; 1° below south); precip. 3.5" (0.5" below avg.; 2" above north). 1-6 Rain, cool. 7-13 Seasonable; showers north. 14-20 Seasonable, showers. 21-31 T-storms, then pleasant.

JUNE 2005: Temp. 71° (1° above avg. east; 1° below west); precip. 2" (1.5" below avg.). 1-5 Sunny, cool. 6-12 Seasonable, t-storms. 13-16 Sunny. 17-22 T-storms, then sunny. 23-30 T-storms, then sunny, warm.

JULY 2005: Temp. 76° (avg.); precip. 6" (2" above avg.). 1-8 Sunny, then t-storms. 9-16 Sunny, warm. 17-20 Warm, humid, t-storms. 21-25 Tropical storm. 26-31 Warm, humid, t-storms.

AUG. 2005: Temp. 75° (1° above avg.); precip. 3" (1" below avg.). 1-9 Warm, humid, t-storms. 10-12 Sunny, comfortable. 13-17 Warm, t-storms. 18-23 Sunny, hot. 24-31 Partly sunny, t-storms.

SEPT. 2005: Temp. 66° (1° below avg.); precip. 5.5" (3" above avg. north; 1" above south). 1-2 Sunny. 3-7 Hurricane. 8-11 Sunny, cool. 12-21 T-storms, then sunny, comfortable. 22-30 Showers, then sunny, cool.

OCT. 2005: Temp. 56° (avg.); precip. 4.5" (1" above avg.). 1-3 Showers. 4-12 Sunny, warm. 13-20 Rain, then sunny, chilly. 21-31 Rain, then showers, cool.

Boston
Hartford
New York
Philadelphia
Baltimore
Atlantic City
Washington
Richmond

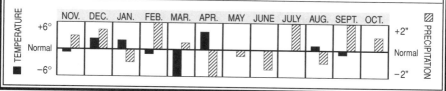

Appalachians

REGION 3 SUMMARY: November through January will be mild, with little snow and milder-than-normal temperatures, but by the end of March, winter will be remembered for above-normal snowfall and below-normal temperatures, on average, especially in the south. The coldest periods will be mid-December, mid-January, and from late February through mid-March. The heaviest snowfalls will occur in early, mid-, and late February and early and mid-March.

After a cold and snowy start, April will be warm, with an early taste of summer in midmonth. Mid- and late May will be warm.

Summer will be cooler and drier than normal. The hottest temperatures will occur in late July and mid- to late August.

A tropical storm will bring heavy rain in the first week of September, especially in the north. Otherwise, September and October will bring near-normal temperatures and precipitation.

NOV. 2004: Temp. 40.5° (2.5° below avg.); precip. 3" (0.5" below avg.). 1-6 Sunny, cool. 7-11 Rain, chilly. 12-14 Cold, flurries. 15-22 Rain, seasonable. 23-30 Sunny, cold, then mild, showers.

DEC. 2004: Temp. 36° (3° above avg. north; 1° above south); precip. 4" (1" above avg.). 1-4 Snow, then sunny. 5-11 Rain, then sunny, mild. 12-16 Rain and snow. 17-23 Sunny, cold, then rain. 24-31 Sunny, then rain to snow.

JAN. 2005: Temp. 30° (2° above avg.); precip. 2.5" (0.5" below avg.). 1-5 Flurries, seasonable. 6-9 Rain south, snow north. 10-13 Snow showers. 14-20 Flurries, cold. 21-24 Rain, mild. 25-31 Sunny, then rain.

FEB. 2005: Temp. 24.5° (avg. north; 7° below south); precip. 4.5" (2" above avg.). 1-5 Warm, rain. 6-8 Cold, snow. 9-15 Sunny, then a snowstorm. 16-18 Flurries. 19-23 Snow, seasonable. 24-28 Heavy snow, cold.

MAR. 2005: Temp. 31° (8° below avg.); precip. 3" (avg.). 1-3 Cold, snow. 4-9 Cold, flurries. 10-14 Cold, snow. 15-20 Cold, snow showers. 21-31 Mild, rain.

APR. 2005: Temp. 54° (4° above avg.); precip. 1.5" (2" below avg.). 1-4 Snow showers, cold. 5-11 Sunny, warm. 12-18 Showers, then sunny, hot. 19-25 T-storms, then cooler. 26-30 Sunny, seasonable.

Elmira ⊙
Scranton ⊙
Harrisburg ⊙
Frederick ⊙
Roanoke ⊙
Asheville ⊙

MAY 2005: Temp. 59° (1° below avg.); precip. 6" (2" above avg.). 1-7 Rain, cool. 8-14 Showers north; sunny, hot south. 15-27 Seasonable, t-storms. 28-31 T-storms, warm.

JUNE 2005: Temp. 66° (2° below avg.); precip. 3" (1" below avg.). 1-5 Sunny, pleasant. 6-12 Partly sunny, t-storms, warm. 13-18 Showers, seasonable. 19-22 Sunny, seasonable. 23-30 Warm, t-storms.

JULY 2005: Temp. 72° (1° below avg.); precip. 3.5" (avg.). 1-6 Sunny, warm. 7-11 T-storms north, sunny south. 12-24 T-storms; cool north, hot south. 25-31 Hot, t-storms.

AUG. 2005: Temp. 73° (2° above avg.); precip. 2.5" (1" below avg.). 1-8 T-storms, warm. 9-13 Sunny, pleasant. 14-16 T-storms. 17-22 Sunny, hot. 23-26 Hot, t-storms. 27-31 Showers; cool north, warm south.

SEPT. 2005: Temp. 63° (1° below avg.); precip. 5.5" (3" above avg. north; 1" below south). 1-3 Sunny, hot. 4-7 Tropical storm. 8-10 Sunny, cool. 11-14 Rain, seasonable. 15-22 Sunny, seasonable. 23-30 Rain, then sunny, cool.

OCT. 2005: Temp. 53° (avg.); precip. 3" (avg.). 1-11 Rain, then sunny, warm. 12-16 Rain, then sunny, cool. 17-20 Chilly, rain to snow. 21-28 Showers, seasonable. 29-31 Rain to snow.

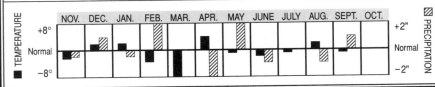

	NOV.	DEC.	JAN.	FEB.	MAR.	APR.	MAY	JUNE	JULY	AUG.	SEPT.	OCT.	

TEMPERATURE +8° Normal ■ −8°

PRECIPITATION +2" Normal −2"

Southeast

REGION 4 SUMMARY: The first half of winter will be near normal, but February and March will be exceptionally cold, with snow and ice storms in northern and central parts of the region. The coldest temperatures will occur in late February and early March—much later than usual. Other cold periods will occur in mid-January and early to mid-February.

April and May will be milder than normal across the north, but cooler than normal in the south. Rainfall will be below normal.

Summer will bring near- or slightly below normal temperatures. Despite a tropical storm that will bring heavy rain in mid- to late July, rainfall will be near normal. The hottest periods will be late June, mid- to late July, and late August.

Expect a hurricane in early September. Otherwise, temperatures and precipitation will be close to normal in September and October.

NOV. 2004: Temp. 53° (2° below avg.); precip. 2" (1" below avg.). 1-5 Sunny, cool. 6-9 Showers, warm. 10-14 Sunny, chilly. 15-22 Seasonable, showers. 23-30 Sunny; cold, then seasonable.

DEC. 2004: Temp. 47° (avg.); precip. 3.5" (avg.). 1-4 Sunny, mild. 5-10 Rain, then sunny. 11-15 Rain, cool. 16-21 Sunny; cold, then mild. 22-25 Rain, then sunny, cold. 26-31 Rain, seasonable.

JAN. 2005: Temp. 45° (1° above avg. north; 1° below south); precip. 6.5" (2" above avg.). 1-6 Rain, then sunny, mild. 7-12 Rain; warm, then seasonable. 13-19 Sunny, cold. 20-25 Heavy rain. 26-31 Sunny, then heavy rain.

FEB. 2005: Temp. 39° (7° below avg.); precip. 5" (1" above avg.). 1-3 Sunny, seasonable. 4-7 Heavy rain; snow north. 8-11 Sunny, cold. 12-19 Rain, chilly. 20-23 Sunny, chilly. 24-28 Rain to snow, then cold.

MAR. 2005: Temp. 48° (7° below avg.); precip. 6.5" (2" above avg.). 1-5 Record cold; snow north, rain south. 6-11 Cold; sunny, then rain; ice north. 12-19 Sunny, chilly. 20-31 Heavy rain, seasonable.

APR. 2005: Temp. 64.5° (3° above avg. north; 0.5° above south); precip. 2" (1" below avg.). 1-5 Sunny, cool. 6-11 Sunny, warm. 12-15 Seasonable; showers, then sunny. 16-20 Showers, then sunny, warm. 21-30 T-storms, then sunny, seasonable.

Raleigh
Columbia
Atlanta
Savannah

MAY 2005: Temp. 70.5° (0.5° below avg.); precip. 3.5" (avg.). 1-4 Showers, cool. 5-14 Sunny; cool, then warm. 15-21 Warm, t-storms. 22-26 Sunny, warm. 27-31 T-storms, seasonable.

JUNE 2005: Temp. 76.5° (0.5° below avg.); precip. 4" (0.5" below avg.). 1-5 T-storms, then sunny, comfortable. 6-10 Sunny, very warm. 11-20 Seasonable, t-storms. 21-24 Sunny, very warm. 25-30 Hot, humid, t-storms.

JULY 2005: Temp. 80.5° (0.5° below avg.); precip. 7" (2" above avg.). 1-8 Seasonable; scattered t-storms. 9-17 Warm, humid; sunny north, t-storms south. 18-21 Very warm, showers. 22-25 Tropical storm. 26-31 Very warm, t-storms.

AUG. 2005: Temp. 79.5° (0.5° above avg.); precip. 4.5" (0.5" below avg.). 1-10 Partly sunny, t-storms, seasonable. 11-15 Sunny, warm. 16-21 Showers, seasonable. 22-31 Partly sunny, warm; t-storms south.

SEPT. 2005: Temp. 73° (2° below avg. north; 0.5° above south); precip. 5.5" (1" above avg.). 1-3 Sunny, warm. 4-7 Hurricane. 8-12 Showers, seasonable. 13-17 Sunny, warm. 18-24 Rain, seasonable. 25-30 Sunny, then showers.

OCT. 2005: Temp. 64.5° (avg. north; 1° above south); precip. 2" (1" below avg.). 1-3 Showers. 4-12 Sunny, warm. 13-19 Showers, then sunny, cool. 20-31 Seasonable, a few showers.

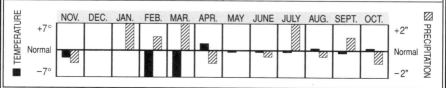

Florida

REGION 5 SUMMARY: Winter will be cold and wet, although a killing freeze in central Florida is unlikely. November will be wet across south Florida, while March will be the wettest month elsewhere. November through January will be cooler than normal, on average, and February and March will be much colder than normal, especially across the north. The coldest temperatures will occur near Thanksgiving, in mid-January, in early to mid-February, and from late February into early March.

Temperatures in April and May will be below normal, on average, despite a warm spell in mid-May. Rainfall will be heavy in the south but below normal in the north.

Summer will bring near-normal temperatures. Rainfall will be near normal in the south, but heavy July thunderstorms will bring well-above-normal rainfall in the north.

Watch for a hurricane in early September. Otherwise, both temperatures and rainfall in September and October will be above normal.

NOV. 2004: Temp. 67° (2° below avg.); precip. 4.5" (2" above avg.). 1-5 Cool, occasional t-storms. 6-10 Sunny, warm. 11-14 Warm, t-storms. 15-18 Sunny, warm. 19-21 T-storms, warm. 22-30 Sunny, cold.

DEC. 2004: Temp. 63.5° (0.5° above avg.); precip. 1.5" (1" below avg.). 1-5 Sunny, chilly. 6-12 Rain, then sunny, warm. 13-22 Mild, showers. 23-31 Sunny, then showers, warm.

JAN. 2005: Temp. 60° (1° below avg.); precip. 3.5" (1" above avg.). 1-10 Showers, then sunny, warm. 11-20 Showers, then sunny, cold. 21-31 Milder, rain.

FEB. 2005: Temp. 56.5° (6° below avg. north; 3° below south); precip. 3.5" (1" above avg.). 1-7 Sunny, then rain. 8-14 Sunny, cold. 15-19 T-storms, warm. 20-23 Rain, seasonable. 24-28 Sunny, cold.

MAR. 2005: Temp. 61.5° (9° below avg. north; 2° below south); precip. 5.5" (6" above avg. north; 1" below south). 1-4 Sunny; cold, then mild. 5-8 Rain, then sunny, cold. 9-13 Heavy rain. 14-18 Sunny, chilly. 19-26 Sunny, warm. 27-31 Rain, warm.

APR. 2005: Temp. 71° (avg.); precip. 4" (3" below avg. north; 6" above south). 1-3 Sunny, warm. 4-8 Sunny, cool. 9-14 Sunny, warm. 15-20 T-storms, warm. 21-30 Seasonable; scattered t-storms.

MAY 2005: Temp. 76° (1° below avg.); precip. 3.5" (0.5" below avg.). 1-3 T-storms, warm. 4-9 Sunny, pleasant. 10-19 Sunny, hot. 20-25 Warm; t-storms, then sunny. 26-31 Seasonable; scattered t-storms.

JUNE 2005: Temp. 80.5° (0.5° below avg.); precip. 5.5" (1" below avg.). 1-6 Sunny, comfortable. 7-9 Sunny, warm. 10-22 Warm, t-storms. 23-30 T-storms, hot.

JULY 2005: Temp. 83° (1° above avg.); precip. 10" (8" above avg. north; 1" below south). 1-12 Seasonable, partly sunny; scattered t-storms. 13-21 Warm; frequent t-storms. 22-31 Hot, t-storms.

AUG. 2005: Temp. 81° (avg.); precip. 7.5" (2" below avg. north; 2" above south). 1-6 Sunny, hot. 7-14 Warm; sunny north, t-storms south. 15-25 Seasonable; scattered t-storms. 26-31 Humid; frequent t-storms.

SEPT. 2005: Temp. 81° (1° above avg.); precip. 12" (5" above avg.). 1-7 Hurricane. 8-14 Sunny, warm. 15-24 Seasonable; sunny north, t-storms south. 25-30 Warm; sunny, then t-storms.

OCT. 2005: Temp. 76.5° (1.5° above avg.); precip. 4" (2" below avg. north; 2" above south). 1-14 Partly sunny, t-storms south; warm. 15-24 Sunny, warm. 25-31 T-storms, then sunny, seasonable.

Jacksonville
Tampa
Orlando
Miami

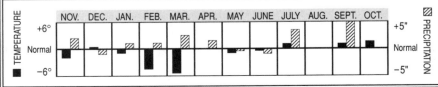

Lower Lakes

REGION 6 SUMMARY: After a cold November, December and January will be milder than normal—but don't be fooled into thinking winter will end early. February and March will be exceptionally cold and snowy. The coldest periods will be mid-November, mid-December, mid-January, and most of February through mid-March. Widespread snowstorms will occur in November (mid-November in the east, early November in the west), mid-January, February, and early and mid-March.

Despite a cold start, April will be mild, with several spells of unusual warmth. May will bring temperatures near normal. Rainfall in April and May will be near normal in the east and below normal in the west.

Summer will be cooler than normal with near-normal rainfall. The hottest weather will occur in mid- to late July and from late August into early September.

Overall, September and October will be cooler and drier than normal.

NOV. 2004: Temp. 36.5° (1° below avg. east; 6° below west); precip. 3" (avg.). 1-4 Sunny, cold. 5-10 Rain and snow. 11-14 Cold; snow east. 15-18 Mild; sunny, then rain. 19-23 Snow, cold. 24-30 Sunny, mild.

DEC. 2004: Temp. 32° (1° above avg. east; 5° above west); precip. 4" (2" above east; avg. west). 1-7 Lake snow, then rainy, mild. 8-12 Sunny, mild. 13-17 Cold; snow showers. 18-25 Rain, mild, then snow showers. 26-31 Seasonable; rain and snow east.

JAN. 2005: Temp. 28° (4° above avg.; avg. east); precip. 3.5" (2" above west; avg. east). 1-5 Snow showers, cold east; sunny, mild west. 6-9 Rain, mild. 10-18 Cold; snow showers. 19-27 Seasonable; snow showers. 28-31 Rain, mild.

FEB. 2005: Temp. 19° (1° below avg. east; 9° below west); precip. 3" (2" above avg. east; avg. west). 1-8 Heavy snow; mild, then cold. 9-12 Snow showers. 13-16 Heavy snow. 17-20 Cold, snow. 21-28 Windy, cold; snow showers.

MAR. 2005: Temp. 28° (8° below avg.); precip. 2" (0.5" below avg. east; 2" below west). 1-9 Snow, then sunny, cold. 10-20 Cold; occasional snow. 21-26 Mild; sunny, then rain. 27-31 Sunny, then rain and snow.

APR. 2005: Temp. 52° (5° above avg.); precip. 2.5" (1" below avg.). 1-5 Snow showers, then sunny. 6-11 T-storms, warm. 12-19 Warm; show-

ers east, sunny west. 20-23 Showers, seasonable. 24-30 Sunny, warm.

MAY 2005: Temp. 57.5° (1° above avg. east; 2° below west); precip. 3.5" (1" above avg. east; 1" below west). 1-8 Chilly, rain. 9-17 Seasonable, showers. 18-28 Sunny, then t-storms, seasonable. 29-31 Sunny, mild.

JUNE 2005: Temp. 63° (4° below avg.); precip. 3.5" (1.5" below avg. east; 2" above west). 1-4 Sunny, cool. 5-12 T-storms; warm, then cool. 13-16 Sunny, seasonable. 17-23 Warm; scattered showers. 24-30 T-storms, then sunny, cool.

JULY 2005: Temp. 70° (2° below avg.); precip. 3.5" (avg.). 1-13 Warm, then cooler; partly sunny; scattered t-storms. 14-18 Seasonable, showers east. 19-23 Sunny east; hot, t-storms west. 24-31 Sunny; cool, then t-storms, warm.

AUG. 2005: Temp. 72° (2° above avg.); precip. 4" (avg.). 1-4 Cool, t-storms. 5-7 Sunny, seasonable. 8-16 Seasonable, a few t-storms. 17-22 Sunny; cool, then warm. 23-31 T-storms, then sunny east; sunny, hot west.

SEPT. 2005: Temp. 63° (avg.); precip. 2.5" (1" below avg.). 1-3 Sunny, hot. 4-8 Showers, cool. 9-14 Seasonable, showers. 15-22 Sunny, warm. 23-30 Cool; showers, then sunny.

OCT. 2005: Temp. 51° (1° below avg.); precip. 2" (avg. east; 1" below west). 1-8 Sunny; cool, then warm. 9-17 Showers, cooler. 18-24 Rain to snow, then sunny, seasonable. 25-31 Rain, then snow.

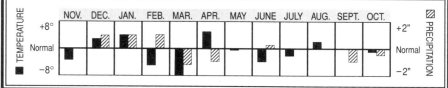

We're looking for people to—

Write Children's Books

By Kristi Holl

I f you've ever dreamed of writing for children, here's your chance to test that dream. . . and find out if you have the aptitude to make it a reality. If you do, we'll teach you how to crack one of today's most rewarding markets for new writers.

The $2 billion children's market

The tremendous recent success of children's books has made the general public aware of what we've known for years: There's a huge market out there. And there's a growing need for new writers trained to create the nearly $2 billion of children's books purchased every year. . . plus the stories and articles needed by more than 600 publishers of magazines for and about children and teenagers.

Who are these needed writers? They're ordinary people like you and me.

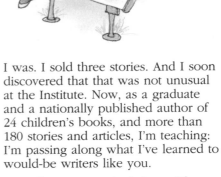

"But am I good enough?"

I was once where you may be now. My occasional thoughts of writing had been pushed down by self-doubt, and I didn't know where to turn for help. Then, on an impulse, I sent for the Institute's free writing aptitude test and it turned out to be the spark I needed. I took their course and my wonderful author-instructor helped me to discover, step-by-step, that my everyday life—probably not much different from yours— was an endless creative resource for my writing!

The promise that paid off

The Institute made the same promise to me that they'll make to you, if you demonstrate basic writing aptitude: *You will complete at least one manuscript suitable to submit to editors by the time you finish the course.*

I really didn't expect to be published before I finished the course, but

---

Kristi Holl, a graduate of our course, has published 24 books and more than 180 stories and articles. She is now an instructor at the Institute.

I was. I sold three stories. And I soon discovered that that was not unusual at the Institute. Now, as a graduate and a nationally published author of 24 children's books, and more than 180 stories and articles, I'm teaching: I'm passing along what I've learned to would-be writers like you.

One-on-one training with your own instructor

My fellow instructors—all of them professional writers or editors—work with their students the same way I work with mine: When you've completed an

Ohio Valley

REGION 7 SUMMARY: November through early February will be milder than normal, with below-normal snowfall. But winter will be relentless from mid-February into early April, with exceptionally cold temperatures and frequent snow the rule. The coldest periods will be early to mid-November, mid-January, and from early February through mid-March. Late February and early March will be especially cold. The snowiest periods will be early December, early to mid-February, and from late February to mid-March.

April will turn warm, with unusually warm temperatures in midmonth. May will bring seasonable temperatures. Summer will be cooler and wetter than normal. The hottest temperatures will occur in mid-July, mid-August, and from late August into early September.

Overall, September and October will be drier and warmer than normal.

NOV. 2004: Temp. 42° (3° below avg.); precip. 3" (0.5" above avg. east; 1.5" below west). 1-4 Sunny, cool. 5-13 Rain, then flurries, record cold. 14-18 Mild; sunny, then rain. 19-24 Cold; snow showers. 25-27 Sunny, mild. 28-30 Rain to snow.

Pittsburgh
Cincinnati
Louisville Charleston

20-22 T-storm, then seasonable. 23-30 Showers, then sunny, seasonable.

DEC. 2004: Temp. 38° (3° above avg.); precip. 3" (0.5" above avg. north; 0.5" below south). 1-3 Snow, then sunny. 4-10 Rain, then sunny, mild. 11-15 Seasonable; rain, then snow. 16-19 Sunny; cold, then mild. 20-25 Mild, then cold; rain showers to snow showers. 26-31 Seasonable; rain and snow east.

JAN. 2005: Temp. 33° (2° above avg.); precip. 2.5" (0.5" below avg.). 1-9 Mild; sunny, then rain. 10-19 Cold; snow showers. 20-26 Mild; showers, then sunny. 27-31 Snow showers, then rain.

FEB. 2005: Temp. 24° (8° below avg.); precip. 3" (1" above avg. east; 0.5" below west). 1-4 Rain, mild. 5-8 Cold; snow east and central. 9-11 Flurries, seasonable. 12-20 Cold, snow. 21-23 Very cold; snow showers. 24-28 Heavy snow, then record cold.

MAR. 2005: Temp. 36° (8° below avg.); precip. 2.5" (1.5" below avg.). 1-6 Very cold, snow. 7-13 Cold; snow showers. 14-20 Cold; snow east and central. 21-26 Mild, showers. 27-31 Rain, then chilly.

APR. 2005: Temp. 59° (5° above avg.); precip. 1.5" (2" below avg.; avg. west). 1-5 Chilly, showers and flurries. 6-11 Warm; sunny, then showers. 12-19 Sunny; cool, then very warm.

MAY 2005: Temp. 61° (2° below avg.); precip. 4.5" (avg.). 1-7 Cool, rain. 8-13 Seasonable; sunny east, t-storms west. 14-24 T-storms, seasonable. 25-31 Sunny, warm.

JUNE 2005: Temp. 69.5° (2.5° below avg.); precip. 7" (3" above avg.). 1-4 Sunny, warm. 5-10 T-storms, seasonable. 11-14 Sunny, seasonable. 15-21 Warm; scattered t-storms. 22-26 T-storms, severe west. 27-30 T-storms, then cool.

JULY 2005: Temp. 75° (1° below avg.); precip. 3" (1" below avg.). 1-8 Sunny, then t-storms, seasonable. 9-13 Sunny, cool, then t-storms east. 14-24 Very warm; scattered t-storms. 25-31 Seasonable; sunny, then t-storms.

AUG. 2005: Temp. 76.5° (2.5° above avg.); precip. 2.5" (1" below avg.). 1-4 T-storms, seasonable. 5-11 Sunny, warm. 12-16 T-storms, seasonable. 17-22 Sunny, very warm. 23-31 T-storms, then sunny, hot.

SEPT. 2005: Temp. 68° (avg. east; 2° above west); precip. 2" (1" below avg.). 1-2 Sunny, hot. 3-8 T-storms, then sunny, cool. 9-14 Seasonable, showers. 15-22 Sunny, warm. 23-30 Showers, seasonable.

OCT. 2005: Temp. 56° (1° above avg. east; 1.5° below west); precip. 2" (0.5" below avg.). 1-8 Showers, then sunny, warm. 9-13 Showers, seasonable. 14-20 Showers, chilly. 21-26 Rain, then sunny, seasonable. 27-31 Rain, then flurries.

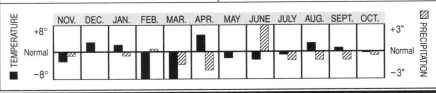

Deep South

REGION 8 SUMMARY: The first half of winter will be colder and drier than normal. Then, February and March will be among the coldest ever, with frequent snow across the north. The snowiest periods will be late December, mid- and late February, and early March. The coldest temperatures will occur in mid-November, mid-January, February, and early March.

April and May will be cooler and drier than normal. Expect much less t-storm activity than usual in the south.

Summer will bring near-normal temperatures, on average, cooler than normal in the north and hotter in the south. The hottest temperatures will occur in late August, with other hot periods in late June, early and mid-July, early August, and early September.

September and October will have near-normal temperatures, with a wet September followed by below-normal rainfall in October.

NOV. 2004: Temp. 51° (4° below avg.); precip. 2" (3" below avg.; 1" above north). 1-7 Sunny; cool, then warm. 8-14 Cool; showers, then sunny. 15-21 T-storms; warm, then cool. 22-24 Sunny, cold. 25-30 Showers, seasonable.

DEC. 2004: Temp. 48° (1° above avg.); precip. 6" (3" above avg. northwest; 1" below southeast). 1-4 Sunny. 5-12 Rain, mild. 13-18 Sunny, seasonable. 19-22 Warm, t-storms. 23-28 Showers, cool. 29-31 Rain; snow north.

JAN. 2005: Temp. 44° (2° above avg. north; 2° below south); precip. 4.5" (0.5" below avg.). 1-5 Sunny, warm. 6-12 Rain, seasonable. 13-19 Sunny, cold. 20-31 Seasonable, rainy.

FEB. 2005: Temp. 36° (10° below avg.); precip. 4" (1" below avg.). 1-5 Sunny, seasonable. 6-18 Cold; rain, snow north. 19-23 Chilly, showers; snow showers north. 24-28 Rain; snow north, then very cold.

MAR. 2005: Temp. 50° (9° below avg. north; 3° below south); precip. 6" (2" below avg. north; 2" above south). 1-5 Cold; snow north, rain south. 6-14 Cold; snow showers north, rain south. 15-20 Sunny; chilly, then seasonable. 21-24 Rain, mild. 25-28 T-storms. 29-31 Sunny.

APR. 2005: Temp. 63.5° (0.5° above avg.); precip. 2.5" (2" below avg.). 1-8 Sunny; cool, then warm. 9-15 Warm, showers. 16-19 Sunny,

warm. 20-27 Seasonable; t-storms, then sunny. 28-30 T-storms.

MAY 2005: Temp. 69° (2° below avg.); precip. 3.5" (1" above avg. northeast; 4" below south). 1-6 Cool, t-storms. 7-11 Sunny, warm. 12-19 Warm; scattered t-storms. 20-25 T-storms, then sunny, warm. 26-31 Warm; scattered t-storms.

JUNE 2005: Temp. 77.5° (0.5° below avg.); precip. 5" (4" above avg. north; 4" below south). 1-8 Warm; scattered t-storms. 9-12 T-storms, then cool north. 13-17 Sunny, hot. 18-23 Very warm; scattered t-storms. 24-30 Sunny, hot.

JULY 2005: Temp. 82° (1° below avg. north; 1° above south); precip. 3" (2" below avg.; 2" above south). 1-10 Partly sunny; scattered t-storms. 11-13 T-storms, cool. 14-24 Hot; scattered t-storms. 25-31 Seasonable, t-storms.

AUG. 2005: Temp. 82° (1° above avg.); precip. 3" (1.5" below avg.). 1-3 T-storms, hot. 4-12 Seasonable; scattered t-storms. 13-19 T-storms, warm. 20-31 Sunny, hot.

SEPT. 2005: Temp. 76° (avg.); precip. 6.5" (2" above avg.). 1-4 Hot, t-storms. 5-11 Cool; sunny, then rain. 12-15 Sunny, warm. 16-22 Showers. 23-27 Sunny, warm. 28-30 T-storms.

OCT. 2005: Temp. 65° (1° above avg. east; 1° below west); precip. 2" (1" below avg.). 1-8 Warm; showers, then sunny. 9-13 Showers, seasonable. 14-19 Sunny; cool, then seasonable. 20-25 Showers. 26-31 Sunny, cool.

Map labels: Nashville, Little Rock, Tupelo, Montgomery, Shreveport, Jackson, Mobile, New Orleans

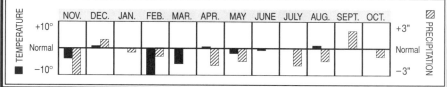

Upper Midwest

REGION 9 SUMMARY: Winter will be colder than normal, with above-normal snowfall in the east and below-normal snowfall in the west. After a cold November, December through early February will be much milder than normal, on average. The remainder of February through mid-March will be exceptionally cold. Other cold periods will occur in late December and mid-January. The snowiest periods will be near Christmas and in late March.

April and May will bring near-normal temperatures and slightly below normal precipitation. Despite a warm spell in mid-April, expect snow in late April in the north and west.

Summer will be drier than normal, with temperatures cooler in the east and hotter than normal in the west. The hottest temperatures will occur in mid- and late July and mid- and late August.

Drier-than-normal weather will continue in September and October, with cool temperatures in the east and near-normal ones in the west.

NOV. 2004: Temp. 24° (4° below avg.); precip. 2" (avg.). 1-4 Sunny, seasonable. 5-11 Cold; snow showers, then sunny. 12-18 Seasonable; sunny, then snow showers. 19-24 Sunny, cold. 25-28 Sunny, mild. 29-30 Snow showers.

DEC. 2004: Temp. 21° (7° above avg.); precip. 1.5" (0.5" above avg.). 1-7 Sunny, mild. 8-15 Mild; snow showers, then sunny. 16-22 Mild; snow showers, then rain. 23-24 Sunny, cooler. 25-31 Snow, then cold, flurries.

JAN. 2005: Temp. 15° (6° above avg.); precip. 0.5" (0.5" below avg.). 1-8 Flurries, then sunny, mild. 9-21 Seasonable, flurries. 22-31 Sunny, mild.

FEB. 2005: Temp. 4° (7° below avg.); precip. 0.5" (0.5" below avg.). 1-7 Flurries; mild, then sunny, cold. 8-10 Mild, flurries. 11-20 Cold; snow showers, then sunny. 21-28 Very cold, flurries.

MAR. 2005: Temp. 20° (7° below avg.); precip. 1" (0.5" below avg.). 1-5 Cold; snow showers. 6-10 Very cold, flurries. 11-19 Cold, flurries. 20-25 Mild, showers. 26-31 Snow, then sunny, seasonable.

APR. 2005: Temp. 40° (1° below avg.); precip. 1.5" (0.5" below avg.). 1-4 Sunny, cold. 5-10 Mild, rain. 11-16 Sunny, warm. 17-23 Rain, cool. 24-30 Cool; sunny, then rain and snow.

MAY 2005: Temp. 55.5° (1° below avg. east; 2° above west); precip. 2.5" (0.5" below avg.). 1-3 Cool, showers. 4-9 Sunny, warm. 10-15 Seasonable, rain. 16-25 Seasonable; sunny, then rain. 26-31 Sunny, seasonable.

JUNE 2005: Temp. 61° (3° below avg.); precip. 3" (1" below avg.). 1-4 Showers, seasonable. 5-17 Cool; sunny, then rainy. 18-21 Sunny, warm. 22-30 Cool, showers.

JULY 2005: Temp. 69.5° (3° below avg. east; 4° above west); precip. 3" (0.5" below avg.). 1-7 Seasonable, t-storms. 8-13 Warm; sunny, then t-storms. 14-18 Sunny, hot. 19-23 T-storms, then sunny, warm. 24-31 Very warm, t-storms.

AUG. 2005: Temp. 70° (3° above avg.); precip. 4" (0.5" above avg.). 1-6 Warm; t-storms, then sunny. 7-10 Sunny; hot, then cool. 11-16 Warm; t-storms, then sunny. 17-23 T-storms, then sunny, cool. 24-31 Sunny, hot.

SEPT. 2005: Temp. 56° (2° below avg.); precip. 2.5" (0.5" below avg.). 1-9 T-storms, then sunny, cool. 10-18 Showers, cool. 19-21 Sunny, seasonable. 22-30 Showers, cool, then sunny, warm.

OCT. 2005: Temp. 46° (2° below avg. east; 2° above west); precip. 1.5" (1" below avg.). 1-5 Sunny, seasonable. 6-10 Showers, then sunny, seasonable. 11-18 Sunny, chilly. 19-24 Seasonable; sunny, then rain. 25-31 Sunny, cool.

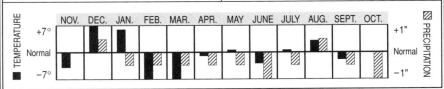

Heartland

REGION 10 SUMMARY: Winter will be exceptionally cold and snowy, despite mild weather from late November through much of January. February and March will be among the coldest and snowiest ever. The coldest periods will be early to mid-November, late December, mid-January, much of February, and early March. Snowstorms will occur in early to mid-January, mid- and late February, and early March.

April and May will bring above-normal temperatures and near-normal rainfall.

Summer temperatures and precipitation will be near normal, on average. The hottest temperatures will occur in early, mid-, and late July and late August. The heaviest thunderstorms will occur in July, with less widespread ones in June and August.

September will start hot. Temperatures will be cooler than normal, on average, in the north and warmer in the south. Rainfall will be below normal. October will be wetter than normal, with near-normal temperatures.

W E A T H E R

NOV. 2004: Temp. 37° (5° below avg.); precip. 1" (1.5" below avg.). 1-3 Sunny, mild. 4-7 Rain to snow. 8-11 Sunny, cold. 12-16 Sunny, mild. 17-23 Rain to snow, then sunny, cold. 24-30 Sunny, mild.

DEC. 2004: Temp. 34° (6° above avg. north; 2° above south); precip. 2.5" (1" above avg.). 1-11 Mild; sunny, then showers. 12-15 Sunny, seasonable. 16-22 Mild; rain; snow north. 23-31 Sunny, cold.

JAN. 2005: Temp. 28° (2° above avg.); precip. 1.5" (0.5" above avg.). 1-8 Mild; sunny, then rain. 9-13 Snow, cold. 14-18 Sunny, cold. 19-28 Flurries, then sunny, mild. 29-31 Seasonable, rain and snow.

FEB. 2005: Temp. 17° (12° below avg.); precip. 1.5" (1" above avg. north; 0.5" below south). 1-2 Sunny, mild. 3-8 Rain to snow, then sunny, cold. 9-12 Flurries, seasonable. 13-22 Snow, cold. 23-28 Snowstorm, then record cold.

MAR. 2005: Temp. 33° (10° below avg.); precip. 1.5" (avg. north; 2" below south). 1-10 Cold, snowy. 11-19 Sunny, cold. 20-22 Sunny, warm. 23-31 T-storms, then sunny, cool.

APR. 2005: Temp. 56° (2° above avg.); precip. 4.5" (1" above avg.). 1-3 Sunny, chilly. 4-10 Mild; sunny, then t-storms. 11-13 Cold; rain; snow north. 14-18 Sunny, warm. 19-27 Cooler; t-storms, then sunny. 28-30 T-storms.

MAY 2005: Temp. 64° (avg.); precip. 3.5" (1"

Des Moines ⊙
Omaha ⊙
Topeka ⊙ ⊙ Kansas City ⊙
St. Louis ⊙

below avg.). 1-7 Sunny, cool. 8-14 Warm; sunny, then t-storms. 15-18 Sunny, warm. 19-25 T-storms, then sunny. 26-31 Seasonable, t-storms.

JUNE 2005: Temp. 71° (2° below avg.); precip. 3.5" (1" below avg.). 1-3 Sunny, warm. 4-12 T-storms, cool. 13-16 Warm; scattered t-storms. 17-21 Sunny, seasonable. 22-25 T-storms, then sunny. 26-30 Cool; scattered t-storms.

JULY 2005: Temp. 77° (avg. north; 2° below south); precip. 5" (1" above avg.). 1-6 Hot, a few t-storms. 7-11 Cool; sunny north, t-storms south. 12-18 Sunny, hot north; t-storms south. 19-23 Seasonable; scattered t-storms. 24-25 Sunny, cool. 26-31 Hot; scattered t-storms.

AUG. 2005: Temp. 78° (2° above avg.); precip. 2.5" (1" below avg.). 1-7 T-storms, then sunny, seasonable. 8-14 Warm, t-storms. 15-25 Warm; sunny south, t-storms north. 26-31 Sunny, hot.

SEPT. 2005: Temp. 67° (3° below avg. north; 3° above south); precip. 2" (1.5" below avg.). 1-3 Hot, then t-storms. 4-8 Sunny, cool. 9-19 T-storms, warm. 20-24 Sunny, seasonable. 25-30 T-storms, then sunny, warm.

OCT. 2005: Temp. 56° (avg.); precip. 4" (1" above avg.). 1-6 Sunny, warm. 7-11 T-storms, then sunny, seasonable. 12-15 T-storms, then sunny, cold. 16-18 Sunny, seasonable. 19-25 T-storms. 26-31 Sunny, seasonable.

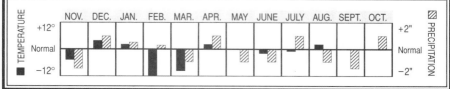

Texas–Oklahoma

REGION 11 SUMMARY: Winter will be cold and dry, with temperatures three to four degrees below normal, on average, and precipitation will be much less than normal. February will be one of the coldest months ever, with the coldest temperatures of the winter in the first part of the month. Other cold periods will occur in late November, late December, mid-January, and mid- and late February. Snowfall will be above normal in the north and east, with the snowiest periods in late December and early, mid-, and late February.

April and May will be warmer and drier than normal, with a major tornado outbreak in late April.

Summer will be rainy, with frequent thunderstorms providing relief from heat but not humidity. Temperatures will be below normal in the north and above normal in the south. The hottest periods will be late June, early and mid-July, and early August.

September and October will be warmer and drier than normal.

NOV. 2004: Temp. 50° (6° below avg.); precip. 1" (2" below avg.). 1-4 Sunny, chilly. 5-11 Rain; mild, then cold, flurries. 12-15 Sunny, milder. 16-19 Rain, then sunny, seasonable. 20-24 Showers and flurries, then sunny, widespread freeze. 25-30 Showers; milder, then sunny, cold.

DEC. 2004: Temp. 49° (3° above avg. north; 1° below south); precip. 3.5" (3" above avg. north; 1" below south). 1-11 Mild; rainy periods, some heavy. 12-15 Sunny, cool. 16-21 Mild, rain. 22-31 Chilly; sunny, then rain, snow north.

JAN. 2005: Temp. 47° (1° above avg.); precip. 2" (avg.). 1-8 Sunny, then rain, warm. 9-15 Rain; snow north, then sunny, cold. 16-22 Mild; cloudy, rain south. 23-31 Seasonable; sunny, then rain.

FEB. 2005: Temp. 38° (10° below avg.); precip. 1" (1" below avg.). 1-4 Sunny, mild. 5-8 Cold, snow and rain. 9-16 Rain, chilly. 17-20 Cold, snow; rain north. 21-28 Rain; snow north, then record cold.

MAR. 2005: Temp. 54.5° (5° above avg. north; 2° below south); precip. 0.5" (2" below avg.). 1-9 Chilly, occasional rain. 10-17 Sunny; chilly, then milder. 18-31 T-Storms, then sunny, warm.

APR. 2005: Temp. 67° (1° above avg.); precip. 3" (avg.). 1-10 Cloudy, warm; scattered t-storms. 11-13 Sunny, cool. 14-20 Warm; scat-

Oklahoma City

Dallas

Houston

San Antonio

tered t-storms. 21-30 Severe t-storms, seasonable.

MAY 2005: Temp. 73° (avg.); precip. 3" (2" below avg.). 1-7 Sunny, cool. 8-13 Warm; scattered t-storms. 14-31 T-storms, then sunny, hot.

JUNE 2005: Temp. 81° (1° above avg.; 1° below north); precip. 6" (2" above avg.). 1-7 Seasonable; scattered t-storms. 8-16 Sunny, hot. 17-22 Heavy t-storms. 23-27 Sunny, hot. 28-30 Sunny south, t-storms north.

JULY 2005: Temp. 83° (2° below avg. north; 2° above south); precip. 3.5" (2" above avg. north; 1" below south). 1-6 Sunny, hot. 7-15 T-storms, seasonable. 16-21 Sunny, hot. 22-27 Sunny north; t-storms, hot south. 28-31 Sunny, hot north; t-storms south.

AUG. 2005: Temp. 81° (1° below avg.); precip. 4" (avg. north; 3" above south). 1-3 Sunny, hot. 4-11 T-storms, comfortable. 12-16 T-storms, cool. 17-21 T-storms, warm. 22-31 Sunny, warm north; t-storms south.

SEPT. 2005: Temp. 77° (1° above avg.); precip. 1.5" (2" below avg.). 1-4 Warm, t-storms. 5-16 Sunny; cool, then hot. 17-21 T-storms, cool. 22-30 Warm; sunny, then t-storms.

OCT. 2005: Temp. 68° (1° above avg.); precip. 5" (1" above avg.). 1-5 Sunny, warm. 6-12 T-storms, warm. 13-17 Sunny, cool. 18-26 T-storms, warm. 27-31 Sunny, seasonable.

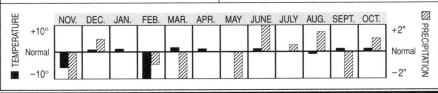

High Plains

REGION 12 SUMMARY: Winter will vary substantially across the region. Montana and Wyoming will be milder than normal, with well below normal snowfall. The Dakotas, Nebraska, and northern Colorado will have below-normal temperatures and snowfall. Kansas, southern Colorado, New Mexico, Texas, and Oklahoma will be colder than normal, with above-normal snowfall. February will be one of the coldest months in history. Other cold periods will be mid-November, late December, mid-January, and early March.

April will bring near-normal temperatures and precipitation, with several spring snowfalls across the north and west. May will be warmer and drier than normal.

Summer will be hot and dry in the north, with ample rainfall and near-normal temperatures in the south. The hottest periods will occur in late June, much of July, and mid- and late August.

September and October will be warmer and drier than normal in the north, and the opposite in the south.

W E A T H E R

NOV. 2004: Temp. 34° (4° below avg. east; avg. west); precip. 1" (0.5" above avg. north; 0.5" below south). 1-5 Sunny, seasonable. 6-11 Cold; snow showers, then sunny. 12-16 Sunny, seasonable. 17-21 Cold, snow. 22-26 Sunny, mild. 27-30 Snow, then cold.

DEC. 2004: Temp. 31.5° (8° above avg. north; 1° above south); precip. 1.5" (avg. northwest; 2" above southeast). 1-7 Sunny, mild. 8-11 Sunny, mild north; rain and ice south. 12-18 Snow showers northeast; sunny, mild west and south. 19-27 Showers, then snow, cold. 28-31 Snow, cold.

JAN. 2005: Temp. 27° (6° above avg. north; 2° below south); precip. 0.5" (0.5" below avg. north; 0.5" above south). 1-6 Mild, sprinkles and flurries. 7-12 Snow, cold. 13-19 Flurries, cold. 20-25 Sunny, mild. 26-31 Snow, then sunny, mild.

FEB. 2005: Temp. 16° (11° below avg.); precip. 1" (0.5" above avg.). 1-6 Mild, rain and snow showers. 7-15 Cold, snowy. 16-28 Cold; snow showers.

MAR. 2005: Temp. 39° (3° below avg. east; 5° above west); precip. 0.5" (0.5" below avg.). 1-11 Changeable; occasional snow. 12-17 Sunny, mild. 18-24 Rain; snow north, then sunny, mild. 25-31 Showers, then sunny, warm days.

APR. 2005: Temp. 48° (avg.); precip. 1.5" (avg.). 1-6 Mild, showers. 7-10 Rain and snow. 11-15 Sunny, seasonable. 16-24 Chilly, rain to snow.

25-30 Chilly; rain; snow north.

MAY 2005: Temp. 61° (3° above avg.); precip. 2" (0.5" below avg.). 1-4 Sunny, cool. 5-8 Sunny, warm. 9-13 Showers, cool. 14-16 Sunny, warm. 17-25 Seasonable, t-storms. 26-31 Warm, showers.

JUNE 2005: Temp. 67° (avg.); precip. 3.5" (1" below avg. northwest; 3" above southeast). 1-6 T-storms, seasonable. 7-17 Scattered t-storms; cool north, hot south. 18-20 Sunny, warm. 21-26 Sunny, hot. 27-30 Cool, t-storms.

JULY 2005: Temp. 74° (5° above avg. north; 1° below south); precip. 1.5" (2" below avg. north; 1" above south). 1-9 Hot; scattered t-storms. 10-27 Hot, sunny. 28-31 T-storms, cooler.

AUG. 2005: Temp. 73° (4° above avg. north; avg. south); precip. 2" (avg.). 1-7 T-storms; cool, then sunny, seasonable. 8-13 Seasonable, t-storms. 14-16 Sunny, hot. 17-20 T-storms north; sunny, hot south. 21-25 Sunny, warm. 26-31 T-storms, then sunny, hot.

SEPT. 2005: Temp. 61.5° (0.5° above avg.); precip. 0.5" (1" below avg.; 2" above south). 1-10 T-storms, then sunny, seasonable. 11-18 T-storms; warm, then chilly. 19-30 Sunny; cool, then warm.

OCT. 2005: Temp. 49.5° (2° above avg. north; 1° below south); precip. 1" (avg.). 1-6 Sunny north, showers south. 7-13 Chilly; sunny north, snow central, rain south. 14-21 Sunny, mild. 22-31 Showers, then sunny, cool.

Billings ⊙
Bismarck ⊙
Rapid City ⊙
Cheyenne ⊙
Denver ⊙
Amarillo ⊙

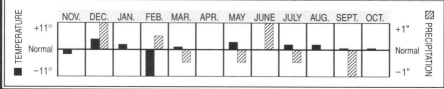

Intermountain

REGION 13 SUMMARY: Winter will be near normal, on average, with near-normal snowfall, below-normal precipitation, and temperatures above normal in the east and below in the west. The coldest periods will be late December, mid-January, and mid-February. Expect snow around Christmas, in early January, early and late February, and early March.

April and May will bring near-normal precipitation, with temperatures near normal in the east and cooler than normal in the west.

Summer will be hot, especially in Montana, Idaho, Wyoming, and Colorado. The hottest periods will occur in late June, mid-July, and early and mid-August. Rainfall will be above normal in the north and close to normal in the south.

September will be warmer and drier than normal. October will be cooler than normal, with near-normal rainfall.

Spokane
Pendleton
Boise
Reno
Salt Lake City
Grand Junction
Flagstaff

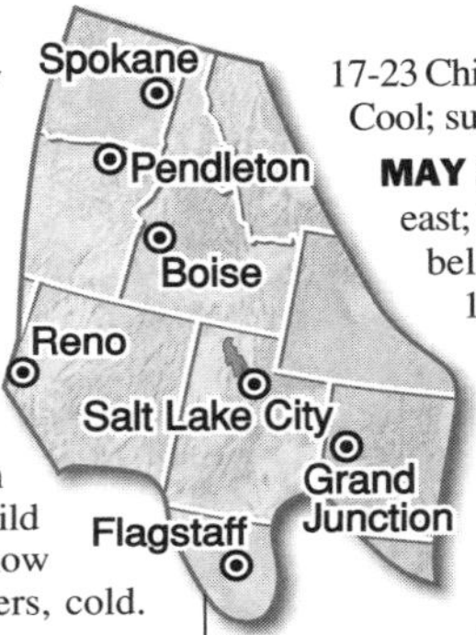

NOV. 2004: Temp. 38.5° (0.5° below avg.); precip. 0.5" (1" below avg.). 1-9 Sunny, seasonable. 10-13 Sunny; cold north, mild south. 14-18 Snow north; sunny, mild south. 19-23 Sunny, mild. 24-30 Rain and snow showers north; cool, sunny south.

DEC. 2004: Temp. 30° (2° above avg. east; 4° below west); precip. 1" (0.5" below avg.). 1-8 Seasonable, rain and snow showers. 9-14 Sunny; mild east, cold west. 15-18 Rain and snow showers, mild. 19-25 Snow showers, cold. 26-31 Very cold; snow, then sunny.

JAN. 2005: Temp. 31.5° (4° above avg. east; 1° below west); precip. 1.5" (avg. east; 0.5" above west). 1-11 Mild, then cold, snowy. 12-14 Sunny, cold. 15-19 Seasonable; snow showers. 20-27 Mild, rain and snow showers. 28-31 Mild; showers north, sunny south.

FEB. 2005: Temp. 29° (4° below avg.); precip. 1.5" (0.5" above avg. east; 0.5" below west). 1-4 Mild, rain and snow showers. 5-14 Cold; snow, then sunny. 15-18 Cold; sunny north, snow showers south. 19-24 Snowstorm, cold. 25-28 Milder, rain and snow showers.

MAR. 2005: Temp. 46° (4° above avg.); precip. 1.5" (avg.). 1-3 Mild; showers; snow north. 4-10 Cold; sunny, then snow. 11-19 Sunny, warm. 20-26 Cool, rainy. 27-31 Sunny, warm.

APR. 2005: Temp. 47° (2° below avg.); precip. 1" (avg.). 1-5 Showers north; sunny, warm south. 6-11 Showers; snow north, then sunny, cool. 12-16 Showers, cool north; sunny, warm south. 17-23 Chilly, rain and snow showers. 24-30 Cool; sunny, then showers.

MAY 2005: Temp. 57° (2° above avg. east; 2° below west); precip. 1" (0.5" below avg.; 1" above northwest). 1-6 Sunny, warm. 7-13 Cold, rain and snow showers. 14-20 Cool; sunny south, showers north. 21-31 Sunny, warm.

JUNE 2005: Temp. 68° (2° above avg.); precip. 0.5" (avg.). 1-5 Seasonable, t-storms. 6-12 Sunny, warm. 13-17 T-storm, then sunny, cool. 18-30 Sunny, warm.

JULY 2005: Temp. 76° (5° above avg. north; 1° above south); precip. 1" (0.5" above avg.). 1-5 Sunny, warm. 6-19 Sunny, hot. 20-23 Hot; scattered t-storms. 24-31 Cool, showers north; t-storms, then sunny, hot south.

AUG. 2005: Temp. 71.5° (1° above avg. east; 2° below west); precip. 1" (0.5" above avg. north; 0.5" below south). 1-7 Sunny, hot. 8-11 T-storms, then sunny, cooler. 12-19 Hot, then t-storms, cool. 20-31 Scattered t-storms; cool northwest, warm elsewhere.

SEPT. 2005: Temp. 64° (2° above avg.); precip. 0.5" (0.5" below avg.). 1-6 Sunny, warm. 7-16 Seasonable; scattered t-storms. 17-30 Sunny, warm.

OCT. 2005: Temp. 49° (2° below avg.); precip. 1" (avg.). 1-10 Rain, then sunny, cool. 11-18 Sunny, mild. 19-25 Cool; showers north. 26-31 Sunny, warm southeast; cool, showers elsewhere.

TEMPERATURE
+4°
Normal
−4°
NOV. DEC. JAN. FEB. MAR. APR. MAY JUNE JULY AUG. SEPT. OCT.
+1"
Normal
−1"
PRECIPITATION

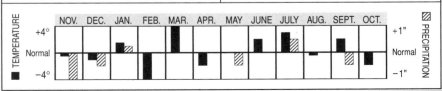

Desert Southwest

REGION 14 SUMMARY: Winter will be milder than normal, especially in the west. March will have temperatures well above normal. Winter rainfall will be above normal, due to widespread showers in December. The coldest periods will be late December, mid-January, and mid-February. The most widespread snowfall will occur in early to mid-January. Other snowy periods in the higher elevations and in the eastern half of the region will occur in early and late December, mid-February, and early to mid-March.

April and May will be warmer and drier than normal, with hot temperatures in late May.

Summer temperatures will be two degrees above normal, on average, with above-normal rainfall in the east and below-normal rainfall in the west. The hottest periods will be mid-June, mid- and late July, and late August.

September will be hot and dry, especially in Arizona and Nevada. October will be wetter and cooler than normal.

NOV. 2004: Temp. 56° (1° below avg. east; 3° above west); precip. 0.1" (0.4" below avg.). 1-6 Showers east; sunny, warm west. 7-10 Cool, showers. 11-19 Sunny, warm. 20-30 Sunny; chilly east, mild west.

DEC. 2004: Temp. 46° (1° below avg.); precip. 1.5" (1" above avg.). 1-6 Seasonable, showers. 7-9 Rain and snow east, sunny west. 10-14 Sunny, mild. 15-19 Mild, rainy. 20-24 Seasonable; rain and snow east, sunny west. 25-31 Showers, then sunny, cold.

JAN. 2005: Temp. 48° (1° above avg.); precip. 0.8" (0.3" above avg.). 1-6 Mild; sunny, then rain. 7-15 Cold; rain and snow, then sunny. 16-25 Sunny, mild. 26-31 Showers, then sunny, seasonable.

FEB. 2005: Temp. 47° (3° below avg.); precip. 0.5" (0.2" above avg. east; 0.2" below west). 1-5 Showers and flurries. 6-11 Sunny, cold. 12-20 Showers and flurries, then sunny, cold. 21-28 T-storms, then sunny, warm.

MAR. 2005: Temp. 62° (5° above avg.); precip. 0.1" (0.4" below avg.). 1-8 Sunny, warm. 9-12 Rain and snow showers. 13-18 Warm; sunny, then t-storms. 19-25 Sunny, warm. 26-31 Showers east, sunny and warm elsewhere.

APR. 2005: Temp. 64° (2° above avg. east; 2° below west); precip. 0.3" (0.2" below avg.). 1-5 Sunny, warm. 6-16 Showers, then sunny, warm. 17-24 Cool; scattered t-storms. 25-30 Seasonable; sunny, then showers.

MAY 2005: Temp. 76° (3° above avg.); precip. 0.2" (0.3" below avg.). 1-3 Sunny, warm. 4-8 Sunny, hot. 9-15 Sunny, seasonable. 16-20 Sunny, cool. 21-31 T-storms, then sunny, hot.

JUNE 2005: Temp. 87° (4° above avg.); precip. 1" (1" above avg. east; 0.1" below west). 1-5 Warm; scattered t-storms. 6-23 Sunny, hot. 24-30 Sunny, warm west; t-storms, cool east.

JULY 2005: Temp. 88° (1° above avg.); precip. 1" (0.5" below avg.; 1" above east). 1-4 Scattered t-storms, not as hot. 5-13 Seasonable, t-storms east; sunny, hot west. 14-20 Seasonable; scattered t-storms. 21-31 Hot; scattered t-storms.

AUG. 2005: Temp. 86° (1° above avg.); precip. 1" (0.5" below avg.). 1-9 Seasonable; scattered t-storms. 10-14 Sunny, seasonable. 15-21 Scattered t-storms; warm east, cool west. 22-31 Scattered t-storms, hot.

SEPT. 2005: Temp. 80° (2° above avg.); precip. 0.5" (0.5" below avg.). 1-9 Scattered t-storms, seasonable east; sunny, hot west. 10-16 Hot; scattered t-storms. 17-22 Sunny; seasonable east, hot west. 23-30 Scattered t-storms, seasonable.

OCT. 2004: Temp. 66.5° (0.5° below avg.); precip. 2" (1" above avg.). 1-12 Cool, t-storms. 13-23 Sunny, warm. 24-28 Sunny; cool, then warm. 29-31 T-storms.

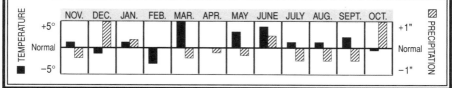

Pacific Northwest

W
E
A
T
H
E
R

REGION 15 SUMMARY: November through March temperatures will be near normal, on average, with near-or below-normal snowfall. Rainfall will be above normal in the north and below normal in the south. The stormiest periods will be mid-November, mid-December, early and late January, late February, and mid- to late March. Expect snow in early to mid-January and late February. The coldest temperatures will occur in early November, late December, early January, and mid-February.

April and May will be cool and wet, with rain in early and late April and mid-May.

Summer will be cooler and drier than normal, on average. The hottest periods will be late June, mid-July, and early August.

September will be warmer and drier than normal, with especially nice weather to start the month. October will be warmer than normal, with above-normal rainfall in the north and below-normal in the south.

NOV. 2004: Temp. 46° (1° below avg.); precip. 7" (3" above avg. north; 2" below south). 1-4 Cool; cloudy north, sunny south. 5-10 Cool; light rain north. 11-16 Stormy; heavy rain, mild. 17-26 Seasonable; occasional rain. 27-30 Chilly; rain north.

DEC. 2004: Temp. 41° (1° below avg.); precip. 5.5" (1" above avg. north; 3" below south). 1-6 Rain, seasonable. 7-12 Mild; rain, heavy north. 13-19 Seasonable; occasional rain. 20-25 Chilly, drizzle and flurries. 26-31 Cold; sunny, then rain.

JAN. 2005: Temp. 45° (3° above avg.); precip. 7" (1" above avg.). 1-8 Cold, rain and snow. 9-15 Partly sunny north, rain and snow south. 16-20 Rain, mild. 21-31 Heavy rain, mild.

FEB. 2005: Temp. 41° (3° below avg.); precip. 4" (1" below avg.). 1-8 Mild, rainy. 9-15 Cool; occasional rain. 16-23 Partly sunny, cold. 24-28 Heavy snow, then rain.

MAR. 2005: Temp. 49° (2° above avg.); precip. 5" (0.5" above avg.). 1-5 Chilly; rain, then partly sunny. 6-10 Seasonable, rainy. 11-19 Partly sunny, warm. 20-26 Heavy rain, seasonable. 27-31 Sunny, warm.

APR. 2005: Temp. 48° (2° below avg.); precip. 4.5" (1.5" above avg.). 1-4 Cool; heavy rain. 5-13 Occasional rain, cool. 14-22 Chilly; light rain. 23-28 Seasonable, sunny. 29-30 Rain, cool.

MAY 2005: Temp. 53° (2° below avg.); precip. 3" (1" above avg.). 1-3 Partly sunny, seasonable. 4-8 Rain, seasonable. 9-20 Cool; occasional rain. 21-31 Sunny, warm.

JUNE 2005: Temp. 60° (avg.); precip. 0.5" (1" below avg.). 1-6 Sunny, pleasant. 7-14 Cool; occasional rain. 15-27 Sunny, seasonable. 28-30 Sunny, hot.

JULY 2005: Temp. 65.5° (1.5° above avg.); precip. 0" (0.5" below avg.). 1-7 Sunny, comfortable. 8-13 Sunny, warm. 14-18 Sunny, seasonable. 19-23 Sunny, hot. 24-31 Cloudy, seasonable.

AUG. 2005: Temp. 62.5° (2.5° below avg.); precip. 2" (1" above avg.). 1-6 Sunny; hot, then seasonable. 7-13 Seasonable; rain, then sunny. 14-31 Cool; occasional rain.

SEPT. 2005: Temp. 62° (1° above avg.); precip. 0.5" (1" below avg.). 1-5 Partly sunny, warm. 6-12 Cool, sprinkles. 13-19 Cool; occasional rain, heavy north. 20-25 Sunny, warm. 26-30 Seasonable, rain.

OCT. 2005: Temp. 54.5° (0.5° above avg.); precip. 3" (1" above avg. north; 1" below south). 1-6 Cool; light rain. 7-12 Sunny, pleasant. 13-19 Mild, rain. 20-27 Cool; rain, heavy south. 28-31 Sunny, seasonable.

Seattle

Portland

Eugene

Eureka

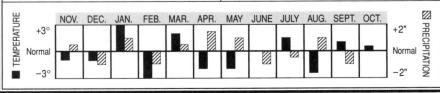

Pacific Southwest

REGION 16 SUMMARY: Winter will be warmer and drier than normal, with temperatures about two degrees above normal, on average, and most of the rain falling in January. The coldest periods will occur in late December, early January, and mid-February. The stormiest periods will occur in mid-December; early, mid-, and late January; and early February.

Expect a storm in mid-April. Otherwise, the month will bring near-normal rainfall, with near-normal temperatures at the coast but cool temperatures in the interior. May will be cloudy, with above-normal temperatures but below-normal rainfall. Late May will be hot across the north.

Summer will be warmer than normal, especially from Los Angeles southward. The hottest periods will be mid- and late June, mid-July, and early to mid-August.

September will bring much-warmer-than-normal temperatures, with several hot periods. October will be rainier than normal, with near-normal temperatures.

W
E
A
T
H
E
R

NOV. 2004: Temp. 62° (4° above avg.); precip. 0.5" (1" below avg.). 1-7 Sunny, warm. 8-14 Partly sunny, seasonable. 15-30 Sunny, warm.

DEC. 2004: Temp. 53° (1° above avg. west; 1° below east); precip. 0.5" (1.5" below avg.). 1-6 Showers, seasonable. 7-13 Sunny, warm. 14-19 Mild, rain. 20-23 Sunny, seasonable. 24-31 Cool; showers, then sunny.

JAN. 2005: Temp. 55.5° (2.5° above avg.); precip. 5" (2" above avg.). 1-9 Rain and t-storms, cool. 10-14 Sunny, seasonable. 15-20 Mild, rain. 21-31 Rain, seasonable.

FEB. 2005: Temp. 55° (avg.); precip. 2" (1" below avg.). 1-4 Stormy; heavy rain. 5-11 Sunny, seasonable. 12-20 Showers north, then sunny, cool. 21-25 Rain, then sunny, cool. 26-28 Cloudy, showers north.

MAR. 2005: Temp. 60.5° (3.5° above avg.); precip. 1.5" (1" below avg.). 1-8 Seasonable; sunny, then showers. 9-15 Sunny, warm. 16-24 Seasonable, rainy. 25-29 Sunny, warm. 30-31 Showers.

APR. 2005: Temp. 58.5° (3° below avg. east; avg. west); precip. 1" (avg.). 1-8 Partly sunny, showers north; seasonable. 9-15 Partly sunny, pleasant. 16-22 Rain, cool. 23-30 Seasonable; sunny, then rain.

MAY 2005: Temp. 66° (2° above avg.); precip. 0.3" (0.2" below avg.). 1-4 Sunny, warm. 5-10

Cloudy; sprinkles north; cooler. 11-16 Sunny; cool east, seasonable west. 17-22 Cloudy; showers north. 23-31 Sunny, hot north; sprinkles south.

JUNE 2005: Temp. 69° (1° above avg.); precip. 0" (0.1" below avg.). 1-4 Sunny, seasonable. 5-13 Sunny; warm north, seasonable south. 14-17 Sunny, warm. 18-21 Sunny, seasonable. 22-30 Sunny, warm.

JULY 2005: Temp. 71.5° (1° below avg. north; 2° above south); precip. 0" (avg.). 1-7 Sunny, cool. 8-13 Hot inland, coastal fog. 14-17 Sunny, hot. 18-31 Sunny, seasonable.

AUG. 2005: Temp. 73° (1° above avg.); precip. 0.1" (avg.). 1-4 Sunny, seasonable. 5-10 Sunny, hot. 11-14 Sunny; hot inland, seasonable coast. 15-22 Sunny; cool inland, seasonable coast. 23-25 Sunny, seasonable. 26-31 Warm; showers north, then sunny.

SEPT. 2005: Temp. 73° (3° above avg.); precip. 0.2" (avg.). 1-5 Scattered t-storms, hot. 6-17 Sunny; hot, then seasonable. 18-22 Hot north, fog south. 23-27 Sunny, seasonable. 28-30 Showers north, hot south.

OCT. 2005: Temp. 65° (avg.); precip. 1" (0.5" above avg.). 1-4 T-storms north; sunny, cool south. 5-14 Sunny, seasonable. 15-20 Showers, seasonable. 21-25 Sunny, warm. 26-31 Rain and t-storms.

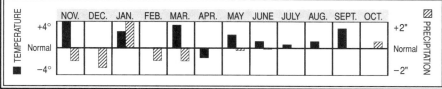

How the Oceans Affect

by Evelyn Browning Garriss

Our Climate

■ At one point in the movie *Jurassic Park,* a mathematician dribbles water across the back of the heroine's hand, demonstrating the chaos theory: Any little bump on her hand would cause the water to flow in a new direction. So, he explained, small things could disrupt the flow of events.

Scientists understand the truth of that moment. Events on opposite sides of the world can cause a storm anywhere in North America; no one factor shapes all the weather. Today, weathermen are looking around the world for interrelated, large-scale weather patterns called teleconnections. They understand that weather is global and are finding, for example, that a minor change of air pressure over the Arctic Ocean can signal a storm that will bury the entire East Coast in snow or bring a lush crop to the fields of Kansas.

Oceans cover 70 percent of the Earth, and only by studying them and their effect on the atmosphere will we understand the conditions shaping our weather.

continued

–Hasler/NASA/GSFC

Why E-l N-i-ñ-o Spells Trouble

Most people are familiar with satellite pictures of the Atlantic Ocean during hurricane season. If conditions are right, you will see a weather pattern off the coast of Africa or in the Caribbean begin to spin and grow into a depression, a tropical storm, or a hurricane. Depending on the wind currents, the storm will remain at sea or aim straight at land. The direction the storm takes is determined by air pressure patterns that are shaped, in part, by warm and cool patches in the ocean.

As far back as the 1400s, the Incas understood the connection between ocean temperatures and large-scale weather patterns. They knew that if the sky over the Pacific Ocean in December was so hazy that they could not see certain stars, the year would be marked by heavy rains and a poor fishing season. They probably didn't know that the haze was caused by warm ocean water, but what they observed and predicted for centuries is

> **As far back as the 1400s, the Incas understood the connection between ocean temperatures and large-scale weather patterns.**

the weather pattern known as El Niño. Even today, people in South America examine the horizon in an effort to predict conditions for the next year.

El Niño became famous in 1997, when the media screamed, "El Niño is coming! El Niño is coming!" They released satellite pictures of a large warm spot in the Pacific Ocean and reported that it would cause an unusually warm winter in the United States and western Canada, floods in the southern states, landslides in California,

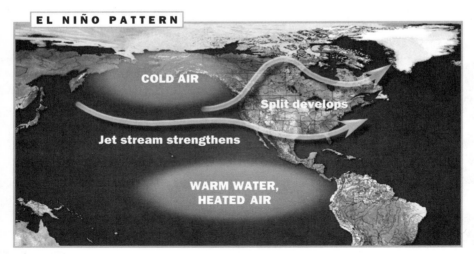

When El Niño is strong, the jet stream splits, bringing warmth to the north and moisture to the south.

drought and fires from Brazil to Mexico, deadly rains and mudslides in Peru, and heavy clouds of smoke to choke Indonesia—and it did!

Scientists have studied El Niño for over a century, and they have learned how it works: Occasionally, the central tropical Pacific Ocean becomes very warm and stays warm for 12 to 18 months. This warm spot slowly flows east until it hits Peru. Then it splits, with a portion flowing north and a portion flowing south.

The air above the unusually warm water heats up and takes in more moisture. As the warm air expands, it changes normal wind currents and alters weather patterns both locally and on a much larger scale. (El Niño can change weather all over the world.)

Scientists call the warm water El Niño, and they call the altered air above it and weather patterns it causes the Southern Oscillation. The entire phenomenon is called the El Niño/Southern Oscillation, or ENSO.

Teleconnection patterns are constantly changing. For a number of reasons—including winds, underwater volcanoes, and deep-sea currents—the Pacific Ocean changes back and forth from the warm El Niño to the chilly La Niña. When the Pacific Ocean cools, the air above the water becomes cooler as well. The change in ocean temperature affects the air pressure over the water, and the ridges and troughs in the atmosphere (which are caused by high and low air pressure) affect the prevailing winds that, in turn, affect our weather.

THE EL NIÑO FORECAST

■

El Niño brings warm winters to Canada and the northern United States.

THE LA NIÑA FORECAST

■

La Niña brings cold winters to Canada and the Pacific Northwest.

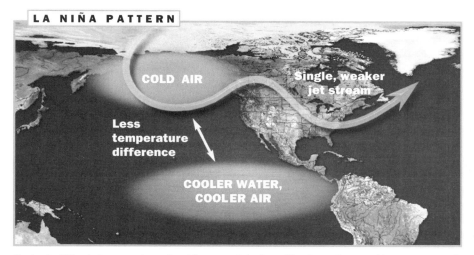

LA NIÑA PATTERN

COLD AIR

Single, weaker jet stream

Less temperature difference

COOLER WATER, COOLER AIR

During La Niña, the jet stream is weak and fluctuates, bringing cold to the northwest and less moisture south.

continued

OCEAN WEATHER BASICS

■ TELECONNECTION: **A recurring large-scale air pressure and circulation pattern that extends over a vast geographical area. (The El Niño/Southern Oscillation, or ENSO, is an example of a teleconnection.)**

■ OSCILLATION: **An air pressure pattern that changes back and forth so that each phase produces a unique, predictable pattern.**

■ EL NIÑO: **The air pressure and circulation patterns that occur when the central and eastern tropical Pacific Ocean waters are warm.**

■ LA NIÑA: **The air pressure and circulation patterns that occur when the central and eastern tropical Pacific Ocean waters are cold.**

Once scientists realized that El Niños and La Niñas could affect global climate, they began analyzing satellite and weather-buoy data from locations all over the world. They also examined old weather records for repeating patterns and discovered other teleconnections and oscillations. Here are five examples:

The **Madden Julian Oscillation** (MJO) is a 40- to 60-day period of alternately strong or weak trade winds that normally blow west. It is named after Roland Madden and Paul Julian, two scientists from the National Center for Atmospheric Research who in 1971 were studying wind patterns in the tropical Pacific. For unknown reasons, these tropical winds sometimes weaken, and the Sun-warmed pulse of ocean water that they usually cause to drift west drifts east. As this pulse of warm water, called a Kelvin wave, moves east—from the coast of Africa across the Indian and Pacific Oceans—it carries changed air patterns above it.

When the wave crashes into South America, the water stops, but the air pattern continues over land northeastward, into the Caribbean atmosphere and across the Atlantic Ocean. Before this cycle is complete, another pulse has already started in the Indian Ocean. Scientists are still studying the MJO. Most agree, however, that when the MJO cycle speeds up and warm Kelvin waves pile up in the Pacific Ocean, we have the start of an El Niño.

> Most scientists agree that when an MJO cycle speeds up and Kelvin waves pile up in the Pacific Ocean, another El Niño is starting.

THE MADDEN JULIAN OSCILLATION FORECAST

■

The MJO usually brings flooding rains (also known as the "Pineapple Express") to the Pacific Northwest and California. In an active hurricane season on the East Coast, it can mean several hurricanes within a few weeks, followed by a long spell with no hurricanes.

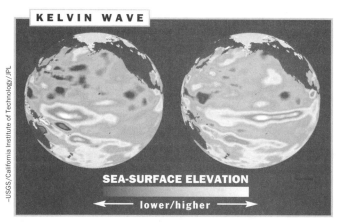

KELVIN WAVE

SEA-SURFACE ELEVATION
◄— lower/higher —►

–USGS/California Institute of Technology/JPL

These satellite images, taken on March 17 (left) and April 6, 1997, depict a Kelvin wave on the equator as it expands into the El Niño of 1997–98.

continued

The **Tropical Atlantic Variability** (TAV) is often called "the El Niño of the Atlantic." Like El Niño, the TAV is associated with trade winds. Unlike El Niño, which travels east, the TAV oscillation runs north and south. Depending on the strength of the southeast trade winds, it alternately warms the ocean water south of the equator, then north, then south again.

When the Atlantic sea-surface temperatures near the equator fluctuate, precipitation patterns change throughout the Atlantic Ocean. Like most oscillations, the TAV is affected by other global weather patterns.

A snapshot of the Tropical Atlantic Variability when it is most conducive to hurricanes (below): *Strong southeast trade winds blow the warm water on the surface of the ocean northwest, over the equator. Warm Atlantic Ocean water energizes storms. (When the southeast trade winds are weak, the warmer waters remain south of the equator.)*

THE TROPICAL ATLANTIC VARIABILITY FORECAST

■

When the TAV causes the water north of the equator to be unusually warm in summer, the warmed water acts as a channel for tropical storms and hurricanes striking the East Coast, especially in the Southeast. Much less is known about the effects of the TAV during winter.

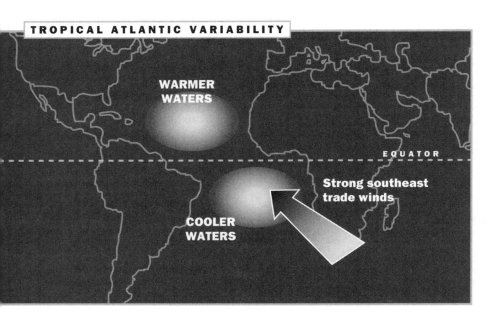

TROPICAL ATLANTIC VARIABILITY

WARMER WATERS

EQUATOR

Strong southeast trade winds

COOLER WATERS

94

continued

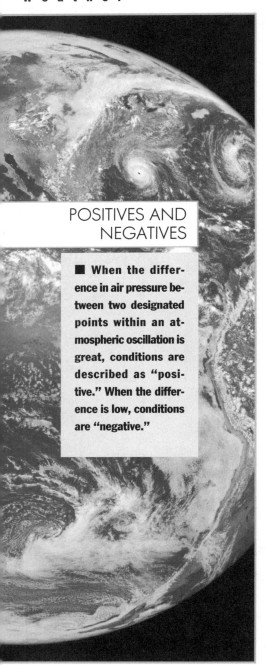

POSITIVES AND NEGATIVES

■ **When the difference in air pressure between two designated points within an atmospheric oscillation is great, conditions are described as "positive." When the difference is low, conditions are "negative."**

The **Pacific/North American** pattern (PNA) is a large teleconnection that dominates weather from Shanghai, China, to Atlanta, Georgia, every month except June and July. The air masses over the warm waters of Hawaii and the cool waters of Alaska's Aleutian Islands start a circulation pattern that sweeps east into North America. There the pattern interacts with a high ridge of air over the northern Rockies and a deep trough over the southern states.

As the PNA turns negative, the airflow becomes more directly west to east.

THE PACIFIC/NORTH AMERICAN PATTERN FORECAST

■

A positive PNA carries tropical moisture into British Columbia, and the United States ends up with cold and stormy weather in the Midwest and Southeast; cold in the East and warmth in the West; and tornadoes—and even snowstorms—along the Gulf Coast, as blasts of polar air meet warm, moist air in the South.

■

A negative PNA carries diminishing amounts of moisture eastward from California, resulting in cold and snowy weather in the West; rain and snow in the plains; and warm and relatively dry weather in the East.

continued

The **Pacific Decadal Oscillation** (PDO) is a change in ocean currents that lasts for 20 to 30 years. It affects not only water temperatures but also air currents overhead. A warm PDO means a warm central Pacific Ocean with cool water in the west, north, and south. During the cool phase, the central waters are cool and the peripheral waters are warm. During the last three decades of the 20th century, we experienced a warm phase.

THE PACIFIC DECADAL OSCILLATION FORECAST

■

A warm PDO may result in more El Niños, more precipitation, and fewer typhoons.

■

A cool PDO results in cool air and less precipitation in the western United States.

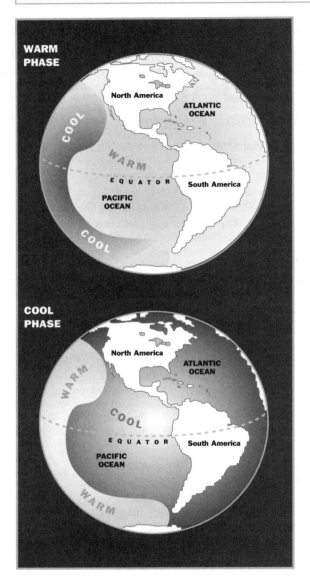

In its warm phase, the PDO brings warm sea-surface temperatures (SSTs) to the North Pacific Ocean, resulting in more precipitation for the western United States. In its cool phase, the PDO brings cool SSTs, resulting in less precipitation.

continued

Embarrassed BY THIN HAIR?

My mother's hair was extremely thin. She was terribly embarrassed by it. You could look right through the hair and see large spots of exposed scalp; and she had split ends. She tried everything available but nothing worked, until we found *Neutrolox*™. Today, my mother's hair looks thick and gorgeous; she looks years younger and she was able to donate her wigs for use by cancer patients.

Neutrolox™ is not just a hair thickening cream; its effective ingredients are the answer to the embarrassing problem of thinning hair and it lets your hair grow fast and naturally. My name is John Peters and I was balding at an extreme rate. After using *Neutrolox*™ we both are getting compliments on our hair for the first time in our lives. It is great for men and women and can be used on color-treated, permed or processed hair. There is nothing like *Neutrolox*™ and it is not yet available in stores. *Neurolox*™ is in a class of it's own.

We honestly believe in *Neutrolox*™ and know you will too! Try Neutrolox™, if you don't agree you get every penny of your money back—no one can beat a 100% no-risk money-back guarantee. To order send $16.95 (plus $3.00 S&H) for a medium, or the most SAVINGS come with the large (you save $9.95) send only $26.95, plus $3.00 S&H for each order to:

Neutrolox, Dept. FA-N2003, BOX 366, Taylor, MI 48180

RINGING in the EARS?
GREAT News For YOU!

If you ever experience ringing in the ears, buzzing, hissing or any other annoying sounds that may be interfering with your life, you should know about *Dr. John's Special Ear Drops*™.

The drops are truly remarkable; for example: 79-year-old Gloria Gains of Richmond, VA writes: "I tried everything available and my doctor told me I would have to live with my trouble. I had trouble sleeping at night and the sounds were driving me out of my mind. Thank God, I seen your advertisement. I hardly notice anything at all anymore and I'm sleeping like a baby. Your drops have been a God-Send."

Thousands of users like Gloria have written to us regarding *Dr. John's Special Ear Drops*™. If your doctor has not been able to help you, I strongly urge you to give *Dr. John's Special Ear Drops*™ a try. You won't be sorry! The drops are guaranteed to be better for you than anything you have ever tried or you will get every cent of your money back, no questions asked. You can't beat that!

To order send $16.95 plus $3.00 S&H (only $19.95) for one bottle. Or order two bottles for the super savings offer only $26.95 plus $3.00 S&H — a total of $29.95. Send to: **Dr. John's Research, Dept. FA-DJ2003, Box 637, Taylor, MI 48180**

Dr. John's Research is celebrating its 26th anniversary this year providing only the best products to its customers. A testimonial reflects the opinion of that individual. Individual results may vary. The Food and Drug Administration does not review claims made on herbal products and the drops are not intended to diagnose, treat, cure or prevent any disease. You should see your doctor if you think you have a disease. If you suffer from ringing in the ears, don't wait a minute longer. Stop suffering.

The **North Atlantic Oscillation** (NAO) affects the eastern United States. This teleconnection sits between the cool atmospheric low over Iceland and the warm high over the Azores.

THE NORTH ATLANTIC OSCILLATION FORECAST

■

In winter, a positive NAO causes Atlantic storms to veer north, and warm, wet winters to occur in the eastern United States and Europe. Northeastern Canada tends to be unusually cold.

In summer, a positive NAO means fewer tropical storms and hurricanes striking the East Coast.

■

In winter, a negative NAO forces cold air into the eastern United States, and causes heavy rains in southern Europe. Northeastern Canada is generally warmer, and areas around the Great Lakes tend to have a cooler, wetter spring.

Studies of a negative NAO in summer have proved inconclusive.

NORTH ATLANTIC OSCILLATION

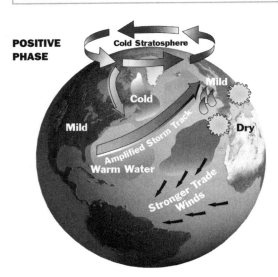

POSITIVE PHASE

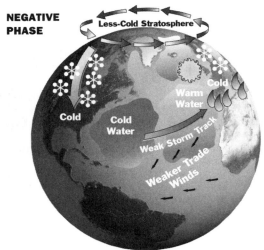

NEGATIVE PHASE

Situated between the cool low pressure over Iceland and the warm high pressure of the Azores, the NAO fluctuates from positive to negative. Extremely low air pressure over Iceland produces a positive NAO and mild winters in the eastern United States. Moderately low air pressure over Iceland results in a negative NAO and harsher winters in the eastern United States.

–diagrams above: Fritz Heide and Jack Cook/WHOI Graphic Services

continued

The oceans constantly change as warm and cool currents flow through them, and those changes are producing a very different climate. We are beginning to understand these patterns and prepare for the outcomes.

So, next time you bake in the West, freeze in the South, or get hit by a storm in New York City, remember: Your weather is caused by changes in the oceans and the atmosphere, and you might as well learn to swim with the current.

The Long-, Long-, Long-Range Forecast

■ An understanding of weather patterns and their effects can put climatic events of the past in perspective and help predict weather over long periods. Here are some hints about how such patterns will affect future conditions:

IN THE EAST

■

The North Atlantic Oscillation (NAO) varies from month to month and year to year. However, scientists are discovering long-term trends. During the 1940s, '50s, and '60s, the NAO was usually negative. In the '70s, '80s, and most of the '90s, the NAO was usually positive. It's becoming negative again. This is bad news for the Great Lakes, Midwest, and East Coast, which will have colder winters. The East Coast will be drier, the Southeast will experience drought, and both regions face an increased risk of hurricanes.

IN THE WEST

■

The Pacific Decadal Oscillation (PDO) also appears to be reversing. In 1999, the PDO entered a cool phase, which has meant less rain and snow for the western United States, Saskatchewan, Alberta, and western British Columbia. If the studies are right, this dry spell will continue for decades. ☐☐

Evelyn Browning Garriss, editor of the *Browning Newsletter,* has been writing, speaking, and consulting about the social and economic impact of climate change for more than 30 years. She tracks weather trends and cycles from her office in New Mexico.

WHAT'S THE WEATHER GOING TO BE TOMORROW?

Personalized local forecasts and long-range predictions, weather history, and more are available 24/7 at **www.almanac.com.** Click on **Article Links 2005** or the "Weather" button.

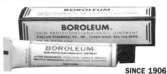

Wafting the Woolly Bugger

Fly-fishing tips from a "pro."

Rhode Island's Bobby Malouin has been fishing for as long as he can remember. He got hooked on fly-fishing at age nine. After fishing all day with a spinning rod and catching only one fish, he noticed that a man with a fly rod had caught three right away.

The first time Bobby tried fly-fishing, he didn't catch anything. A fellow fisherman gave him 20 flies and told him which ones to use. That same day, another fisherman gave him a fly vest and a reel on the condition that he not give up the sport. He didn't; he got his own vise for fly-tying and has been fly-fishing and tying his own flies ever since.

Now, Bobby spends much of his free time fly-fishing or -tying or talking about doing both. He goes fishing at least three times a week in season, watches fishing shows on television, and attends fly-tying courses. He estimates that he knows more than 200 recipes, or fly patterns, by heart, and says that he'd like to teach the sport and the art of fly-tying. (A local tackle shop has asked him to in-

struct.) In 2003, he entered a competition sponsored by United Fly Tyers Inc. that involved making flies selected from a list of recipes at home as well as creating flies at the competition. He won top prize, something that will come in handy in a couple of years: a $1,000 scholarship for college. You see, Bobby is only 15.

Bobby Malouin has no shortage of tackle.

by Galen H. McGovern

Whether you're just starting out or simply need to bone up on your techniques, you might take heed of Bobby's best advice:

■ **Ask any local fisherman about which flies are best to use, or get your dip net out and find out for yourself.** A dip net is usually dragged across the lake-, river-, or streambed to catch nymphs, emerging insects, and other aquatic life. It works especially well after you've turned over stones, wood, and other matter on the bottom.

■ **When learning to tie, start big and easy to get the basic technique down.** Try Woolly Buggers, Woolly Worms, and Montanas.

■ **When nothing seems to be working, try the Pheasant Tail.** Bobby adds a copper thorax to it, which helps the fly to sink faster, head down, in the water.

■ **Don't worry about losing your flies**—you can just tie more.

■ **The color of a fly has a lot to do with catching fish.** If the fly doesn't look like what the fish are feeding on, they won't go for it. Woolly Buggers work very well, and Bobby always puts flash—a shiny, sparkly material—on the sides of his.

■ **The time of year and weather conditions determine which flies work best.** In 2003, when the trout were hitting wet flies or nymphs, Bobby had good luck with heavily weighted flies in olive and black. The fish seemed to be deeper in the water, perhaps due to the abundance of rain. For more advice on the best times and conditions, see "Best Fishing Days," page 108.

continued

Wind Wisdom

Wind from the south, hook in the mouth.

Wind from the east, bite the least.

Wind from the north, further off.

Wind from the west, bite the best.

Woolly Bugger

Pheasant Tail

Best Catches

The first fish Bobby Malouin caught using a fly he himself had tied was a big rainbow trout on a Pheasant Tail. His first successful use of a store-bought fly was with a Muddler Minnow.

–photos above: *Fly Tying Made Clear and Simple* by Skip Morris, Frank Amato Publications

■ **Practice your technique.** Bobby has done a lot of casting in his backyard with a crude fly (to help straighten the line out) with the hook clipped off (to help avoid injuries).

■ **Mash down the barbs on your hooks.** This makes a smaller hole in the fish's mouth, and you won't lose the fish as long as you keep pressure on the line when you're bringing the fish in.

■ **Fish in places where fish hide or stay to save energy:** undercut banks, obstructions, on the side of the current, in front of and behind rocks. Never fish from upstream to downstream; stirred-up debris will scare the fish.

■ **Wear polarized sunglasses;** they'll help you see the fish.

■ **Have patience.** You'll get better as you go.

Why Fish?

A survey in *The Splash,* newsletter of the National Fresh Water Fishing Hall of Fame (Hayward, Wisconsin), revealed how anglers' reasons for fishing shifted over a 20-year period:

Year	Food	Companionship (with family and friends, not just the fish)	Relaxation
1980	28%	19%	14%
2000	5%	33%	35%

Galen H. McGovern is a writer and environmental consultant in Rhode Island.

Fishing Folklore

Eat the eyes of a fish, and you'll never be afraid of the dark.

Some fishermen consider it unlucky to eat a fish from tail to head.

To restock fishing grounds: Eat half of the first fish you take, and then throw the uneaten part back into the water. The next year, the entire fish will return to the same place and wait to be caught again.

It's good luck to spit on your hook, and good luck to spit into the mouth of the first fish you catch (both promise an abundant catch). It's bad luck to spit into the water in front of you (which will drive fish away).

Don't let your shadow fall on the water while you are fishing (you'll scare the fish away).

Fish bite best at night, and if you play a fiddle or guitar then, the fish will come to the top because they love the music.

□□

Black Listed Cancer Treatment Could Save Your Life

As unbelievable as it seems the key to stopping many cancers has been around for over 30 years. Yet it has been banned. Blocked. And kept out of your medicine cabinet by the very agency designed to protect your health—the FDA.

In 1966, the senior oncologist at a prominent New York hospital rocked the medical world when he developed a serum that **"shrank cancer tumors in 45 minutes!"** 90 minutes later they were gone... Headlines hit every major paper around the world. Time and again this life saving treatment worked miracles, but the FDA ignored the research and hope he brought and shut him down.

You read that right. He was not only shut down—but also forced out of the country where others benefited from his discovery. How many other treatments have they been allowed to hide?

Decades ago, European research scientist Dr. Johanna Budwig, a six-time Nobel Award nominee, discovered a totally natural formula that not only protects against the development of cancer, but has helped people all over the world diagnosed with incurable cancer—now lead normal lives.

After 30 years of study, Dr. Budwig discovered that the blood of seriously ill cancer patients was deficient in certain substances and nutrients. Yet, healthy blood always contained these ingredients. It was the lack of these nutrients that allowed cancer cells to grow wild and out of control.

It has been shown that by simply eating a combination of two natural and delicious foods (found on page 134) not only can cancer be prevented—but in some cases it was actually healed! "Symptoms of cancer, liver dysfunction, and diabetes were completely alleviated." Remarkably, what Dr. Budwig discovered was a totally natural way for eradicating cancer.

However, when she went to publish these results so that everyone could benefit—**she was blocked by manufacturers with heavy financial stakes!** For over 10 years now her methods have proved effective—yet she is denied publication—blocked by the giants who don't want you to read her words.

What's more, the world is full of expert minds like Dr. Budwig who have pursued cancer remedies and come up with remarkable natural formulas and diets that work for hundreds and thousands of patients. *How to Fight Cancer & Win* author William Fischer has studied these methods and revealed their secrets for you—so that you or someone you love may be spared the horrors of conventional cancer treatments.

As early as 1947, Virginia Livingston, M.D., isolated a cancer-causing microbe. She noted that every cancer sample analyzed contained it.

This microbe—a bacteria that is actually in each of us from birth to death—multiplies and promotes cancer when the immune system is weakened by disease, stress, or poor nutrition. Worst of all, the microbes secrete a special hormone protector that short-circuits our body's immune system—allowing the microbes to grow undetected for years. No wonder so many patients are riddled with cancer by the time it is detected. But there is hope even for them...

Throughout the pages of *How to Fight Cancer & Win* you'll meet real people who were diagnosed with cancer—suffered through harsh conventional treatments—turned their backs on so called modern medicine—only to be miraculously healed by natural means! Here is just a sampling of what others have to say about the book.

"We purchased *How to Fight Cancer & Win*, and immediately my husband started following the recommended diet for his just diagnosed colon cancer. He refused the surgery that our doctors advised. Since following the regime recommended in the book he has had no problems at all, cancer-wise. If not cured, we believe the cancer has to be in remission." —*Thelma B.*

"As a cancer patient who has been battling lymphatic cancer on and off for almost three years now, I was very pleased to stumble across *How to Fight Cancer & Win*. The book was inspiring, well-written and packed with useful information for any cancer patient looking to maximize his or her chances for recovery." —*Romany S.*

"I've been incorporating Dr. Budwig's natural remedy into my diet and have told others about it. Your book is very informative and has information I've never heard about before. Thanks for the wonderful information." —*Molly G.*

Claim your book today and you will be one of the lucky few who no longer have to wait for cures that get pushed "underground" by big business and money hungry giants.

To get your copy of *How to Fight Cancer & Win* go to www.agorahealthbooks.com/farm2 or call **1-888-821-3609 and ask for code P6E93** to order by credit card. Or write "Fight Cancer—Dept. P6E93" on a plain piece of paper with your name, address, phone number (in case we have a question about your order) and mail it with a check for $19.95 plus $5.00 shipping to: **Agora Health Books, Dept. P6E93, P.O. Box 925 Frederick, MD 21705-9838**

If you are not completely satisfied, return the book within one year for a complete and total refund—no questions asked. This will probably be the most important information you and your loved ones receive—so order today!

ID#P6E93

Best Fishing Days and Times

■ **The best times to fish are when the fish are naturally most active. The Sun,** Moon, tides, and weather all influence fish activity. For example, fish tend to feed more at sunrise and sunset. During a full Moon, tides are higher than average and fish tend to feed more. However, most of us go fishing when we can get the time off, not because it is the best time. But there *are* best times, according to fishing lore:

The Best Days for 2005, when the Moon is between new and full:

January 10–25
February 8–23
March 10–25
April 8–24
May 8–23
June 6–22
July 6–21
August 4–19
September 3–17
October 3–17
November 1–15
December 1–15
December 30–31

■ One hour before and one hour after high tides, and one hour before and one hour after low tides. (The times of high tides for Boston are given on pages 180–202; also see pages 232–233. Inland, the times for high tides correspond with the times the Moon is due south. Low tides are halfway between high tides.)

■ During the "morning rise" (after sunup for a spell) and the "evening rise" (just before sundown and the hour or so after).

■ When the barometer is steady or on the rise. (But even during stormy periods, the fish aren't going to give up feeding. The smart fisherman will find just the right bait.)

■ When there is a hatch of flies—caddis flies or mayflies, commonly. (The fisherman will have to match *his* fly with the hatching flies or go fishless.)

■ When the breeze is from a westerly quarter rather than from the north or east.

■ When the water is still or rippled, rather than during a wind.

Tackle-Box Checklist

✔ Fishing line
✔ Bobbers
✔ Swivels, to keep fishing line from twisting
✔ Leaders
✔ Sinkers
✔ Different sizes of hooks
✔ Pliers, to help remove hooks
✔ Stringer, to hold all the fish you catch
✔ Sharp knife
✔ Ruler/scale
✔ Flashlight
✔ First-aid kit
✔ Insect repellent
✔ Sunscreen

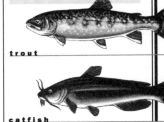

trout

catfish

salmon

New lure's catch rate may be too high for some tournaments.

Out-fishes other bait 19 to 4 in one contest.

Uses aerospace technology to mimic a real fish.

Swims with its tail.

New lure swims like a real fish--nearly triples catch in Florida contest.

ORLANDO, FL— A small company in Connecticut has developed a new lure that mimics the motion of a real fish so realistically eight professionals couldn't tell the difference between it and a live shad when it "swam" toward them on retrieval. The design eliminates wobbling, angled swimming and other unnatural motions that problem other hard bait lures. It swims upright and appears to propel itself with its tail.

Curiously, the company may have designed it too well. Tournament fishermen who have used it said it's possible officials will not allow it in contests where live bait is prohibited. They claim it swims more realistically than anything they have ever seen. If so, that would hurt the company's promotional efforts. Winning tournaments is an important part of marketing a new lure.

Fish would probably prefer to see it restricted. I watched eight veteran fishermen test the new lure (called The KickTail™) on a lake outside Orlando FL for about four hours. Four used the KickTail and four used a combination of their favorite lures and shiners (live bait). The four using the KickTail caught 41 fish versus 14 for the other four. In one boat the KickTail won 19 to 4. The KickTail also caught bigger fish, which suggests it triggers larger, less aggressive fish to strike.

The KickTail's magic comes from a patented technology that breaks the tail into five segments. As water rushes by on retrieval, a little-known principle called aeronautical flutter causes the tail to wag left and right, as if the lure were propelling itself with its tail. Unlike other hard baits, the head remains stationary— only the tail wags. A company spokesman told me this.

"Marine biologists will tell you that the more a lure swims like a real fish, the more fish it will catch. Well, the only live thing the KickTail doesn't do is breathe. It's always swimming wild and free. Fish can't stand it. We've seen fish that have just eaten go for the KickTail. It's like having another potato chip."

Whether you fish for fun or profit, if you want a nearly 3 to 1 advantage, I would order now before the KickTail becomes known. The company even guarantees a refund, if you don't catch more fish and return the lures within 30 days. There are three versions: a floater, a diver and a "dying shad" with a weed guard. Each lure costs $9.95 and you must order at least two. There is also a "Super 10-Pack" with additional colors for only $79.95, a savings of almost $20.00. S/h is only $6.00 no matter how many you order.

To order call **1-800-873-4415** or click **www.ngcsports.com** anytime of any day or send a check or M.O. (or cc number and exp. date) to NGC Sports (**Dept. KT-764**), 60 Church Street, Yalesville, CT 06492. CT orders add sales tax. The KickTail is four inches long and works in salt and fresh water.

Tracker's Guide

Off for a walk in the woods? Keep an eye out for signs of these woodland creatures.

text compiled by Sarah Perreault

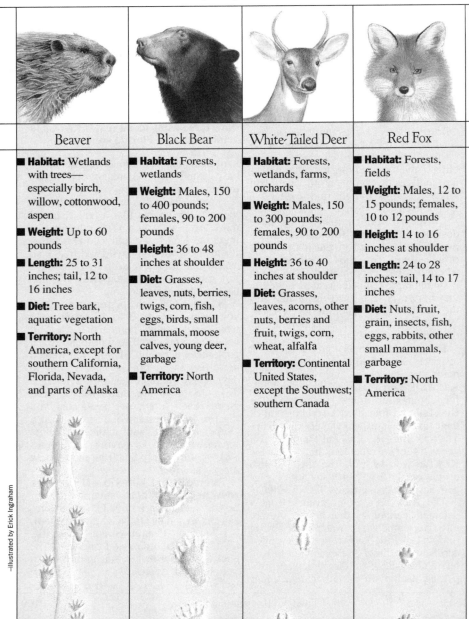

Beaver	Black Bear	White-Tailed Deer	Red Fox
■ **Habitat:** Wetlands with trees—especially birch, willow, cottonwood, aspen ■ **Weight:** Up to 60 pounds ■ **Length:** 25 to 31 inches; tail, 12 to 16 inches ■ **Diet:** Tree bark, aquatic vegetation ■ **Territory:** North America, except for southern California, Florida, Nevada, and parts of Alaska	■ **Habitat:** Forests, wetlands ■ **Weight:** Males, 150 to 400 pounds; females, 90 to 200 pounds ■ **Height:** 36 to 48 inches at shoulder ■ **Diet:** Grasses, leaves, nuts, berries, twigs, corn, fish, eggs, birds, small mammals, moose calves, young deer, garbage ■ **Territory:** North America	■ **Habitat:** Forests, wetlands, farms, orchards ■ **Weight:** Males, 150 to 300 pounds; females, 90 to 200 pounds ■ **Height:** 36 to 40 inches at shoulder ■ **Diet:** Grasses, leaves, acorns, other nuts, berries and fruit, twigs, corn, wheat, alfalfa ■ **Territory:** Continental United States, except the Southwest; southern Canada	■ **Habitat:** Forests, fields ■ **Weight:** Males, 12 to 15 pounds; females, 10 to 12 pounds ■ **Height:** 14 to 16 inches at shoulder ■ **Length:** 24 to 28 inches; tail, 14 to 17 inches ■ **Diet:** Nuts, fruit, grain, insects, fish, eggs, rabbits, other small mammals, garbage ■ **Territory:** North America

–Illustrated by Erick Ingraham

Hydrogen Peroxide Can Heal What?

The DIRT CURE

FOR A

WINTER

COUGH

AND

OTHER MEANS

TO

HOMEMADE

HEALTH

and

HAPPINESS

The Dirt Cure

Proof that laboring in the soil is the most invigorating and healthful of all exercises.

Find a piece of land on which there are blueberry and other small bushes and in which there are numerous small stones. When that land is covered with about a foot of snow but is not frozen solid, shovel off the snow. Then cut down the bushes and dig out the stones, turning up fresh and pure soil. Pause occasionally to take up two fistfuls of soil, bring them close to your face, and, with your mouth wide open, inhale the scent of the fresh earth.

Continue until you have cleared half an acre, and you will find yourself strong and hale, and entirely rid of your cough.

In 1849, this procedure brought relief to a 57-year-old farmer who had been afflicted with a severe cough for several winters.

–The Old Farmer's Almanac archives

–illustrated by Carolyn Croll

PANTRY POTIONS

These easy, economical remedies provide relief to the mind, body, and pocketbook.

BEET ROUGE

If someone compliments you by saying that you look "as red as a beet," smile wisely to yourself.

1 beet
2 to 3 tablespoons powdered starch or rice powder

Wash, dry, and peel a ripe red beet. Press the beet against a grater until all the juice is extracted. To this liquid, add finely powdered starch or rice powder until the desired shade is obtained. Spread the mixture onto a platter, cover with cheesecloth, and set in a sunny place until completely dry. Store in an airtight container. **Makes 3 to 4 tablespoons.**

Apply the powder to your cheeks as you would store-bought rouge.

–The Old Farmer's Almanac archives

■

SUGAR SCRUB

Use this sweet mixture to exfoliate the dead skin that makes you look dull and flaky—unless, of course, you want to look dull and flaky!

1 tablespoon granulated sugar
1 teaspoon warm water

Place sugar in the palm of your hand. Add water drop by drop to make a paste. **Makes about 1 tablespoon.**

Gently rub the abrasive sugar scrub over your face and neck (avoiding your eyes), and massage lightly with your fingertips. Rinse with warm water followed by cool water. Just a spoonful of sugar actually helps control oil buildup, cleanses clogged pores, and works as an antibacterial.

■

CHERRY LIP BALM

A dab of this lip balm heals and soothes chapped lips, giving you quick relief and reason to smile.

3 tablespoons shortening, such as Crisco
1 packet cherry Kool-Aid
1 empty 35-mm film canister, washed and dried

Place shortening in a ceramic mug or bowl and heat in a microwave oven for 1 minute (or until the shortening liquefies). Empty the packet of Kool-Aid into the melted shortening and stir well until dissolved. Carefully pour the colored liquid into the film canister, cap tightly, and refrigerate overnight. In the morning, you've got tasty, homemade lip balm. ∎

DEODORANT CREAM
Don't let "B.O." be your one-way ticket to doom as the object of hushed scorn and ridicule!

2 teaspoons baking soda
2 teaspoons cornstarch
2 teaspoons petroleum jelly

Mix the baking soda, cornstarch, and petroleum jelly well. Heat in a double boiler over low heat and stir until a smooth cream forms. Pour the cream into a small container with a tight-fitting lid and let cool. **Makes about 3 ounces.**
Apply with fingers.

∎

HOT-SAUCE LINIMENT
When applied topically as a rubdown, this powerful liniment, made with Tabasco sauce (which contains the alkaloid capsaicin), provides warm, soothing relief from congestion, sprains, and muscle- and backaches.

Note: Gum myrrh and goldenseal may be available in your local health food store.

2 tablespoons Tabasco or other hot-pepper sauce
2 cups apple cider vinegar
2 ounces gum myrrh
1 ounce dried goldenseal

Mix the Tabasco sauce, vinegar, myrrh, and goldenseal in a saucepan and boil gently for 10 minutes. Let cool, and pour into a sanitized glass bottle. Cap tightly. Place the bottle in a dark place for one week, shaking twice a day. **Makes about two cups.** ☐☐

The scrub, balm, deodorant, and liniment recipes are excerpted from Joey Green's Incredible Country Store *by Joey Green (Rodale Inc., 2004; paperback, $19.95) and printed with the permission of the publisher. Available at www.rodale.com and wherever books are sold.*

TRY THIS FANCY FOOTWORK

Need to get more exercise but worn out by workouts? Go to **www.almanac.com** and click on **Article Links 2005** to find the Relocation Shuffle and Dance Tips.

DEFEAT DIABETES—REGAIN CONTROL

If you suffer from Type 2 Diabetes you may experience anger, hopelessness, depression, loss of pleasure in life or even feel threatened by daily activities. A new book, *Defeating Diabetes,* gives you answers—how to reverse the limitations of diabetes, ways to recover your vitality, and how to regain pleasure in living.

You will get the latest facts about Type 2 Diabetes—the condition, its symptoms, what causes it, and new ways to defeat the limitations it imposes. Even more, in a caring and methodical fashion, the book reveals up-to-date information: what carbohydrates you can eat safely, how to monitor your intake with ease, and how to design the optimum diabetes diet.

The book guides you in day-to-day wellness: diet facts, food references, practical and delicious menus, and exercises that you can easily add to your daily routine. Written by a registered dietician and a doctor, this book goes far beyond the basic guidelines and rules. You'll discover new secrets for healthy living that put you back in control.

You'll learn the essentials: fitness habits that work, ways to get better sleep and feel rested, how to reduce stress, and secrets for emotional recovery and health. This book delivers a new message of hope for the 18 million Type 2 Diabetes sufferers in the US.

Satisfied readers report: "I am astonished that by changing my diet I enjoy eating and feel great!" This reader adds, "I'm off of the expensive drugs and feeling better than I have in years, all because of diet and exercise."

You can improve the quality of life regardless of your age. Start today and **order** *Defeating Diabetes.* Send name, address, copy of ad, with check or money order for $14.95, *plus $3.25 P&H (CA residents add $1.08 tax).* Credit cards: send number & expiration date. Mail to: United Research Publishers, Dept. DB-OF-A4, 132 North El Camino Real, Encinitas, CA 92024. Order on-line: **www.urpublishers.com**
Our 100% Guarantee: Return within 90 days for a refund if not fully satisfied!

NEW ARTHRITIS RELIEF
Safe, Natural & Drug-Free

If you suffer from pain or inflammation in your joints or bones, stiff or difficult movement, or aches in surrounding muscle, then a new book, *Conquering Arthritis, Osteoporosis and Other Degenerative Diseases,* can help.

This book gives you vital facts about arthritis. It reveals the truth about treatments and gives new hope for reversing symptoms with *all-natural methods. Conquering Arthritis* challenges use of prescription drugs and tells why some drugs may actually cause more harm than good.

This book explains arthritis. It covers the different types of arthritis, the variety of causes for each type, the symptoms for each type, and the full range of treatments available. It reveals new information on how toxins in the foods, medicines and products we use each day can produce symptoms and disease progression.

You'll discover new, vital ways to promote healing—why body detoxification should be the *first step to better health,* how specific foods may reduce pain while others can cleanse, and how inexpensive nutritional supplements can support symptom relief. It covers the importance of certain exercises that can help reverse degeneration. It shows how acupuncture can bring fast relief and why reflexology helps healing.

This book gives new answers for the estimated 57 million Americans who suffer from arthritis. It can help improve your quality of life in these ways: reduced costs and risks associated with expensive drugs, reduced pain, and increased mobility.

One reader writes: "I am astonished that inflammation has been reduced by changing my diet." Another reader adds, "I do not dread getting out of bed in the morning. I can move with freedom again."

Regardless of your age or type of arthritis *Conquering Arthritis* can help. **Order today:** send name, address, copy of ad with check or money order for $16.95, *plus $3.25 P&H (CA residents add $1.23 tax).* Credit cards: send number & expiration date. Mail today to: United Research Publishers, Dept. AR-OF-A4, 132 North El Camino Real, Encinitas, CA 92024. Order on-line: **www.urpublishers.com**
Our 100% Guarantee: Return within 90 days for a refund if not fully satisfied!

▶ Troubled by pet hairs on your furniture? Put on a rubber glove and run your hand in one direction over the surface. The hairs will form a thin rope that's easy to pick up.

▶ Got unsightly silverware? Polish it with the juice of a banana skin puréed in a blender.

Don't Throw That Away!

▶ **When tomato sauce turns a good plastic container pink, fill it with warm water, drop in one or two denture-cleaning tablets, wait 20 minutes, and rinse. (The tablets also work well for cleaning toilets.)**

▶ If you spill red wine on a tablecloth or carpet, sprinkle the stain liberally with salt and leave it alone until the salt turns red. Then shake out and wash the tablecloth or vacuum the carpet.

If your string of pearls has lost its luster, clean it carefully with a soft cloth dipped in olive oil. Wipe off oil before wearing.

▶ When silk flowers get dusty, put them in a paper bag with several table-spoons of salt and shake gently for two minutes to clean them.

▶ **To clean pine pitch from your hands, rub them well with a glob of mayonnaise, then wash.**

REUSE, REFRESH, RECYCLE.

▶ Give new life to any feather pillow by putting it in the dryer with three clean tennis balls on low heat for ten minutes.

▶ Boil old toothbrushes in water for four minutes and use them for cleaning golf clubs, bird feeders, and fish tanks, or for getting off the last bits of corn silk from fresh ears.

▶ **Pull a clean cotton sock over your hand to wash or dry the dishes. Or, wear one on your hand to dust railings and chair rungs. Or, protect especially fragile Christmas ornaments by putting them in old socks.**

▶ Refresh household sponges by soaking them in cold salt water for ten minutes.

▶ Sprinkle baking soda on carpets to deodorize them. Leave it on for an hour and then vacuum.

▶ Is your toaster toast? Unplug it, cut off the cord, clean out the crumbs, and use it to hold bills and other mail.

▶ **Use an old pair of panty hose to strain old paint, removing any lumps or debris that might otherwise mar your paint job.**

▶ Use clean, squeeze-type ketchup and mustard containers for decorating cakes. Their spouts are great for writing and drawing with cake icing.

COMPILED BY GEORGIA ORCUTT

Georgia Orcutt has been a contributor to *The Old Farmer's Almanac* and its family of publications for years.

117

Amusement

On the 50th anniversary of Albert Einstein's death, advice on

HOW TO BE A GENIUS

(or at least a little smarter than you are now) • by Tony Velocci

–Emilio Segre Visual Archives/ American Institute of Physics

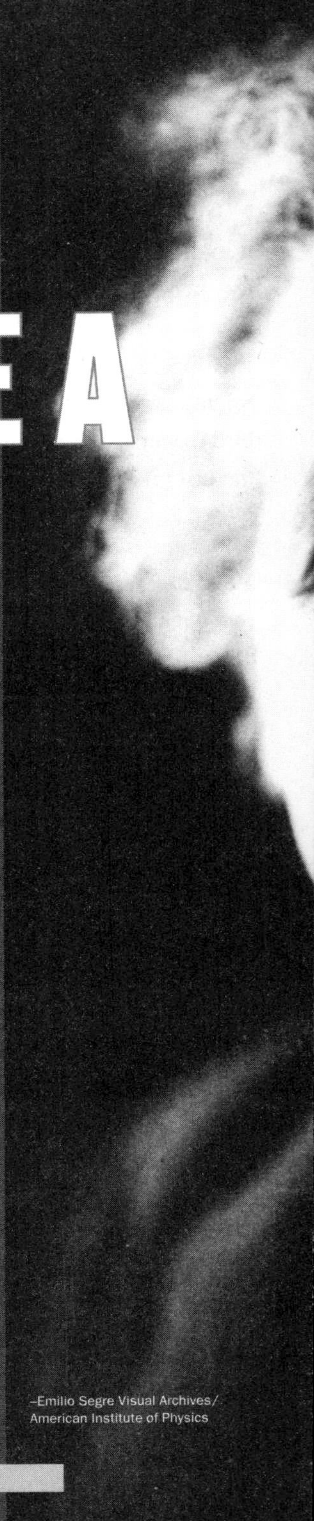

For centuries, people with extraordinary intellect have demonstrated an amazing ability to invent, to explain the seemingly inexplicable, and to conceptualize ideas that have had a profound impact on society. Meanwhile, the rest of us have often looked on in awe, wondering, How did he or she do that? What does it take to be a genius?

Consider this: You may possess some of the same traits that distinguished some of history's most famous thinkers. All you need to know is *how* to reach your potential.

1 THINK IN MOVING PICTURES.

Genius is an African who dreams up snow.

–Vladimir Nabokov, Russian-born American writer (1899–1977)

Visualization is a kind of mental movie. In their mind's eye, geniuses see concepts as theater rather than as still photography. Einstein wrote, "My particular ability does not lie in mathematical calculation, but rather in visualizing effects, possibilities, and consequences."

CONTINUED

ALBERT EINSTEIN

SIR ISAAC NEWTON

MADAME MARIE CURIE

SIGMUND FREUD

WOLFGANG AMADEUS MOZART

SOCRATES

THOMAS EDISON

2 COMBINE THE NEW WITH THE OLD.

In every work of genius, we recognize our own rejected thoughts: They come back to us with a certain alienated majesty.

–Ralph Waldo Emerson, American writer
(1803–1882)

By describing an unfamiliar object or idea using a familiar concept or thing, deep thinkers have found that they can break out of a stale perspective. To help formulate his theory of relativity, Einstein imagined himself riding on a beam of light while holding a mirror in front of him or standing on a platform while a train passed by.

3 FIND SIMILARITIES.

Genius, in one respect, is like gold —numbers of persons are constantly writing about both, who have neither.

–Charles Caleb Colton, English writer
(1780–1832)

The ability to make juxtapositions has inspired great intellects to see things that remain hidden to others—an outcome commonly known as the "Ah-ha!" moment. For instance, Leonardo da Vinci drew a connection between a stone hitting water and the sound of a bell, leading him to conclude that sound travels in waves.

4 TRUST YOUR HUNCHES.

True genius is a mind of large general powers, accidentally determined to some particular direction.

–Samuel Johnson, English writer
(1709–1784)

Geniuses commonly know without being able to say how they know. Claude Bernard, the founder of modern physiology, wrote that everything purposeful in scientific thinking begins with feeling.

5 DON'T GIVE UP!

Genius is nothing but a great aptitude for patience.

–Georges-Louis de Buffon, French naturalist
(1707–1788)

Einstein was once asked what the difference was between him and the average person. He said that if you asked the average person to find a needle in the haystack, the person would stop when he found a needle. Einstein said that he, on the other hand, would comb through the entire haystack looking for all the possible needles. "It's not that I'm smart, it's just that I stay with the problems longer," he said.

CONTINUED

Kill Foot Pain Dead!

Total Relief Guaranteed– Risk-Free.

Don't blame foot pain on your shoes! Most foot pain comes from misalignment of the bones in your feet.

Foot pain begins when your foot's balance and natural elasticity is gone. Corns, calluses, bunions, even hammertoes can develop, as well as toe cramps, fallen arches, burning skin, tender blisters, flaking and chafing. Ankle, leg, knee, hip - even lower back pain, can result from improper foot alignment. And when your feet hurt, you hurt all over.

Now! No More Foot Pain. Guaranteed!

Featherspring® Foot Supports, a remarkable discovery from Europe are unlike anything you have ever tried. First, they are *custom-formed* for your feet and your feet only! Secondly, they help restore and maintain the elastic support you had when you were younger. They actually help realign your feet, while absorbing shock and relieving pain.

© Featherspring, 712 N. 34th Street, Seattle, WA 98103-8881

For over 40 years, Feathersprings have brought blessed relief to more than 3,000,000 foot pain sufferers world wide. No other foot support has ever given so much relief to so many people.

It doesn't matter whether you are a woman or man, whether your feet are size 4 or 14, what width your foot is, how low or high your arches are, how old you are or how long you've had foot pain... we know Feathersprings will work for you.

Visit our web site at www.featherspring.com

Guaranteed To Kill Your Foot Pain Dead! We'll Prove It To You Risk Free!

If you are bothered by aches and pains of the feet, legs, or lower back, we state without reservation that Feathersprings will bring you relief or *you risk nothing.*

Send today for FREE Fact Kit.

Cut out and mail in the coupon below TODAY for FREE information, including details of our risk-free money back guarantee.

Custom–Formed Feathersprings end foot pain... once and for all!

6 JUST DO IT . . . AGAIN . . . AND AGAIN.

Genius is an infinite love of taking pains.

–Sir James Matthew Barrie, Scottish writer (1860–1937)

Wolfgang Amadeus Mozart wrote more than 600 pieces of music, and Johann Sebastian Bach produced a cantata every week. Thomas Edison gave himself and his assistants patent quotas. (His personal tally was a record of 1,093, which has yet to be beaten.) Einstein published nearly 250 scientific papers; the third one earned him a doctorate from the University of Zurich and the fourth brought him the 1921 Nobel Prize for physics.

7 BREAK THE RULES.

Rules and models destroy genius and art.

–William Hazlitt, English writer (1778–1830)

Problems stump the average person because he or she gets stuck in a "rule rut." That's when ingrained patterns of thinking—erroneous assumptions, half-truths, personal experience, misplaced generalities—are mistaken for truth and all conflicting ideas are ignored. The great new ideas are just outside of the prevailing thought.

8 FANTASIZE.

It takes a lot of time to be a genius, you have to sit around so much doing nothing, really doing nothing.

–Gertrude Stein, American writer (1874–1946)

122

IQ Fact and Fiction

■ The first intelligence quotient, or IQ, tests were conducted in the early 1900s by Alfred Binet on students in France in order to determine individual potential. Binet's initial scoring system was later revised to involve dividing a student's test results by the average result achieved by his or her age group, and multiplying that by 100. A student achieving at his or her age group was determined to have an IQ of 100.

■ A 140 (or above) IQ does not mean that a person is a genius. No reputable testing source uses an IQ number to classify someone in that category. The myth probably originated in the 1920s when Stanford University professor Lewis Terman, developer of the Stanford-Binet IQ test, used students with IQs above 140 for research.

Einstein said, "When I examine myself and my methods of thought, I come to the conclusion that the gift of fantasy has meant more to me than my talent for absorbing positive knowledge." He used his imagination to push beyond what is familiar and look at problems from many different perspectives.

CONTINUED

Learn. Earn.

The top ten reasons why training at home is the smart way to learn new career skills.

1 You can choose from Specialized Associate Degree and Career Diploma programs in today's hottest fields.

2 You can access study materials, exams, grades, instructor help, and more online.

3 You study at your own pace, in your own place, eliminating the need to ever commute to classes.

4 You'll have round-the-clock access to helpful, experienced instructors by phone or e-mail.

5 You take your exams when you decide you're ready — by telephone, online, or by mail.

6 You'll earn your degree or diploma from a school accredited by the Accrediting Commission of the Distance Education and Training Council. Education Direct is also accredited by the Middle States Commission on Secondary Schools for our high school and vocational-technical programs.

7 You'll earn continuing education units (CEUs) approved by the International Association for Continuing Education and Training.

8 Over 13 million students from the U.S. and abroad have chosen Education Direct training programs.

9 Over half of the Fortune 500 companies have used the simple, step-by-step Education Direct method to train their employees.

10 Your program can help you begin a new career, advance in your current one, or even open your own business, where you can make more money doing work you love!

624A

Get **FREE** facts on the program of your choice by calling

1-800-572-1685 ext. 4340,

by visiting our website at

www.EduDirect-usa.com
(online enter ID# AA2S94T),

or by mailing the coupon below.

THOMSON
EDUCATION DIRECT

Dept. AA2S94T
925 Oak Street
Scranton, PA 18515-0700

Please send me free facts, color brochure, and full information on how I can train at home for the career I have chosen. I understand I am under no obligation. **CHECK ONE BOX ONLY.**

HEALTH
- ☐ 03 Child Day Care Mgmt.
- ☐ 24 Dental Assistant
- ☐ 405 Early Childhood Education*
- ☐ 94 Fitness and Nutrition
- ☐ 409 Health Information Technology*
- ☐ 381 Medical Insurance Clerk
- ☐ 23 Medical Office Assistant
- ☐ 39 Medical Transcriptionist
- ☐ 383 Occupational Therapy Aide
- ☐ 84 Pharmacy Technician
- ☐ 146 Physical Therapy Aide
- ☐ 88 Veterinary Assistant
- ☐ 396 Veterinary Technician**

FINANCE & BUSINESS
- ☐ 61 Accounting*
- ☐ 390 Bookkeeping
- ☐ 60 Business Management*
- ☐ 406 Criminal Justice*
- ☐ 15 Home Inspector
- ☐ 68 Hospitality Management*
- ☐ 412 Human Resources Management

- ☐ 08 Paralegal
- ☐ 401 Paralegal Studies*
- ☐ 70 Small Business Owner

HIGH SCHOOL
- ☐ 07 High School

TECHNOLOGY
- ☐ 64 Applied Computer Science*
- ☐ 54 AutoCAD®
- ☐ 105 Computer Graphic Artist
- ☐ 53 Desktop Publishing & Design
- ☐ 404 E-Commerce Administration**
- ☐ 65 Electrical Engineering Technology**
- ☐ 407 Graphic Design Technology**
- ☐ 403 Internet Multimedia & Design**
- ☐ 27 PC Repair
- ☐ 38 PC Specialist
- ☐ 83 Web Page Designer
- ☐ 402 Web Programming**

MECHANICS
- ☐ 04 Auto Repair Technician
- ☐ 06 Electrician
- ☐ 14 HVAC Technician
- ☐ 62 Mechanical Engineering Technology**
- ☐ 89 Small Engine Repair

OTHER EXCITING PROGRAMS
- ☐ 104 Carpenter
- ☐ 59 Catering/Gourmet Cooking
- ☐ 63 Civil Engineering Technology**
- ☐ 42 Dressmaking and Design
- ☐ 30 Floral Design
- ☐ 76 Freelance Writer
- ☐ 145 Home Remodeling and Repair
- ☐ 05 Hotel/Restaurant Management

- ☐ 12 Interior Decorator
- ☐ 56 Pet Groomer
- ☐ 40 Photographer
- ☐ 151 Plumber
- ☐ 58 Private Investigator
- ☐ 160 Professional Bridal Consultant
- ☐ 102 Professional Landscaper
- ☐ 31 Professional Locksmithing
- ☐ 26 Teacher Aide
- ☐ 35 Travel Agent
- ☐ 22 Wildlife/Forestry Conservation

*Associate in Specialized Business Degree Program

**Associate in Specialized Technology Degree Program

NAME_____ AGE_____

STREET_____ APT.#_____

CITY/STATE_____ ZIP_____

PHONE (____)_____ E-MAIL_____

9 HOLD THAT THOUGHT.

A good memory is an essential ingredient of genius.

–John Ferguson, Scottish writer
(1851–1899)

Anders Ericsson, a psychologist at Florida State University, believes that a talent for storing information about particular topics is the ingredient essential for expert performance in any field. He also believes that such a skill can be developed at will. Exceptionally bright people place important pieces of information into their long-term memories in a way that makes the information accessible to working-memory processes.

10 HAVE FUN!

Genius is the capacity to evade hard work.

–Elbert Green Hubbard, American writer
(1856–1915)

Arthur Molella, director of the Smithsonian Institution's Lemelson Center for the Study of Invention and Innovation, has observed: "The sense of play is the essence of inventive activity. Invention begins in the joyful, free association of the mind."

Tony Velocci is a New Jersey–based magazine writer who has covered topics ranging from deep-sea treasure hunting to energy exploration on Alaska's North Slope.

How Can You Tell If You're a Genius?

■ **You can't tell—exactly.** According to Mensa, the international society of highly intelligent people, "genius" can not be measured; tests can not capture the diverse areas of aptitude and creativity exhibited by brilliant people. You can see how close you come to being Mensa material, however. Among the more than 200 tests (and minimum scores) accepted for membership are the following:

TEST	MINIMUM SCORE
Graduate Record Exam (GRE)	
Through June 30, 1994	1250
July 1, 1994, and after	1875
Miller Analogies Test (raw score)	66
Graduate Management Admissions Test (GMAT) (total score by %)	95
College SAT (math plus verbal)	
Through September 30, 1974	1300
October 1, 1974, through January 31, 1994	1250
February 1, 1994, and after	N/A*

*not accepted (Mensa considers SATs taken on or after February 1, 1994, to be achievement tests measuring knowledge, not inductive and deductive reasoning.)

□□

SEE HOW SMART YOU ARE
To learn about measuring IQ and to take a Mensa quiz, go to **www.almanac.com** and click on **Article Links 2005.**

Do You Have Diabetes?
Are You on Medicare?

If you answered "yes" to both questions,
the cost of your diabetes testing supplies may be covered.*

Call 1-800-986-1740

Know the facts about Medicare coverage for individuals with diabetes.
Liberty Medical Supply is the nation's leader in home delivery of diabetes testing supplies. We are a Medicare participating provider. You could be eligible for our complete direct to your home delivery program of diabetes testing supplies, and the cost may be covered by Medicare.

No up-front costs.* You pay no money up-front when you order diabetes testing supplies from Liberty. With qualified supplemental insurance, you may owe nothing at all.

No claim forms to fill out.
We will bill Medicare and your supplemental insurance company for you.

No charge for shipping.
Your order will be delivered to your home with no charge for shipping. You won't have to stand in pharmacy lines or go out in bad weather.

To learn if you are eligible, call us toll-free:
1-800-986-1740

*Deductibles and co-payments apply. Liberty's Family of Companies also provides respiratory medications and supplies, prescription medications and A1c testing, and shoes for people with diabetes.

We Deliver Better Health

LIBERTY

A PolyMedica Company

The Best Places to Meet

For some people, meeting others—especially significant others—is a breeze. The rest of us really have to work at it. It's worth the effort, say the "experts" (obviously, those with a mate). Having someone special in your life can help you live longer, stay healthier, and generally be happier. What they don't tell you is *where* to meet someone; we do. We polled those in the know. Some of their theories may surprise you.

by Jeff Brein

Someone

The Big City

■ According to Census 2000, the 18-and-over population of the United States was made up of 108 million women and 101 million men. If you're looking for women, pack your bags for Chicago, Los Angeles, or New York City. If you're on a quest for a man, head to Salinas, California; Fort Lauderdale, Florida; or Paradise, Nevada.

The Small City

■ Specifically, Seward, Alaska. Tiny Seward (pop. approx. 3,000) caters to single women by offering them a great shot at finding Mr. Right—for a price. Marilyn Sutherland runs the Polar Bear Jumpoff Festival Bachelor (and Bachelorette) Auction each January as a public service to her community (and a local charity).

"The average man fetches between $100 and $500, although several years ago, a woman from Texas phoned in her offer of $700 for an eligible tour boat operator. She happily trudged north that summer to make good on her successful bid," Sutherland says.

To date, several pairings have actually ended in happy marriages. Interested? The next auction is set for January 21, 2005. Call 907-224-5230 for bidding rules and details.

Not enough choices? With 11 million men and nearly 12 million women over the age of 18 in Canada, single women searching for that special someone might want to travel to the Yukon, the Northwest Territories, or Nunavut, which has the highest male-to-female ratio in Canada. Other provinces—especially Nova Scotia, Prince Edward Island, and Quebec—hold the most promise for men looking for women.

Your Computer

■ "Computer dating is not just safe—it works," says Dr. Karen Adams, coauthor of the *Online Dating Survival Guide*.

"It used to be that more men were looking than women, but now it's about even. The good news is that the guys are no longer all geeks."

(continued)

Adams's advice seems right on target. Online dating service www.match.com has an average of 23,000 new people enroll every day; www.matchmaker.com has lured 9.5 million hopeful romantics to its site.

Users need to follow a few simple safety rules: Never give out your e-mail address (this is where the services come in), always meet in public places, exchange and verify a home telephone number (to see if a husband or wife answers), and do your best to keep expectations in check. It's also wise not to reveal too much about yourself too soon. Save some surprises for your first meeting.

Here's one last tip: Post your picture. People who do get 80 percent more hits than those who don't—that is, except for the guy who proudly displayed a snapshot of himself next to a former girlfriend whose head had been snipped out.

BEST PLACE
Away From Home

■ "Travel is an inherently romantic activity and provides fertile ground for all kinds of serendipitous encounters," says Peter Guttman, author of *Worlds to Imagine: Dream Journeys for Romantic Travelers.*

Guttman's favorite meeting places include trains (the rails provide a hypnotic sound track) and white-water rafting trips (think campfires and twinkling stars).

"When journeying the planet, always look for spots where the locals and visitors mingle, particularly at sunset," Guttman says.

Paris Permenter, former contributing editor for *Honeymoon Magazine* and cofounder of www.lovetripper.com, suggests a captive environment where people share an adventure together from start to finish. "Join a cruise or tour, and you're together from beginning to end," she says. "Singles resorts are terrible places to meet, because people are coming and going all the time. When you get there, it's like arriving late to a party."

Look for smaller ships or tour groups, preferably where classes and seminars are held. (Intelligent and inquisitive people are usually more outgoing.) If you're under 50, try South America. Older? Head for Europe.

BEST PLACE
Your Own Neighborhood

■ GinaMaria Jerome, who has written extensively on finding common ground and establishing instant rapport with others, claims that "the best place to meet

someone is where you are doing what you love to do. Chances are you'll be happy, in a good mood, and the best you can be."

(continued)

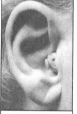

Try a bookstore if you're looking for a woman (more than half of all books are bought by women). If you're on the prowl for a man, take up line dancing—which will show observant males that you like to dance. This may be just enough to prompt otherwise-shy prospects to join in and approach you. Also, simple tasks like walking the dog or jogging work well.

Jerome's idea of the absolute best place to meet someone is on your feet. "Stand in line, especially at a movie, show, or sporting event. You already have something in common with everyone nearby, you have plenty of time on your hands, and you're generally headed in the same direction," she says.

Finally, don't give up on the places that mothers have been recommending for generations: church, college, and the country club. After all, moms know best.

Jeff Brein lives on an island near Seattle, Washington. He was introduced to his wife by a friend more than 30 years ago at a college party and has happily spent most of his adult life avoiding bachelor auctions, Internet dating, and standing in lines.

Spinning the Bottle of Love

Looking for romance? Here are some tips on where to find it from Trish McDermott, vice president of romance at www.match.com. If you're . . .

A FELLOW WHO'S A FLIRT:
Women in the Kansas City, Kansas, and Oklahoma City, Oklahoma, metro areas will be most responsive.

A MAN WHO DOESN'T SMOKE:
61.3 percent of women in San Francisco, California, are looking for you.

A MAN WITH BLUE EYES:
Women in Knoxville, Tennessee, will have their eyes on you.

A BROWN-EYED GUY:
Head to Memphis, Tennessee.

A WOMAN WHO LIKES COCKTAILS:
Austin, Texas, is your best chance for finding a man.

A REDHEADED WOMAN:
You'll do better at meeting men in Albuquerque, New Mexico.

A WOMAN WITH BABY-BLUE EYES:
You'll attract more attention in Oklahoma City, Oklahoma, or Grand Rapids, Michigan.

A WOMAN WITH HAZEL EYES:
You'll find the best pickings in San Antonio, Texas.

A WOMAN BOASTING A FEW ADDED POUNDS:
Albuquerque, New Mexico, men most appreciate a little extra to love.

Long-term care coverage
Who needs it; How to find the right policy

Americans are living longer than ever and are now facing the important decision of whether to purchase long-term care insurance. Most people buy this coverage to protect their assets, preserve their independence and provide quality care.

In general, long-term care protection makes sense for those with assets of $100,000 to $2 million. Those with less can rely on Medicaid. Those with more can usually pay the costs themselves.

With over 100 policies on the market — each with different benefits, premiums, exclusions and application requirements — it pays to comparison shop. According to respected *Money Magazine* financial editor, Jean Chatzky, "Your best bet is to get quotes from at least three companies." In addition, you should consider a policy with at least a three-year term — the average time people need care.

Look for a daily benefit that would cover the average daily nursing-facility cost in your area. The national average is $155 per day, or over $55,000 per year.* However, in some areas it can run twice as much. Look for an elimination period (the time before your benefits begin) of 90 days.

Smart Money Tip

Remember, this is catastrophic coverage. Most people who need the insurance can afford the cost of care for three months. Plus, this approach lowers your cost — in some cases by as much as 30% per year. Equally important, insist on insurers rated "A" or better by A.M. Best and "strong" by Standard & Poor's and Moody's.

If you'd like to receive three quotes with just one call, Long-Term Care Quote℠ will provide them — free of charge. The company, which has been recommended in *Consumers Digest, Kiplinger's* and on NBC — will ask for basic information on your age, health and location, then shop up to 15 top-rated carriers on your behalf. You'll get details and quotes on the three best policies for you and a copy of *The Consumer's Guide to Long-Term Care Insurance*. Plus, no agent will call or visit.

To request your free policy comparisons and personalized quotes, either write to Long-Term Care Quote℠, 25 South Arizona Place, Suite 560, Chandler, AZ 85225 (please include your date of birth and Special Code #506), visit www.LongTermCareQuote.com or call toll-free 1-800-587-3279.

*The Guide to Long-Term Care Insurance by The Health Insurance Association of America, 2003; Writing agent Robert W. Davis; CA License #0B78024. All inquiries will be kept strictly confidential. Not available in TX.

Winning Essays in the 2004 Essay Contest

The Best Decision I Ever Made

Just a pinch of spice goes a long way, my mother always told me when I... mean for baking; so... walk backwards to school or change the part... hair or buy records by musici... of all because of her li... "pinch" never

First Prize

Just a pinch of spice goes a long way, my mother always told me when I was growing up. She didn't just mean for baking; sometimes she would make me walk backwards to school or change the part in my hair or buy records by musicians I'd never heard of—all because of her little "pinch" mantra.

When my seventh-grade teacher held a pair-off bake-off in 1952, I was eager to partner up with my best friend and get cooking. Then I noticed that Hank, the shiest boy in town, had no partner at all. I could almost hear my mother saying, "Just a pinch . . ."

After taking a moment to shed my teenage dignity, I decided to sign up with Hank. We walked home together and spent the whole afternoon baking batches of peppercorn cookies, trying to get just the right mix. And it turned out that we did: We beat all my friends and won first place in our class.

The real prize was my marriage to Hank 15 years later, an everyday reminder of how my mother's words have added flavor to my life. And Hank and I have had those cookies to spice up all of our Christmases together ever since the seventh grade.

–Su Sinhababu, Malvern, Pennsylvania

Second Prize

I called to say good-bye." With these five words, an educational experience was launched. The caller didn't realize that he was sparking a relationship that would connect the world of war to a locked facility for adolescent delinquents far away in New Hampshire.

It was Mike, my daughter's 23-year-old former boot-camp buddy, who had just received orders to ship out to Iraq. Unfortunately, she wasn't home. As I offered to take a message, the teacher in me couldn't pass up the opportunity to reach out for the history that was unfolding. "Can you write to my students during your deployment?" I asked.

Mike's letters generated opportunities to teach geography, cultural customs, law, ethics, the economic impact of war, the role of oil in an industrial world, and foreign policy, each time with me asking, "How does this affect Mike, our pen pal?"

The war and locations such as Umm

Qasr and Basra became familiar. Mike's letters opened new doors, and a fellowship was explored with kids who rarely experience heroism.

The more Mike shared himself with the students, the more they examined their own paths to rehabilitation.

Time stood still when Mike returned in uniform to shake each student's hand in gratitude. There wasn't a dry eye.

–*Jackie Kramer, Manchester, New Hampshire*

Third Prize

One day in August 1997, I unwittingly made a decision that probably saved the lives of my entire family.

That morning, I had bought a secondhand, old-fashioned, ladies' bicycle. By nature, I am a messy, disorganized pack rat who leaves behind a trail of stuff. Always the procrastinator, I had left the bike in the yard.

After supper, my farmer husband needed a ride to the wheat field. Rain had been forecast, so he was anxious to continue harvesting. As we began buckling our three small boys into our car, I noticed my bike. Totally uncharacteristically, I felt an urge to put it away before we left. I debated mentally for a moment, and then hurriedly parked the bike in the shed.

Grumbling about wasted time, my husband started the car. Immediately came horrible shrieks and a thick dust cloud. A teenager's speeding car had clipped a pickup, become airborne, and rolled several times across our driveway before finally landing in a ditch. I'm convinced that God inspired me to move that bicycle, which delayed our departure by a minute. Otherwise, we certainly could have been crushed as we pulled out of our little lane.

–*Sharon Ambrose, Butler, Pennsylvania*

Announcing the 2005 Essay Contest

MY REMODELING DISASTER

In 200 words or less, please tell us your favorite story about renovating or remodeling your home.

ESSAY AND RECIPE CONTEST RULES

Cash prizes (first prize, $100; second prize, $75; third prize, $50) will be awarded for the best original essays on the subject "My Remodeling Disaster" and for the best recipes using oatmeal (amateur cooks only, please). All entries become the property of Yankee Publishing Inc., which reserves all rights to the material. The deadline for entries is Friday, January 28, 2005. Please type all entries. Label "Essay Contest" or "Recipe Contest" and send to The Old Farmer's Almanac, P.O. Box 520, Dublin, NH 03444; or e-mail (subject: Essay Contest or Recipe Contest) to almanac@yankeepub.com. Include your name, mailing address, and e-mail address. Winners will be announced in *The 2006 Old Farmer's Almanac* and posted on our Web site, www.almanac.com.

HOW TO WIN at PET

by Martie Majoros

■ When it comes to shows, there is a competition for nearly every type of animal—but don't expect success to happen overnight. Just as athletes commit to years of training for an event, you and your animal may have to spend some time preparing for a show.

To help you get started, here is advice from people whose animals have spent some time in the winner's circle. If the training and grooming seem like a lot of work, remember that it's not about winning or losing. It's about having fun.

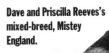

Dave and Priscilla Reeves's mixed-breed, Mistey England.

Cats

THE OWNERS
Dave and Priscilla Reeves of Lorida, Florida, began raising and showing cats in 2000.

THE SHOW
The 2002 American Cat Fanciers Association annual meeting in Philadelphia, Pennsylvania; Mistey England, their eight-year-old, won Best Household Pet honors.

BREAKFAST OF CHAMPIONS
A commercial blend of chicken, salmon, potatoes, duck, turkey, carrots, and peas.

HEALTH AND HYGIENE
The Reeveses spend about $20,000 on veterinarian bills and $2,600 for cat litter annually. Each month, they go through 2,000 pounds of cat litter for their many felines.

–Dave Reeves

BEAUTY TIPS

Become familiar with the particular grooming techniques and products for your breed. The Reeveses use three different soaps for each shampooing: to remove grease and oil, to remove

Specialty judge Mike Wilcox handles a Seal Point Siamese.

–ACFA

SHOWS and COUNTY FAIRS

residue from the previous shampoo, and to create a glistening effect. A special conditioner leaves the cat's fur soft and smooth.

INSIDER'S ADVICE

In the Best Household Pet category, there are no breed standards. Animals are judged solely on personality and grooming, so they need to be extremely clean and comfortable around people.

THE WINNING PERSONALITY

One that is affectionate, "talks" a lot, and isn't afraid of new people, says Dave Reeves.

Cattle

THE OWNERS

Deb and Mark Core of Pleasantville, Iowa, grew up showing livestock and continued to show in college. Their daughters, Bailey and Kennedy, now show Maine-Anjou cattle.

–The American Maine-Anjou Association

The Core family shows Maine-Anjou cattle like this one.

THE SHOWS

4-H shows, the Louisville and Denver livestock shows, and others.

BREAKFAST OF CHAMPIONS

A basic diet of protein, corn, and oats, adjusted according to the animal's age so that it will fill out at the right time.

HEALTH AND HYGIENE

In hot weather, keep animals indoors during the day, with fans on them, if necessary; allow them to exercise and stretch in a pen at

135

night. Avoid keeping them on cement, as that can lead to stiff-legged cattle; the ideal animal is flexible and able to take long strides.

BEAUTY TIPS

Prior to a show, the Cores often wash their Maine-Anjou cattle with Joy dishwashing detergent and brush them as much as three times a day. They rinse the animals well to avoid flaky skin, and Deb clips their coats to bring out their lines and accentuate their muscles.

INSIDER'S ADVICE

"Decide on your level of commitment. We do 15 to 20 shows a year. The county fair may be enough for some people," says Deb Core.

THE WINNING PERSONALITY

"You simply need to accept the fact that the first time [the cattle] go to a show, they will probably be kind of like a kid at their first day of school—a little scared, and maybe not behaving exactly like they did at home."

hen, Robin, received first prize in the 4-H competition.

BREAKFAST OF CHAMPIONS

Baby chicks are fed a high-protein food until they are about 18 weeks old, and then a combination feed that contains corn and soybean meal.

HEALTH AND HYGIENE

Wash hens with a mild dish detergent and use a final rinse of lemon juice and water to bring out the highlights in their feathers. As the feathers are drying, arrange them so that they are all going in the same direction, with no tips sticking out.

BEAUTY TIP

Rub a mixture of canola oil and rosemary on the hens' legs to kill any mites and to make them shine.

INSIDER'S ADVICE

"Even if you're not planning on showing your hens, it's always good to handle them anyway, so that they won't be skittish when you feed or wash them." Seltzer

Chickens

THE OWNER

Twelve-year-old Catherine Seltzer began showing poultry when she was nine years old.

THE SHOW

The 2003 Cheshire County Fair in Keene, New Hampshire; her

Catherine Seltzer with
Cleo, an Americana hen.

–Greg Seltzer

Families Have Saved Up To 50% On Heating Costs

And never have to buy fuel — wood, oil, gas, kerosene — ever again!

REPLACE OLD & INEFFICIENT HEAT

Hydro-Sil is a unique room-by-room heating system that can **save you hundreds of dollars** in home heating costs. It can replace or supplement your electric heat, gas or oil furnace and woodstoves.

Hydro-Sil heating works like this: inside the heater case is a sealed copper tube filled with a harmless silicone fluid that will never spill, leak, boil or freeze. **It's permanent. You'll never run out.** Running through the liquid is a variable watt hydroelectric element that is *only* being supplied a *proportional* amount of power on an *as-needed basis*. When Hydro-Sil is turned on, the silicone liquid is quickly heated, and with its heat retention qualities, continues to heat after the Hydro element shuts off. Hydro-Sil's room-by-room technology greatly increases energy savings and comfort.

Many Families are Benefitting — You can too!

• **F. Smalley (Mass):** *"A company that advertises the truth* saved me 50% compared to my gas heat. I found it hard to believe until my power bill came. Thanks a million!"

• **R. Hanson (Ind):** "I cannot begin to tell you how pleased I am with Hydro-Sil... the first time in 25 years our electric bill was reduced... *saved $635, over 40%!"*

• **A. Consalves (Mass):** "We updated our existing standard electric heat, removing 20 electric heaters and replacing them with Hydro-Sil. *Wow – what a difference!* We received a substantial reduction of our electric bill. I have recommended Hydro-Sil to many people!"

ORDER BY: PHONE • WEBSITE • MAIL
☐Check ☐MasterCard ☐VISA
800-627-9276 OR **www.hydrosil.com**

**MAIL TO: HYDRO-SIL, P.O. BOX 662,
FORT MILL, SC 29715**

Seasonal Discount Available Now!

Your benefits with Hydro-Sil:

• **Slash Heating Cost** – Up to 50%
• **Lifetime Warranty** – no service calls
• **Safe** – complete peace of mind
• **Clean** – no fumes – no smoke
• **U.L. Listed**
• **Preassembled** – ready to use
• **No furnaces** – ducts – chimney
• **Portable (110V) or permanent (220V)**
• **Whole House Heating or Single Room**
• **Room by Room Control**

PERMANENT 220 VOLT	Approx. Area To Heat	Discount Price	Quantity
8´ 2000 watts	250-300 sq. ft.	$279	
6´ 1500 watts	180-250 sq. ft.	$249	
5´ 1250 watts	130-180 sq. ft.	$229	
4´ 1000 watts	100-130 sq. ft.	$209	
3´ 750 watts	75-100 sq. ft.	$189	
2´ 500 watts	50-75 sq. ft.	$169	
Thermostats – CALL for options and exact heater needed			
PORTABLE 110 VOLT – Thermostat Included			
5´ Hydro–Max 750 -1500 watts		$219	
4´ Convector – Dual watt		$179	
3´ 750 watts – Silicone		$179	
$15.00 shipping per heater		$ _____	
Total Amount		$ _____	

Acct. No. _____ Ex. _____

Name _____

Address _____

Phone _____

recommends handling young chicks every other day for 5 to 15 minutes.

THE WINNING PERSONALITY

A hen that is most representative of the breed, is well mannered, and handles easily.

Dogs

THE OWNERS

Mary Ann Kerr of Cumming, Georgia, bought her first Pembroke Welsh corgi nearly 20 years ago for her ten-year-old son to show. The small size of the dog made it easier for the young child to handle. Since then, the Kerrs have raised and shown numerous corgis.

THE SHOW

Their corgi, Jack Frost, won the American Kennel Club Championship in 2003.

BREAKFAST OF CHAMPIONS

A good basic dog food with chicken or beef listed as the main ingredient.

HEALTH AND HYGIENE

Before a show, bathe and brush the dog. Trim its nails with a Dremel sander, leaving just a small amount of nail showing. "You don't want to hear too many clicks as the dog walks across the floor," says Kerr.

BEAUTY TIP

Use a special whitening shampoo to brighten up the corgi's characteristic white chest fur.

INSIDER'S ADVICE

There are nutritious dog foods in all price ranges. "Just do what is good for you. Do what's comfortable for you and what your budget will allow."

THE WINNING PERSONALITY

One that is true to the breed's characteristics. Corgis were bred to herd cattle. In one show, the Kerrs' dog broke away from the handler in the exhibition ring and began herding the other dogs and handlers. The judge awarded the dog Best of Breed.

Fish

THE OWNER

Charlie Drew, a member of the Hamilton and District Aquarium Society in Ontario, Canada, started raising and showing tropical fish when he was 11 years old. Today, he has more than 80 aquariums and raises nearly 8,000 fish each year to sell to wholesalers and fish stores.

The Kerrs' Pembroke Welsh corgi, Jack Frost.

–Richard and Mary Ann Kerr

—fish photos: Charlie Drew

Some of Charlie Drew's tropical fish: a Hi-fin Black Swordtail *(top);* a Pigeon Blood Discus *(above).*

THE SHOW

The Hamilton and District Aquarium Society Show; in 2002, he won first prize in the Characins & Amphibians category. Over the past 50 years, his fish have received several hundred awards.

BREAKFAST OF CHAMPIONS

A pinch of frozen brine shrimp, three times a day.

BEAUTY TIP

No special grooming required. Select only the most representative of the breed to show.

INSIDER'S ADVICE

Make sure there is nothing in the tank that can cut a fish's fins. Once, transferring a fish to a smaller tank, Drew used a plastic container instead of a net to scoop the fish out of the tank. He acci-

dentally cut the tip of a fin with the edge of the container, and ruined the fish for the show. To encourage a specific fish to grow, keep it in its own tank. Change 30 percent of the water each time fish are fed.

THE WINNING PERSONALITY

"If a fish swims around a lot and holds its fins up like its variety should, it has [an advantage] over some fish that don't swim actively," says Drew.

Rats

THE OWNER

Karen Robbins, president of the American Fancy Rat and Mouse Association (AFRMA), began raising rats and mice 30 years ago.

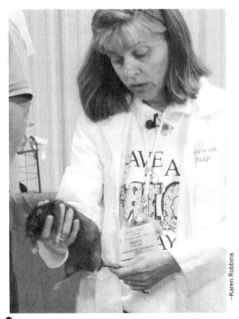

—Karen Robbins

Karen Robbins holds a pet rat at the America's Family Pet Expo rat show in April 2003.

(c o n t i n u e d)

THE SHOW

California's Orange County Fair; for the past seven years, her rats have won Best of Show.

BREAKFAST OF CHAMPIONS

High-quality pellet food, available at most pet stores; treats, such as whole-wheat bread, shredded wheat, and Total cereal; and fresh fruits and vegetables. Avoid dry dog food; it will make the rat's coat look greasy.

HEALTH AND HYGIENE

Rats are very clean and spend much of their time grooming themselves. Of course, if a rat is dirty, give it a bath.

BEAUTY TIP

The perfect rat is "pleasing to the eye, with good outline and inquisitive attention. Its body should be long and racy in appearance, and show strong bone. The loin should be well arched," according to the AFRMA guidelines.

INSIDER'S ADVICE

Handle rats and mice every day, beginning the day they are born, to accustom them to people.

THE WINNING PERSONALITY

The ideal rat is curious and active. Some judges prefer an animal that has been trained to give kisses, to walk a tightrope, or to jump up on its owner. □□

Martie Majoros is the research editor at *The Old Farmer's Almanac.*

THE SURVEY SAYS ...

Dogs and cats are our most favored pet companions. To learn more about life with these four-legged friends, go to **www.almanac.com** and click on **Article Links 2005.**

For information about advertising in *The Old Farmer's Almanac,* please call Sherin Wight at *800-729-9265, ext. 137.*

Gestation and Mating Table

	Proper Age for First Mating	Period of Fertility (years)	Number of Females for One Male	Period of Gestation (days)	
				AVERAGE	RANGE
Ewe	90 lb. or 1 yr.	6		147 / 151[1]	142–154
Ram	12–14 mo., well matured	7	50–75[2] / 35–40[3]		
Mare	3 yr.	10–12		336	310–370
Stallion	3 yr.	12–15	40–45[4] / Record 252[5]		
Cow	15–18 mo.[6]	10–14		283	279–290[7] 262–300[8]
Bull	1 yr., well matured	10–12	50[4] / Thousands[5]		
Sow	5–6 mo. or 250 lb.	6		115	110–120
Boar	250–300 lb.	6	50[2] / 35–40[3]		
Doe goat	10 mo. or 85–90 lb.	6		150	145–155
Buck goat	Well matured	5	30		
Bitch	16–18 mo.	8		63	58–67
Male dog	12–16 mo.	8	8–10		
Queen cat	12 mo.	6		63	60–68
Tom cat	12 mo.	6	6–8		
Doe rabbit	6 mo.	5–6		31	30–32
Buck rabbit	6 mo.	5–6	30		

[1]For fine wool breeds. [2]Hand-mated. [3]Pasture. [4]Natural. [5]Artificial. [6]Holstein and beef: 750 lb.; Jersey: 500 lb. [7]Beef; 8–10 days shorter for Angus. [8]Dairy.

Incubation Period of Poultry (days)	**Maximum Life Span of Animals in Captivity (years)**	
Chicken 21	Cat (domestic) 34	Duck (domestic) 23
Duck 26–32	Chicken (domestic) 25	Goat (domestic) 20
Goose 30–34	Dog (domestic) 29	Goose (domestic) 20
Guinea 26–28		Horse 62
		Rabbit . . . . 18+

	Estral/Estrous Cycle (including heat period)		Length of Estrus (heat)		Usual Time of Ovulation	When Cycle Recurs if Not Bred
	AVERAGE	RANGE	AVERAGE	RANGE		
Mare	21 days	10–37 days	5–6 days	2–11 days	24–48 hours before end of estrus	21 days
Sow	21 days	18–24 days	2–3 days	1–5 days	30–36 hours after start of estrus	21 days
Ewe	16½ days	14–19 days	30 hours	24–32 hours	12–24 hours before end of estrus	16½ days
Goat	21 days	18–24 days	2–3 days	1–4 days	Near end of estrus	21 days
Cow	21 days	18–24 days	18 hours	10–24 hours	10–12 hours after end of estrus	21 days
Bitch	24 days		7 days	5–9 days	1–3 days after first acceptance	Pseudo-pregnancy
Cat		15–21 days	3–4 days, if mated	9–10 days, in absence of male	24–56 hours after coitus	Pseudo-pregnancy

THE MAN WHO COULDN'T STOP WALKING

How a health regimen became an obsession.

by Joyce Litz

I n 1860, on a lark, Edward Payson Weston agreed to walk 478 miles from Boston to Washington, D.C., for Abraham Lincoln's inauguration, if Lincoln beat Steven A. Douglas in the presidential election.

On February 22, 1861, 21-year-old Weston began his trek; he arrived in Washington 11 days later. He missed the inauguration by only a few hours, but the event launched his career as a leading sports figure of the 19th and early 20th centuries—an outcome few would have predicted.

When Weston was born on March 15, 1839, he weighed only four-and-a-half pounds and wasn't expected to live. As a child, he was weak and slight of build. His life changed when he was 15, and he and his parents moved from their home in Providence, Rhode Island, to Boston. There, a friend who was a sports trainer began to work with him. The trainer took him off coffee, put him on a diet of vegetables and milk, and urged him to take short walks every day. Before long, the walks lengthened and Weston was hooked.

When he was 20, Weston was hired by the *New York Herald,* first as a messenger boy and later as a police

—The Granger Collection

Weston, at age 38 *(above)* and at age 85 *(right, wearing gaiters).* A showman when walking, he delighted the public with his unflagging endurance and his dapper attire.

—Culver Pictures

Weston on his first walk from Portland, Maine, to Chicago in 1867 *(right)*. In 1907, at the age of 68 *(below)*, he repeated this walk, adding 19 miles yet cutting 29 hours off his time.

–The Granger Collection

–Culver Pictures

reporter. His lively step enabled him to get to an incident and back quickly, sometimes before his rivals.

Newspaper coverage of the walk to Washington made Weston a household name and helped him land a job delivering mail (on foot) from Boston and New York to federal army troops in the capital during the Civil War.

At age 28, Weston accepted his first official challenge—to walk 1,326 miles from Portland, Maine, to Chicago within 30 consecutive days. Motivated by $10,000 in prize money offered by a Maine walking club, he began the event as its only contestant on October 29. Crowds lined the route to cheer him, fueling what newspapers called "pedestrian mania." He beat the deadline by 1 hour, 20 minutes (excluding Sundays), earning the nickname "Yankee Clipper." He was deluged with invitations to take part in race-walking events at country fairs and New York City tracks and to give

lectures on the joys of walking.

The walks and speaking engagements brought Weston a lot of attention, which he relished. Dressed in his customary attire—high gaiters, a hat, and a black velvet tunic on which he displayed his many medals—and with a small riding crop in hand, he delighted the public.

In distance events, often hundreds of miles, he was unbeatable. Many surpassed his speed, but none could equal his endurance. He could walk five miles per hour, on average, for days and weeks. He set his best records on the primitive country roads of the United States and Great Britain—not on level indoor tracks.

One of his most amazing performances may be the six-day, 550-mile contest in London's Agricultural Hall in 1879. After walking long and hard—and in the lead—for four days, Weston fell into bed for a two-hour nap, but his coach let him sleep for six hours. When he awoke refreshed, he learned that he was 13 miles behind his nearest competitor. He walked the remaining 127 miles in 24 hours, setting a world record of 141 hours, 44 minutes for the total 550-mile walk and spurring thunderous applause from onlookers.

On 100 days from 1883 to 1884, he walked 50 miles a day for the Church of England (and lectured on temperance in the evenings)—but never on Sundays. When he was young, his mother, a deeply religious person, had cautioned him never to walk on Sunday. He had promised he would not.

At age 67, Weston agreed for the second time to be examined by 30 doctors who were curious about how he maintained his stamina. In preparation, he walked 100 miles, from Philadelphia to New York, finishing in 23 hours, 54 minutes—just an hour or so before the exam. The doctors discovered that his muscles still had the same elasticity, his lungs the same breathing capacity, and his eyes the same alertness that other physicians had found 35 years before.

Pedestrian Habits

■ Weston's gait was his own—a smooth step with slightly bent knees that he called a "flat-foot shuffle."

■ To relax, he placed a riding crop behind his back, hooked in his elbows; it made him feel as if he were sitting down while he walked.

Weston's Advice to Walkers:

"Get a pair of comfortable shoes. Then let your feet find their natural position, whether they toe in or out. Let the stride be easy and don't try to lengthen it."

(continued)

Indeed, Weston seemed not to age. At age 68, he repeated the walk from Portland, Maine, to Chicago. Although the route was 19 miles longer, he cut 29 hours off his time.

He followed that with an even more ambitious walk. On his 70th birthday, he began a 3,895-mile "ocean-to-ocean" tramp across the country along a northern route. He fought tornadoes and strong winds across the Midwest and late-spring blizzards in the Rocky and Sierra Nevada mountains. He spent four miles on his hands and knees following a railroad track through the Rockies, "too frail to stand up to the raging winds," according to a *New York Times* story. He finished in 104 days, seven hours, and later said that it was the most frightening walk of his career.

On the return trip, he took a southern route. Following railroad tracks for 2,500 miles, he averaged 60 miles a day. After 76 days, 23 hours, Weston arrived in New York City "at a fast gait and [not] at all fatigued," according to a *New York Times* reporter. He was awarded an

Think You Can Beat Him?

■ Edward Payson Weston participated in more than 1,000 walking contests. He preferred challenges where he could walk alone on country roads but also participated in six-day "go-as-you please" races. The following feats set records:

YEAR	ROUTE/LOCATION	DISTANCE	TIME (excluding Sundays)
1861	Boston to Washington, D.C.	478 miles	10 days, 4 hours
1867	Portland, Maine, to Chicago	1,326 miles	24 days, 22 hours, 40 minutes
1871	Empire Rink, New York City	400 miles	4 days, 23 hours, 32 minutes
1871	St. Louis Track, Missouri	200 miles (including 2 miles backward)	1 day, 17 hours
1874	Barnum's Roman Hippodrome, New York City	115 miles	24 consecutive hours
1874	Industrial Hall, Newark, New Jersey	515 miles	6 consecutive days
1879	Agricultural Hall, London	550 miles	5 days, 21 hours, 44 minutes
1907	Portland, Maine, to Chicago	1,345 miles	23 days, 17 hours
1909	New York City to San Francisco	3,895 miles	104 days, 7 hours
1910	Santa Monica, California, to New York City	3,600 miles	76 days, 23 hours
1913	New York City to Minneapolis, Minnesota	1,546 miles	51 days
1922	Buffalo, New York, to New York City	495 miles	29 days

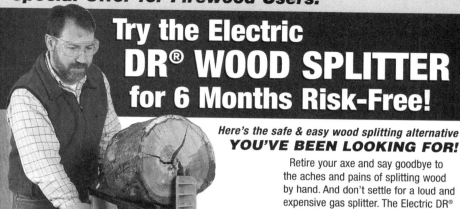

undisclosed amount of prize money and a bonus for beating his own schedule. (Weston didn't have a regular job, and his family—his wife and, eventually, three children—often struggled to make ends meet.)

In his mid-70s, Weston walked around the country, delivering his lecture, "The Vicissitudes of a Walker," to enthusiastic audiences and talking of making a comeback. That wasn't to be, however. Ten years later, robbers broke into his farmhouse near Highland, New York, and while fighting them off he was shot in the leg.

Soon after the incident, he moved to Philadelphia. He was destitute when Anne Nichols, the author of the Broadway play *Abie's Irish Rose,* heard about his plight. Although she had never met him, she set up a $30,000 trust fund for him. He returned to Brooklyn, where in November 1927, at age 88, he was hit by a taxicab while walking across the street. He was confined to a wheelchair and eventually to his bed. Edward Payson Weston died at the age of 90.

Joyce Litz, great-granddaughter of Edward Payson Weston, is the author of *Montana Frontier: One Woman's West* (University of New Mexico Press, 2004), a biography of his daughter, Lillian Weston Hazen.

Steps to Good Health

■ Studies show that walking can . . .

- **improve circulation**
- **improve the immune system**
- **help prevent and control diabetes**
- **aid breathing**
- **help control weight**

■ This chart shows the approximate number of calories expended by a 100-, 150-, and 200-pound person walking for one hour at a given pace:

	100 lb.	150 lb.	200 lb.
Walking 2 mph	160	240	312
Walking 3 mph	210	320	416
Walking 4.5 mph	295	440	572

Stepping Out(doors)

■ Walking on gravel or grass burns slightly more calories than walking on a treadmill. □ □

Foot Notes

One mile equals 5,280 feet. An average walker strides, or takes, about 2,200 steps for every mile, and an average stride, or step, is two to three feet in length.

One way to measure your stride is to walk a measured distance of 25 feet, counting your steps as you go. Divide 25 by the number of steps. The result is the length of your stride in feet.

THE WALKER'S WAYS

Edward Payson Weston maintained a strict diet all his life and had other rituals. To learn more about him and the health benefits of walking, go to www.almanac.com and click on **Article Links 2005.**

Learn to tune-up your computer and keep it in tip-top condition.

Protect your privacy and keep your personal information from being stolen!

Trace your family tree back to its roots … even if they're in another country!

"Easy Computing for Seniors!"

A Step-by-Step Handbook from Start-up to Shut-down!

(By Frank K. Wood)

If you want to conquer your fear of computers, protect your privacy, earn money, avoid computer viruses and find what you want on the Internet, you need *"Easy Computing for Seniors: A Step-by-Step Handbook from Start-up to Shut-Down,"* an informative new book just released to the public by FC&A Publishing in Peachtree City, Georgia.

Written especially for the pre-computer generation, the easy-to-understand tricks, tips and "how-tos" make this an essential book for seniors … or anyone!

▶ Surf the web and snatch up bargains by the bagful.

▶ Send e-mails — with photo attachments — anywhere in the world.

▶ Balance your checkbook and even create a budget — in just minutes.

▶ Keep accurate, up-to-date medical and prescription medicine records safe and sound — yet easily accessible when you or a loved one need them.

▶ Order your groceries — shop for clothes and gifts without ever leaving the comforts of your home!

▶ Keep in touch with family and friends — absolutely free — no long distance or toll charges!

▶ Take college classes — for fun or for a degree — the choice is yours!

▶ Find old friends — fast! Be your own private detective. It's easy!

▶ Overcome your fears (and anxieties) — and become a computer whiz in just a few days — guaranteed!

▶ Not sure what kind of computer you need — no problem, here's how to get the right one without paying an arm and a leg!

▶ Don't understand "computer-ese" — this book explains it all.

▶ Afraid of buttons and gadgets? — No worry, you'll overcome your fears and know what to do in no time flat!

Learn all these amazing secrets and more. To order a copy, just return this notice with your name and address and a check for $9.99 plus $3.00 shipping and handling to: **FC&A, Dept. TOF-05,** 103 Clover Green, Peachtree City, GA 30269. We will send you a copy of *"Easy Computing for Seniors: A Step-by-Step Handbook from Start-up to Shut-Down."*

You get a no-time-limit guarantee of satisfaction or your money back.

You must cut out and return this notice with your order. Copies will not be accepted!

IMPORTANT — FREE GIFT OFFER EXPIRES IN 30 DAYS

All orders mailed within 30 days will receive a free gift, *"241 Computer Terms You Need to Know,"* guaranteed. Order right away!

©FC&A 2004

Cooking With Condiments

BY MATT WOHL

Matt Wohl, executive director of Arts Alive in Burlington, Vermont, has been collecting and cooking with condiments for years.

How many times have you been at a restaurant and pocketed a few extra of those little crackers packages? Or jam tubs? Or sugar packets for your coffee? If you're like most people, you rarely use these. The crackers get crushed in your pocket. The jam sits in your refrigerator. And the sugar goes into the glove compartment of your car, never to be seen again.

Now imagine those small portions as the main ingredients of recipes, and you might start bringing home a few extras on purpose.

Cookies With Jam

10 packets saltine crackers (2 crackers each)
1/4 teaspoon cinnamon
1/2 teaspoon vanilla powder, optional
16 pats or rosettes butter (approximately 1 teaspoon each), softened
40 packets sugar (a scant 3/4 teaspoon each) water
8 to 10 sleeves or minitubs strawberry, raspberry, or apricot jam; grape jelly; or orange marmalade (approximately 1 tablespoon each)

■ Preheat oven to 350°F. Using a dry cloth or paper towel, gently brush off as much salt from the surface of the saltines as you can (or use unsalted, if you can find them). Crush crackers in a food processor or blender until they have the consistency of flour. Add cinnamon and vanilla powder. Mix, and set aside. Blend butter and sugar in a bowl until smooth. Add cracker crumbs. Combine. The mixture will be dry and clumpy. Add a few drops of water, and mix. Batter will be dry.

Shape the dough into one-inch balls. Place on an ungreased cookie sheet. Dough will spread out to about two to three inches, so space accordingly.

–illustrated by Renée Quintal Daily

Bake for 8 minutes or until light brown. Remove cookies from the oven and cool them on the baking sheet. Cover a plate or rack with a paper towel and place the cooled cookies on the towel.

Spread a layer of jam on top of single cookies or combine two to make sandwich cookies. **Makes 8 to 10 sandwich cookies.**

Tomato Soup

Note: The vinegar content of the ketchup varies among packagers and may affect the consistency and quality of the soup.

4 containers (1 ounce each) half-and-half
3 to 4 packets ketchup
1/2 cup warm water
1 packet black pepper (optional)

■ Pour half-and-half into a mug and microwave 15 seconds (get the liquid hot, not boiling). Mix ketchup and water. Slowly add ketchup mixture to half-and-half (if added too quickly, curdling can result). Return to microwave and heat to desired temperature. Season with pepper, if desired. **Serves 1.**

TIPS FROM A CONDIMENT CONNOISSEUR

■ Butter take-homes are not all the same size, so be ready to adjust the recipe.

■ Packaged condiments are best.

■ Just as cuisine varies across the country, so does the selection of condiments available. Experiment and enjoy! □□

PACKETS ON PARADE

The packaging of food products in small portions is an industry, an art form, and a genre of collectibles. To view hundreds of condiment packets, including some from other parts of the world, go to **www.almanac.com** and click on **Article Links 2005.**

Your Fresh Fruits and Vegetables Need Water!

FREE INFO!

Now, have all the chlorine free water you need with a well you drilled yourself!

Since 1962, thousands of happy gardeners and homewners around the world have discovered the **Hydra-Drill™** secret. They drilled their own wells and their gardens prove it! You can, too.

Call or write us today and we'll send you a big, free package of information about drilling your own well with the **Hydra-Drill™**. We carry everything you need for your home water requirements, including pumps and tanks.

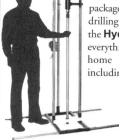

Ask about our "How to..." video

Call Today for **FREE** Water Well Drilling Information Package

1-800-333-7762
ask for operator 8570
www.deeprock.com

$\mathcal{B}$arbecue, $\mathcal{B}$iscuits, $\mathcal{B}$eyond

GOOD COOKING, SOUTHERN-STYLE.

BY ALICE CARY

The words "Southern" and "cooking" go together like pecan and pie, with signature dishes ranging from ambrosia and angel pies to zephyrinas (a cracker made from biscuit dough, originating in Charleston, South Carolina).

Just what makes a dish Southern? Cooks agree on the secrets, if not the details: farm-fresh ingredients, first and foremost. Next, cooking that is both creative and practical, and served up with Southern-style hospitality. There's history, too—as there is with all things Southern—which means that recipes draw from a blend of cultures, including Native American, European, and African.

Whether you're in the mood for hearty stew, barbecue, or something sweet, here's a hearty trio of cooking styles.

MAMA DIP'S "DUMP COOKING"

One of the happiest moments for Mildred Council—better known as Mama Dip—occurred in 1938, when she was about nine years old. One morning, as her family was leaving the house to plow and plant, her father said to her, "You stay here and fix a little something to eat." "I had already been dreaming about cooking," she writes in her book, *Mama Dip's Kitchen*, "and I could hardly wait to tell my playmates."

Mama Dip has been cooking ever since, most recently in her Chapel Hill, North Carolina, restaurant, Mama Dip's Kitchen, where she has won a legion of fans. Mama Dip is a master of what she calls "dump cooking," which means "no recipes, just measure by eye and feel and taste and testing." These two recipes from her book result from her dump-cooking style and have been tested for accuracy. Says Mama Dip: "Use what you have. Try it dif-

ferent ways. Use your imagination. Treat the recipes like sewing patterns— stretch or alter them to fit."

■ *Mildred Council was nicknamed "Dip" as a child because she had arms long enough to reach into the rain barrel to scoop up a big dipperful of water.*

BRUNSWICK STEW

2 pounds pork neck bones	6 cups finely chopped potatoes
1 chicken (2 pounds), cut up, or chicken parts	2 cans (16 ounces each) tomatoes, chopped, with juice
1 cup chopped onion	1 tablespoon seasoned salt
3 cups okra	1 teaspoon crushed red pepper
3 cups corn	
2 packages (10 ounces each) frozen baby lima beans	

■ Rinse the neck bones under running water and put them in a large (1½-gallon) pot. Cover with water. Let come to a boil, then cook for 30 minutes. Put the chicken into the pot, adding water if necessary to cover. Continue cooking until the chicken is tender, about 45 minutes. Take out the pork and chicken. Skim off the fat, strain the liquid, and return it to the pot. Add 1 quart water and all the vegetables and seasonings. Remove the pork and chicken meat from the bones and cut the chicken meat into pieces. Put the meat back in the pot and let cook slowly for 1 hour. **Serves 12 to 15.**

SPRING VEGETABLE POT

1 pound small new potatoes	1 small can (5 ounces) evaporated milk
2 cups fresh green peas, shelled	2 tablespoons flour
6 asparagus spears, each cut into 4 pieces	1/4 cup water
	salt and pepper, to taste
1/4 cup (1/2 stick) butter, cut into pieces	

■ Scrape or peel the potatoes. Cook the peas at a slow boil in a quart of water for 30 minutes. Add the potatoes, and

153

add some hot water to the pot, if needed, to cover the vegetables. Boil for 20 minutes more. Add the asparagus and butter and simmer until the asparagus is tender, about 10 minutes. Add the evaporated milk. Mix together the flour and water and add the paste to the pot a little at a time to thicken the liquid into a cream sauce. Add salt and pepper. Cover and turn off the heat. Let sit for about 10 minutes to let the flavor ripen. **Serves 6.**

ISLAND FLAVORS, GULLAH TREATS

As an 11-year-old girl growing up on Daufuskie Island, South Carolina, Sallie Ann Robinson was known for making light and feathery biscuits. Now her cookbook, *Gullah Home Cooking the Daufuskie Way*, celebrates the ways of life and the recipes families shared on her island. As she explains, "the way we lived, life was gathering, growing, and preparing food."

Robinson's cooking isn't fancy, but it's satisfying: "Whether you grew up in a high-rise or a tin-roofed shack," she says, her dishes "will sho'nuff stick to your ribs."

Gullah Home Cooking the Daufuskie Way by Sallie Ann Robinson. Copyright © 2003 by Sallie Ann Robinson.

Gullah Home Cooking *the* Daufuskie way
smokin' Joe Butter Beans, ol' 'Fuskie Fried Crab Rice, sticky-Bush Blackberry Dumpling, & other sea Island Favorites
SALLIE ANN ROBINSON
foreword by Pat Conroy

■ *Gullah, a way of speaking that blends English and African languages, is unique to Daufuskie Island. For example, "remember" is "famemba" and a burlap bag is a "croaker sack."*

HAND-TOSSED FLUFFY BISCUITS

2 cups sifted all-purpose flour
3 teaspoons baking powder
1 teaspoon salt
5 tablespoons shortening, such as Crisco
3/4 cup whole milk or buttermilk
2 medium eggs

■ Preheat oven to 350°F. Mix the dry ingredients together and cut in the shortening. Slowly mix in the milk and eggs until combined. Sprinkle some flour on your table or counter or a large cutting board, knead the dough five or six times, and then roll it out to a thickness of ¼ inch or more. Using a biscuit cutter, cut into 2-inch rounds. Place on an ungreased cookie sheet. Bake for 20 to 30 minutes, until golden brown, then brush on melted butter or margarine if you like. Serve immediately, with butter, honey, jelly, syrup, or whatever you want. **Makes about 10 biscuits.**

BARBECUE SPARERIBS

Note: Bottled barbecue sauce will do. Or, search www.almanac.com/food to find a barbecue sauce recipe and make your own.

15 to 20 sparerib pieces
salt and pepper, to taste
paprika, to taste
1/4 cup cooking oil
1 medium onion, sliced

1 stalk celery, chopped
1 medium green bell pepper, cut into wedges
2 cups hot water
barbecue sauce

■ Buy cut-up spareribs or cut up a slab yourself into pieces that will fit in a medium-large pot. Wash the spareribs and pat dry, then sprinkle with salt, pepper, and paprika. Put ribs and oil in the pot. Set the pot over medium heat, add half the onion, half the celery, and half the bell pepper, and stir-fry a couple of minutes. Add the hot water and boil 20 to 30 minutes. This will give you tender and juicy ribs.

Preheat oven to 350°F. Take the ribs from the pot and place them in a baking pan. Pour the barbecue sauce of your choice, along with the remaining onion, celery, and bell pepper, over the ribs and bake 30 to 45 minutes—or grill them over a low fire, brushing with sauce, 10 to 15 minutes. Then sit down for some sweet, tender, finger-lickin' eatin', and take your time, because they are so-o-o-o good. **Serves 4 to 6.**

(continued)

PRESERVING THE HERITAGE

Bill Neal always fessed up to eating possum and grits. "When we no longer eat these foods, we no longer will be Southerners," he explained. Before Neal died in 1991 at age 41, he had already attracted fans through his books and with Crook's Corner, his restaurant in Chapel Hill, North Carolina. His primer on baking, *Biscuits, Spoonbread, & Sweet Potato Pie*, praises the multitude of influences on Southern kitchens. "This hybrid cooking is the most intriguing to me," he wrote. "It reveals the ingenuity and creativity of the Southern cook."

Biscuits, Spoonbread, & Sweet Potato Pie by Bill Neal. Copyright © 1990 by Bill Neal.

All excerpts are used by permission of the University of North Carolina Press. Visit www.uncpress.unc.edu or call 800-848-6224 for more information.

■ *"When I cook[ed], I [was] constantly telling my children something like 'This is your grandmother's biscuit.' I mean[t] it isn't just something to fill up their stomachs; it's part of the way crafts, traditions, and cultures have been perpetuated for thousands of years—one generation teaching the next. Almost everyone has a special recipe from a grandmother or an aunt that means more than how it tastes."* –Bill Neal

FUDGE PIE

2 ounces unsweetened chocolate
1/2 cup (1 stick) butter
2 eggs
7/8 cup sugar
1/4 cup all-purpose flour
1/4 teaspoon salt
1 teaspoon vanilla extract
1 tablespoon dark rum, brandy, or bourbon
1/2 cup chopped pecans or black walnuts (optional)

■ Preheat oven to 350°F. Melt the chocolate and butter in a double boiler. Beat the eggs until foamy. Slowly add the sugar and beat well. Sift the flour and salt together. Stir into

The Old Farmer's Almanac Blue Ribbon RECIPES
PRESENTS

With everything from appetizers to desserts, you're sure to find a dish for every appetite and occasion.

★ 90 award-winning recipes from America's country fairs

★ 160 pages, hardbound, FULL-COLOR cover

★ Makes a GREAT GIFT!

Only $14.95*

the batter gently. Add the melted chocolate, vanilla, liquor, and nuts if desired. Stir just until smooth and pour into a well-buttered 9-inch pie pan. Bake for 30 minutes, until the top is puffed and the center is just set. Serve with sour cream or ice cream. **Serves 8.**

BROWN SUGAR SHORTBREAD

1 cup (2 sticks) butter　　**1/8 teaspoon salt**
1 cup light-brown sugar　　**Chocolate Glaze (optional)**
2 cups flour

■ Preheat oven to 325°F. Beat the butter until light. Add the brown sugar and cream well. Mixture should be light and not grainy. Add flour and salt a bit at a time, but quickly. Do not overbeat at this point. As soon as dough is well blended, turn into a $9\frac{1}{2}$-inch-diameter springform pan. Spread smoothly and evenly. Prick all over with a three-prong fork. Bake for about 35 minutes, until barely brown. Cut into 16 wedges before completely cooled, but allow to age a day, stored in an airtight container, before serving. **Makes 16 wedges.**

CHOCOLATE GLAZE

2 ounces semisweet chocolate
1 1/2 tablespoons butter
1 teaspoon strong coffee
2 tablespoons sieved powdered sugar
pinch of salt

■ Combine all ingredients in the top of a double boiler. Heat gently until the chocolate is melted and the mixture is smooth upon stirring. Cool slightly before using. Spread chocolate glaze evenly over the middle part of the shortbread, leaving a $\frac{1}{2}$-inch margin around the outer edge. **Makes 1/2 cup.**　　☐☐

Alice Cary grew up in a family where biscuits, chicken and dumplings, Brunswick stew, and custard were standard fare. For many years, her grandmother owned and ran a small West Virginia grocery store that featured homemade baked goods.

Indiana Firm Discovers:

Special ^New^ cream for arthritis

(SPECIAL)–A small company in central Indiana has developed a special cream that relieves arthritis pain in minutes, even chronic arthritis pain—deep in the joints. The product which is called **PAIN BUST·R-II**, is one of the fastest acting therapeutic formulas ever developed in the fight against arthritis. Immediately upon application it goes to work by penetrating deep to the areas most affected—the joints themselves, bringing fast relief where relief is needed most. Men and women who have suffered arthritis pain for years are reporting incredible results with this product. Even a single application seems to work remarkably well in relieving pain and bringing comfort to cramped, knotted joints. *PAIN BUST·R-II was researched and formulated to be absorbed directly into the joints and muscles—where the pain originates. Long-time arthritis sufferers will be glad to know that this formula will help put an end to agonizing days and sleepless nights. It is highly recommended by users who have resumed daily activities and are enjoying life again.

Read what our users have to say:

"I use **PAIN BUST** because I suffer from tension in my back and shoulders. I can't praise your product enough, I've used other ointments, but they don't seem to work as fast nor last as long. Thank you. Thank you...Thank you!"   *C.K.F.*

"Last night when I went to sleep I rubbed some **PAIN BUST** on my sore aching knee. 15 minutes later I fell sound asleep and woke 8 hours later with absolutely no pain. I wish I knew about **PAIN BUST** long ago." *B.M.S.*

NO-RISK FREE TRIAL
We Trust You — Send No Money!

TO ORDER: Just write **"PAIN BUST·R-II"** on a sheet of paper and send it along with your name, address and the number of tubes you wish to order. We will promptly ship you 1 large tube for $7.95, 2 large tubes for $13.90 or 3 large tubes for only $19.35 *(SAVES $4.50)*. Prices include all shipping and handling. We will enclose an invoice and if for any reason you wish to cancel your order, simply mark Cancel on the invoice and there will be no charge to you. You don't even have to bother returning the merchandise. Send for your NO-RISK FREE TRIAL ORDER today to:
Continental Quest/Research Corp.
220 W. Carmel Dr. - Dept. OFA-05
Carmel, IN 46032.

©2000 Continental Quest/Research Corp.

Winning Recipes in the 2004 Recipe Contest

Apples

Apple-Stuffed Baked Fish

1 cup peeled, cored, and grated Golden
   Delicious apple
1/2 cup grated carrot
1/2 cup minced green onion
2 tablespoons fresh lemon juice
1/4 teaspoon ground ginger
1/4 teaspoon ground mustard
1/4 teaspoon salt
1/4 teaspoon black pepper
1/8 teaspoon dried thyme
4 white fish fillets (cod, sole, or other,
   4 to 5 ounces each)
1/2 cup chicken broth or water

■ Preheat oven to 400°F. Lightly oil a small roasting pan. In a medium bowl, combine the first nine ingredients; mix well. Spread apple mixture over the fillets; carefully roll up. Place stuffed fillets, seam side down, in oiled pan. Pour broth over fillets; cover with aluminum foil and bake 10 to 15 minutes, or until fish is opaque and barely flakes. **Serves 4.**

–Art Sager, Agassiz, British Columbia

Apple-and-Pork Burger Delights

Burgers:
1 pound ground pork
1 Granny Smith apple
1 Golden Delicious apple
1/8 teaspoon cloves
1/8 teaspoon cinnamon
1/8 teaspoon cumin
3 garlic cloves, minced
1/2 tablespoon cilantro, chopped
1/2 bunch green onions, chopped
1 tablespoon balsamic vinegar
1/2 to 1 cup bread crumbs
1/2 cup olive oil

Slaw Topping:
1 Granny Smith apple
1 Golden Delicious apple
1/2 tablespoon cilantro, chopped
1/2 bunch green onions, chopped
1 tablespoon balsamic vinegar
drizzle of olive oil
salt and pepper, to taste

Note: Peel, core, and grate all of the apples in this recipe.

■ For burgers: In a medium bowl, mix the first ten ingredients and about ½ cup of the bread crumbs. (Add more crumbs if too wet; slightly moist is better. Otherwise, the burgers will be tough and dry.) Mix thoroughly. Make into 4 to 6 patties. Refrigerate for about 30 minutes.

For slaw topping: In a small bowl, mix the apples, cilantro, onions, and vinegar. Drizzle with olive oil and season with salt and pepper to taste. Set aside.

Put ½ cup olive oil in a large skillet on medium heat. Place burgers in pan and cook 20 to 25 minutes, turning once.

When burgers are done, serve them with the slaw topping. **Serves 4 to 6.**

–Ginger Moreno, Rancho Palos Verdes, California

Easy Three-Bowl Apple Cake

4 apples, peeled, cored, and diced
1 3/4 cups sugar
1 1/2 tablespoons lemon juice
3 cups flour
2 teaspoons baking soda
2 teaspoons cinnamon
dash of salt
2 eggs
1 cup oil
1 1/2 teaspoons vanilla extract

■ Preheat oven to 350°F. Grease a 9x13-inch pan.

In bowl 1: Combine first three ingredients; mix well.

In bowl 2: Sift flour together with baking soda, cinnamon, and salt.

In bowl 3: Mix lightly beaten eggs, oil, and vanilla.

Add bowl 3 to bowl 1; stir well. Combine with bowl 2; mix well (batter will be stiff). Pour into prepared pan. Bake 45 minutes, or until a tester comes out clean. **Makes about 20 pieces.**

–Helen D. Lomupo, Gilboa, New York

Delicious-Apple Ice Cream Topping

2 Delicious apples, peeled, cored, and
**   chopped into 1/4-inch pieces**
2 tablespoons butter
2 tablespoons light-brown sugar
1/2 cup sugar
3 tablespoons orange juice
2 tablespoons honey
1 teaspoon cinnamon
1/4 cup dark corn syrup
2 tablespoons spiced rum (optional)

■ Melt butter in 1-quart sauce pan. Add all ingredients, except rum. Bring to a boil. Reduce heat to low and simmer uncovered 15 minutes, stirring occasionally. Remove from heat and stir in rum. Let stand for 3 minutes before serving over ice cream. **Makes about 2 cups.**

–Jim Smith, Littleton, Colorado

Calcutta Apple Chutney

4 large, firm, Granny Smith apples, peeled,
**   cored, and chopped**
1 sweet onion, peeled and chopped
2 teaspoons mustard seeds
1 cup golden raisins
1 cup light-brown sugar, firmly packed
2 serrano chilies, seeded, stemmed, and
**   minced**
4 cloves garlic, minced
2 tablespoons crystallized ginger, minced
zest and juice of 1 lemon
1/2 cup pear nectar

■ Place apples in a large saucepan. Add remaining ingredients and cook over medium heat for 5 to 8 minutes, stirring occasionally. Reduce heat to low, and cook for an additional 10 to 15 minutes, stirring occasionally. **Makes 4 to 5 cups.**

–Elaine Sweet, Dallas, Texas

□ □

HAVE AN APPLE A DAY

Go to **www.almanac.com** and click on **Article Links 2005** for more tasty contest recipes.

OUR MYSTERIOUS,

"We will . . . gain a new foothold on the Moon and . . . prepare for new journeys to the worlds beyond our own."

–George W. Bush, 43rd U.S. president, January 14, 2004

With plans in the works for man to return to the Moon by 2020, what better time to review some facts and folklore about this celestial body? by Bob Berman

Lunar Statistics

DIAMETER: 2,160 miles

★ This is about the distance from Washington, D.C., to the Rocky Mountains.

AVERAGE ORBITAL SPEED: 2,287 miles per hour

★ This number is very close to the Moon's diameter, making it the only known celestial body that moves through space at its own width per hour. This motion is readily visible from Earth, even to the naked eye, as the Moon shifts its position against the background stars.

–illustrated by Renée Quintal Daily

MAJESTIC MOON

–National Space Science Data Center

**SYNODIC PERIOD, OR LUNAR MONTH:
29 days, 12 hours, 44 minutes, 2.8 seconds**
★ This is the average period from one new Moon to the next.

ROTATION PERIOD: 27 days, 7 hours, 43 minutes, 11.5 seconds
★ This spin-time of the Moon on its own axis is identical to the time it takes the Moon to revolve around Earth, which is why the Moon always keeps almost the same face toward us. (See "The Near Side," page 165.)

MASS: 81.3 times smaller than Earth's
★ Its total mass is 500 quintillion tons.

ALBEDO: Approximately 0.12
★ Just 12 percent of the sunlight strik-

Neil Armstrong took this picture of Edwin Aldrin on the Moon during the Apollo 11 *mission in July 1969.*

ing the Moon is reflected; the Moon's surface has about the same shininess as soil. By comparison, the albedo of snow is 0.75, and that of Jupiter, 0.51.

(c o n t i n u e d)

MAGNITUDE: –12.7 in full phase
★ Each magnitude on the standard scale is 2.5 times brighter than the next; so compared with the brightest star, Sirius, whose magnitude is –1.5, the Moon is more than 250,000 times brighter.

SURFACE TEMPERATURES: Daytime, 235°F typically, 273°F maximum; nighttime, can drop to –275°F
★ This day/night range of about 500 degrees is more than five times greater than what is found in extreme desert areas of Earth, but is typical of an airless world.

DISTANCE FROM EARTH: 238,857 miles (mean), with variations of over 30,000 miles

SURFACE GRAVITY: 5.3 feet per second
★ On the Moon, an object would fall less than three feet in one second and about 11 feet in two seconds. On Earth, an object would fall 64 feet in two seconds.

ESCAPE VELOCITY: 1.48 miles per second
★ To escape the Moon's gravity, a rocket must achieve a speed of about 1.5 miles per second, or 5,328 miles per hour. To escape Earth, a rocket requires a velocity of nearly 7 miles per second, or 25,000 miles per hour.

Fly Me to the Moon . . .

★ Readers perusing the Almanac 51 years ago would have read this item:

J. P. Colbert of the University of Nebraska is confident that before this century is up the trip [to the Moon] will take but a mere nine hours out, with two hours at the Moon for sightseeing, and thirteen hours in which to coast back. –The Old Farmer's Almanac, *1954*

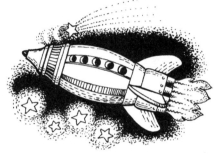

Scientists inform us that travel to the Moon will take three to four days each way for the foreseeable future.

★   ★   ★

It's Not Cheese

★ This table shows the similarities and differences in the composition of the crusts of the Moon and Earth. Note that the Moon's surface is a combination of cratered, light-color highlands and smooth, dark-color maria.

Percentage of Various Elements in the Crust of the Moon and Earth

	OXYGEN	SILICON	IRON	MAGNESIUM	ALUMINUM	CALCIUM AND POTASSIUM
Moon Highlands	61.1	16.2	4.5	4.0	10.2	6.1
Moon Maria	60.6	16.8	1.8	5.3	6.6	4.7
Earth	61.7	21.0	1.9	1.8	6.4	3.3

Reprinted from *Dynamic Astronomy*, 5th ed., by Robert T. Dixon (Prentice Hall, 1989).

The Near Side

★ The full Moon nearly always displays the same features to us. This is essentially

-National Space Science Data Center

because the time it takes for the Moon to rotate once on its axis is identical to the time it takes for it to revolve once around the Earth. This is a special circumstance particular to the Moon, inasmuch as we see both hemispheres of all the other bodies in the solar system as they rotate. Because of a phenomenon called libration, an apparent slight wobble resulting from the Moon's elliptical orbit, we can see about 59 percent of its surface over time. To see an animation of what libration is, go to www.inconstantmoon.com/not_libr _ac.htm.

The lunar features that are most visible to the naked eye are the ancient lava flows that filled some of its older craters—enormous, smooth, dark, frozen seas, also known as maria. The lava came from the Moon's interior. After the Moon was formed four billion years ago, it was repeatedly hit by meteors. These impacts liquefied its inside. As subsequent large meteors hit and cracked the Moon's surface, lava from its man-

tle flowed up through the cracks made by the crashes. Today the Moon is cold and dead inside.

The Far Side

★ On October 4, 1959, Russia's *Luna 3* was launched toward the Moon, where it later became the first vehicle to send back images of the Moon's far side. Surprise! The distant hemisphere looked entirely different: Instead of maria, this side has many craters—scars received during its first few hundred million years of life.

The Dark Side?

★ There is no continually dark "side" of the Moon. Every part of the Moon has both day and night in half-month intervals.

The man who has seen the rising Moon break out of the clouds at midnight has been present like an archangel at the creation of light and of the world.

–Ralph Waldo Emerson, American writer (1803–1882)

(c o n t i n u e d)

Somewhere Over the Moonbow

★ A moonbow is a rare nighttime event. The Moon must be clearly visible in one part of the sky while rain falls in the opposite part. Like a rainbow, a moonbow is an enormous arc in the sky—but it is much less intense than a solar rainbow. It usually appears spooky white, although all of the spectral colors are present. (The colors

This moonbow in the Virgin Islands was captured with a 30-second exposure.

will show up photographically on high-speed film sufficiently exposed.) The size of the moonbow depends on the Moon's height: the lower the Moon, the bigger the moonbow. The tallest moonbows occur when the Moon is within an hour of rising or setting.

Why Does It Look So Big?

★ Who hasn't turned down a road to confront a low, horizon-hugging Moon that seems enormous? This is the famous "Moon illusion."

Many people assume that this common effect is caused by our atmosphere magnifying the image, but the explanation is far simpler. When the Moon is high overhead, it is dwarfed by the vast hemisphere of the heavens. By contrast,

when the Moon is low, it is viewed in proximity to earthly objects, such as chimneys or trees, whose size and shape provide scale.

Want to make the Moon illusion vanish? To reduce the Moon from enormous to ordinary, use a paper tube like the kind that holds paper towels. Close one eye and look through the tube at the enlarged Moon. It will appear normal. Now close the eye in the tube and open your other eye. The Moon appears huge again. Observe the Moon with the tube when it's high and again when it's low in the sky. The Moon will appear to be the same size both times.

A Marvelous Night for a Moon Dog

★ When the Moon is low in the sky, a bright "false Moon"—a well-defined saucer of brilliant moonlight—may hover off to its side. Sometimes, these "saucers" are distinct bright spots attached to a halo around the Moon at a point 22 degrees to its right or left—or

This moon dog appeared at the Moon's far right, off Montauk Point, Long Island (N.Y.).

–photo: Martin Turner

166

Lunar Lore

★ Myths and legends about the Moon abound. While they are not scientific, they have a long and colorful history. Here are two:

TO HAVE WEALTH: Collect water in the light of a waxing Moon and put it into a silver dish. Place the dish so that the Moon is reflected in the water, and dip your hands into the water. As your hands dry, imagine money flowing to you. It should come within this lunar cycle.

TO LOSE WEIGHT: Draw an outline of your desired body shape. Around this, draw an outline of the shape you are now. When the Moon is full, press your fingers along the larger outline and smooth it down to the figure inside, symbolically removing unwanted pounds. Do this for two weeks, while the Moon wanes. Repeat until the desired outcome is achieved. ☐☐

This lunar lore is taken from Many Moons *by Diane Brueton (Prentice Hall Press, 1991).*

★ ★ ★

YOUR TICKET TO THE MOON

To learn more about the Moon in history and lore, go to **www.almanac.com** and click on **Almanac Links 2005.**

on both sides at once. Often, however, they may seem to appear without the halo. By day, with the Sun, one of these phenomena is called a parhelion, or sun dog. By night, it is called a paraselene, or moon dog. Look for a moon dog when you see high, thin, cirrus clouds near the Moon.

Bob Berman's latest book is *Strange Universe* (Henry Holt and Company, 2003).

Astronomical Glossary

Aphelion (Aph.): The point in a planet's orbit that is farthest from the Sun.

Apogee (Apo.): The point in the Moon's orbit that is farthest from Earth.

Celestial Equator (Eq.): The circle around the celestial sphere that is halfway between the celestial poles. It can be thought of as the plane of Earth's equator projected out onto the sphere.

Celestial Sphere: An imaginary sphere projected into space that represents the entire sky, with an observer on Earth at its center. All celestial bodies other than Earth are imagined as being on its inside surface.

Conjunction: The time at which two or more celestial bodies appear closest in the sky. (Dates for conjunctions are given in the **Right-Hand Calendar Pages 181–203**; sky sightings of closely aligned bodies are given in the **SKY WATCH** section of the **Left-Hand Calendar Pages 180–202**.) **Inferior (Inf.):** Mercury or Venus is between the Sun and Earth. **Superior (Sup.):** The Sun is between a planet and Earth.

Declination: The celestial latitude of an object in the sky, measured in degrees north or south of the celestial equator; analogous to latitude on Earth. The Almanac gives the Sun's declination at noon.

Dominical Letter: A letter from A to G, denoting Sundays in the ecclesiastical calendar for a given year, determined by the date on which the first Sunday falls. If it falls on January 1, the letter (for the year) is A; if it falls on January 2, the letter is B; and so on.

Eclipse, Lunar: The full Moon enters the shadow of Earth, which cuts off all or part of the sunlight reflected off the Moon. **Total:** The Moon passes completely through the **umbra** (central dark part) of Earth's shadow. **Partial:** Only part of the Moon passes through the umbra. **Penumbral:** The Moon passes through only the penumbra (area of partial darkness surrounding the umbra).

Eclipse, Solar: Earth enters the shadow of the new Moon, which cuts off all or part of the Sun's light. **Total:** Earth passes through the umbra (central dark part) of the Moon's shadow, resulting in totality for observers within a narrow band on Earth. **Annular:** The Moon appears silhouetted against the Sun, with a ring of sunlight showing around it. **Partial:** The Moon blocks only part of the Sun.

Ecliptic: The apparent annual path of the Sun around the celestial sphere. The plane of the ecliptic is tipped $23\frac{1}{2}°$ from the celestial equator.

Elongation: The difference in degrees between the celestial longitudes of a planet and the Sun. **Greatest Elongation (Gr. Elong.):** The greatest apparent distance of a planet from the Sun, as seen from Earth.

Epact: A number from 1 to 30 that indicates the Moon's age on January 1 at Greenwich, England; used for determining the date of Easter.

Equinox: When the Sun crosses the celestial equator. This occurs two times each year: **Vernal** around March 21 and **Autumnal** around September 23.

Evening Star: A planet that is above the western horizon at sunset and less than 180° east of the Sun in right ascension.

Golden Number: A number in the 19-year cycle of the Moon, used for determining the date of Easter. (Approximately every 19 years, the Moon's phases occur on the same dates.) Add 1 to any given year and divide by 19; the remainder is the Golden Number. If there is no remainder, the Golden Number is 19.

Julian Period: A period of 7,980 years beginning January 1, 4713 B.C. Devised in 1583 by Joseph Scaliger, it provides a chronological basis for the study of ancient history. To find the Julian year, add 4,713 to any year.

Midnight: Astronomical midnight is the

time when the Sun is opposite its highest point in the sky (noon). Midnight is neither A.M. nor P.M., although 12-hour digital clocks typically display midnight as 12:00 A.M. On a 24-hour time cycle, 00:00, rather than 24:00, usually indicates midnight.

Moon on Equator: The Moon is on the celestial equator.

Moon Rides High/Runs Low: The Moon is highest above or farthest below the celestial equator.

Moonrise/Moonset: When the Moon rises above/sets below the horizon.

Moon's Phases: The changing appearance of the Moon, caused by the different angles at which it is illuminated by the Sun. **First Quarter:** Right half (in Northern Hemisphere) of the Moon is illuminated. **Full:** The Sun and the Moon are in opposition; the entire disk of the Moon is illuminated. **Last Quarter:** Left half (in Northern Hemisphere) of the Moon is illuminated. **New:** The Sun and the Moon are in conjunction; the entire disk of the Moon is darkened.

Moon's Place, Astronomical: The actual position of the Moon within the constellations on the celestial sphere. **Astrological:** The astrological position of the Moon within the zodiac according to calculations made more than 2,000 years ago. Because of precession of the equinoxes and other factors, this is not the Moon's actual position in the sky.

Morning Star: A planet that is above the eastern horizon at sunrise and less than 180° west of the Sun in right ascension.

Node: Either of the two points where a body's orbit intersects the ecliptic. **Ascending:** The body is moving from south to north of the ecliptic. **Descending:** The body is moving from north to south of the ecliptic.

Occultation (Occn.): When the Moon or a planet eclipses a star or planet.

Opposition: The Moon or a planet appears on the opposite side of the sky from the Sun (elongation 180°).

Perigee (Perig.): The point in the Moon's orbit that is closest to Earth.

Perihelion (Perih.): The point in a planet's orbit that is closest to the Sun.

Precession: The slowly changing position of the stars and equinoxes in the sky resulting from variations in the orientation of Earth's axis.

Right Ascension (R.A.): The celestial longitude of an object in the sky, measured eastward along the celestial equator in hours of time from the vernal equinox; analogous to longitude on Earth.

Roman Indiction: A number in a 15-year cycle, established January 1, A.D. 313, as a fiscal term. Add 3 to any given year in the Christian era and divide by 15; the remainder is the Roman Indiction. If there is no remainder, it is 15.

Solar Cycle: A period of 28 years in the Julian calendar, at the end of which the days of the month return to the same days of the week.

Solstice, Summer: The Sun reaches its greatest declination ($23\frac{1}{2}°$) north of the celestial equator. **Winter:** The Sun reaches its greatest declination ($23\frac{1}{2}°$) south of the celestial equator.

Stationary (Stat.): The apparent halted movement of a planet against the background of the stars shortly before it appears to move backward/westward (retrograde motion) or forward/eastward (direct motion).

Sun Fast/Slow: When a sundial reading is behind (slow) or ahead of (fast) clock time.

Sunrise/Sunset: The visible rising and setting of the Sun's upper limb across the unobstructed horizon of an observer whose eyes are 15 feet above ground level.

□□

The Visible Planets

■ Listed here for Boston are the times (EST/EDT) of the visible rising and setting of the planets Venus, Mars, Jupiter, and Saturn on the 1st, 11th, and 21st of each month and December 31st. The approximate times of their visible rising and setting on other days can be found by interpolation. The capital letters that appear beside the times are Key Letters and are used to convert the times for other localities **(see pages 176 and 235)**. For definitions of morning and evening stars, see the **Astronomical Glossary on page 168**.

Venus

After the transit in 2004, Venus has an off year in 2005.
It is visible with difficulty as a low, predawn morning star during the first 20 days of January, hides behind the Sun for the next three months, and emerges as a brightening evening star in western twilight from May until year's end. It never gets higher than 20 degrees, only about half of last year's prominence. The cloud-covered world will be unusually spectacular in late fall for Southern Hemisphere observers, but not for those in the Northern Hemisphere. Still, it will attract attention, especially during the two months before its greatest brilliancy on December 9th.

Jan. 1 ......rise	5:39	E	Apr. 1 ....**set**	**6:09**	C	July 1 ....**set**	**9:57**	E	Oct. 1 ....**set**	**8:05**	A
Jan. 11 .....rise	5:57	E	Apr. 11 .....**set**	**7:33**	D	July 11......**set**	**9:52**	D	Oct. 11......**set**	**7:58**	A
Jan. 21....rise	6:11	E	Apr. 21 ....**set**	**7:58**	D	July 21......**set**	**9:44**	D	Oct. 21......**set**	**7:55**	A
Feb. 1 ......rise	6:18	E	May 1 ....**set**	**8:24**	D	Aug. 1......**set**	**9:30**	D	Nov. 1.......**set**	**6:57**	A
Feb. 11 ....rise	6:19	D	May 11 .....**set**	**8:49**	E	Aug. 11.....**set**	**9:16**	C	Nov. 11.....**set**	**7:01**	A
Feb. 21 ....rise	6:16	C	May 21 .....**set**	**9:12**	E	Aug. 21.....**set**	**9:01**	C	Nov. 21.....**set**	**7:06**	A
Mar. 1 ....rise	6:10	D	June 1 ......**set**	**9:34**	E	Sept. 1 ....**set**	**8:44**	B	Dec. 1 ....**set**	**7:08**	A
Mar. 11....rise	6:00	D	June 11 ....**set**	**9:48**	E	Sept. 11 ...**set**	**8:29**	B	Dec. 11......**set**	**7:01**	A
Mar. 21....rise	5:48	C	June 21 .....**set**	**9:55**	E	Sept. 21 ...**set**	**8:16**	B	Dec. 21 .....**set**	**6:42**	A
									Dec. 31 .....**set**	**6:05**	A

Mars

This is an excellent year for Mars. Mars opens the year
as an inconspicuous orange "star" in Scorpius, and then brightens steadily as it chugs all the way to Aries. Becoming brilliant by summer and very brilliant in early fall, it will appear about half the apparent size of Jupiter and may be large enough for surface features to be viewed through a telescope. Although not as close and brilliant as during its historic meeting with Earth in 2003, Mars attains a fine November opposition high in the sky for Northern Hemisphere observers. This will be the closest Mars will be to Earth until 2018.

Jan. 1 ......rise	4:28	E	Apr. 1 ......rise	3:00	E	July 1.......rise	12:43	A	Oct. 1.......**rise**	**8:21**	A
Jan. 11 .....rise	4:23	E	Apr. 11 .....rise	3:42	D	July 11.....rise	12:19	A	Oct. 11.....**rise**	**7:37**	A
Jan. 21....rise	4:18	E	Apr. 21 ....rise	3:23	D	July 21....**rise**	**11:54**	B	Oct. 21.....**rise**	**6:49**	A
Feb. 1 ......rise	4:11	E	May 1 ......rise	3:03	D	Aug. 1......**rise**	**11:27**	B	Nov. 1......**rise**	**4:53**	A
Feb. 11 ....rise	4:03	E	May 11 .....rise	2:42	D	Aug. 11.....**rise**	**11:02**	B	Nov. 11.....set	6:09	D
Feb. 21 ....rise	3:53	E	May 21 ....rise	2:20	D	Aug. 21....**rise**	**10:35**	B	Nov. 21.....set	5:15	D
Mar. 1 ....rise	3:45	E	June 1 ......rise	1:55	C	Sept. 1 ....**rise**	**10:07**	B	Dec. 1 .....set	4:28	D
Mar. 11....rise	3:32	E	June 11 ....rise	1:32	C	Sept. 11 ...**rise**	**9:37**	B	Dec. 11 ....set	3:46	D
Mar. 21....rise	3:18	E	June 21 ....rise	1:09	C	Sept. 21 ...**rise**	**9:03**	A	Dec. 21 ....set	3:12	D
									Dec. 31 ....set	2:43	D

Boldface—P.M.; Lightface—A.M.

Jupiter

Jupiter starts the year in Virgo, rising around midnight, and comes up two hours earlier each succeeding month. It reaches opposition on April 3, when it rises at sunset and makes its brightest appearance of the year. It remains up most of the night until summer, but can be seen only during the first half of the night. Jupiter is low in the west in September, slips behind the Sun in October, and reemerges in the predawn east in December, when it crosses into Libra.

Jan. 1	rise	12:23	C	Apr. 1	**rise**	**6:09**	C	July 1	set	12:34	C	Oct. 1	**set**	**7:06**	B

Jan. 1 ......rise 12:23 C Apr. 1 ......**rise 6:09** C July 1 ....set 12:34 C Oct. 1 ....**set 7:06** B
Jan. 11 .....**rise 11:44** C Apr. 11 .....set 6:05 B July 11 .....**set 11:57** C Oct. 11 ......**set 6:31** B
Jan. 21 .....**rise 11:07** C Apr. 21 .....set 5:23 C July 21 .....**set 11:20** B Oct. 21 ......**set 5:57** B
Feb. 1 ......**rise 10:25** C May 1 ......set 4:41 C Aug. 1 .....**set 10:40** B Nov. 1 .....rise 5:37 D
Feb. 11 ....**rise 9:45** C May 11 .....set 4:00 C Aug. 11 ....**set 10:04** B Nov. 11 ...rise 5:08 D
Feb. 21 ....**rise 9:03** C May 21 .....set 3:19 C Aug. 21 ....**set 9:28** B Nov. 21 ...rise 4:40 D
Mar. 1 ......**rise 8:29** C June 1 ......set 2:35 C Sept. 1 ......**set 8:50** B Dec. 1 ......rise 4:11 D
Mar. 11 ....**rise 7:44** C June 11 .....set 1:55 C Sept. 11 ....**set 8:15** B Dec. 11 ....rise 3:42 D
Mar. 21 ....**rise 6:59** C June 21 .....set 1:16 C Sept. 21 ....**set 7:40** B Dec. 21 ....rise 3:12 D
 Dec. 31 ....rise 2:41 D

Saturn

This is a superb year for the ringed planet. It is brightest in January, reaches opposition on January 13th, and remains prominent in Gemini until early spring. By late June it is low in the west, where it has a striking conjunction with Mercury and Venus on the 24th. It is invisible behind the Sun in July, but returns in August as a predawn star in the east. It gains attention again in November when it rises before midnight. By early December, it is up by 9:00 P.M. and visible the rest of the night.

Jan. 1 ......**rise 5:18** A Apr. 1 ......set 2:04 E July 1 ....**set 9:29** E Oct. 1 ......rise 1:35 A
Jan. 11 .....**rise 4:35** A Apr. 11 .....set 2:26 E July 11 .....**set 8:54** E Oct. 11 ....rise 1:00 A
Jan. 21 .....set 6:48 E Apr. 21 .....set 1:48 E July 21 .....**set 8:19** E Oct. 21 ....rise 12:21 A
Feb. 1 ....set 6:02 E May 1 ......set 1:11 E Aug. 1 .....rise 5:00 A Nov. 1 ......**rise 10:40** A
Feb. 11 .....set 5:20 E May 11 .....set 12:30 E Aug. 11 ....rise 4:27 A Nov. 11 ....**rise 10:02** A
Feb. 21 .....set 4:39 E May 21 .....**set 11:54** E Aug. 21 ....rise 3:54 A Nov. 21 ....**rise 9:23** A
Mar. 1 ......set 4:06 E June 1 ......**set 11:15** E Sept. 1 .....rise 3:18 A Dec. 1 ......**rise 8:43** A
Mar. 11 ....set 3:26 E June 11 .....**set 10:39** E Sept. 11 ...rise 2:44 A Dec. 11 ....**rise 8:02** A
Mar. 21 ....set 2:47 E June 21 .....**set 10:04** E Sept. 21 ...rise 2:10 A Dec. 21 ....**rise 7:21** A
 Dec. 31 ....**rise 6:38** A

Mercury

Mercury is best viewed when it's near the edge of its orbit, farthest from the Sun, just as its orbit slants upward from the horizon at its greatest angle. It meets those requirements this year 30 to 45 minutes after sunset, low in the west from February 27 to March 22, and from mid-June to mid-July. In the eastern sky, 30 to 45 minutes before sunrise, the best viewing opportunities are January 1–15, August 15–September 5, and December 1–25. Mercury and Venus are extremely close together on June 25th, and may even merge into a single "star."

DO NOT CONFUSE ■ *Venus with Jupiter during their close meetings in late August and early September. Venus is much brighter.* ■ *Mercury with Saturn during their three-way meetings with Venus in late June. Mercury is slightly orange and a bit brighter than Saturn.* ■ *Mars with the nearby orange star Antares at the beginning of January. Though their colors match, Antares is a little brighter.*

Eclipses

■ There will be four eclipses in 2005, two of the Sun and two of the Moon. Solar eclipses are visible only in certain areas and require eye protection to be viewed safely. Lunar eclipses are technically visible from the entire night side of Earth, but during a penumbral eclipse, the dimming of the Moon's illumination is slight.

APRIL 8: annular–total eclipse of the Sun.
Only the partial phase will be visible, and this only from the southern United States. The eclipse will begin between 5:30 P.M. and 6:00 P.M. EDT (2:30 P.M. and 3:00 P.M. PDT), depending on location, and will last about one hour.

APRIL 24: penumbral eclipse of the Moon.
The beginning of the penumbral phase will be visible in North America and Hawaii; the end will be visible in western North America and Hawaii. The Moon enters penumbra at 3:50 A.M. EDT (12:50 A.M. PDT) and leaves penumbra at 8:00 A.M. EDT (5:00 A.M. PDT).

OCTOBER 3: annular eclipse of the Sun.
This eclipse will not be visible in North America.

OCTOBER 17: partial eclipse of the Moon.
The beginning of the umbral phase will be visible in central and western North America and Hawaii. The end will be visible in western North America and Hawaii. The Moon enters penumbra at 5:51 A.M. EDT (2:51 A.M. PDT) and enters umbra at 7:34 A.M. EDT (4:34 A.M. PDT). The Moon leaves umbra at 8:33 A.M. EDT (5:33 A.M. PDT) and leaves penumbra at 10:15 A.M. EDT (7:15 A.M. PDT).

FULL-MOON DATES

	2005	2006	2007	2008	2009
Jan.	25	14	3	22	10
Feb.	23	12	2	20	9
Mar.	25	14	3	21	10
Apr.	24	13	2	20	9
May	23	13	2 & 31	19	9
June	22	11	30	18	7
July	21	10	29	18	7
Aug.	19	9	28	16	5
Sept.	17	7	26	15	4
Oct.	17	6	26	14	4
Nov.	15	5	24	13	2
Dec.	15	4	23	12	2 & 31

Solar Eclipse Dates, 2005–2024

DATE	REGIONS WITH VISIBLE TOTALITY
2005 Apr. 8	S. Pacific Ocean
2006 Mar. 29	Africa, Turkey, Russia
2008 Aug. 1	Northern Canada, Greenland, Siberia, China
2009 July 22	India, China, central Pacific Ocean
2010 July 11	S. Pacific Ocean, southern South America
2012 Nov. 13	Australia, S. Pacific Ocean
2013 Nov. 3	Atlantic Ocean, central Africa
2015 Mar. 20	N. Atlantic Ocean, Arctic
2016 Mar. 9	Southeast Asia, N. Pacific Ocean
2017 Aug. 21	United States
2019 July 2	S. Pacific Ocean, South America
2020 Dec. 14	S. Pacific Ocean, South America
2021 Dec. 4	Antarctica
2023 Apr. 20	Indonesia, Australia
2024 Apr. 8	Mexico, United States, Canada

Bright Stars

Transit Times

■ This table shows the time (EST or EDT) and altitude of a star as it transits the meridian (i.e., reaches its highest elevation while passing over the horizon's south point) at Boston on the dates shown. The transit time on any other date differs from that of the nearest date listed by approximately four minutes per day. To find the time of a star's transit for your location, convert its time at Boston using Key Letter C.*

Time of Transit (EST/EDT)   Boldface–P.M.
Lightface–A.M.

Star	Constellation	Magnitude	Jan. 1	Mar. 1	May 1	July 1	Sept. 1	Nov. 1	Altitude (degrees)
Altair	Aquila	0.8	**12:48**	8:56	5:57	1:57	**9:49**	**4:49**	56.3
Deneb	Cygnus	1.3	**1:39**	9:47	6:47	2:48	**10:40**	**5:40**	92.8
Fomalhaut	Psc. Aus.	1.2	**3:54**	**12:02**	9:02	5:02	12:54	**7:55**	17.8
Algol	Perseus	2.2	**8:05**	**4:13**	**1:13**	9:13	5:09	12:09	88.5
Aldebaran	Taurus	0.9	**9:32**	**5:40**	**2:40**	10:40	6:36	1:37	64.1
Rigel	Orion	0.1	**10:10**	**6:18**	**3:18**	11:18	7:15	2:15	39.4
Capella	Auriga	0.1	**10:12**	**6:20**	**3:20**	11:20	7:17	2:17	93.6
Bellatrix	Orion	1.6	**10:21**	**6:29**	**3:29**	11:29	7:25	2:26	54.0
Betelgeuse	Orion	var. 0.4	**10:51**	**6:59**	**3:59**	11:59	7:55	2:56	55.0
Sirius	Can. Maj.	−1.4	**11:41**	**7:49**	**4:49**	**12:49**	8:45	3:45	31.0
Procyon	Can. Min.	0.4	12:38	**8:42**	**5:43**	**1:43**	9:39	4:39	52.9
Pollux	Gemini	1.2	12:44	**8:48**	**5:49**	**1:49**	9:45	4:45	75.7
Regulus	Leo	1.4	3:07	**11:11**	**8:12**	**4:12**	**12:08**	7:08	59.7
Spica	Virgo	var. 1.0	6:24	2:32	**11:28**	**7:28**	**3:24**	10:24	36.6
Arcturus	Boötes	−0.1	7:14	3:22	12:19	**8:19**	**4:15**	11:15	66.9
Antares	Scorpius	var. 0.9	9:27	5:35	2:35	**10:32**	**6:28**	**1:28**	21.3
Vega	Lyra	0	11:35	7:43	4:43	12:39	**8:35**	**3:36**	86.4

Risings and Settings

■ To find the time of a star's rising at Boston on any date, subtract the interval shown at right from the star's transit time on that date; add the interval to find the star's setting time. To find the rising and setting times for your city, convert the Boston transit times above using the Key Letter* shown at right before applying the interval. The directions in which the stars rise and set, shown for Boston, are generally useful throughout the United States.

Deneb, Algol, Capella, and Vega are circumpolar stars—they never set but appear to circle the celestial north pole.

Star	Interval (h. m.)	Rising Key	Rising Dir.	Setting Key	Setting Dir.
Altair	6:36	B	EbN	E	WbN
Fomalhaut	3:59	E	SE	D	SW
Aldebaran	7:06	B	ENE	D	WNW
Rigel	5:33	D	EbS	B	WbS
Bellatrix	6:27	B	EbN	D	WbN
Betelgeuse	6:31	B	EbN	D	WbN
Sirius	5:00	D	ESE	B	WSW
Procyon	6:23	B	EbN	D	WbN
Pollux	8:01	A	NE	E	NW
Regulus	6:49	B	EbN	D	WbN
Spica	5:23	D	EbS	B	WbS
Arcturus	7:19	A	ENE	E	WNW
Antares	4:17	E	SEbE	A	SWbW

*The values of Key Letters are given in the Time Corrections table (page 235).

-Beth Krommes

The Twilight Zone

How to determine the length of twilight and the times of dawn and dark.

■ Twilight is the time preceding sunrise and again following sunset, when the sky is partially illuminated. The three ranges of twilight are defined according to the Sun's position below the horizon. Civil twilight ends when the Sun is 6 degrees below the horizon (visually, the horizon is clearly defined). Nautical twilight ends when the Sun is 12 degrees below the horizon (the horizon is indistinct). Astronomical twilight ends when the Sun is 18 degrees below the horizon (sky illumination is imperceptible). Dawn and dark occur when the Sun is more than 18 degrees below the horizon and there is no illumination from the Sun.

LENGTH OF TWILIGHT (hours and minutes)

LATITUDE	Jan. 1 to Apr. 10	Apr. 11 to May 2	May 3 to May 14	May 15 to May 25	May 26 to July 22	July 23 to Aug. 3	Aug. 4 to Aug. 14	Aug. 15 to Sept. 5	Sept. 6 to Dec. 31
25° N to 30° N	1 20	1 23	1 26	1 29	1 32	1 29	1 26	1 23	1 20
31° N to 36° N	1 26	1 28	1 34	1 38	1 43	1 38	1 34	1 28	1 26
37° N to 42° N	1 33	1 39	1 47	1 52	1 59	1 52	1 47	1 39	1 33
43° N to 47° N	1 42	1 51	2 02	2 13	2 27	2 13	2 02	1 51	1 42
48° N to 49° N	1 50	2 04	2 22	2 42	—	2 42	2 22	2 04	1 50

TO DETERMINE THE LENGTH OF TWILIGHT: The length of twilight changes with latitude and the time of year and is independent of time zones. Use the **Time Corrections table, page 235,** to find the latitude of your city or the city nearest you. Use that figure in the chart above with the appropriate date to calculate the length of twilight in your area.

TO DETERMINE WHEN DAWN OR DARK WILL OCCUR: Calculate the sunrise/sunset times for your locality, using the instructions in **How to Use This Almanac, page 176.** Subtract the length of twilight from the time of sunrise to determine when dawn breaks. Add the length of twilight to the time of sunset to determine when dark descends.

E X A M P L E :

Boston, Mass. (latitude 42° 22')

Sunrise, August 1	5:37 A.M.
Length of twilight	−1:52
Dawn breaks	3:45 A.M. EDT
Sunset, August 1	8:03 P.M.
Length of twilight	+1:52
Dark descends	9:55 P.M. EDT

Principal Meteor Showers

SHOWER	BEST VIEWING	POINT OF ORIGIN	DATE OF MAXIMUM*	PEAK RATE (/HR.)**	ASSOCIATED COMET
Quadrantid	Predawn	N	Jan. 4	80	—
Lyrid	Predawn	S	Apr. 22	12	Thatcher
Eta Aquarid	Predawn	SE	May 4	20	Halley
Delta Aquarid	Predawn	S	July 30	10	—
Perseid	Predawn	NE	Aug. 11–13	75	Swift-Tuttle
Draconid	Late evening	NW	Oct. 9	6	Giacobini-Zinner
Orionid	Predawn	S	Oct. 21–22	25	Halley
Taurid	Late evening	S	Nov. 9	6	Encke
Leonid	Predawn	S	Nov. 18	20	Tempel-Tuttle
Andromedid	Late evening	S	Nov. 25–27	5	Biela
Geminid	All night	NE	Dec. 13–14	65	—
Ursid	Predawn	N	Dec. 22	12	Tuttle

*May vary by one or two days in either direction.   **Approximate.

How to Use This Almanac

The calendar pages (180–203) are the heart of *The Old Farmer's Almanac*. They present astronomical data and sky sightings for the entire year and are what make this book a true almanac, a "calendar of the heavens." In essence, these pages are unchanged since 1792, when Robert B. Thomas published his first edition. The long columns of numbers and symbols reveal all of nature's precision, rhythm, and glory—an astronomical look at the year 2005.

The Seasons of the Year

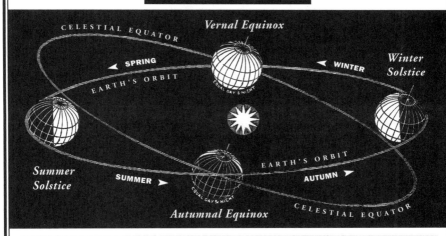

THE SEASONS OF 2005

Spring .... March 20, 7:33 A.M. EST	Fall .... September 22, 6:23 P.M. EDT
Summer .... June 21, 2:46 A.M. EDT	Winter .... December 21, 1:35 P.M. EST

■ The seasons occur because as the Earth revolves around the Sun, its axis is always tilted at 23.5 degrees from the perpendicular and remains in the same orientation relative to the Sun. This tilt causes different latitudes on Earth to receive varying amounts of sunlight throughout the year.

In the Northern Hemisphere, the summer solstice (around June 21) marks the beginning of summer and occurs when the North Pole is tilted toward the Sun. The winter solstice (around December 21) marks the beginning of winter and occurs when the North Pole is tilted away from the Sun. In the Southern Hemisphere, the summer solstice occurs around December 21, and the winter solstice, around June 21.

The equinoxes occur when the hemispheres equally face the Sun and receive equal amounts (12 hours each) of daylight and darkness. The vernal equinox marks the beginning of spring, and the autumnal equinox marks the beginning of autumn.

continued

The Left-Hand Calendar Pages • 180–202

S A M P L E   M O N T H

SKY WATCH ☆ *The box at the top of each Left-Hand Calendar Page describes the best times to view celestial highlights, including conjunctions, meteor showers, and planets. (The dates on which select astronomical events occur appear on the Right-Hand Calendar Pages.)*

1 **2** **3** **4** **5** **6** **7** **8**

For an explanation of this page, see page 176; for values of Key Letters, see page 235.

Day of Year	Day of Month	Day of Week	☼ Rises h. m.	Key	☼ Sets h. m.	Key	Length of Day h. m.	Sun Fast m.	Declination of Sun ° ′	High Tide Boston Light—A.M. Bold—P.M.	☽ Rises h. m.	Key	☽ Sets h. m.	Key	Place	Age
305	1	Sa.	6 17	D	4 38	B	10 21	32	14 s. 27	4½ 4¾	1 ^P_M 46	E	11 ^P_M 28	B	CAP	7
306	2	E	6 18	D	4 37	B	10 19	32	14 46	5¾ 6	2 16	E	—	—	CAP	8
307	3	M.	6 20	D	4 35	B	10 15	32	15 05	6¾ 7	2 40	D	12 ^A_M 37	C	AQU	9

The Left-Hand Calendar Pages, as shown above, contain daily Sun and Moon rise and set times, the length of day, high tide times, the Moon's place and age, and more for Boston. Examples of how to calculate astronomical times are shown below.

1 To calculate the sunrise/sunset times for your locale: Each sunrise/sunset time is assigned a Key Letter whose value is given in minutes in the **Time Corrections** table on **page 235.** Find your city in the table, or the city nearest you, and add or subtract those minutes to/from Boston's sunrise or sunset time given.

E X A M P L E :

■ To find the time of sunrise in Denver, Colorado, on the first day of the month:

Sunrise, Boston, with Key Letter D (above)	6:17 A.M. EST
Value of Key Letter D for Denver (p. 236)	+ 11 minutes
Sunrise, Denver	6:28 A.M. MST

2 To determine your city's length of day, find the sunrise/sunset Key Letter values for your city on **page 235.** Add or

ATTENTION, READERS: *All times given in this edition of the Almanac are for Boston, Massachusetts, and are in Eastern Standard Time (EST), except from 2:00 A.M., April 3, until 2:00 A.M., October 30, when Eastern Daylight Time (EDT) is given. Key Letters (A–E) are provided so that you can calculate times for other localities.*

subtract the sunset value to/from Boston's length of day. Then simply *reverse* the sunrise sign (from minus to plus, or plus to minus) and add or subtract this value to/from the result of the first step.

E X A M P L E :

■ To find the length of day in Richmond, Virginia:

Length of day, Boston (above)	**10:21**
Sunset Key Letter B for Richmond (p. 238)	**+ 32**
	10:53
Reverse sunrise Key Letter D for Richmond (p. 238, +17 to –17)	**– 17**
Length of day, Richmond (10 hr., 36 min.)	**10:36**

3 Use the Sun Fast column to change sundial time to clock time in Boston. A sundial reads natural time, or Sun time, which is neither Standard nor Daylight time except by coincidence. *Subtract* the minutes given in the Sun Fast column (except where the number is preceded by an asterisk [*], in which case *add* the minutes) to get Boston clock time, and use Key Letter C in the table on **page 235** to convert the time to your city.

C
A
L
E
N
D
A
R

E X A M P L E :

■ To change sundial time to clock time in Boston, or Salem, Oregon:

Sundial reading: (Boston or Salem)	12:00 noon
Subtract Sun Fast (p. 176)	– 32 minutes
Clock time, Boston	11:28 A.M. EST
Use Key Letter C for Salem (p. 238)	+ 27 minutes
Clock time, Salem	11:55 A.M. PST

4 This column gives the degrees and minutes of the Sun from the celestial equator at noon EST or EDT.

5 This column gives the times of high tides in Boston. For example, the first high tide occurs at 4:30 A.M. and the second occurs at 4:45 P.M. (A dash indicates that high tide occurs on or after midnight and so is recorded on the next day.) Figures for calculating high tide times and heights for localities other than Boston are given in the Tide Corrections table on **page 232.**

–Beth Krommes

6 To calculate the moonrise/moonset times for localities other than Boston, follow the example in the next column, making a correction for longitude (see table, above right). For the longitude of your city, **see page 235.** (Note: A dash in the moonrise/moonset columns indicates that rise or set times occur on or after midnight and are recorded on the next day.)

LONGITUDE OF CITY	CORRECTION MINUTES
58°–76°	0
77°–89°	+1
90°–102°	+2
103°–115°	+3
116°–127°	+4
128°–141°	+5
142°–155°	+6

E X A M P L E :

■ To determine the time of moonrise in Lansing, Michigan:

Moonrise, Boston, with Key Letter E (p. 176)	1:46 P.M. EST
Value of Key Letter E for Lansing (p. 237)	+ 54 minutes
Correction for Lansing longitude 84° 33'	+ 1 minute
Moonrise, Lansing	2:41 P.M. EST

Use the same procedure to determine the time of moonset.

7 The Moon's Place is its *astronomical* placement in the heavens. (This should not be confused with the Moon's *astrological* place in the zodiac, as explained on **page 229.**) All calculations in this Almanac are based on astronomy, not astrology, except for the information on **pages 227–229.**

In addition to the 12 constellations of the zodiac, this column may indicate others: Auriga **(AUR),** a northern constellation between Perseus and Gemini; Cetus **(CET),** which lies south of the zodiac, just south of Pisces and Aries; Ophiuchus **(OPH),** a constellation primarily north of the zodiac but with a small corner between Scorpius and Sagittarius; Orion **(ORI),** a constellation whose northern limit first reaches the zodiac between Taurus and Gemini; and Sextans **(SEX),** which lies south of the zodiac except for a corner that just touches it near Leo.

8 The last column gives the Moon's Age, which is the number of days since the previous new Moon. (The average length of the lunar month is 29.53 days.)

continued

The Right-Hand Calendar Pages • 181–203

CALENDAR

SAMPLE MONTH

- Weather prediction rhyme.
- Day of the month.
- Day of the week.
- The bold letter in this column is the Dominical Letter, a traditional ecclesiastical designation for Sunday. In this sample, the letter is E, because the first Sunday of the year fell on the fifth day of January. The Dominical letter for 2005 is **B**.
- Notable celestial events appear as these symbols. (See opposite page for an explanation of symbols.)
- Sundays and special holy days generally appear in this typeface.
- Religious feasts generally appear in this typeface.
- Civil holidays generally appear in this typeface.
- Noteworthy historical events, folklore, and legends appear in this typeface.
- Proverbs, poems, and adages appear in this typeface.
- First high tide at Boston on this sample day is 10.8 feet; second high tide is 10.3 feet.

What moistens the lip
and what brightens the eye?
What calls back the past,
like the rich pumpkin pie? –J. G. Whittier

D. M.	D. W.	Dates, Feasts, Fasts, Aspects, Tide Heights	Weather ↓
1	Sa.	All Saints' • Sadie Hawkins Day • ☌♆☾ • Tides {9.2 10.1	*A*
2	**E**	21st S. af. P. • ☌♅☾ • Tides {9.1 9.8 •	*scoop*
3	M.	All Souls' • ☌♂☾ • First national auto show, held in New York City, 1900 •	*of*
4	Tu.	Election Day • James Ritty received a patent for a cash register, 1879 •	*vanilla*
5	W.	☾ on Eq. • Bryan Adams born, 1959 • Tides {9.6 9.6 •	*on*
6	Th.	*The barber shows you the mirror, but it's too late to raise a squawk.* • {9.9 9.6	*northern*
7	Fr.	Last spike of the transcontinental Canadian Pacific Railway driven at Craigellachie, B.C., 1885	*hills*
8	Sa.	**Full Beaver** ○ • **Eclipse** ☾ • ♅ stat. • Tides {10.1 9.4	*gives*
9	**E**	22nd S. af. P. • ☾ at ☊ • Sally Tompkins born, 1833	*the*
10	M.	☾ at apo. • S.S. *Edmund Fitzgerald* sank in storm, entire crew of 29 lost, 1975 •	*snow-*
11	Tu.	St. Martin • **Veterans Day** • Indian Summer • Tides {9.1 10.0	*blower*
12	W.	Largest iceberg on record (208x60 miles) discovered by U.S.S. *Glacier*, 1956 •	*salesman*
13	Th.	☾ rides high • ☌♄☾ • Tides {8.6 9.6 •	*thrills.*
14	Fr.	First performance of a Western theatrical production in North America, 1606 • {8.4 9.4 •	*The*
15	Sa.	Explorer Zebulon Pike spotted a mountain he called Grand Peak, later renamed Pikes Peak, 1806	*sight*
16	**E**	23rd S. af. P. • Skunks hibernate now. • Tides {8.3 9.2 •	*of*
17	M.	St. Hugh of Lincoln • Computer mouse patented, 1970 • {8.4 9.2	*white,*
18	Tu.	☌♃☾ • Captain Nathaniel B. Palmer discovered Antarctica, 1820 •	*however*
19	W.	*If there be ice in November that will bear a duck, There will be nothing thereafter but sleet and muck.*	*meager,*
20	Th.	☾ on Eq. • First nighttime photograph taken from airplane, 1925 • {10.0 10.0	*makes*
21	Fr.	North Carolina became the 12th state, 1789 • Tides {10.8 10.3 •	*the*
22	Sa.	Statue of Liberty began role as first U.S. lighthouse to use electricity, 1886 • {11.5 10.6	*skiers*

☞ *For explanations of Almanac terms, see the glossaries on pages 168, 204, and 234.*

Predicting Earthquakes

–Beth Krommes

■ Note the dates in the **Right-Hand Calendar Pages** when the Moon rides high or runs low. The date of the high begins the most likely five-day period of earthquakes in the Northern Hemisphere; the date of the low indicates a similar five-day period in the Southern Hemisphere. Also noted are the two days each month when the Moon is on the celestial equator, indicating the most likely time for earthquakes in both hemispheres.

■ Throughout the **Right-Hand Calendar Pages** are groups of symbols that represent notable celestial events. The symbols and names of the principal planets and aspects are:

☉	**Sun**	♆	**Neptune**
○ ● ☾	**Moon**	♇	**Pluto**
☿	**Mercury**	☌	**Conjunction (on the same celestial longitude)**
♀	**Venus**		
⊕	**Earth**		
♂	**Mars**	☊	**Ascending node**
♃	**Jupiter**	☋	**Descending node**
♄	**Saturn**	☍	**Opposition (180 degrees from Sun)**
♅	**Uranus**		

EXAMPLE:

☌♅☾ next to the second day of the month (see opposite page) means that on that date a conjunction (☌) of Uranus (♅) and the Moon (☾) occurs: They are aligned along the same celestial longitude and appear to be closest together in the sky.

Earth at Perihelion and Aphelion

■ Earth will be at *perihelion,* or 91,403,167 miles from the Sun, on January 1, 2005. Earth will be at *aphelion,* or 94,512,074 miles from the Sun, on July 4, 2005.

CALENDAR

2005 Calendar Highlights

Movable Religious Observances

Septuagesima Sunday	**January 23**
Shrove Tuesday	**February 8**
Ash Wednesday	**February 9**
Palm Sunday	**March 20**
Good Friday	**March 25**
Easter	**March 27**
First day of Passover	**April 24**
Rogation Sunday, Orthodox Easter	**May 1**
Ascension Day	**May 5**
Whitsunday–Pentecost	**May 15**
Trinity Sunday	**May 22**
Vesak	**May 23**
Corpus Christi	**May 29**
Rosh Hashanah, First day of Ramadan	**October 4**
Yom Kippur	**October 13**
First Sunday of Advent	**November 27**
First day of Chanukah	**December 26**

Chronological Cycles

Dominical Letter	**B**
Epact	**19**
Golden Number (Lunar Cycle)	**11**
Roman Indiction	**13**
Solar Cycle	**26**
Year of Julian Period	**6718**

–Beth Krommes

Eras

ERA	YEAR	BEGINS
Byzantine	**7514**	**September 14**
Jewish (A.M.)*	**5766**	**October 4**
Chinese (Lunar) [Year of the Rooster]	**4703**	**February 9**
Roman (A.U.C.)	**2758**	**January 14**
Nabonassar	**2754**	**April 22**
Japanese	**2665**	**January 1**
Grecian (Seleucidae)	**2317**	**September 14 (or October 14)**
Indian (Saka)	**1927**	**March 22**
Diocletian	**1722**	**September 11**
Islamic (Hegira)*	**1426**	**February 10**

**Year begins at sunset the evening before.*

SKY WATCH ☆ *Saturn begins the year at its biggest and brightest, reaching opposition on the 13th. In Gemini, it's high overhead at midnight. Jupiter, in Virgo, starts rising before midnight. The remaining bright planets gather in the predawn east: Venus and Mercury are very close together 30 to 45 minutes before dawn in an exceptionally long-lived conjunction best seen during the first half of the month. Hovering just above them is Mars, not quite as bright as nearby Antares, in Scorpius. Mars quickly moves into Ophiuchus for the rest of the month. Earth reaches its near point to the Sun (perihelion) on the year's opening day, which hasn't happened in centuries.*

☾	Last Quarter	3rd day	12th hour	46th minute
●	New Moon	10th day	7th hour	3rd minute
☽	First Quarter	17th day	1st hour	57th minute
○	Full Moon	25th day	5th hour	32nd minute

Times are given in Eastern Standard Time.

For an explanation of this page, see page 176; for values of Key Letters, see page 235.

Day of Year	Day of Month	Day of Week	Rises h. m.	Key	Sets h. m.	Key	Length of Day h. m.	Sun Fast m.	Declination of Sun ° '	High Tide Boston Light—A.M. Bold—P.M.		Rises h. m.	Key	Sets h. m.	Key	Place	Age
1	1	Sa.	7 14	E	4 23	A	9 09	12	22 s.57	2¾	3	10ᴹ17	C	10ᴬ46	D	LEO	21
2	2	**B**	7 14	E	4 23	A	9 09	12	22 52	3½	3¾	11ᴹ22	D	11 06	C	VIR	22
3	3	M.	7 14	E	4 24	A	9 10	11	22 46	4¼	4½	—	–	11 25	C	VIR	23
4	4	Tu.	7 14	E	4 25	A	9 11	11	22 40	5	5½	12ᴹ29	E	11ᴬ46	B	VIR	24
5	5	W.	7 14	E	4 26	A	9 12	10	22 33	6	6½	1 40	E	12ᴾ11	B	VIR	25
6	6	Th.	7 13	E	4 27	A	9 14	10	22 25	6¾	7½	2 55	E	12 41	A	LIB	26
7	7	Fr.	7 13	E	4 28	A	9 15	9	22 17	7¾	8½	4 14	E	1 19	A	SCO	27
8	8	Sa.	7 13	E	4 29	A	9 16	9	22 09	8¾	9½	5 33	E	2 11	A	OPH	28
9	9	**B**	7 13	E	4 30	A	9 17	9	22 01	9½	10¼	6 46	E	3 17	A	SAG	29
10	10	M.	7 13	E	4 31	A	9 18	8	21 52	10½	11¼	7 48	E	4 35	A	SAG	0
11	11	Tu.	7 12	E	4 33	A	9 21	8	21 43	11½	—	8 35	E	5 58	B	CAP	1
12	12	W.	7 12	E	4 34	A	9 22	7	21 33	12¼	12¼	9 12	E	7 21	B	CAP	2
13	13	Th.	7 12	E	4 35	A	9 23	7	21 22	1	1¼	9 40	D	8 39	D	AQU	3
14	14	Fr.	7 11	E	4 36	A	9 25	7	21 12	1¾	2¼	10 05	D	9 53	D	AQU	4
15	15	Sa.	7 11	E	4 37	A	9 26	6	21 00	2¾	3	10 26	C	11ᴹ03	D	PSC	5
16	16	**B**	7 10	E	4 38	A	9 28	6	20 49	3¾	4	10 47	B	—		PSC	6
17	17	M.	7 10	E	4 40	A	9 30	6	20 38	4½	5	11 08	B	12ᴬ12	E	PSC	7
18	18	Tu.	7 09	E	4 41	A	9 32	5	20 26	5½	6	11 32	B	1 19	E	ARI	8
19	19	W.	7 09	E	4 42	A	9 33	5	20 13	6½	7	11ᴬ59	A	2 26	E	ARI	9
20	20	Th.	7 08	E	4 43	A	9 35	5	20 00	7¼	8	12ᴾ32	A	3 31	E	TAU	10
21	21	Fr.	7 07	E	4 44	A	9 37	4	19 46	8¼	9	1 11	A	4 34	E	TAU	11
22	22	Sa.	7 07	E	4 46	A	9 39	4	19 32	9	9¾	1 59	A	5 31	E	AUR	12
23	23	**B**	7 06	D	4 47	A	9 41	4	19 18	9¾	10½	2 53	A	6 21	E	GEM	13
24	24	M.	7 05	D	4 48	A	9 43	4	19 03	10½	11¼	3 54	A	7 03	E	GEM	14
25	25	Tu.	7 04	D	4 49	A	9 45	3	18 48	11¼	11¾	4 57	B	7 38	E	CAN	15
26	26	W.	7 03	D	4 51	A	9 48	3	18 33	11¾	—	6 02	B	8 07	E	CAN	16
27	27	Th.	7 02	D	4 52	A	9 50	3	18 18	12¼	12½	7 06	C	8 31	E	LEO	17
28	28	Fr.	7 02	D	4 53	A	9 51	3	18 03	1	1	8 10	D	8 52	D	LEO	18
29	29	Sa.	7 01	D	4 55	A	9 54	3	17 46	1½	1¾	9 14	D	9 11	D	VIR	19
30	30	**B**	7 00	D	4 56	A	9 56	2	17 30	2¼	2½	10 19	D	9 30	C	VIR	20
31	31	M.	6 59	D	4 57	A	9 58	2	17 s.13	2¾	3¼	11ᴾ27	D	9ᴬ50	C	VIR	21

JANUARY HATH 31 DAYS • 2005

Open the door, though the wild winds blow,
Take the child in and make him cozy.
Take him in and hold him dear,
He is the wonderful glad New Year. –Dinah Maria Mulock Craik

D. M.	D. W.	Dates, Feasts, Fasts, Aspects, Tide Heights	Weather ↓
1	Sa.	New Year's Day • **Holy Name** • ⊕ at perihelion • { 8.7 / 9.3	*Hands*
2	**B**	**2nd S. af. Ch.** • ☾ on Eq. • *From small beginnings come great things.*	*un-*
3	M.	☌♃☾ • George Washington defeated British in Battle of Princeton, N.J., 1777	*mittened*
4	Tu.	**St. Elizabeth Ann Seton** • ☾ at ☋ • Tides { 9.2 / 8.6 •	*get*
5	W.	Twelfth Night • Babe Ruth sold to New York Yankees, 1920 • { 9.6 / 8.6 •	*frost-*
6	Th.	**Epiphany** • Albany designated capital of N.Y., 1797 • Tides { 10.0 / 8.7	*bitten.*
7	Fr.	Distaff Day • ☌♂☾ • Galileo discovered first three moons of Jupiter, 1610 •	*Rays*
8	Sa.	☌☿☾ • ☌♀☾ • Lewis and Clark saw a 105-foot-long whale skeleton in NW Oregon, 1806	*of*
9	**B**	**1st S. af. Ep.** • ☾ runs low • Tides { 11.5 / 9.7 •	*sun*
10	M.	Plough Monday • **New** ● • ☾ at perig. • Florida seceded from the Union, 1861	*are*
11	Tu.	☌♆☾ • First discotheque opened, Los Angeles, 1963 • { 12.0 / — •	*inter-*
12	W.	John Hancock, first to sign Declaration of Independence, born, 1737 • { 10.2 / 11.9	*mittent,*
13	Th.	**St. Hilary** • ☌☿♀ • ☌♅☾ • ♄ at ☍ • { 10.4 / 11.6	*mixed*
14	Fr.	Astronomer Edmond Halley died, 1742 • Blizzard hit Chicago, 1918 • Tides { 10.4 / 11.1	*with*
15	Sa.	☾ on Eq. • *Trust the man who sings in his bathtub.* • Tides { 10.3 / 10.4	*swirly*
16	**B**	**2nd S. af. Ep.** • Tides { 10.1 / 9.7 •	*flurries*
17	M.	**Martin Luther King Jr.'s Birthday (observed)** • ☾ at ☊ • { 9.9 / 9.0	*spittin'.*
18	Tu.	*N.Y. Daily Mirror* columnist Walter Winchell debuted on radio, 1926 • Tides { 9.6 / 8.5 •	*For*
19	W.	Temperature dropped 50 degrees in Portsmouth, N.H., 1810 • Actress Jean Stapleton born, 1923	*man*
20	Th.	First major U.S. geology book debuted, 1809 • Tides { 9.4 / 8.1 •	*or*
21	Fr.	*To question a wise man is the beginning of wisdom.* • Tides { 9.4 / 8.1 •	*beast,*
22	Sa.	**St. Vincent** • President Lyndon B. Johnson died, 1973 • Tides { 9.5 / 8.3 •	*it's*
23	**B**	**Septuagesima** • ☾ rides high • ☾ at apo. • { 9.7 / 8.4	*hardly*
24	M.	☌♄☾ • Moving picture of a solar eclipse taken from dirigible over Long Island, 1925 •	*fittin',*
25	Tu.	**Conversion of Paul** • **Full Wolf** ○ • S.S. *City of Boston* disappeared, 1870 •	*but*
26	W.	**Sts. Timothy & Titus** • *Fog in January brings a wet spring.* • { 10.0 / — •	*it*
27	Th.	Author Lewis Carroll born, 1832 • Last performance of "Peter Pan" at N.Y.C.'s Imperial Theater, 1951	*shows*
28	Fr.	**St. Thomas Aquinas** • U.S. Coast Guard established, 1915 • Tides { 9.0 / 9.9	*no*
29	Sa.	Geologist William Edmond Logan became first Canadian-born knight, 1856 • { 9.1 / 9.7 •	*sign*
30	**B**	**Sexagesima** • ☾ on Eq. • Cellist Lynn Harrell born, 1944 • { 9.3 / 9.4	*of*
31	M.	☾ at ☋ • ☌♃☾ • Raccoons mate now. • { 9.4 / 9.1 •	*quittin'!*

Farmer's Calendar

■ In an age of many too many experts dispensing much too much wisdom, the modern weather report takes on some of the antique role of folklore. Forecasts on radio and TV, and in the daily papers, become the subjects of discussion and debate on their own, in place of the old weather signs. The latter we increasingly forget, if we're aware of them at all. Significant behavior on the part of squirrels, mice, and small birds; the many sky signs and cloud signs; the feel and direction of the wind—all these grow more and more obsolete as predictors. Today at the village store, you hear from your neighbor A, who tells you that the Boston news is predicting six inches of snow for tonight. Another, B, who listens to the White River station, announces that up there they are saying ten; and a third, C, contributes the report from St. Johnsbury, where a foot is down already.

It might seem that we have here yet another inevitable exchange of tradition and individual observation for a cold and charmless technology. Not necessarily, however. For anyone who still has a smattering of the old weather lore, modern meteorology may add to the satisfaction of reading nature's signs. When I see on an otherwise fairly clear night a ring of haze circling the Moon, I know that I can expect rain or snow on the morrow. I go indoors and turn on the radio. Lo and behold, there's the weatherman warning of the coming storm. So ancient wisdom isn't lost, but merely placed at a remove in the process of forecasting. It used to predict the weather. Now it predicts the prediction.

SKY WATCH ☆ *Venus and Mercury, last month's predawn performers, are now too close to the Sun to be seen. Mars, in Sagittarius all month, is still not very bright as it climbs higher in predawn twilight. Brilliant Jupiter is up in the east by 10:00 P.M. and out all night thereafter. Saturn is February's highlight world, nicely up in the northeast at nightfall and high overhead at 10:00 P.M., almost directly above blue-white Sirius, the only star that outshines the ringed world. The Moon hovers close to greenish Uranus on the 9th (binoculars needed), near Saturn on the 19th, and alongside Jupiter on the 26th. The year's brightest concentration of stars—centered on Orion—now hovers prominently high at nightfall.*

☾ Last Quarter	2nd day	2nd hour	27th minute
● New Moon	8th day	17th hour	28th minute
☽ First Quarter	15th day	19th hour	16th minute
○ Full Moon	23rd day	23rd hour	54th minute

Times are given in Eastern Standard Time.

For an explanation of this page, see page 176; for values of Key Letters, see page 235.

Day of Year	Day of Month	Day of Week	☼ Rises h. m.	Key	☼ Sets h. m.	Key	Length of Day h. m.	Sun Fast m.	Declination of Sun ° '	High Tide Boston Light—A.M. Bold—P.M.	☽ Rises h. m.	Key	☽ Sets h. m.	Key	Place	Age
32	1	Tu.	6 58	D	4 59	A	10 01	2	16 s. 56	3½ 4	—	–	10♈12	B	VIR	22
33	2	W.	6 57	D	5 00	A	10 03	2	16 38	4¼ 5	12♍38	E	10 39	B	LIB	23
34	3	Th.	6 55	D	5 01	A	10 06	2	16 21	5¼ 6	1 53	E	11 12	A	LIB	24
35	4	Fr.	6 54	D	5 02	A	10 08	2	16 03	6¼ 7	3 10	E	11♈55	A	SCO	25
36	5	Sa.	6 53	D	5 04	A	10 11	2	15 44	7¼ 8	4 24	E	12♍52	A	SAG	26
37	6	**B**	6 52	D	5 05	A	10 13	2	15 26	8¼ 9¼	5 29	E	2 03	A	SAG	27
38	7	M.	6 51	D	5 06	A	10 15	1	15 08	9¼ 10	6 23	E	3 24	B	SAG	28
39	8	Tu.	6 50	D	5 08	B	10 18	1	14 49	10¼ 11	7 04	E	4 48	B	CAP	0
40	9	W.	6 48	D	5 09	B	10 21	1	14 29	11¼ 11¾	7 37	E	6 10	C	AQU	1
41	10	Th.	6 47	D	5 10	B	10 23	1	14 10	12 —	8 03	D	7 28	D	AQU	2
42	11	Fr.	6 46	D	5 12	B	10 26	1	13 50	12¾ 1	8 27	D	8 43	D	AQU	3
43	12	Sa.	6 45	D	5 13	B	10 28	1	13 30	1½ 1¾	8 48	C	9 54	E	CET	4
44	13	**B**	6 43	D	5 14	B	10 31	1	13 09	2¼ 2¾	9 10	B	11♍05	E	PSC	5
45	14	M.	6 42	D	5 15	B	10 33	1	12 49	3 3½	9 33	B	—	–	ARI	6
46	15	Tu.	6 40	D	5 17	B	10 37	1	12 28	4 4½	9 59	A	12♈13	E	ARI	7
47	16	W.	6 39	D	5 18	B	10 39	1	12 07	4¾ 5½	10 30	A	1 21	E	TAU	8
48	17	Th.	6 38	D	5 19	B	10 41	2	11 46	5¾ 6½	11 08	A	2 26	E	TAU	9
49	18	Fr.	6 36	D	5 21	B	10 45	2	11 25	6¾ 7½	11♈53	A	3 25	E	TAU	10
50	19	Sa.	6 35	D	5 22	B	10 47	2	11 04	7¾ 8½	12♍45	A	4 18	E	AUR	11
51	20	**B**	6 33	D	5 23	B	10 50	2	10 42	8½ 9¼	1 44	A	5 03	E	GEM	12
52	21	M.	6 32	D	5 24	B	10 52	2	10 20	9½ 10	2 47	B	5 40	E	CAN	13
53	22	Tu.	6 30	D	5 26	B	10 56	2	9 58	10¼ 10¾	3 52	B	6 10	E	CAN	14
54	23	W.	6 29	D	5 27	B	10 58	2	9 36	10¾ 11¼	4 57	C	6 35	E	LEO	15
55	24	Th.	6 27	D	5 28	B	11 01	2	9 14	11½ 11¾	6 02	C	6 57	D	LEO	16
56	25	Fr.	6 26	D	5 29	B	11 03	2	8 52	12 —	7 07	D	7 17	D	LEO	17
57	26	Sa.	6 24	D	5 31	B	11 07	3	8 30	12½ 12¾	8 12	D	7 36	C	VIR	18
58	27	**B**	6 23	D	5 32	B	11 09	3	8 07	1 1¼	9 19	E	7 56	C	VIR	19
59	28	M.	6 21	D	5 33	B	11 12	3	7 s. 45	1½ 2	10♍29	E	8♈17	B	VIR	20

FEBRUARY HATH 28 DAYS • 2005

Snow in the country—snow in the town,
Silently, silently sinking down;
Everywhere, everywhere fast-falling snow,
Dazzling the eyes with its crystalline glow! –Jennie E. Haight

D. M.	D. W.	Dates, Feasts, Fasts, Aspects, Tide Heights	Weather ↓
1	Tu.	St. Brigid • First dental college incorporated, Baltimore, Md., 1840 • {9.5 / 8.8	*Mild,*
2	W.	Candlemas • Groundhog Day • ♃ stat. • Tides {9.6 / 8.5	*then*
3	Th.	☌♆☉ • *When life gives you scraps, make quilts.* • {9.8 / 8.4	*groundhog-*
4	Fr.	Ice storm hit Mass., N.H., and Maine, 1959 • Pianist Liberace died, 1987 • {10.0 / 8.4	*wild!*
5	Sa.	St. Agatha • ☌♂☾ • J. Witherspoon, N.J. delegate to Continental Congress, born, 1723	*It's*
6	**B**	Quinquagesima • ☾ runs low • Tides {10.8 / 9.2	*biting*
7	M.	☾ at perig. • Plow manufacturer John Deere born, 1804 • {11.3 / 9.7 •	*and*
8	Tu.	Shrove Tuesday • New ● • Tides {11.7 / 10.2 •	*whiting:*
9	W.	Ash Wednesday • Chinese New Year • {11.8 / 10.6	*Suddenly*
10	Th.	**Islamic New Year** • France ceded Canada to Great Britain, 1763 • Tides {11.8 / — •	*it's*
11	Fr.	☾ on Eq. • *I Love Lucy* won an Emmy for Best Situation Comedy, 1954 • {10.8 / 11.5	*inviting!*
12	Sa.	Gala carnival at first U.S. skating rink, Madison Square Garden, N.Y.C., 1879 • Tides {10.8 / 10.9	*Cover*
13	**B**	1st S. in Lent • ☾ at ☊ • *What the eyes see, the heart believes.* •	*up,*
14	M.	St. Valentine • Sts. Cyril & Methodius • ☌♆♀	*Cupid!*
15	Tu.	Susan B. Anthony born, 1820 • First mustard manufactured in U.S. advertised, 1768 • {9.9 / 8.7	*It's*
16	W.	Ember Day • Ventriloquist Edgar Bergen born, 1903 • Tides {9.4 / 8.2 •	*the*
17	Th.	Winter's back breaks. • National Congress of Mothers, later known as the PTA, founded, 1897	*windchill*
18	Fr.	Ember Day • Jefferson Davis inaugurated as provisional president of Confederate states, 1861	*factor,*
19	Sa.	Ember Day • ☾ rides high • Jockey Eddie Arcaro born, 1916 • {9.0 / 7.9	*stupid!*
20	**B**	2nd S. in Lent • ☾ at apo. • ☌♄☾ • {9.2 / 8.1	*The*
21	M.	**George Washington's Birthday (observed)** • Dedication of Washington Monument, 1885	*warmest*
22	Tu.	George Washington born, 1732 • Fistfight erupted in U.S. Senate, 1902 • {9.7 / 8.8	*place*
23	W.	**Full Snow** ○ • Liberty Bell developed final, irreparable crack, 1846 • Tides {9.9 / 9.1	*is*
24	Th.	St. Matthias • Thomas Edison married Mina Miller, 1886 •	*cyberspace.*
25	Fr.	☌♅☉ • First state tax on gasoline, Oreg., 1919 • {10.1 / — •	*Down-*
26	Sa.	☾ on Eq. • President Lincoln signed uniform currency bill, 1863 • {9.6 / 10.0 •	*loading*
27	**B**	3rd S. in Lent • ☾ at ☋ • ☌♃☾	*a coastal*
28	M.	43 inches of snow fell in Rochester, N.Y., 1900 • *February makes a bridge and March breaks it.*	*coating!*

Many a good argument is ruined by some fool who knows what he is talking about.
–Marshall McLuhan, Canadian philosopher (1911–1980)

Farmer's Calendar

■ I live in a very old house, and when it's cold outside, it's cold inside. Living in it takes a little extra doing then. You have to adapt to a cold house, just as you have to adapt to snow and ice outdoors. After a good many years in this place, I have learned the winter drill pretty well. I know which windows need newspapers stuffed around them against the draft, which rooms to close off, and which warm up on a sunny day. I become able to tell precisely how much more firewood we'll burn on a day of 5 below than on a day of 10 above. (Answer: disproportionately more.) The driver of the heating oil truck that delivers to this house owns four plaid shirts, and I get to know and admire each of them.

Some years, the kind of cold that imposes a way of life, even indoors, makes only a tentative, fleeting visit, but other years, it's in the game for real money. (Ask the oil man—or ask his boss.) Nights go down to 15, 20 below, and the cold endures for weeks. That kind of weather requires further adaptation. I put on a woolen watch cap. At first, I feel like a fool wearing a winter hat indoors. I feel like an extra in *On the Waterfront*. But the hat works. It keeps me warm. Soon, I forget I'm wearing it.

It's surprising how quickly and completely we learn the cold. After a week below zero, 20 feels balmy, and 30, like a heat wave. The watch cap comes off. The woodpile's daily dwindling slows. The oil man doesn't drop by as he used to. I kind of miss him.

THE THIRD MONTH • 2005

SKY WATCH ☆ *Everything meshes for Mercury as it offers its best display of the year. Straight above the sunset point in the faint constellation Pisces, it's the only "star" low in deepening twilight, 40 minutes after sunset. The Moon acts as guide on the 11th, floating just left of the broiling ruddy world. Mercury is most brilliant when it's on the far side of its orbit, during the first 10 days of the month. At nightfall, Jupiter is about to rise and Saturn stands high overhead. Saturn will remain visible most of the night and Jupiter all of the night. The Moon hovers near Saturn on the 18th and 19th, and near Jupiter on the 25th and 26th. Spring begins with the vernal equinox on the 20th, at 7:33 A.M. EST.*

☾ Last Quarter	3rd day	12th hour	36th minute
● New Moon	10th day	4th hour	10th minute
☽ First Quarter	17th day	14th hour	19th minute
○ Full Moon	25th day	15th hour	58th minute

Times are given in Eastern Standard Time.

For an explanation of this page, see page 176; for values of Key Letters, see page 235.

Day of Year	Day of Month	Day of Week	☀ Rises h. m.	Key	☀ Sets h. m.	Key	Length of Day h. m.	Sun Fast m.	Declination of Sun ° '	High Tide Boston Light—A.M. Bold—P.M.		☽ Rises h. m.	Key	☽ Sets h. m.	Key	Place	Age
60	1	Tu.	6 19	D	5 34	B	11 15	3	7 s. 22	2¼	2¾	11ᴹ42	E	8♎41	B	LIB	21
61	2	W.	6 18	D	5 35	B	11 17	3	6 59	3	3½	—	–	9 11	A	LIB	22
62	3	Th.	6 16	D	5 37	B	11 21	4	6 36	3¾	4½	12♎57	E	9 50	A	SCO	23
63	4	Fr.	6 14	D	5 38	B	11 24	4	6 13	4¾	5½	2 10	E	10 40	A	OPH	24
64	5	Sa.	6 13	D	5 39	B	11 26	4	5 50	6	6¾	3 17	E	11♎43	A	SAG	25
65	6	**B**	6 11	D	5 40	B	11 29	4	5 26	7	7¾	4 13	E	12ᴹ58	B	SAG	26
66	7	M.	6 10	D	5 41	B	11 31	4	5 03	8	9	4 58	E	2 18	B	CAP	27
67	8	Tu.	6 08	D	5 43	B	11 35	5	4 40	9¼	9¾	5 33	E	3 40	C	CAP	28
68	9	W.	6 06	D	5 44	B	11 38	5	4 16	10	10¾	6 02	D	5 00	C	AQU	29
69	10	Th.	6 04	D	5 45	B	11 41	5	3 53	11	11½	6 26	D	6 16	D	AQU	0
70	11	Fr.	6 03	D	5 46	B	11 43	5	3 29	11¾	—	6 48	C	7 30	E	PSC	1
71	12	Sa.	6 01	C	5 47	B	11 46	6	3 05	12¼	12½	7 10	C	8 43	E	PSC	2
72	13	**B**	5 59	C	5 49	B	11 50	6	2 42	1	1½	7 33	B	9 54	E	ARI	3
73	14	M.	5 58	C	5 50	B	11 52	6	2 18	1¾	2¼	7 58	B	11ᴹ05	E	ARI	4
74	15	Tu.	5 56	C	5 51	B	11 55	7	1 54	2½	3	8 28	A	—	–	TAU	5
75	16	W.	5 54	C	5 52	B	11 58	7	1 31	3¼	3¾	9 03	A	12♎12	E	TAU	6
76	17	Th.	5 52	C	5 53	B	12 01	7	1 07	4	4¾	9 45	A	1 16	E	TAU	7
77	18	Fr.	5 51	C	5 54	B	12 03	7	0 43	5	5¾	10 36	A	2 12	E	AUR	8
78	19	Sa.	5 49	C	5 56	B	12 07	8	0 s. 19	6	7	11ᴹ33	A	3 00	E	GEM	9
79	20	**B**	5 47	C	5 57	C	12 10	8	0 n. 04	7	7¾	12♎35	B	3 40	E	CAN	10
80	21	M.	5 46	C	5 58	C	12 12	8	0 28	8	8¾	1 39	B	4 12	E	CAN	11
81	22	Tu.	5 44	C	5 59	C	12 15	9	0 52	8¾	9½	2 44	C	4 39	E	LEO	12
82	23	W.	5 42	C	6 00	C	12 18	9	1 15	9½	10	3 50	C	5 02	D	LEO	13
83	24	Th.	5 40	C	6 01	C	12 21	9	1 39	10¼	10¾	4 55	D	5 22	D	LEO	14
84	25	Fr.	5 39	C	6 02	C	12 23	10	2 02	11	11¼	6 01	D	5 41	D	VIR	15
85	26	Sa.	5 37	C	6 03	C	12 26	10	2 26	11½	11¾	7 09	E	6 01	C	VIR	16
86	27	**B**	5 35	C	6 05	C	12 30	10	2 49	12¼	—	8 19	E	6 21	B	VIR	17
87	28	M.	5 33	C	6 06	C	12 33	10	3 13	12½	1	9 32	E	6 45	B	VIR	18
88	29	Tu.	5 32	C	6 07	C	12 35	11	3 36	1	1¾	10ᴹ47	E	7 13	A	LIB	19
89	30	W.	5 30	C	6 08	C	12 38	11	3 59	1¾	2½	—	–	7 49	A	SCO	20
90	31	Th.	5 28	C	6 09	C	12 41	11	4 n. 23	2½	3¼	12♎02	E	8♎35	A	OPH	21

MARCH HATH 31 DAYS • 2005

Again rejoicing Nature sees
Her robe assume its vernal hues,
Her leafy locks wave in the breeze,
All freshly steep'd in morning dews. –Robert Burns

D. M.	D. W.	Dates, Feasts, Fasts, Aspects, Tide Heights	Weather ↓
1	Tu.	St. David • *All is not butter that comes from the cow.* • {10.0 / 9.2 •	*Beware!*
2	W.	St. Chad • Martha Washington Hotel, for women only, opened in N.Y.C., 1903 •	*This*
3	Th.	Anne Mansfield Sullivan began teaching deaf/blind Helen Keller, 1887 • {10.0 / 8.5	*month*
4	Fr.	*Every man knows best where his own shoe pinches.* • Tides {9.9 / 8.4 •	*comes*
5	Sa.	St. Piran • ☾ runs low • Boston Massacre, 1770 • Tides {10.0 / 8.4	*in*
6	**B**	4th S. in Lent • ☌♂☾ • {10.2 / 8.8	*like*
7	M.	St. Perpetua • ☾ at perig. • ☌♆☾ • Tides {10.6 / 9.4 •	*a*
8	Tu.	Supreme Court justice Oliver Wendell Holmes Jr. born, 1841 • Tides {11.0 / 10.0 •	*polar*
9	W.	Battle of U.S.S. *Monitor* and U.S.S. *Merrimack* (renamed C.S.S. *Virginia*) ended in draw, 1862 • {11.3 / 10.5	*bear!*
10	Th.	New ● • Thomas Jefferson became U.S. minister to France, 1785 • {11.5 / 10.9	*Some*
11	Fr.	☾ on Eq. • ☌☿☾ • N.Y. Public Library co-architect Thomas Hastings born, 1860	*relief,*
12	Sa.	St. Gregory the Great • ☾ at ☊ • ☿ Gr. Elong. (18° E.) • {11.1 / 11.0	*but*
13	**B**	5th S. in Lent • Harvard University renamed for clergyman John Harvard, 1639	*all*
14	M.	**Pure Monday** • Warren Harding became first U.S. president to file income tax return, 1923 •	*too*
15	Tu.	Beware the ides of March. • Dr. Wallace E. Howell was hired by N.Y.C. to make rain, 1950 •	*brief—*
16	W.	Norman Thagard became first American to visit Russian space station *Mir*, 1995 • {9.8 / 8.6 •	*don't*
17	Th.	St. Patrick • British forces evacuated Boston, 1776 • {9.3 / 8.0 •	*put*
18	Fr.	☾ rides high • Single tornado struck Mo., Ill., and Ind., killing 695 people, 1925 • {8.9 / 7.8	*away*
19	Sa.	St. Joseph • ☾ at apo. • ☌♄☾ • ☿ stat. • {8.7 / 7.7	*that*
20	**B**	Palm Sunday • **Sunday of Orthodoxy** • **Vernal Equinox**	*shovel,*
21	M.	♄ stat. • *In spring, no one thinks of the snow that fell last year.* • Tides {9.0 / 8.3	*chief!*
22	Tu.	Elisha Graves Otis installed first commercial passenger elevator, in N.Y.C. store, 1857 • {9.3 / 8.7	*Next*
23	W.	Edmonton, Alberta, reached a toasty 22.2°C (72°F), 1889 • Tides {9.6 / 9.1 •	*in*
24	Th.	Maundy Thursday • Singer Elvis Presley inducted into Army, 1958 • {9.8 / 9.6	*line:*
25	Fr.	Good Friday • **Full Worm** ○ • ☾ on Eq. • {10.0 / 9.9	*heavy*
26	Sa.	☌♃☾ • Poet Walt Whitman died, 1892 • Tides {10.1 / 10.2 •	*rains.*
27	**B**	Easter • ☾ at ☋ • ♇ stat. • Tides {10.0 / —	*Better*
28	M.	Easter Monday • *Better give a penny than lend twenty.* • Tides {10.5 / 9.9	*unclog*
29	Tu.	☿ in inf. ☌ • Vesta, brightest asteroid, discovered, 1807 • {10.6 / 9.6	*those*
30	W.	♀ in sup. ☌ • Official opening of Canada's first subway (Toronto), 1954 • {10.6 / 9.3	*storm*
31	Th.	Daylight Saving Time observed for first time in U.S., 1918 • Tides {10.5 / 9.0 •	*drains!*

Farmer's Calendar

■ Went to Town Meeting last year. Wished I hadn't. American democracy in its purest form is frightening stuff.

The meeting itself wasn't the problem. The usual crowd did the usual business with the usual expedition, coffee and doughnuts provided by the Ladies' Aid. But then, the next day, I read the account of our meeting in the local newspaper. "Herman Bond spoke in favor of the article authorizing the Town to purchase a new dump truck," I read. That sounds harmless enough, except that it wasn't Herman who spoke, it was Arthur Hemingway; and Arthur didn't speak in favor of the article, he spoke against it. I know all this because— remember— I was there. Hence my distress.

So often, when we read news reports of events that we ourselves have witnessed, we find that the reports get these events more or less wrong— and if this happens in the small affairs that we have direct knowledge of, why not in the large affairs of the nation and world? Are press accounts of them full of error, too? There's no reason to think otherwise.

American democracy depends on informed deliberation by its citizens. Ensuring that the people are informed on the issues of their time, so that their deliberations can have some measure of confidence and intelligence, is the job of the nation's press. But if reporting by the press on the crucial issues should be as faulty as we discover it to be on the noncrucial ones, then isn't the journey of our democracy a ride to who knows where? It remains for us to hang on tight.

THE FOURTH MONTH • 2005

SKY WATCH ☆ *This is Jupiter's month, as it reaches opposition in Virgo on the 3rd. Now rising at sunset, the night's very brightest "star" at magnitude –2.5 dominates the southeast before positioning itself halfway up the southern sky at midnight. Saturn is high up at nightfall and then slowly sinks into the west, setting by 2:00 A.M. Mars, now in Capricornus, is still a predawn object in the east but is slowly brightening; it's near the Moon on the 4th. A total solar eclipse on the 8th, visible only in the South Pacific, will appear as a partial solar eclipse in the southern half of the United States. Venus is invisible behind the Sun; Mercury is a morning star not worth the bother.*

☾	Last Quarter	1st day	19th hour	50th minute
●	New Moon	8th day	16th hour	32nd minute
☽	First Quarter	16th day	10th hour	37th minute
○	Full Moon	24th day	6th hour	6th minute

After 2:00 A.M. on April 3, Eastern Daylight Time (EDT) is given.

For an explanation of this page, see page 176; for values of Key Letters, see page 235.

Day of Year	Day of Month	Day of Week	☼ Rises h. m.	Key	☼ Sets h. m.	Key	Length of Day h. m.	Sun Fast m.	Declination of Sun ° '	High Tide Boston Light—A.M.	Bold—P.M.	☽ Rises h. m.	Key	☽ Sets h. m.	Key	☽ Place	☽ Age
91	1	Fr.	5 26	B	6 10	C	12 44	12	4 N.46	3½	**4¼**	1 A.M. 11	E	9 A.M. 34	A	SAG	22
92	2	Sa.	5 25	B	6 11	C	12 46	12	5 09	4½	**5½**	2 09	E	10 A.M. 44	A	SAG	23
93	3	**B**	6 23	B	7 12	C	12 49	12	5 32	6¾	**7½**	3 56	E	1 P.M. 01	B	CAP	24
94	4	M.	6 21	B	7 14	C	12 53	13	5 55	7¾	**8½**	4 33	E	2 20	B	CAP	25
95	5	Tu.	6 20	B	7 15	D	12 55	13	6 18	9	**9½**	5 03	E	3 38	C	AQU	26
96	6	W.	6 18	B	7 16	D	12 58	13	6 40	10	**10½**	5 28	D	4 54	D	AQU	27
97	7	Th.	6 16	B	7 17	D	13 01	13	7 03	10¾	**11¼**	5 50	D	6 07	D	PSC	28
98	8	Fr.	6 15	B	7 18	D	13 03	14	7 26	11¾	—	6 12	C	7 20	E	PSC	0
99	9	Sa.	6 13	B	7 19	D	13 06	14	7 48	12	**12½**	6 34	B	8 32	E	PSC	1
100	10	**B**	6 11	B	7 20	D	13 09	14	8 10	12¾	**1¼**	6 58	B	9 44	E	ARI	2
101	11	M.	6 10	B	7 22	D	13 12	14	8 32	1½	**2**	7 25	B	10 P.M. 54	E	ARI	3
102	12	Tu.	6 08	B	7 23	D	13 15	15	8 54	2¼	**2¾**	7 58	A	—	–	TAU	4
103	13	W.	6 06	B	7 24	D	13 18	15	9 16	2¾	**3½**	8 38	A	12 A.M. 01	E	TAU	5
104	14	Th.	6 05	B	7 25	D	13 20	15	9 38	3¾	**4¼**	9 26	A	1 02	E	AUR	6
105	15	Fr.	6 03	B	7 26	D	13 23	15	9 59	4½	**5¼**	10 21	A	1 54	E	GEM	7
106	16	Sa.	6 01	B	7 27	D	13 26	16	10 20	5½	**6¼**	11 A.M. 21	A	2 37	E	GEM	8
107	17	**B**	6 00	B	7 28	D	13 28	16	10 41	6¼	**7¼**	12 P.M. 25	B	3 12	E	CAN	9
108	18	M.	5 58	B	7 29	D	13 31	16	11 02	7¼	**8**	1 29	B	3 41	E	LEO	10
109	19	Tu.	5 57	B	7 31	D	13 34	16	11 23	8¼	**9**	2 34	C	4 05	E	LEO	11
110	20	W.	5 55	B	7 32	D	13 37	17	11 43	9¼	**9¾**	3 39	D	4 26	D	LEO	12
111	21	Th.	5 54	B	7 33	D	13 39	17	12 03	10	**10¼**	4 45	D	4 45	D	VIR	13
112	22	Fr.	5 52	B	7 34	D	13 42	17	12 24	10¾	**11**	5 52	D	5 05	C	VIR	14
113	23	Sa.	5 51	B	7 35	D	13 44	17	12 43	11½	**11½**	7 02	E	5 25	C	VIR	15
114	24	**B**	5 49	B	7 36	D	13 47	17	13 03	**12**	—	8 16	E	5 47	B	VIR	16
115	25	M.	5 48	B	7 37	D	13 49	18	13 23	12¼	**12¾**	9 32	E	6 14	B	LIB	17
116	26	Tu.	5 46	B	7 38	D	13 52	18	13 42	1	**1½**	10 P.M. 49	E	6 48	A	SCO	18
117	27	W.	5 45	B	7 40	D	13 55	18	14 01	1¾	**2¼**	—	–	7 31	A	SCO	19
118	28	Th.	5 43	B	7 41	D	13 58	18	14 20	2½	**3¼**	12 A.M. 02	E	8 27	A	SAG	20
119	29	Fr.	5 42	B	7 42	D	14 00	18	14 39	3¼	**4¼**	1 05	E	9 34	A	SAG	21
120	30	Sa.	5 41	B	7 43	D	14 02	18	14 N.57	4¼	**5¼**	1 A.M. 56	E	10 A.M. 50	B	SAG	22

APRIL HATH 30 DAYS • 2005

Gladness is born of the April weather,
And the heart is as light as a wind-tossed feather.
Who could be sad on a day like this?
The care that vexed us no longer is. –Eben Eugene Rexford

D. M.	D. W.	Dates, Feasts, Fasts, Aspects, Tide Heights	Weather ↓
1	Fr.	All Fools' • ☾ runs low • *Trouble rides a fast horse.* • Tides {10.3 / 8.7	*Fools*
2	Sa.	*American Farmer* journal founded, 1819 • Tap dancer Charles "Honi" Coles born, 1911 •	*slush*
3	**B**	☌♂☾ • ♃ at ☍ • **Daylight Saving Time begins, 2:00 A.M.** • {10.0 / 8.8 •	*in*
4	M.	Annunciation • ☾ at perig. • ☌♆☾ • {10.1 / 9.2 •	*where*
5	Tu.	☌♅☾ • New York Chamber of Commerce formed, 1768 • Tides {10.4 / 9.8	*angels*
6	W.	U.S. entered World War I by declaring war on Germany, 1917 • Tides {10.6 / 10.4 •	*hover.*
7	Th.	☾ on Eq. • ☌☿☾ • *The fiddle makes the feast.* • {10.8 / 10.8	*Hallelujah!*
8	Fr.	**New ● • Eclipse ☉** • ☾ at ☊ • {10.9 / —	*Winter's*
9	Sa.	First baseball game in Houston Astrodome, 1965 • Tides {11.1 / 10.7 •	*over!*
10	**B**	**3rd S. of Easter** • ☿ stat. • Tides {11.2 / 10.4 •	*It's*
11	M.	First Easter Egg roll at the White House, 1878 • Circus showman James A. Bailey died, 1906 •	*been*
12	Tu.	☌♂♆ • Dr. Peter Safer, originator of C.P.R., born, 1924 • Tides {10.7 / 9.5 •	*so*
13	W.	Thomas Jefferson born, 1743 • *Plough deep and you will have plenty of corn.* • {10.3 / 9.0	*rotten,*
14	Th	☾ rides high • President William H. Taft threw a pitch to open the baseball season, 1910 •	*we've*
15	Fr.	☌♄☾ • Last day U.S. silver coins allowed to circulate in Canada, 1870 • {9.3 / 8.1	*almost*
16	Sa.	☾ at apo. • Annie Oakley hit 100 clay targets in a row, setting women's record, 1922	*forgotten*
17	**B**	**4th S. of Easter** • Tides {8.8 / 8.0 •	*skies*
18	M.	Lighted fishing pole patented, 1978 • Strong earthquake hit San Francisco, 1906 • {8.8 / 8.2	*of*
19	Tu.	Spring peepers heard in Dublin, N.H., 1941 • John C. Miles won Boston Marathon, 1926 • {8.9 / 8.6	*blue*
20	W.	George Clinton became first U.S. vice president to die in office, 1812 • Tides {9.1 / 9.0 •	*and*
21	Th.	☾ on Eq. • *David Dows,* largest five-masted schooner of its time, launched, 1881 • {9.4 / 9.6	*clouds*
22	Fr.	☌♃☾ • Symphony Society of N.Y. began first European tour by U.S. orchestra, 1920 •	*like*
23	Sa.	St. George • ☾ at ☋ • Tides {9.8 / 10.5 •	*cotton!*
24	**B**	**First day of Passover** • **Full Pink ○** • **Eclipse ☾** • Robert B. Thomas born, 1766 •	
25	M.	St. Mark • N.Y. first state to require auto license plates, 1901 • Tides {10.8 / 10.0	*Even a*
26	Tu.	☿ Gr. Elong. (27° W.) • *Every path has its puddle.* • Tides {11.1 / 9.9 •	*shower*
27	W.	Arbor Day founder Julius Sterling Morton died, 1902 • Shad bush blooms now. • {11.1 / 9.7	*can't*
28	Th.	☾ runs low • Ethel Catherwood, Olympic gold-medal winner in 1928 for high jump, born, 1909 •	*make*
29	Fr.	☾ at perig. • Weather device TOTO hit by weak tornado, 1984 • Tides {10.9 / 9.2	*us*
30	Sa.	Law passed to have name of Boulder Dam restored to Hoover Dam, 1947 • {10.6 / 9.1 •	*glower!*

There is no genius without a mixture of madness.
–Seneca, the Younger, Roman philosopher

Farmer's Calendar

■ On the famous 18th of April in 1775—230 years ago—the British infantry marched west out of Boston to seize a cache of arms they believed rebellious colonists had collected at Concord. A couple of hours ahead of them rode Paul Revere, a Boston silversmith and political activist, who warned the countryside of the armed approach that precipitated the violent beginning of the American adventure in nationhood.

Also on the road that night, and on the same mission as the immortal Revere, were the considerably less immortal William Dawes and Samuel Prescott. Dawes was a tanner, then about age 30; Prescott, a few years younger. Both had ridden from Boston as well to warn of the British approach. In fact, according to a recent history of those extraordinary days, there were a good dozen riders giving the alarm that night. And a good thing it was, too, for Revere and Dawes didn't spread word of the British sortie very far. Only Prescott made it all the way to Concord, which had been the original objective of all.

It is the nature of history, when studied with care, to prove that human events are seldom as simple as we've been told, and to show that the heroic acts of legend, drama, and patriotic verse are never quite the whole story. Paul Revere was not one man, but many. We ought not to be downhearted, however, for that fact does not for a moment diminish the event or impair its high drama and momentous importance. Let yourself be swept up by the excitement. Enjoy the game, but know the score.

THE FIFTH MONTH • 2005

SKY WATCH ☆ *Jupiter continues to blaze brilliantly nearly all night long. It is closely joined by the Moon on the 19th in a fine conjunction. Saturn floats well up in the west at nightfall and sets around midnight. Venus, in Taurus, now slowly reemerges as an evening star, extremely low in the west a half hour after sunset; the thin crescent Moon floats alongside it on the 8th. In the postmidnight shift, Mars, now in dim Aquarius, hovers next to Uranus from the 14th to the 17th; use binoculars to view the orange-and-green planetary combo. The Moon joins Mars on the 31st.*

☾	Last Quarter	1st day	2nd hour	24th minute
●	New Moon	8th day	4th hour	45th minute
☽	First Quarter	16th day	4th hour	57th minute
○	Full Moon	23rd day	16th hour	18th minute
☾	Last Quarter	30th day	7th hour	47th minute

Times are given in Eastern Daylight Time.

For an explanation of this page, see page 176; for values of Key Letters, see page 235.

Day of Year	Day of Month	Day of Week	Rises h. m.	Key	Sets h. m.	Key	Length of Day h. m.	Sun Fast m.	Declination of Sun ° '	High Tide Boston Light—A.M. **Bold—P.M.**		Rises h. m.	Key	Sets h. m.	Key	Place	Age
121	1	**B**	5 39	B	7 44	D	14 05	18	15 N.15	5½	6¼	2♈36	E	12 M08	B	CAP	23
122	2	M.	5 38	B	7 45	D	14 07	19	15 33	6½	7¼	3 07	E	1 25	C	AQU	24
123	3	Tu.	5 37	B	7 46	D	14 09	19	15 51	7½	8¼	3 32	D	2 40	D	AQU	25
124	4	W.	5 35	A	7 47	D	14 12	19	16 08	8¾	9¼	3 55	D	3 53	D	AQU	26
125	5	Th.	5 34	A	7 48	D	14 14	19	16 25	9¾	10	4 16	C	5 04	D	CET	27
126	6	Fr.	5 33	A	7 49	D	14 16	19	16 42	10½	11	4 37	B	6 15	E	PSC	28
127	7	Sa.	5 32	A	7 51	D	14 19	19	16 58	11½	11½	4 59	B	7 25	E	ARI	29
128	8	**B**	5 30	A	7 52	D	14 22	19	17 15	12¼	—	5 25	B	8 36	E	ARI	0
129	9	M.	5 29	A	7 53	D	14 24	19	17 31	12¼	1	5 55	A	9 45	E	TAU	1
130	10	Tu.	5 28	A	7 54	D	14 26	19	17 46	1	1¾	6 32	A	10 49	E	TAU	2
131	11	W.	5 27	A	7 55	D	14 28	19	18 02	1¾	2¼	7 17	A	11 M45	E	TAU	3
132	12	Th.	5 26	A	7 56	D	14 30	19	18 17	2½	3	8 10	A	—	—	AUR	4
133	13	Fr.	5 25	A	7 57	D	14 32	19	18 32	3¼	3¾	9 08	A	12 M32	E	GEM	5
134	14	Sa.	5 24	A	7 58	D	14 34	19	18 46	4	4¾	10 11	B	1 10	E	CAN	6
135	15	**B**	5 23	A	7 59	E	14 36	19	19 00	4¾	5½	11♈15	B	1 41	E	CAN	7
136	16	M.	5 22	A	8 00	E	14 38	19	19 14	5¾	6½	12 P19	C	2 07	E	LEO	8
137	17	Tu.	5 21	A	8 01	E	14 40	19	19 28	6½	7¼	1 23	C	2 29	D	LEO	9
138	18	W.	5 20	A	8 02	E	14 42	19	19 41	7½	8	2 28	D	2 49	D	LEO	10
139	19	Th.	5 19	A	8 03	E	14 44	19	19 53	8½	8¾	3 33	D	3 08	C	VIR	11
140	20	Fr.	5 18	A	8 04	E	14 46	19	20 06	9¼	9½	4 41	E	3 27	C	VIR	12
141	21	Sa.	5 17	A	8 05	E	14 48	19	20 18	10	10¼	5 53	E	3 48	B	VIR	13
142	22	**B**	5 16	A	8 06	E	14 50	19	20 30	10¾	11	7 09	E	4 13	B	LIB	14
143	23	M.	5 15	A	8 07	E	14 52	19	20 41	11¾	11¾	8 28	E	4 44	A	LIB	15
144	24	Tu.	5 15	A	8 08	E	14 53	19	20 53	12½	—	9 45	E	5 24	A	SCO	16
145	25	W.	5 14	A	8 09	E	14 55	19	21 03	12½	1¼	10 55	E	6 16	A	OPH	17
146	26	Th.	5 13	A	8 10	E	14 57	19	21 14	1¼	2	11 P52	E	7 21	A	SAG	18
147	27	Fr.	5 13	A	8 11	E	14 58	19	21 24	2¼	3	—	—	8 36	B	SAG	19
148	28	Sa.	5 12	A	8 11	E	14 59	18	21 33	3¼	4	12♈36	B	9 56	B	CAP	20
149	29	**B**	5 11	A	8 12	E	15 01	18	21 42	4¼	5	1 10	E	11♈15	C	CAP	21
150	30	M.	5 11	A	8 13	E	15 02	18	21 51	5¼	6	1 37	D	12 M31	C	AQU	22
151	31	Tu.	5 10	A	8 14	E	15 04	18	22 N.00	6¼	7	2♈00	D	1 P44	D	AQU	23

MAY HATH 31 DAYS • 2005

I think if you listen closely
In the sweet glad days of spring,
With the song of the brook, the breeze, and the birds,
You can hear the flowers sing. –Helen Isabel Moorhouse

D. M.	D. W.	Dates, Feasts, Fasts, Aspects, Tide Heights	Weather ↓
1	B	**Rogation S.** • **Orthodox Easter** • **May Day** • ☌♆☾	*In*
2	M.	**Sts. Philip & James** • ☌♂☾ • Tides { 10.1 / 9.4 •	*gentle*
3	Tu.	**Invention of the Holy Cross** • ☌♅☾ • Tides { 10.0 / 9.8 •	*mist*
4	W.	☾ on Eq. • *Always put the saddle on the right horse.* • Tides { 10.1 / 10.2 •	*the*
5	Th.	**Ascension** • **Cinco de Mayo** • Flash flood in Fort Worth, Tex., 1995 •	*tulips*
6	Fr.	☌☿☾ • ☾ at ☊ • *Hindenburg* exploded, 1937 • { 10.2 / 10.9	*glisten,*
7	Sa.	Wagon-mounted fire escape ladder patented, 1878 • First inaugural ball, 1789 •	*jonquils*
8	B	**1st S. af. Asc.** • **New ●** • Tides { 10.0 / — •	*glow,*
9	M.	**St. Gregory of Nazianzus** • *No weather is ill if the wind is still.* • { 11.0 / 9.7	*and*
10	Tu.	Mother's Day first celebrated in Grafton, W.Va., and Philadelphia, Pa., 1908 • { 10.8 / 9.5 •	*listen!*
11	W.	Sheila Burnford, author of *The Incredible Journey*, born, 1918 • Tides { 10.5 / 9.1 • **Three**	*As*
12	Th.	☾ rides high • Charles Sherrill first demonstrated a crouching start for sprinters, 1888 • **Chilly**	*the*
13	Fr.	☌♄☾ • Cyrus Hall McCormick, inventor of a reaper, died, 1884 • **Saints**	*earth*
14	Sa.	☾ at apo. • ☌♂♅ • First manned U.S. space station launched, 1973 • { 9.4 / 8.4 •	*at*
15	B	**Whit S.** • **Pentecost** • Tides { 9.1 / 8.3 •	*last*
16	M.	*When fortune knocks upon the door, open it widely.* • Tides { 8.9 / 8.4 •	*unhardens,*
17	Tu.	Senate Watergate Committee began public hearings, 1973 • Tides { 8.8 / 8.6 •	*roto-*
18	W.	Ember Day • TWA was first airline to fly the Douglas DC-2 aircraft, 1934 • { 8.8 / 9.0	*tillers*
19	Th.	**St. Dunstan** • ☾ on Eq. • ☌♃☾ • ♆ stat. • { 9.0 / 9.4	*knead*
20	Fr.	Ember Day • ☾ at ☋ • First Lady Dolley Madison born, 1768 • { 9.1 / 9.9 •	*the*
21	Sa.	Ember Day • James Gladstone, first Canadian aboriginal senator, born, 1887 • { 9.4 / 10.4	*gardens.*
22	B	**Trinity** • Train of 100-plus wagons left Independence, Mo., for Oregon, 1843 •	*Lilacs*
23	M.	**Vesak** • **Victoria Day (Canada)** • **Full Flower ○** • Tides { 9.7 / 11.3 •	*lift*
24	Tu.	Canada's first medical graduate awarded degree by McGill University, 1833 • Tides { 9.8 / —	*their*
25	W.	**St. Bede** • Tornado leveled Udall, Kans., 83 lives lost, 1955 • Tides { 11.5 / 9.9	*purple*
26	Th.	☾ runs low • ☾ at perig. • *A bird in the hand is messy.* • { 11.6 / 9.8 •	*arches*
27	Fr.	Frontiersman "Wild Bill" Hickok born, 1837 • Tides { 11.5 / 9.7 •	*over*
28	Sa.	☌♆☾ • *On With the Show* debuted in N.Y.C., first all-color talking picture, 1929 •	*the*
29	B	**Corpus Christi** • Ocean liner *Empress of Ireland* sank, 1914 •	*Memorial*
30	M.	**Memorial Day (observed)** • ☌♅☾ • Aviator Wilbur Wright died of typhoid fever, 1912	*Day*
31	Tu.	**Visit. of Mary** • ☌♂☾ • Tides { 10.1 / 9.9 •	*marchers.*

Farmer's Calendar

■ *May Day.* High time to start preparing the vegetable patch for this year's planting. I pick up the long-handled spade and set out up the hill to the garden. The brown earth, hummocked and heaved by months of frost, looks reluctant to be tilled, but I stick in the spade and begin to make a row. Soon I am well into the task: thrust, lever, lift, turn. Presently, the familiar aches and pains of middle age associated with spring work make themselves felt—as contrasted with the equally familiar, but quite distinctive, aches and pains of summer, fall, and winter work. How do the young do it? To work all day without a stitch, without a twinge? It can't be easy.

Time for a break. I look around the garden. A chickadee is busily making a nest in a little hole in one of the old locust posts that hold the garden fence. Not a good idea, perhaps. The hole is the right size and height, but it looks southwest. By August, the sun will beat on that post all afternoon. Those chickadees will find that they have built a very hot nursery. Perhaps the little ones will be gone by then.

I spot some green sprigs at the bottom of the garden. They're carrot tops. Last year the snow came early, and these carrots never got harvested. I pull them up. For some reason, my carrots don't do the way a carrot ought to do. They have arms and legs, whiskers and tentacles. They look less like carrots than like some kind of odd, orange creature of the sea bottom. Here in landlocked Vermont, in a garden far—very far—above the tide line, has appeared a school of gaudy vegetable squid.

SKY WATCH ☆ *Mercury, by midmonth, becomes a very low evening star right after sunset. A bit higher up, Venus improves while crossing into Gemini. The Moon joins it on the 7th, forms a triangle with Venus and Saturn on the 8th, floats alongside Saturn on the 9th, is near Jupiter on the 15th, and joins brightening Mars in the early hours of the 29th. A super three-way meeting of Mercury, Venus, and Saturn happens 30 to 60 minutes after sunset on the 24th, low in the west. Venus and Mercury get even closer together on the 25th, and on the 26th they seem to merge into one dazzling "star," with Saturn just below. Summer arrives with the solstice on the 21st, at 2:46 A.M. EDT.*

● New Moon	6th day	17th hour	55th minute
☽ First Quarter	14th day	21st hour	22nd minute
○ Full Moon	22nd day	0 hour	14th minute
☾ Last Quarter	28th day	14th hour	23rd minute

Times are given in Eastern Daylight Time.

For an explanation of this page, see page 176; for values of Key Letters, see page 235.

Day of Year	Day of Month	Day of Week	☼ Rises h. m.	Key	☼ Sets h. m.	Key	Length of Day h. m.	Sun Fast m.	Declination of Sun ° '	High Tide Boston Light—A.M. Bold—P.M.	☽ Rises h. m.	Key	☽ Sets h. m.	Key	Place	Age
152	1	W.	5 10	A	8 15	E	15 05	18	22 N.08	7¼ 8	2♑21	C	2♏54	D	PSC	24
153	2	Th.	5 09	A	8 15	E	15 06	18	22 16	8½ 8¾	2 42	B	4 04	E	PSC	25
154	3	Fr.	5 09	A	8 16	E	15 07	18	22 23	9¼ 9¾	3 04	B	5 13	E	ARI	26
155	4	Sa.	5 09	A	8 17	E	15 08	17	22 30	10¼ 10½	3 28	B	6 23	E	ARI	27
156	5	**B**	5 08	A	8 17	E	15 09	17	22 36	11 11¼	3 56	A	7 32	E	TAU	28
157	6	M.	5 08	A	8 18	E	15 10	17	22 42	12 —	4 30	A	8 37	E	TAU	0
158	7	Tu.	5 08	A	8 19	E	15 11	17	22 48	12 12½	5 12	A	9 36	E	TAU	1
159	8	W.	5 07	A	8 19	E	15 12	17	22 54	12½ 1¼	6 01	A	10 27	E	AUR	2
160	9	Th.	5 07	A	8 20	E	15 13	16	22 59	1¼ 2	6 58	A	11 08	E	GEM	3
161	10	Fr.	5 07	A	8 21	E	15 14	16	23 04	2 2¾	8 00	A	11♏42	E	CAN	4
162	11	Sa.	5 07	A	8 21	E	15 14	16	23 08	2¾ 3½	9 04	B	—	—	CAN	5
163	12	**B**	5 07	A	8 22	E	15 15	16	23 11	3½ 4¼	10 07	B	12♏09	D	LEO	6
164	13	M.	5 07	A	8 22	E	15 15	16	23 15	4¼ 5	11♏11	C	12 32	D	LEO	7
165	14	Tu.	5 07	A	8 22	E	15 15	15	23 17	5 5¾	12♏14	C	12 52	D	LEO	8
166	15	W.	5 07	A	8 23	E	15 16	15	23 20	6 6½	1 17	D	1 11	C	VIR	9
167	16	Th.	5 07	A	8 23	E	15 16	15	23 22	6¾ 7¼	2 22	D	1 30	C	VIR	10
168	17	Fr.	5 07	A	8 24	E	15 17	15	23 24	7¾ 8	3 31	E	1 49	C	VIR	11
169	18	Sa.	5 07	A	8 24	E	15 17	15	23 25	8½ 8¾	4 44	E	2 12	B	VIR	12
170	19	**B**	5 07	A	8 24	E	15 17	14	23 26	9½ 9¾	6 01	E	2 39	B	LIB	13
171	20	M.	5 07	A	8 24	E	15 17	14	23 26	10¼ 10½	7 20	E	3 14	A	SCO	14
172	21	Tu.	5 07	A	8 25	E	15 18	14	23 26	11¼ 11¼	8 34	E	4 00	A	OPH	15
173	22	W.	5 08	A	8 25	E	15 17	14	23 25	12 —	9 39	E	5 01	A	SAG	16
174	23	Th.	5 08	A	8 25	E	15 17	14	23 25	12¼ 1	10 30	E	6 14	A	SAG	17
175	24	Fr.	5 08	A	8 25	E	15 17	13	23 24	1 1¾	11 09	E	7 36	B	CAP	18
176	25	Sa.	5 09	A	8 25	E	15 16	13	23 23	2 2¾	11♏39	E	8 58	B	CAP	19
177	26	**B**	5 09	A	8 25	E	15 16	13	23 21	3 3¾	—	—	10 18	C	AQU	20
178	27	M.	5 09	A	8 25	E	15 16	13	23 18	4 4¾	12♏04	D	11♏33	D	AQU	21
179	28	Tu.	5 10	A	8 25	E	15 15	12	23 15	5 5½	12 26	C	12♏46	D	PSC	22
180	29	W.	5 10	A	8 25	E	15 15	12	23 12	6 6½	12 47	C	1 56	E	PSC	23
181	30	Th.	5 11	A	8 25	E	15 14	12	23 N.08	7 7½	1♏09	B	3♏06	E	PSC	24

C A L E N D A R

JUNE HATH 30 DAYS • 2005

Fair and green is the marsh in June;
Wide and warm in the sunny noon.
The flowering rushes fringe the pool
With slender shadows, dim and cool. –Antoinette Alcott Bassett

D. M.	D. W.	Dates, Feasts, Fasts, Aspects, Tide Heights	Weather ↓
1	W.	☾ on Eq. • Invention of photosensitive glass announced, 1947 • { 9.8 10.2	*Butterflies*
2	Th.	☾ at ☊ • Swimming pool formally accepted as addition to White House, 1933 • { 9.6 10.4	*flutter*
3	Fr.	☿ in sup. ☌ • Automobile manufacturer Ransom Eli Olds born, 1864 • { 9.5 10.6 •	*and*
4	Sa.	*The ambitious bullfrog puffed and puffed until he burst.* • { 9.4 10.7 •	*bumblebees*
5	**B**	**3rd S. af. P.** • ♃ stat. • Tides { 9.4 10.7	*bumble—*
6	M.	D-Day, 1944 • **New** ● • First Pa. Horticultural Society exhibition, 1829	*thunder-*
7	Tu.	Two men left N.Y.C. for 54-day row across Atlantic, 1896 • Tides { 9.1 — •	*storms*
8	W.	☾ rides high • ☌♀☾ • Architect Frank Lloyd Wright born, 1869 • { 10.4 9.0	*begin*
9	Th.	**Orthodox Ascension** • ☌♄☾ • Tornado in Worcester, Mass., 1953	*to*
10	Fr.	Ben Franklin's kite and key experiment, 1752 • Tides { 10.1 8.8 •	*rumble.*
11	Sa.	**St. Barnabas** • ☾ at apo. • Part of Meigg's Wharf in San Francisco washed away, 1864	*It's*
12	**B**	**4th S. af. P.** • Bandleader Archie Bleyer born, 1909 • { 9.6 8.6	*getting*
13	M.	**Shavuot** • ♇ at ☍ • *Plain dealing is best.* • { 9.3 8.7 •	*hotter—*
14	Tu.	**St. Basil** • Strawberries are ripe about now in southern N.H. • { 9.1 8.8 •	*college*
15	W.	☾ on Eq. • ♅ stat. • Magna Carta signed, 1215 • Tides { 8.9 9.0 •	*grads*
16	Th.	☾ at ☋ • ☌♃☾ • Hail, 17 inches in circumference, fell in Dubuque, Iowa, 1882	*sing*
17	Fr.	Sir Francis Drake landed on the Pacific Coast, 1579 • Tides { 8.8 9.8 •	*Alma*
18	Sa.	James Montgomery Flagg, illustrator of Uncle Sam "I Want You for U.S. Army" poster, born, 1877	*Mater.*
19	**B**	**5th S. af. P.** • **Orthodox Pentecost** •	*"Boom!"*
20	M.	*You can't sell the cow and have the milk.* • Telegraph patented, 1840 • { 9.3 11.1 •	*go*
21	Tu.	**Summer Solstice** • Ferris wheel debuted, 1893 • Tides { 9.5 11.5 •	*summer's*
22	W.	**St. Alban** • **Full Strawberry** ○ • ☾ runs low •	*opening*
23	Th.	☾ at perig. • *Better sense in the head than cents in the pocket.* • Tides { 11.8 9.9	*guns,*
24	Fr.	**Nativ. John the Baptist** • **Midsummer Day** • { 11.9 10.1 •	*while*
25	Sa.	☌♆☾ • ☌♀♄ • Actress June Lockhart born, 1925 • { 11.7 10.2	*parents*
26	**B**	**6th S. af. P.** • **Orthodox All Saints'** • ☌☿♄ •	*lose*
27	M.	☌☿♀ • 100°F in Fort Yukon, Alaska, 1915 • { 11.0 10.3 •	*daughters*
28	Tu.	**St. Irenaeus** • ☾ on Eq. • Molly Pitcher manned cannon, 1778 • { 10.5 10.3	*and*
29	W.	**Sts. Peter & Paul** • ☾ at ☊ • ☌♂☾ • { 9.9 10.3	*gain*
30	Th.	*Life never stands still: If you don't advance, you recede.* • Tides { 9.5 10.3 •	*sons.*

Behind every successful man stands a surprised mother-in-law.
–Hubert Humphrey, American politician

Farmer's Calendar

■ Go to a country auction, and you will see alchemy at work: Dross is transmuted into gold. The auctioneer is the alchemist. Observe how he works. He holds up some item that should have gone to the dump years ago, an empty pipe tobacco tin, say. He asks for an opening bid of ten dollars. No response from the audience. He asks for five dollars. Silence. One dollar? A hand goes up. Two? Another hand. Four? Another. In the next thirty seconds, the tin, which rationally is worth maybe a dime, recovers the absurdly high price it failed to open at, and in another minute or less the auctioneer knocks it down for twenty bucks.

The wizardry of auctioneering isn't found in high-price, high-brow affairs where elegant people watch French Impressionist canvases go for millions. There, the worth of items for auction is high, and the auctioneer's job is to drive it higher. These events may be of interest to students of money, but to students of humanity, the real show is under a tent on a village green. In that setting, you see the auction's essence. It's a magic show. The auctioneer is an illusionist, like the stage magician; but unlike the latter, his illusion isn't of material reality. The auctioneer's illusion is the illusion of value. And just as in the familiar magic show, where the onlookers watch the beautiful assistant sawn in two and then made whole, it isn't really the auctioneer who makes the illusion, it's the audience. We see what we are led to see, and when we are led by an expert, we may see strange sights.

JULY

The Seventh Month • 2005

SKY WATCH ☆ *The month begins with Venus and Mercury still very close together, in Cancer, low in the west at dusk. They continue their eye-catching side-by-side performance until the 10th, after dangling beneath the crescent Moon on the 8th. Venus crosses into Leo at midmonth and is near its main star Regulus on the 22nd. Saturn has slipped behind the Sun and can not be seen, while Jupiter is low in the southwest at dusk and visible until midnight. The real news is Mars, now seriously brightening to magnitude zero as it slips into Pisces after nipping a corner of the lesser-known constellation Cetus. Rising by 1:00* A.M.*, it dominates the wee hours.*

●	New Moon	6th day	8th hour	2nd minute
☽	First Quarter	14th day	11th hour	20th minute
○	Full Moon	21st day	7th hour	0 minute
☾	Last Quarter	27th day	23rd hour	19th minute

Times are given in Eastern Daylight Time.

For an explanation of this page, see page 176; for values of Key Letters, see page 235.

Day of Year	Day of Month	Day of Week	☼ Rises h. m.	Key	☼ Sets h. m.	Key	Length of Day h. m.	Sun Fast m.	Declination of Sun ° '	High Tide Boston Light—A.M.	Bold—P.M.	☽ Rises h. m.	Key	☽ Sets h. m.	Key	☽ Place	☽ Age
182	1	Fr.	5 11	A	8 25	E	15 14	12	23N.04	8	**8½**	1 A.M. 32	B	4 P.M. 15	E	ARI	25
183	2	Sa.	5 12	A	8 25	E	15 13	12	22 59	9	**9¼**	1 58	B	5 23	E	ARI	26
184	3	**B**	5 12	A	8 24	E	15 12	11	22 54	10	**10**	2 30	A	6 29	E	TAU	27
185	4	M.	5 13	A	8 24	E	15 11	11	22 49	10¾	**10¾**	3 09	A	7 30	E	TAU	28
186	5	Tu.	5 14	A	8 24	E	15 10	11	22 44	11½	**11½**	3 56	A	8 23	E	AUR	29
187	6	W.	5 14	A	8 24	E	15 10	11	22 38	**12¼**	—	4 51	A	9 07	E	GEM	0
188	7	Th.	5 14	A	8 23	E	15 09	11	22 31	12¼	**1**	5 51	A	9 43	E	GEM	1
189	8	Fr.	5 15	A	8 23	E	15 08	11	22 24	1	**1½**	6 54	B	10 12	E	CAN	2
190	9	Sa.	5 16	A	8 22	E	15 06	10	22 17	1½	**2¼**	7 58	B	10 36	E	LEO	3
191	10	**B**	5 17	A	8 22	E	15 05	10	22 09	2¼	**3**	9 01	C	10 56	D	LEO	4
192	11	M.	5 18	A	8 21	E	15 03	10	22 01	3	**3½**	10 04	C	11 15	D	LEO	5
193	12	Tu.	5 19	A	8 21	E	15 02	10	21 53	3¾	**4¼**	11 A.M. 06	D	11 34	C	VIR	6
194	13	W.	5 19	A	8 20	E	15 01	10	21 45	4½	**5**	12 P.M. 09	D	11 P.M. 52	C	VIR	7
195	14	Th.	5 20	A	8 20	E	15 00	10	21 36	5¼	**5¾**	1 15	E	—	–	VIR	8
196	15	Fr.	5 21	A	8 19	E	14 58	10	21 26	6	**6½**	2 24	E	12 A.M. 13	B	VIR	9
197	16	Sa.	5 22	A	8 18	E	14 56	10	21 16	7	**7¼**	3 37	E	12 37	B	LIB	10
198	17	**B**	5 23	A	8 18	E	14 55	9	21 06	8	**8¼**	4 53	E	1 07	A	LIB	11
199	18	M.	5 23	A	8 17	E	14 54	9	20 55	9	**9¼**	6 10	E	1 47	A	SCO	12
200	19	Tu.	5 24	A	8 16	E	14 52	9	20 44	10	**10**	7 19	E	2 39	A	SAG	13
201	20	W.	5 25	A	8 15	E	14 50	9	20 33	10¾	**11**	8 17	E	3 47	A	SAG	14
202	21	Th.	5 26	A	8 15	E	14 49	9	20 22	11¾	—	9 02	E	5 06	B	SAG	15
203	22	Fr.	5 27	A	8 14	E	14 47	9	20 09	12	**12¾**	9 37	E	6 31	B	CAP	16
204	23	Sa.	5 28	A	8 13	E	14 45	9	19 58	12¾	**1½**	10 05	D	7 54	C	AQU	17
205	24	**B**	5 29	A	8 12	E	14 43	9	19 45	1¾	**2½**	10 29	D	9 15	D	AQU	18
206	25	M.	5 30	A	8 11	E	14 41	9	19 32	2¾	**3¼**	10 51	C	10 31	D	PSC	19
207	26	Tu.	5 31	A	8 10	D	14 39	9	19 18	3¾	**4¼**	11 12	B	11 A.M. 44	D	PSC	20
208	27	W.	5 32	A	8 09	D	14 37	9	19 05	4½	**5**	11 P.M. 35	B	12 P.M. 56	E	PSC	21
209	28	Th.	5 33	A	8 08	D	14 35	9	18 51	5½	**6**	—	–	2 06	E	ARI	22
210	29	Fr.	5 34	A	8 07	D	14 33	9	18 36	6½	**7**	12 A.M. 01	B	3 16	E	ARI	23
211	30	Sa.	5 35	A	8 06	D	14 31	9	18 22	7½	**8**	12 31	A	4 23	E	TAU	24
212	31	**B**	5 36	A	8 05	D	14 29	9	18N.07	8¾	**8¾**	1 A.M. 08	A	5 P.M. 25	E	TAU	25

JULY HATH 31 DAYS • 2005

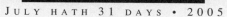

How many songs, O summer wind,
How many songs you know
Of fair, sweet things in your wanderings,
As over the earth you go. –Ina Donna Coolbrith

D. M.	D. W.	Dates, Feasts, Fasts, Aspects, Tide Heights	Weather ↓
1	Fr.	**Canada Day** • First sales tax in U.S. began in W. Va., 1921 • Tides {9.1 / 10.3 •	*At*
2	Sa.	Amelia Earhart and Frank Noonan disappeared during flight over Pacific Ocean, 1937 • {8.9 / 10.3	*worst,*
3	**B**	**7th S. af. P.** • Dog Days begin. • *Don't look for perfume in the doghouse.*	*a*
4	M.	**Independence Day** • Tides {8.8 / 10.2 •	*cloudburst.*
5	Tu.	☾ rides high • ⊕ at aphelion • "Sudden gust" in N.E. Mass., 1643 •	*Good*
6	W.	**New ●** • *Pennsylvania Evening Post* first newspaper to publish Declaration of Independence, 1776	*news*
7	Th.	☌☿♀ • Sir Arthur Conan Doyle, Sherlock Holmes author, died, 1930 • {10.2 / 8.8 •	*for*
8	Fr.	☾ at apo. • ☌☿☾ • ☌♀☾ • ☿ Gr. Elong. (26° E.)	*ball games*
9	Sa.	John F. Blondel received patent for doughnut cutter, 1872 • Tides {10.0 / 8.9 •	*and*
10	**B**	**8th S. af. P.** • *Ants are very busy before rain.* •	*barbecues!*
11	M.	Confederate Gen. Jubal Early's army reached Frederick, Md., 1864 • Tides {9.7 / 9.0	*Batten*
12	Tu.	☾ on Eq. • Dwight Eisenhower became first U.S. president to fly in helicopter, 1957 • {9.5 / 9.1	*down*
13	W.	☌♃☾ • Cornscateous air is everywhere. • Tides {9.2 / 9.2 •	*for*
14	Th	**Bastille Day** • ☾ at ☋ • Tides {8.9 / 9.4 •	*heaven's*
15	Fr.	**St. Swithin** • First Buddhist temple established in U.S., 1904 • Tides {8.7 / 9.7	*heavy*
16	Sa.	Mary Baker Eddy, founder of Christian Science, born, 1821 • Tides {8.6 / 10.0 •	*metal*
17	**B**	**9th S. af. P.** • Two triple plays by Minnesota Twins, 1990 •	*sound!*
18	M.	Aurora, Ill., received 16.91 inches of rain in 24 hours, 1996 • Tides {8.8 / 10.8 •	*You'll*
19	Tu.	Poet Rose Alnora Hartwick Thorpe died, 1939 • Tides {9.1 / 11.2 •	*need*
20	W.	☾ runs low • Hank Aaron hit 755th home run, 1976 • Tides {9.5 / 11.6 •	*an*
21	Th.	**Full Buck** ○ • ☾ at perig. • Canada's first public railway opened, 1836 •	*ocean*
22	Fr.	**St. Mary Magdalene** • ☌♆☾ • ☿ stat. • {10.2 / — •	*of*
23	Sa.	☌♄☉ • ☌♅☾ • Union Act approved, merging Upper and Lower Canada, 1840	*suntan*
24	**B**	**10th S. af. P.** • *It is good to go afoot with a horse in hand.* • {11.9 / 10.7	*lotion.*
25	M.	**Sts. James & Christopher** • ☾ on Eq. • Tides {11.5 / 10.8 •	*Run*
26	Tu.	**St. Anne** • ☾ at ☊ • *The hook without bait catches no fish.* • {10.9 / 10.7	*for*
27	W.	☌♂☾ • Comedian Bob Hope died, 2003 • Tides {10.3 / 10.5 •	*shelter!*
28	Th.	The metric system became legal in the U.S., 1866 • Tides {9.6 / 10.3 •	*Cool:*
29	Fr.	**St. Martha** • Prince Charles married Lady Diana Spencer, 1981 • {9.1 / 10.0 •	*We*
30	Sa.	Hawaii's first English-language newspaper published, 1836 • Tides {8.7 / 9.9 •	*won't*
31	**B**	**11th S. af. P.** • Astrogeologist's ashes deposited on Moon, 1999 •	*swelter.*

Farmer's Calendar

■ Today you don't see raccoons in this neighborhood in quite the numbers they formerly attained. The cause of their decline may be a disease that has led to a temporary scarcity, but other factors may also be at work. For one thing, from the coon point of view, the commons hereabouts aren't what they used to be. I have seen to that.

As the head produce gardener on this place, I have the job of raising fresh and nutritious vegetables of all kinds for the good health of the local fauna. In the past, my annual production always included sweet corn. No crop is easier to grow, or to eat. Everybody loves fresh garden corn, but nobody loves it as much as a raccoon. This I discovered after many years of carefully tending a stand of corn, only to have it devoured by coons, usually on the night before I had planned to harvest.

I tried every way I could learn of to keep the coons out of the corn. I wasn't alone. In those days, you could get a Ph.D. from the University of Vermont in coon-repelling. Nothing worked. You were told to lay newspapers down among the corn plants, because the coons wouldn't walk on them. The coons read the papers and ate the corn. You were told to spray shaving cream about the corn patch. The coons arrived as usual, shaved, and ate the corn.

At last I did what I find works best in such situations: I gave up. I quit planting corn. Shortly thereafter, the coon population crashed. Maybe it's time to take up corn again, but I think I will leave that to another gardener.

THE EIGHTH MONTH • 2005

SKY WATCH ☆ *Mercury, returning to the predawn east at midmonth as a morning star, dangles just below Saturn, which has reemerged in its new home of Cancer; the pair is best seen from the 20th to the 27th. As evening twilight fades, Venus brightens and is now conspicuous, if low; it closely meets the Moon on the 7th. Jupiter sinks farther into the west and is near the Moon on the 9th. Venus approaches Jupiter the final week of August and hangs out spectacularly close to it on the 31st. Mars doubles in brightness as it clips Cetus en route into Aries. The year's best meteor shower, the Perseids, will be wonderful on the night of August 11–12, especially after midnight.*

●	New Moon	4th day	23rd hour	5th minute
☽	First Quarter	12th day	22nd hour	38th minute
○	Full Moon	19th day	13th hour	53rd minute
☾	Last Quarter	26th day	11th hour	18th minute

Times are given in Eastern Daylight Time.

For an explanation of this page, see page 176; for values of Key Letters, see page 235.

Day of Year	Day of Month	Day of Week	☼ Rises h. m.	Key	☼ Sets h. m.	Key	Length of Day h. m.	Sun Fast m.	Declination of Sun ° '	High Tide Boston Light—A.M.	Bold—P.M.	☽ Rises h. m.	Key	☽ Sets h. m.	Key	☽ Place	☽ Age
213	1	M.	5 37	A	8 03	D	14 26	9	17N.52	9½	**9¾**	1 A.M. 52	A	6 P.M. 20	E	TAU	26
214	2	Tu.	5 38	A	8 02	D	14 24	9	17 37	10½	**10½**	2 45	A	7 07	E	AUR	27
215	3	W.	5 39	A	8 01	D	14 22	9	17 21	11¼	**11¼**	3 44	A	7 44	E	GEM	28
216	4	Th.	5 40	A	8 00	D	14 20	9	17 05	**12**	—	4 46	B	8 15	E	CAN	0
217	5	Fr.	5 41	A	7 59	D	14 18	10	16 49	12	**12½**	5 50	B	8 40	E	CAN	1
218	6	Sa.	5 42	A	7 57	D	14 15	10	16 32	12½	**1¼**	6 54	B	9 02	D	LEO	2
219	7	**B**	5 43	A	7 56	D	14 13	10	16 15	1¼	**1¾**	7 57	C	9 21	D	LEO	3
220	8	M.	5 44	A	7 55	D	14 11	10	15 58	1¾	**2¼**	8 59	D	9 39	D	LEO	4
221	9	Tu.	5 45	A	7 53	D	14 08	10	15 41	2½	**3**	10 01	D	9 57	C	VIR	5
222	10	W.	5 46	A	7 52	D	14 06	10	15 23	3¼	**3½**	11 A.M. 05	E	10 17	B	VIR	6
223	11	Th.	5 47	A	7 51	D	14 04	10	15 05	4	**4¼**	12 P.M. 12	E	10 39	B	VIR	7
224	12	Fr.	5 48	A	7 49	D	14 01	11	14 47	4¾	**5**	1 21	E	11 05	A	LIB	8
225	13	Sa.	5 49	A	7 48	D	13 59	11	14 29	5½	**5¾**	2 34	E	11 P.M. 39	A	LIB	9
226	14	**B**	5 50	A	7 46	D	13 56	11	14 11	6½	**6¾**	3 49	E	—	–	SCO	10
227	15	M.	5 52	B	7 45	D	13 53	11	13 52	7½	**7¾**	5 00	E	12 A.M. 24	A	OPH	11
228	16	Tu.	5 53	B	7 43	D	13 50	11	13 33	8½	**8¾**	6 02	E	1 23	A	SAG	12
229	17	W.	5 54	B	7 42	D	13 48	11	13 14	9½	**9¾**	6 52	E	2 36	A	SAG	13
230	18	Th.	5 55	B	7 40	D	13 45	12	12 55	10½	**10¾**	7 31	E	3 58	B	CAP	14
231	19	Fr.	5 56	B	7 39	D	13 43	12	12 35	11½	**11¾**	8 03	E	5 23	B	CAP	15
232	20	Sa.	5 57	B	7 37	D	13 40	12	12 15	**12¼**	—	8 29	D	6 46	C	AQU	16
233	21	**B**	5 58	B	7 36	D	13 38	12	11 55	12½	**1¼**	8 52	C	8 06	D	AQU	17
234	22	M.	5 59	B	7 34	D	13 35	13	11 35	1½	**2**	9 14	B	9 23	D	PSC	18
235	23	Tu.	6 00	B	7 33	D	13 33	13	11 15	2¼	**2¾**	9 37	B	10 38	E	PSC	19
236	24	W.	6 01	B	7 31	D	13 30	13	10 54	3¼	**3¾**	10 02	B	11 A.M. 51	E	ARI	20
237	25	Th.	6 02	B	7 30	D	13 28	13	10 33	4¼	**4½**	10 31	A	1 P.M. 03	E	ARI	21
238	26	Fr.	6 03	B	7 28	D	13 25	14	10 12	5	**5½**	11 06	A	2 13	E	TAU	22
239	27	Sa.	6 04	B	7 26	D	13 22	14	9 51	6	**6½**	11 P.M. 48	A	3 18	E	TAU	23
240	28	**B**	6 05	B	7 25	D	13 20	14	9 30	7¼	**7½**	—	–	4 16	E	TAU	24
241	29	M.	6 06	B	7 23	D	13 17	15	9 09	8¼	**8¼**	12 A.M. 39	A	5 06	E	AUR	25
242	30	Tu.	6 07	B	7 21	D	13 14	15	8 47	9¼	**9¼**	1 36	A	5 46	E	GEM	26
243	31	W.	6 08	B	7 20	D	13 12	15	8N.25	10	**10**	2 A.M. 38	A	6 P.M. 19	E	CAN	27

AUGUST

AUGUST HATH 31 DAYS • 2005

And from the hot field's farthest edge
The cricket's soft refrain
With mellow accent tells the tale
That August's here again. –Helen Maria Winslow

D. M.	D. W.	Dates, Feasts, Fasts, Aspects, Tide Heights	Weather ↓
1	M.	**Lammas Day** • *When trout refuse bait or fly, there ever is a storm nigh.*	"Delugin's"
2	Tu.	☾ rides high • Street letter boxes installed in Boston and N.Y.C., first in U.S., 1858 • {8.5 / 9.9	of
3	W.	National Basketball Association formed from merger, 1949 • Tides {8.6 / 10.0	grandeur!
4	Th.	New ● • ☾ at apo. • George Washington became a Master Mason, 1753 •	You
5	Fr.	☿ in inf. ☌ • *A mariner must have his eye upon rocks and sands as well as upon the North Star.*	can't
6	Sa.	**Transfiguration** • Asteroids renamed to honor final Shuttle *Columbia* crew, 2003 •	stand
7	**B**	**12th S. af. P.** • Peace Bridge opened, 1927 • {10.1 / 9.2 •	your
8	M.	**St. Dominic** • ☌ ♀ ☾ • ♆ at ☍ • {9.9 / 9.3 •	ground
9	Tu.	☾ on Eq. • Lassen Volcanic National Park, Calif., established, 1916 • {9.7 / 9.4 •	when
10	W.	**St. Lawrence** • ☾ at ☋ • ☌ ♃ ☾ • Tides {9.5 / 9.5 •	Thor's
11	Th.	**St. Clare** • Dog Days end. • *Don't keep a dog and bark yourself.* •	hammer
12	Fr.	Marjorie Gestring, at age 13, won Olympic gold medal for springboard diving, 1936 • {8.9 / 9.7	pounds.
13	Sa.	Samuel Leeds Allen granted patent for Flexible Flyer sled, 1889 • Tides {8.7 / 9.8 •	Every
14	**B**	**13th S. af. P.** • Massive blackout affected parts of North America, 2003	night
15	M.	**Assumption** • ☿ stat. • Emperor Napoleon Bonaparte born, 1769 • {8.5 / 10.3	the
16	Tu.	☾ runs low • Trade between Union and Confederate states prohibited, 1861 • {8.8 / 10.7	anvil
17	W.	Cat Nights begin. • Hurricane Diane hit Carolina Beach, N.C., 1955 • {9.1 / 11.2	chorus!
18	Th.	☌ ♆ ☾ • Charles Wilkes began expedition to South Pole, 1838 • {9.7 / 11.6	Has
19	Fr.	Full Sturgeon ○ • ☾ at perig. • Tides {10.2 / 11.9 •	someone
20	Sa.	☌ ♅ ☾ • Poet Edgar Albert Guest born, 1881 • Pope Pius X died, 1914 • {10.7 / —	got
21	**B**	**14th S. af. P.** • ☾ on Eq. • Tides {11.9 / 11.0 •	it in
22	M.	☾ at ☊ • Theodore Roosevelt became first U.S. president to ride in an automobile, 1902	for us?
23	Tu.	☿ Gr. Elong. (18° W.) • *There's more to riding than a pair of boots.* • Tides {11.3 / 11.1 •	Hot,
24	W.	**St. Bartholomew** • Treaty of Cordoba signed, granting Mexico independence from Spain, 1821	but
25	Th.	☌ ♂ ☾ • New Orleans, La., founded, 1718 • Tides {9.9 / 10.5 •	not for
26	Fr.	Tornado hit train on bridge in Dearborn County, Ind., 1864 • Tides {9.3 / 10.0 •	long:
27	Sa.	Town of York in Upper Canada founded (renamed Toronto in 1834), 1793 • {8.7 / 9.7 •	Chilly
28	**B**	**15th S. af. P.** • First successful U.S. vineyard established in Ky., 1798	nights
29	M.	**St. John the Baptist** • ☾ rides high • Tides {8.2 / 9.4 •	bring
30	Tu.	Boston reached 99°F, 1973 • *Asking costs nothing.* • {8.2 / 9.5 •	autumn
31	W.	☾ at apo. • ☌ ♄ ☾ • ♅ at ☍ • Tides {8.4 / 9.6 •	on.

Farmer's Calendar

■ The wood nymph butterfly *(Cercyonis pegala)* is common over the eastern half of the country anywhere there are meadows and woods edges. It's a variable species, but in my northern area it's fairly small, about the size of a big postage stamp. It's the color of milk chocolate and has at the corner of each wing an elongated yellow patch enclosing a pair of dark eyespots. Its caterpillar looks like a tiny bit of some fruit candy: green with long yellow stripes.

Every butterfly has its own way of flying. The wood nymph's flight is loose and floppy, now fast, now slow, as it wanders low over the sunlit meadows. It has an odd tic in its habit of flight. The butterfly alights frequently, and when it does it invariably hitches or pivots itself around on its perch before resting, just as an old-fashioned lady, on seating herself, might automatically gather her skirts around from behind her. Some butterflies are supposed to position themselves so as to avoid having their wings cast a shadow as they light, but the wood nymph's quick sidestep doesn't seem to do that.

For me, the wood nymph is important as one of the first signs of the changing season. It appears each year in late July or early August, at the height of the high summer. The sun is hot, the woods rich in green shade, the days end in long, soft twilight. But when I see the first wood nymph, I know that in another month the leaves will have begun to turn. Just when it seems that the summer must go on forever, this quiet little butterfly arrives to whisper, *No, it won't.*

SKY WATCH ☆ *Venus and Jupiter are striking as they hover very close together on the 1st, low in the southwest in fading evening twilight, joined on the 6th by the crescent Moon. Virgo's blue star Spica gets in on the action too, just below Venus. By month's end, Jupiter has sunk too low to be easily seen. The big news is Mars, which again doubles in brightness and breaks the magnitude −1 barrier. Up before 10:00 P.M. at midmonth, it stops its eastward motion and begins retrograding among the stars of Aries. Darkness lengthens at its fastest annual rate, by three minutes nightly in most locations. Autumn begins with the equinox on the 22nd, at 6:23 P.M. EDT.*

●	New Moon	3rd day	14th hour	45th minute
☽	First Quarter	11th day	7th hour	37th minute
○	Full Moon	17th day	22nd hour	1st minute
☾	Last Quarter	25th day	2nd hour	41st minute

Times are given in Eastern Daylight Time.

For an explanation of this page, see page 176; for values of Key Letters, see page 235.

Day of Year	Day of Month	Day of Week	☼ Rises h. m.	Key	☼ Sets h. m.	Key	Length of Day h. m.	Sun Fast m.	Declination of Sun ° '	High Tide Boston Light—A.M. Bold—P.M.		☽ Rises h. m.	Key	☽ Sets h. m.	Key	Place	Age
244	1	Th.	6 10	B	7 18	D	13 08	16	8 N. 04	10¾	10¾	3 ♈42	B	6 ᴘ45	E	CAN	28
245	2	Fr.	6 11	B	7 16	D	13 05	16	7 42	11½	11½	4 46	B	7 08	D	LEO	29
246	3	Sa.	6 12	B	7 15	D	13 03	16	7 20	12	—	5 49	C	7 27	D	LEO	0
247	4	**B**	6 13	B	7 13	D	13 00	16	6 58	12¼	12½	6 52	D	7 46	D	LEO	1
248	5	M.	6 14	B	7 11	D	12 57	17	6 35	12¾	1¼	7 55	D	8 04	C	VIR	2
249	6	Tu.	6 15	B	7 09	D	12 54	17	6 13	1½	1¾	8 58	E	8 22	B	VIR	3
250	7	W.	6 16	B	7 08	D	12 52	17	5 51	2	2¼	10 04	E	8 43	B	VIR	4
251	8	Th.	6 17	B	7 06	D	12 49	18	5 28	2¾	3	11 ♒12	E	9 08	B	VIR	5
252	9	Fr.	6 18	B	7 04	C	12 46	18	5 06	3½	3¾	12 ᴘ23	E	9 39	A	LIB	6
253	10	Sa.	6 19	B	7 02	C	12 43	19	4 43	4¼	4½	1 36	E	10 18	A	SCO	7
254	11	**B**	6 20	B	7 01	C	12 41	19	4 20	5	5¼	2 47	E	11 ᴍ10	A	OPH	8
255	12	M.	6 21	B	6 59	C	12 38	19	3 57	6	6½	3 50	E	—	–	SAG	9
256	13	Tu.	6 22	B	6 57	C	12 35	20	3 34	7¼	7½	4 44	E	12 ♈15	A	SAG	10
257	14	W.	6 23	B	6 55	C	12 32	20	3 11	8¼	8½	5 26	E	1 31	B	SAG	11
258	15	Th.	6 24	B	6 54	C	12 30	20	2 48	9¼	9½	6 00	E	2 53	B	CAP	12
259	16	Fr.	6 25	B	6 52	C	12 27	21	2 25	10¼	10½	6 27	D	4 15	C	AQU	13
260	17	Sa.	6 26	B	6 50	C	12 24	21	2 02	11	11½	6 51	D	5 36	D	AQU	14
261	18	**B**	6 27	B	6 48	C	12 21	21	1 39	12	—	7 14	C	6 55	D	PSC	15
262	19	M.	6 28	B	6 46	C	12 18	22	1 15	12¼	12¾	7 37	B	8 12	E	PSC	16
263	20	Tu.	6 30	C	6 45	C	12 15	22	0 52	1¼	1½	8 01	B	9 28	E	PSC	17
264	21	W.	6 31	C	6 43	C	12 12	22	0 29	2	2¼	8 29	A	10 43	E	ARI	18
265	22	Th.	6 32	C	6 41	C	12 09	23	0 N. 05	2¾	3	9 02	A	11 ♈56	E	TAU	19
266	23	Fr.	6 33	C	6 39	C	12 06	23	0 S. 18	3¾	4	9 42	A	1 ᴘ06	E	TAU	20
267	24	Sa.	6 34	C	6 38	C	12 04	23	0 41	4½	4¾	10 31	A	2 08	E	TAU	21
268	25	**B**	6 35	C	6 36	C	12 01	24	1 05	5½	5¾	11 ᴘ26	A	3 02	E	AUR	22
269	26	M.	6 36	C	6 34	C	11 58	24	1 28	6½	6¾	—	–	3 45	E	GEM	23
270	27	Tu.	6 37	C	6 32	C	11 55	25	1 51	7¾	7¾	12 ♈27	A	4 21	E	GEM	24
271	28	W.	6 38	C	6 31	B	11 53	25	2 15	8½	8¾	1 31	B	4 49	E	CAN	25
272	29	Th.	6 39	C	6 29	B	11 50	25	2 38	9½	9½	2 35	B	5 13	D	LEO	26
273	30	Fr.	6 40	C	6 27	B	11 47	26	3 S. 01	10¼	10¼	3 ♈39	B	5 ᴘ33	D	LEO	27

SEPTEMBER HATH 30 DAYS • 2005

Through sunny days and yellow weeks,
With clouds that melt in tears,
The glory of the harvest speaks
In all the silken ears. –J. Hazard Hartzell

D. M.	D. W.	Dates, Feasts, Fasts, Aspects, Tide Heights	Weather ↓
1	Th.	Last passenger pigeon, Martha, died at the Cincinnati Zoological Garden, Ohio, 1914 • { 8.7 / 9.8	*Here's*
2	Fr.	☌♀♃ • ♇ stat. • Japan formally surrendered, ending WWII, 1945	*what's*
3	Sa.	New ● • First successful penny paper, *N.Y. Sun,* began publication, 1833 •	*topical—*
4	B	16th S. af. P. • Actress Irene Dunne died, 1990 • { 10.0 / 9.5 •	*a*
5	M.	Labor Day • ☾ on Eq. • *Rest is the sweet sauce of labor.* • Tides { 10.0 / 9.7 •	*storm*
6	Tu.	☾ at ☋ • ☌♃☾ • Pilgrims set sail for New World, 1620 • { 9.9 / 9.8	*that's*
7	W.	☌♀☾ • Steamer *Lady Elgin* collided with schooner on Lake Michigan, 1860 •	*tropical!*
8	Th.	Margaret Gorman of Washington, D.C., became first Miss America, 1921 • { 9.5 / 10.0	*Students*
9	Fr.	St. Omer • Writer Phyllis Whitney born, 1903 • Tides { 9.2 / 10.0 •	*wear*
10	Sa.	*An apple a day keeps the doctor away—unless it's a green one.* • Tides { 8.9 / 10.0 •	*their*
11	B	17th S. af. P. • Terrorist attacks on U.S., 2001 • { 8.6 / 10.0 •	*gloomy*
12	M.	☾ runs low • Henry Hudson began exploration of what is later named the Hudson River, 1609	*faces,*
13	Tu.	Commodore John Barry, father of the American navy, died, 1803 • Tides { 8.6 / 10.3 •	*while*
14	W.	Holy Cross • World's largest airship, *Graf Zeppelin II,* made its first flight, 1938	*we*
15	Th.	☌♆☾ • British occupied New York, 1776 • Tides { 9.4 / 11.0 •	*watch*
16	Fr.	☾ at perig. • ☌♅☾ • James Pierpont's "Jingle Bells" copyrighted, 1857	*the*
17	Sa.	Full Harvest ○ • ☿ in sup. ☌ • Tides { 10.7 / 11.6 •	*pennant*
18	B	18th S. af. P. • ☾ on Eq. • Tides { 11.2 / — •	*races.*
19	M.	☾ at ☊ • Bruno R. Hauptmann charged with kidnap-murder of Lindbergh baby, 1934 •	*So*
20	Tu.	St. Eustace • Billy Jean King won battle-of-the-sexes tennis match vs. Bobby Riggs, 1973 •	*long,*
21	W.	St. Matthew • Ember Day • "Bugs Bunny" animator Chuck Jones born, 1912	*summer!*
22	Th.	Harvest Home • **Autumnal Equinox** • ☌♂☾ • Tides { 10.2 / 10.8 •	*Cool*
23	Fr.	Ember Day • Psychologist Sigmund Freud died, 1939 • Tides { 9.5 / 10.3 •	*and*
24	Sa.	Ember Day • Black Friday financial crisis, 1869 • { 8.9 / 9.8 •	*glummer.*
25	B	19th S. af. P. • ☾ rides high • Tides { 8.4 / 9.3 •	*The*
26	M.	*Little pigs eat great potatoes.* • Frontiersman Daniel Boone died, 1820 • { 8.1 / 9.1	*smell*
27	Tu.	St. Vincent de Paul • Mark McGwire hit 70th home run of season, 1998 • { 8.1 / 9.1	*of*
28	W.	☌♄☾ • ☾ at apo. • Gorilla escaped Boston zoo, rested at bus stop, 2003 •	*apple*
29	Th.	St. Michael • $387,500 paid for Lou Gehrig's last baseball glove, 1999 • { 8.5 / 9.4	*pies*
30	Fr.	St. Sophia • Woodchucks hibernate now. • Tides { 8.9 / 9.6 •	*satisfies.*

How many apples fell on Newton's head before he took the hint?
–Robert Frost, American poet

Farmer's Calendar

■ Fossil-hunting scientists working in remote northeastern China not long ago came up with the remains of a creature one paleontologist here described as "bizarre." Imagine an iguana who, invited to a costume party, has made the unfortunate decision to dress up as a chicken. *Microraptor gui,* as the scientists have called their discovery, lived 125 million years ago. It was a reptile, three feet long, with feathers on the trailing edges of its four hind legs and at the end of its long tail. Whether or not it could fly is unknown. Some paleontologists speculate that, while it didn't take flight like a bird, *M. gui* could climb trees and then descend through the air in an extended glide, like a flying squirrel.

So science is here proposing an ungainly union of lizard, pigeon, and squirrel, a misbegotten farrago that looks like the work of an idle afternoon spent among nature's spare parts. You wouldn't credit such an animal—but there are the thing's bones. The fossil record seems to be the unconscious mind of nature, a phantasmagoria of images, ideas, and memories roiling about behind the rational, intelligible face of nature's waking life. What are the dragons of myth but the dinosaurs? What are the beasts of fairy tale but the great bears, mammoths, and ground sloths of the Ice Age? No man ever saw a plesiosaur, but we have found our own sea monster in the Jurassic. However improbable the beast, some guy with a rock hammer and a whisk broom is, at this moment, digging it out of the ground in a dry and distant land.

THE TENTH MONTH • 2005

SKY WATCH ☆ *Mercury is close to the horizon as an evening star. Venus brightens to become dazzling in Libra but remains low in the southwest as evening twilight fades. Jupiter vanishes behind the Sun on the 22nd. Saturn is quite high now at dawn. Mars is the headliner: The red planet rises around 8:00 P.M. at midmonth and doubles its brightness yet again. It breaks the magnitude –2 barrier and is bested in brilliance only by Venus. The Milky Way, our own galaxy, now is highest at nightfall. A beautiful edgewise view can be seen in country skies during October's Moonless opening week. An annular eclipse of the Sun on the 3rd is visible in Europe and Africa but not North America.*

●	New Moon	3rd day	6th hour	28th minute
☽	First Quarter	10th day	15th hour	1st minute
○	Full Moon	17th day	8th hour	14th minute
☾	Last Quarter	24th day	21st hour	17th minute

After 2:00 A.M. on October 30, Eastern Standard Time (EST) is given.

For an explanation of this page, see page 176; for values of Key Letters, see page 235.

Day of Year	Day of Month	Day of Week	☼ Rises h. m.	Key	☼ Sets h. m.	Key	Length of Day h. m.	Sun Fast m.	Declination of Sun ° '	High Tide Boston Light—A.M.	**Bold—P.M.**	☽ Rises h. m.	Key	☽ Sets h. m.	Key	☽ Place	☽ Age
274	1	Sa.	6 41	C	6 25	B	11 44	26	3 s.25	10¾	**11**	4 A.M. 42	C	5 P.M. 52	D	LEO	28
275	2	**B**	6 43	C	6 24	B	11 41	26	3 48	11½	**11¾**	5 45	D	6 10	C	VIR	29
276	3	M.	6 44	C	6 22	B	11 38	26	4 11	**12**	—	6 49	D	6 29	B	VIR	0
277	4	Tu.	6 45	C	6 20	B	11 35	27	4 34	12¼	**12½**	7 55	E	6 49	B	VIR	1
278	5	W.	6 46	C	6 19	B	11 33	27	4 57	1	**1**	9 03	E	7 12	B	VIR	2
279	6	Th.	6 47	C	6 17	B	11 30	27	5 20	1½	**1¾**	10 14	E	7 41	A	LIB	3
280	7	Fr.	6 48	C	6 15	B	11 27	28	5 43	2¼	**2½**	11 A.M. 27	E	8 18	A	SCO	4
281	8	Sa.	6 49	C	6 13	B	11 24	28	6 06	3	**3¼**	12 P.M. 38	E	9 05	A	SCO	5
282	9	**B**	6 50	C	6 12	B	11 22	28	6 29	4	**4**	1 44	E	10 04	A	SAG	6
283	10	M.	6 51	C	6 10	B	11 19	29	6 52	4¾	**5**	2 39	E	11 P.M. 15	A	SAG	7
284	11	Tu.	6 53	C	6 08	B	11 15	29	7 15	6	**6**	3 24	E	—	–	SAG	8
285	12	W.	6 54	C	6 07	B	11 13	29	7 37	7	**7¼**	3 59	E	12 A.M. 33	B	CAP	9
286	13	Th.	6 55	C	6 05	B	11 10	29	8 00	8	**8¼**	4 28	D	1 53	B	CAP	10
287	14	Fr.	6 56	D	6 04	B	11 08	30	8 22	9	**9¼**	4 52	D	3 12	C	AQU	11
288	15	Sa.	6 57	D	6 02	B	11 05	30	8 44	10	**10¼**	5 15	C	4 30	D	AQU	12
289	16	**B**	6 58	D	6 00	B	11 02	30	9 06	10¾	**11¼**	5 37	C	5 46	D	PSC	13
290	17	M.	7 00	D	5 59	B	10 59	30	9 28	11½	—	6 00	B	7 02	E	PSC	14
291	18	Tu.	7 01	D	5 57	B	10 56	30	9 50	12	**12¼**	6 27	B	8 18	E	ARI	15
292	19	W.	7 02	D	5 56	B	10 54	31	10 12	12¾	**1**	6 58	A	9 33	E	ARI	16
293	20	Th.	7 03	D	5 54	B	10 51	31	10 33	1¾	**1¾**	7 35	A	10 46	E	TAU	17
294	21	Fr.	7 04	D	5 53	B	10 49	31	10 54	2½	**2½**	8 21	A	11 A.M. 54	E	TAU	18
295	22	Sa.	7 06	D	5 51	B	10 45	31	11 16	3¼	**3¼**	9 14	A	12 P.M. 52	E	TAU	19
296	23	**B**	7 07	D	5 50	B	10 43	31	11 37	4	**4¼**	10 14	A	1 41	E	GEM	20
297	24	M.	7 08	D	5 48	B	10 40	31	11 57	5	**5¼**	11 P.M. 18	B	2 20	E	GEM	21
298	25	Tu.	7 09	D	5 47	B	10 38	31	12 18	6	**6¼**	—	–	2 51	E	CAN	22
299	26	W.	7 10	D	5 45	B	10 35	32	12 38	7	**7**	12 A.M. 22	B	3 16	E	CAN	23
300	27	Th.	7 12	D	5 44	B	10 32	32	12 59	7¾	**8**	1 26	B	3 38	D	LEO	24
301	28	Fr.	7 13	D	5 43	B	10 30	32	13 19	8¾	**9**	2 29	C	3 57	D	LEO	25
302	29	Sa.	7 14	D	5 41	B	10 27	32	13 38	9½	**9¾**	3 32	D	4 15	D	LEO	26
303	30	**B**	6 15	D	4 40	B	10 25	32	13 58	9	**9½**	3 36	D	3 33	C	VIR	27
304	31	M.	6 17	D	4 39	B	10 22	32	14 s.17	9¾	**10¼**	4 A.M. 41	E	3 P.M. 53	B	VIR	28

OCTOBER HATH 31 DAYS • 2005

The dead leaves fall like noiseless rain,
The air is calm and warm and sweet;
Upon the woodland and the plain
The ghost of summer rests her feet. –Clinton Scollard

D. M.	D. W.	Dates, Feasts, Fasts, Aspects, Tide Heights	*Weather* ↓
1	Sa.	St. Gregory • ♂ stat. • Game 1 in first World Series, 1903 • { 9.3 9.8 •	*In*
2	B	20th S. af. P. • ☾ on Eq. • Tides { 9.7 9.9 •	*every*
3	M.	New ● • Eclipse ☉ • ☾ at ☋ • { 10.0 — •	*pond,*
4	Tu.	Rosh Hashanah • **First day of Ramadan** • Tides { 9.9 10.2 •	*lake,*
5	W.	*Better to be the head of a lizard than the tail of a dragon.* • Tides { 9.8 10.4 •	*and*
6	Th.	☌♀♃ • Actress Bette Davis died, 1989 • Tides { 9.7 10.4 •	*river,*
7	Fr.	☌♀☾ • Cornell University welcomed its first students, 1868 • { 9.4 10.4	*autumn*
8	Sa.	Edward V. Rickenbacker, World War I flying ace, born, 1890 • Tides { 9.2 10.3	*colors*
9	B	21st S. af. P. • ☾ runs low • { 8.9 10.2 •	*shimmer;*
10	M.	**Columbus Day** • **Thanksgiving Day (Canada)** • Tides { 8.7 10.1 •	*neither*
11	Tu.	*Juliana,* first steam-powered ferry in U.S., began service, 1811 • Tides { 8.6 10.1 •	*rain*
12	W.	☌♆☾ • Singer John Denver died, 1997 • Tides { 8.8 10.2 •	*nor*
13	Th.	Yom Kippur • Jewish organization B'nai B'rith founded, 1843 • { 9.3 10.4 •	*dust*
14	Fr.	☾ at perig. • ☌♅☾ • Lester Pearson won Nobel Peace Prize, 1957 • { 9.9 10.7	*of*
15	Sa.	☾ on Eq. • First U.S. fishing magazine, *American Angler,* published, 1881 • { 10.5 10.9	*snow*
16	B	22nd S. af. P. • ☾ at ☊ • Tides { 11.1 11.0 •	*dims*
17	M.	St. Ignatius of Antioch • **Full Hunter's** ○ • **Eclipse** ☾ •	*the*
18	Tu.	St. Luke • Succoth • Tides { 5.3 6.4 •	*jack-o-lantern's*
19	W.	☌♂☾ • *Be silent and pass for a philosopher.* • Tides { 10.6 11.4 •	*glow.*
20	Th.	Laurel and Hardy's *The Flying Deuces* debuted, 1939 • Tides { 10.2 11.1 •	*Summer*
21	Fr.	Portland, Maine, received 13.32 inches of rain in 24 hours, 1996 • { 9.7 10.6	*returns,*
22	Sa.	☾ rides high • ☌♃☉ • First recorded solar eclipse, China, 2136 B.C. •	*and*
23	B	23rd S. af. P. • *Life never gets a goldfish down.* •	*lingers—*
24	M.	Canadian schooner *Bluenose* won International Fishermen's Trophy, 1921 • { 8.3 9.2 •	*then*
25	Tu.	☌♄☾ • Little brown bats hibernate now. • Tides { 8.1 8.9 •	*the*
26	W.	☾ at apo. • ♆ stat. • R. Krueger became World Rock Paper Scissors champion, 2003	*curtain*
27	Th.	DuPont announced invention of nylon, 1938 • Tides { 8.4 8.9 •	*closes,*
28	Fr.	Sts. Simon & Jude • St. Louis, Mo., police first in U.S. to use fingerprinting, 1904	*pulled*
29	Sa.	☾ on Eq. • Merchandiser Fred Lazarus Jr. born, 1884 • Tides { 9.1 9.3 •	*by*
30	B	24th S. af. P. • ☾ at ☋ • **Daylight Saving Time ends, 2:00 A.M.**	*icy*
31	M.	All Hallows' Eve • St. Wolfgang • *Every pumpkin is known by its stem.*	*fingers.*

Farmer's Calendar

■ "Not even wrong," is a term scientists use to heap scorn on bad theory. A hypothesis or proposed account of reality that is dismissed as being not even wrong is not, perhaps, false as to fact or reasoning, but somehow radically, irremediably irrelevant. The criticism works on the profoundest level and goes beyond the truth and logic of an idea to cast doubt on its fundamental perception, its standpoint, almost its sanity.

The understanding that a position can be subject to flaws deeper than falsehood or fallacy provides the climax to one of the world's great philosophical dramas, the story of Job. In the Bible, Job is the prosperous herdsman whom the Lord tests so cruelly. For no reason, because of no offense of Job's, the Lord strips him of his property, his family, and his health. Prostrate with suffering and grief, Job demands to know why an innocent and upright man like himself should be put in such pain by a just God. Various counselors attempt to answer his question, none satisfactorily. At last, in one of the most astonishing passages in the Bible, the Lord speaks to Job and tells him, in effect, that he doesn't get it. "Where wast thou when I laid the foundations of the earth?" the Lord asks Job. "Hast thou entered into the springs of the sea? Doth the eagle mount up at thy command?" He goes on to invite Job to consider the majesty, intricacy, and perfection of God's creation and to reflect that, by comparison, Job's remonstrances on the injustice of his condition are as nothing. They are not false, but unimportant. They are not even wrong.

NOVEMBER

THE ELEVENTH MONTH • 2005

SKY WATCH ☆ *Mars comes to opposition on the 7th. At a brilliant magnitude –2.3, it rises at sunset, is out all night, and is quite high at midnight in Aries. The nearly full Moon joins Mars on the 14th. Venus achieves greatest elongation on the 3rd, but its 47-degree solar separation is wasted, since it's south of the ecliptic and not very high. Still, watch it closely when it meets the Moon on the 5th. Saturn rises before 11:00 P.M. at midmonth; it floats alongside the Moon on the 21st. Jupiter, above the crescent Moon on the 29th, returns as a predawn planet low in the east. November's on-again, off-again Leonid meteor showers will definitely be "off" this year; even if they do appear, they'll be ruined by an almost-full Moon.*

●	New Moon	1st day	20th hour	25th minute
☽	First Quarter	8th day	20th hour	57th minute
○	Full Moon	15th day	19th hour	57th minute
☾	Last Quarter	23rd day	17th hour	11th minute

Times are given in Eastern Standard Time.

For an explanation of this page, see page 176; for values of Key Letters, see page 235.

Day of Year	Day of Month	Day of Week	☼ Rises h. m.	Key	☼ Sets h. m.	Key	Length of Day h. m.	Sun Fast m.	Declination of Sun ° '	High Tide Boston Light—A.M.	Bold—P.M.	☽ Rises h. m.	Key	☽ Sets h. m.	Key	☽ Place	☽ Age
305	1	Tu.	6 18	D	4 37	B	10 19	32	14 s. 37	10¼	**10¾**	5 A.M. 49	E	4 P.M. 15	B	VIR	0
306	2	W.	6 19	D	4 36	B	10 17	32	14 56	11	**11½**	7 00	E	4 43	A	LIB	1
307	3	Th.	6 20	D	4 35	B	10 15	32	15 14	11½	—	8 14	E	5 17	A	LIB	2
308	4	Fr.	6 21	D	4 34	B	10 13	32	15 33	12¼	**12¼**	9 28	E	6 01	A	SCO	3
309	5	Sa.	6 23	D	4 32	B	10 09	32	15 52	1	**1**	10 37	E	6 58	A	OPH	4
310	6	**B**	6 24	D	4 31	B	10 07	32	16 10	1¾	**2**	11 A.M. 36	E	8 06	A	SAG	5
311	7	M.	6 25	D	4 30	B	10 05	32	16 27	2¾	**2¾**	12 P.M. 24	E	9 22	B	SAG	6
312	8	Tu.	6 27	D	4 29	A	10 02	32	16 44	3¾	**3¾**	1 01	E	10 40	B	CAP	7
313	9	W.	6 28	D	4 28	A	10 00	32	17 02	4¾	**5**	1 31	E	11 P.M. 58	B	CAP	8
314	10	Th.	6 29	D	4 27	A	9 58	32	17 18	5¾	**6**	1 56	D	—	–	AQU	9
315	11	Fr.	6 30	D	4 26	A	9 56	32	17 35	6¾	**7**	2 18	D	1 A.M. 14	C	AQU	10
316	12	Sa.	6 32	D	4 25	A	9 53	31	17 51	7¾	**8**	2 40	C	2 28	D	PSC	11
317	13	**B**	6 33	D	4 24	A	9 51	31	18 07	8½	**9**	3 02	B	3 42	D	PSC	12
318	14	M.	6 34	D	4 23	A	9 49	31	18 23	9½	**10**	3 26	B	4 56	E	ARI	13
319	15	Tu.	6 35	D	4 22	A	9 47	31	18 38	10¼	**10¾**	3 55	A	6 10	E	ARI	14
320	16	W.	6 36	D	4 21	A	9 45	31	18 53	11	**11½**	4 29	A	7 24	E	TAU	15
321	17	Th.	6 38	D	4 20	A	9 42	31	19 08	11¾	—	5 11	A	8 35	E	TAU	16
322	18	Fr.	6 39	D	4 20	A	9 41	31	19 22	12¼	**12¼**	6 02	A	9 38	E	TAU	17
323	19	Sa.	6 40	D	4 19	A	9 39	30	19 36	1	**1**	7 00	A	10 32	E	AUR	18
324	20	**B**	6 41	D	4 18	A	9 37	30	19 49	1¾	**1¾**	8 03	B	11 15	E	GEM	19
325	21	M.	6 43	D	4 17	A	9 34	30	20 02	2½	**2¾**	9 08	B	11 A.M. 50	E	CAN	20
326	22	Tu.	6 44	D	4 17	A	9 33	30	20 15	3½	**3½**	10 12	B	12 P.M. 17	E	CAN	21
327	23	W.	6 45	D	4 16	A	9 31	29	20 28	4¼	**4½**	11 P.M. 15	B	12 40	D	LEO	22
328	24	Th.	6 46	D	4 16	A	9 30	29	20 39	5¼	**5¼**	—	–	1 00	D	LEO	23
329	25	Fr.	6 47	D	4 15	A	9 28	29	20 52	6	**6¼**	12 A.M. 18	C	1 19	D	LEO	24
330	26	Sa.	6 48	D	4 14	A	9 26	28	21 03	6¾	**7¼**	1 20	D	1 37	C	VIR	25
331	27	**B**	6 50	E	4 14	A	9 24	28	21 14	7½	**8**	2 24	D	1 55	B	VIR	26
332	28	M.	6 51	E	4 14	A	9 23	28	21 24	8¼	**8¾**	3 30	E	2 16	B	VIR	27
333	29	Tu.	6 52	E	4 13	A	9 21	27	21 34	9	**9½**	4 40	E	2 42	A	VIR	28
334	30	W.	6 53	E	4 13	A	9 20	27	21 s. 44	9¾	**10¼**	5 A.M. 54	E	3 P.M. 13	A	LIB	29

NOVEMBER

NOVEMBER HATH 30 DAYS • 2005

There comes the sound of childish feet
And childish laughter loud and sweet,
And little hands stretch eager palms
To beg the firelight's golden alms. –James Berry Bensel

D. M.	D. W.	Dates, Feasts, Fasts, Aspects, Tide Heights	Weather ↓
1	Tu.	**All Saints'** • New ● • First national weather service in U.S. began operation, 1870	*Teeth-*
2	W.	**All Souls'** • *To the brave man every land is a native country.* • { 10.6 / 9.6	*chattering,*
3	Th.	☌☿☾ • ☿ Gr. Elong. (24° E.) • ♀ Gr. Elong. (47° E.) • { 10.8 / — •	*then*
4	Fr.	Sunspot 486 produced record-breaking X28-class solar flare, 2003 • Tides { 9.6 / 10.9 •	*a*
5	Sa.	☌♀☾ • Susan B. Anthony cast her ballot, earning a fine, 1872 •	*spattering.*
6	**B**	**25th S. af. P.** • ☾ runs low • Tides { 9.2 / 10.7 •	*Too*
7	M.	♂ at ☍ • Former U.S. First Lady Eleanor Roosevelt died, 1962 • { 9.0 / 10.5	*good*
8	Tu.	Election Day • ☌♆☾ • Abraham Lincoln reelected as U.S. president, 1864 •	*to*
9	W.	☾ at perig. • Al Capp's Sadie Hawkins Day first celebrated, 1938 • { 9.0 / 10.1 •	*be*
10	Th.	☌♅☾ • U.S. Marine Corps established, 1775 • Tides { 9.3 / 10.0 •	*true;*
11	Fr.	**St. Martin of Tours** • **Veterans Day** • Tides { 9.7 / 10.0 •	*skies*
12	Sa.	**Sadie Hawkins Day** • Indian Summer • ☾ on Eq. • ☾ at ☊ • { 10.2 / 10.1	*of*
13	**B**	**26th S. af. P.** • Thousands of meteors fell per hour, 1833 •	*cobalt*
14	M.	☿ stat. • *You can not make a crab walk straight.* • Tides { 11.1 / 10.1 •	*blue,*
15	Tu.	**Full Beaver** ○ • ☌♂☾ • Astronomer Sir William Herschel born, 1738 •	*and*
16	W.	♅ stat. • President Nixon approved construction of an Alaskan pipeline, 1973 •	*warmer,*
17	Th.	**St. Hugh of Lincoln** • Sculptor Auguste Rodin died, 1917 • Tides { 11.1 / —	*too!*
18	Fr.	U.S. railroads adopted four standard time zones, 1883 • *Necessity sharpens industry.* •	*Make*
19	Sa.	☾ rides high • Hudson Bay Co. ceded territory to Canada, 1869 • Tides { 9.2 / 10.4 •	*the*
20	**B**	**27th S. af. P.** • Yo-yo patented, 1866 • { 8.9 / 10.0 •	*best*
21	M.	☌♄☾ • *Wonder is the seed of science.* • Tides { 8.6 / 9.5 •	*of*
22	Tu.	♄ at stat. • National Hockey League formed, 1917 • Tides { 8.4 / 9.2 •	*it—*
23	W.	**St. Clement** • ☾ apo. • Horseshoe-manufacturing machine patented, 1835	*you're*
24	Th.	**Thanksgiving** • ☿ in inf. ☌ • Tides { 8.3 / 8.7 •	*likely*
25	Fr.	First sword-swallower performance in U.S., 1817 • *After feasting, fasting.* • { 8.5 / 8.6 •	*not*
26	Sa.	☾ on Eq. • Public streetcar service began in N.Y.C., 1832 • Tides { 8.8 / 8.7 •	*to*
27	**B**	**1st S. of Advent** • ☾ at ☋ • Tides { 9.2 / 8.8 •	*like*
28	M.	*Who throws a stone at the sky may have it fall on his head.* • Tides { 9.7 / 9.0 •	*the*
29	Tu.	☌♃☾ • Committee of Secret Correspondence organized by 2nd Continental Congress, 1775	*rest*
30	W.	**St. Andrew** • Meteorite hit woman in her home, Sylacauga, Ala., 1954 • { 10.5 / 9.3	*of it!*

Food is our common ground, a universal experience.
–James Beard, American chef

Farmer's Calendar

■ "The pleasure that is in sorrow," a poet has written, "is sweeter than the pleasure of pleasure itself." Hence the beauty of the fall of the year, and hence our particular delight in the spectacle it presents to our senses. It's a spectacle of decline, deterioration, and bereavement—a melancholy spectacle. We respond to it for that very reason. We love the fall because of its melancholy, not in spite of it.

The sweet sadness of the year's end doesn't set in until most of the autumn leaves are gone from the trees. The autumn colors are too bright and too busy to have the effect, though they point to it. It's when the leaves are brown, and few, and the branches and trunks of the trees are gray that they begin to produce the emotional tone of this season, the tone of loss. The low skies of November, the dun ponds and frozen brooks, are a dark setting.

But although the season has a sorrowful character, it isn't a depressing time. On the contrary: The atmosphere of these last weeks before winter comes is the antithesis of depression. The senses—the feelings—become more receptive, educated by the stripped-down, impoverished look of the land. Maybe the last leaves, long dead, that hang on the trees are few in number, but you consider each one of them. Maybe the subdued little salt-and-pepper birds of November don't know many songs, but they have a companionable presence the brighter summer birds lack. In a part of the year that withholds the occasions for high spirits, the pleasure that we take is the pleasure of reflection, and it's keen, because it goes down deep.

DECEMBER

THE TWELFTH MONTH • 2005

SKY WATCH ☆ *Venus reaches greatest brilliancy on the 9th at magnitude –4.6, after hovering near the crescent Moon on the 4th. It moves from Sagittarius to Capricornus, then retrogrades and falls toward the Sun. Mars, out nearly all night, is magnificent. Mercury has a nice predawn apparition. Jupiter, just above it all month, enters Libra, its home for the next year. Saturn rises at around 8:00 P.M. at midmonth and brightens beyond the zero-magnitude threshold in advance of its opposition next month. The midmonth Geminid meteors are spoiled by a bright Moon. Winter begins with the solstice on the 21st, at 1:35 P.M. EST.*

●	New Moon	1st day	10th hour	1st minute
☽	First Quarter	8th day	4th hour	36th minute
○	Full Moon	15th day	11th hour	15th minute
☾	Last Quarter	23rd day	14th hour	36th minute
●	New Moon	30th day	22nd hour	12th minute

Times are given in Eastern Standard Time.

For an explanation of this page, see page 176; for values of Key Letters, see page 235.

Day of Year	Day of Month	Day of Week	☼ Rises h. m.	Key	☼ Sets h. m.	Key	Length of Day h. m.	Sun Fast m.	Declination of Sun ° '	High Tide Boston Light—A.M.	Bold—P.M.	☽ Rises h. m.	Key	☽ Sets h. m.	Key	☽ Place	☽ Age
335	1	Th.	6 54	E	4 13	A	9 19	27	21 s. 53	10½	**11**	7 A.M. 09	E	3 P.M. 54	A	SCO	0
336	2	Fr.	6 55	E	4 12	A	9 17	26	22 02	11¼	**11¾**	8 22	E	4 47	A	OPH	1
337	3	Sa.	6 56	E	4 12	A	9 16	26	22 11	**12**	—	9 27	E	5 54	A	SAG	2
338	4	**B**	6 57	E	4 12	A	9 15	26	22 19	12¾	**12¾**	10 20	E	7 10	B	SAG	3
339	5	M.	6 58	E	4 12	A	9 14	25	22 27	1½	**1¾**	11 02	E	8 29	B	CAP	4
340	6	Tu.	6 59	E	4 12	A	9 13	25	22 34	2½	**2½**	11 A.M. 34	E	9 48	C	CAP	5
341	7	W.	7 00	E	4 12	A	9 12	24	22 40	3¼	**3½**	12 P.M. 01	D	11 P.M. 04	C	AQU	6
342	8	Th.	7 00	E	4 11	A	9 11	24	22 46	4¼	**4¾**	12 23	D	—	–	AQU	7
343	9	Fr.	7 02	E	4 12	A	9 10	23	22 52	5¼	**5¾**	12 45	C	12 A.M. 18	D	PSC	8
344	10	Sa.	7 03	E	4 12	A	9 09	23	22 58	6¼	**6¾**	1 06	B	1 30	E	PSC	9
345	11	**B**	7 03	E	4 12	A	9 09	23	23 03	7¼	**7¾**	1 29	B	2 42	E	PSC	10
346	12	M.	7 04	E	4 12	A	9 08	22	23 07	8¼	**8¾**	1 55	B	3 55	E	ARI	11
347	13	Tu.	7 05	E	4 12	A	9 07	22	23 11	9	**9¾**	2 26	A	5 08	E	ARI	12
348	14	W.	7 06	E	4 12	A	9 06	21	23 15	9¾	**10½**	3 05	A	6 19	E	TAU	13
349	15	Th.	7 07	E	4 12	A	9 05	21	23 18	10½	**11¼**	3 52	A	7 25	E	TAU	14
350	16	Fr.	7 08	E	4 13	A	9 05	20	23 20	11¼	—	4 48	A	8 22	E	AUR	15
351	17	Sa.	7 08	E	4 13	A	9 05	20	23 22	12	**12**	5 50	A	9 10	E	GEM	16
352	18	**B**	7 09	E	4 13	A	9 04	19	23 24	12¾	**12¾**	6 54	B	9 48	E	CAN	17
353	19	M.	7 10	E	4 14	A	9 04	19	23 26	1½	**1½**	7 59	B	10 18	E	CAN	18
354	20	Tu.	7 10	E	4 14	A	9 04	18	23 26	2	**2¼**	9 03	C	10 42	E	LEO	19
355	21	W.	7 11	E	4 15	A	9 04	18	23 26	2¾	**3**	10 05	C	11 03	D	LEO	20
356	22	Th.	7 11	E	4 15	A	9 04	17	23 26	3½	**3¾**	11 P.M. 06	D	11 22	D	LEO	21
357	23	Fr.	7 11	E	4 16	A	9 05	17	23 25	4¼	**4½**	—	–	11 40	C	VIR	22
358	24	Sa.	7 11	E	4 16	A	9 05	16	23 24	5¼	**5½**	12 A.M. 08	D	11 A.M. 58	C	VIR	23
359	25	**B**	7 12	E	4 17	A	9 05	16	23 23	6	**6¼**	1 12	E	12 P.M. 17	B	VIR	24
360	26	M.	7 12	E	4 18	A	9 06	15	23 21	6¾	**7¼**	2 19	E	12 40	B	VIR	25
361	27	Tu.	7 12	E	4 18	A	9 06	15	23 18	7½	**8¼**	3 29	E	1 08	A	LIB	26
362	28	W.	7 13	E	4 19	A	9 06	14	23 15	8½	**9**	4 44	E	1 44	A	LIB	27
363	29	Th.	7 13	E	4 20	A	9 07	14	23 12	9¼	**10**	5 59	E	2 31	A	SCO	28
364	30	Fr.	7 13	E	4 21	A	9 08	13	23 07	10	**10¾**	7 09	E	3 33	A	SAG	0
365	31	Sa.	7 13	E	4 21	A	9 08	13	23 s. 03	10¾	**11½**	8 A.M. 09	E	4 P.M. 47	A	SAG	1

December hath 31 days • 2005

Life is mostly froth and bubble;
Two things stand like stone:
Kindness *in another's trouble,*
Courage *in your own.* –Adam Lindsay Gordon

D. M.	D. W.	Dates, Feasts, Fasts, Aspects, Tide Heights	Weather ↓
1	Th.	New ● • Scrabble trademark registered, 1948 • Tides {10.9 / 9.4} •	*Cold*
2	Fr.	St. Viviana • "In God We Trust" promoter Charles E. Bennett born, 1910 • {11.1 / 9.5} •	*and*
3	Sa.	☾ runs low • ☿ stat. • Discovery of "Pumpkin Papers" secret documents announced, 1948	*snowy!*
4	B	**2nd S. of Advent** • ☌♀☾ • {9.5 / 11.3} •	*Colder*
5	M.	☾ at perig. • ☌♆☾ • U.S. president Martin Van Buren born, 1782 •	*and*
6	Tu.	St. Nicholas • *No sweet without sweat.* • Tides {9.4 / 10.8} •	*snowier!*
7	W.	St. Ambrose • **National Pearl Harbor Remembrance Day** • ☌♅☾ •	*Not*
8	Th.	"In Flanders Fields" poem published, 1915 • Tides {9.6 / 10.0} •	*quite*
9	Fr.	☾ on Eq. • ☾ at ☊ • ♀ Gr. Bril. • Canada's first coin club formed, 1862 •	*as*
10	Sa.	St. Eulalia • ♂ stat. • Mississippi became the 20th state, 1817 • {10.0 / 9.5} •	*cold,*
11	B	**3rd S. of Advent** • UNICEF established, 1946 • {10.3 / 9.4}	*but*
12	M.	☌♂☾ • ☿ Gr. Elong. (21° W.) • Tides {10.6 / 9.3} •	*probably*
13	Tu.	St. Lucia • *One today is worth two tomorrows.* • Tides {10.7 / 9.3} •	*blowier!*
14	W.	Halcyon Days • Ember Day • *National Velvet* premiered, 1944 • {10.8 / 9.3} •	*Guess:*
15	Th.	**Full Cold** ○ • ☌♇☉ • Philadelphia streets first cleaned by machine, 1854 •	*a*
16	Fr.	Ember Day • ☾ rides high • Current Cape Hatteras, N.C., lighthouse began operation, 1870	*mess!*
17	Sa.	Ember Day • *The wise understand half a word.* • Tides {9.1 / 10.4} •	*Had*
18	B	**4th S. of Advent** • National Anti-Saloon League founded, 1895	*enough?*
19	M.	☌♄☾ • Mark Twain received a patent for suspenders, 1871 • {8.8 / 9.9} •	*That's*
20	Tu.	☾ at apo. • Louisiana Purchase finalized, 1803 • Tides {8.7 / 9.6} •	*tough!*
21	W.	St. Thomas • **Winter Solstice** • Crossword puzzle debuted, 1913 • {8.6 / 9.3} •	*Same*
22	Th.	Beware the Pogonip. • First string of Christmas tree lights created, 1882 • Tides {8.5 / 8.9}	*stuff,*
23	Fr.	☾ on Eq. • ♀ stat. • *Daylight now lengthens to the extent of a gnat's yawn.* •	*only*
24	Sa.	☾ at ☋ • Treaty of Ghent, agreement to end War of 1812, signed, 1814 • {8.7 / 8.4}	*harder!*
25	B	**Christmas Day** • Explorer Samuel de Champlain died, 1635 •	*2006*
26	M.	First day of Chanukah • **Boxing Day (Canada)** • ☌♃☾ •	*could*
27	Tu.	St. John • *The Howdy Doody Show* debuted, 1947 • Tides {9.6 / 8.5} •	*be*
28	W.	Holy Innocents • "A Neglected Anniversary" bathtub hoax published, 1917 •	*worse—*
29	Th.	☌☿☾ • Gaslights first used at the White House, 1848 • Tides {10.6 / 9.0} •	*better*
30	Fr.	New ● • ☾ runs low • –48°F, Mazama and Winthrop, Wash., 1968 •	*fill your*
31	Sa.	St. Sylvester • *With bounteous cheer, conclude the year.* • {11.4 / 9.6} •	*larder!*

Farmer's Calendar

■ The coming around each year of winter is the chief seasonal fact of life in this part of the country. The necessity for responding to prolonged cold, ice, and snow is the condition of man's existence in the north, and our responses are deeply ingrained in us. The onset of winter may overtake or otherwise confound our preparations, but it doesn't surprise us. Others react differently.

The first real snow of the year always seems to take the two dogs on this place by surprise. They're little, low-built creatures; to them, a couple of inches of snow are no joke. Leaving the house early on the first snowy morning, they stop short. They apparently have no memory of snow from past years. Soon, they sally forth, but where yesterday morning they dashed out into the yard at full tilt, now they move slowly, tentatively, through the new snow. Soon, being dogs, they figure out that you can eat snow. This is a revelation, because, unlike the other things they like to eat—that is, practically everything—the snow is available in unlimited and unrestricted quantities. The pair of them plow along through the stuff, happily rooting, tossing, and chomping.

The family cats also make the annual rediscovery of snow, but their reaction is more human. They are disenchanted. The boldest cat leaves the house, steps into the snow. She pauses. She raises one foot, then another, and shakes it. Then she stalks resignedly on. She doesn't try to eat the snow. She doesn't pretend to like it. Perhaps she understands that in five or six months, it will be gone.

Glossary of Almanac Oddities

■ Many readers have expressed puzzlement over the rather obscure notations that appear on our **Right-Hand Calendar Pages (181–203).** These "oddities" have long been fixtures in the Almanac, and we are pleased to provide some definitions. (Once explained, they may not seem so odd after all!)

–Beth Krommes

Ember Days (Movable): The Almanac traditionally marks the four periods formerly observed by the Roman Catholic and Anglican churches for prayer, fasting, and the ordination of clergy. These Ember Days are the Wednesdays, Fridays, and Saturdays that follow in succession after (1) the First Sunday in Lent; (2) Whitsunday–Pentecost; (3) the Feast of the Holy Cross, September 14; and (4) the Feast of St. Lucia, December 13. The word *ember* is perhaps a corruption of the Latin *quatuor tempora,* "four times."

Folklore has it that the weather on each of the three days foretells the weather for three successive months; that is, for September's Ember Days, Wednesday forecasts weather for October, Friday for November, and Saturday for December.

Distaff Day (January 7): This was the first day after Epiphany, when women were expected to get back to their spinning. (Plough Monday was the day the men returned to work, and every few years, Distaff Day and Plough Monday fall on the same day.) A distaff is the staff for holding the flax or wool in spinning, and it symbolized the domestic sphere. "The distaff side" indicated the women. One traditional proverb notes that "Yule is come and Yule is gone, and we have feasted well; so Jack must to his flail again and Jenny to her wheel."

Plough Monday (January): The first Monday after Epiphany was called Plough Monday because it was the day that men returned to their plough, or daily work, after the Christmas holiday. It was customary for farm laborers to draw a plough through the village, soliciting money for a "plough-light," which was kept burning in the parish church all year. In some areas, the custom of blessing the plough is maintained.

Three Chilly Saints (May): Mamertus, Pancras, and Gervais were three early Christian saints. Because their feast days, on May 11, 12, and 13, respectively, are traditionally cold, they have come to be known as the Three Chilly Saints. An old French saying translates to: "St. Mamertus, St. Pancras, and St. Gervais do not pass without a frost."

Midsummer Day (June 24): Although it occurs near the summer solstice, to the farmer this day is the midpoint of the growing season, halfway between planting and harvest and an occasion for festivity. The English church considered it a "Quarter Day," one of the four major divisions of the liturgical year. It also marks the feast day of St. John the Baptist.

Cornscateous Air (July): First used by early almanac makers, this term signifies warm, damp air. Though it signals ideal climatic conditions for growing corn, it also poses a danger to those affected by asthma, pneumonia, and other respiratory problems.

Dog Days (July 3–August 11): These are the hottest and most unhealthy days of the year. Also known as Canicular Days, the name derives from the Dog Star, Sirius. The traditional timing of Dog Days is the 40 days beginning July 3 and ending August 11, coinciding with the heliacal (at sunrise) rising of Sirius.

Lammas Day (August 1): From the Old English "hlaf maesse," meaning "loaf mass," Lammas Day marked the beginning of the harvest. Traditionally, loaves of bread were baked from the first-ripened grain and brought to the churches to be consecrated. Through the centuries, "loafmass" became "Lammas." In Scotland, Lammastide fairs became famous as the time when trial marriages could be made. These marriages could end after a year with no strings attached.

Cat Nights Begin (August 17): This term harks back to the days when people believed in witches. An old Irish legend says that a witch could turn into a cat and regain herself eight times, but on the ninth time, August 17, she couldn't change back, hence the saying: "A cat has nine lives." Because August is a "yowly" time for cats, this may have prompted the speculation about witches on the prowl in the first place.

Harvest Home (September): In Europe and Britain, the conclusion of the harvest each autumn was once marked by festivals of fun, feasting, and thanksgiving known as "Harvest Home." It was also a time to hold elections, pay workers, and collect rents. These festivals usually took place around the time of the au-

tumnal equinox. Certain groups in this country, particularly the Pennsylvania Dutch, have kept the tradition alive.

St. Luke's Little Summer (October): A spell of warm weather that occurs about the time of the saint's feast day, October 18, this period is sometimes referred to as Indian summer.

Indian Summer (November): A period of warm weather following a cold spell or a hard frost, Indian summer can occur between St. Martin's Day (November 11) and November 20. Although there are differing dates for its occurrence, for more than 200 years the Almanac has adhered to the saying "If All Saints' brings out winter, St. Martin's brings out Indian summer." As for the origin of the term, some say it comes from the early Native Americans, who believed that the condition was caused by a warm wind sent from the court of their southwestern god, Cautantowwit.

Halcyon Days (December): About 14 days of calm weather follow the blustery winds of autumn's end. The ancient Greeks and Romans believed them to occur around the time of the winter solstice, when the halcyon, or kingfisher, was brooding. In a nest floating on the sea, the bird was said to have charmed the wind and waves so that the waters were especially calm during this period.

Beware the Pogonip (December): The word *pogonip* is a meteorological term used to describe an uncommon occurrence—frozen fog. The word was coined by Native Americans to describe the frozen fogs of fine ice needles that occur in the mountain valleys of the western United States and Canada. According to Indian tradition, breathing the fog is injurious to the lungs.

Holidays and Observances

A selected list of commemorative days, with federal holidays denoted by *.

Jan. 1	New Year's Day*
Jan. 17	Martin Luther King Jr.'s Birthday *(observed)** Benjamin Franklin's Birthday
Jan. 19	Robert E. Lee Day *(Ark., Fla., Ky., La., S.C.)*
Feb. 2	Groundhog Day Guadalupe-Hidalgo Treaty Day *(N.Mex.)*
Feb. 8	Mardi Gras *(Baldwin & Mobile Counties, Ala.; La.)*
Feb. 12	Abraham Lincoln's Birthday
Feb. 14	St. Valentine's Day
Feb. 15	Susan B. Anthony's Birthday *(Fla.; Wis.)*
Feb. 21	George Washington's Birthday *(observed)**
Mar. 1	Town Meeting Day *(Vt.)*
Mar. 2	Texas Independence Day
Mar. 15	Andrew Jackson Day *(Tenn.)*
Mar. 17	St. Patrick's Day Evacuation Day *(Suffolk Co., Mass.)*
Mar. 28	Seward's Day *(Alaska)*
Apr. 2	Pascua Florida Day
Apr. 13	Thomas Jefferson's Birthday
Apr. 18	Patriots Day *(Maine; Mass.)*
Apr. 21	San Jacinto Day *(Tex.)*
Apr. 22	Earth Day
Apr. 29	National Arbor Day
May 1	May Day
May 5	Cinco de Mayo
May 8	Mother's Day Truman Day *(Mo.)*
May 21	Armed Forces Day
May 22	National Maritime Day
May 23	Victoria Day *(Canada)*
May 30	Memorial Day *(observed)**
June 5	World Environment Day
June 11	King Kamehameha I Day *(Hawaii)*
June 14	Flag Day

June 17	Bunker Hill Day *(Suffolk Co., Mass.)*
June 19	Father's Day Emancipation Day *(Tex.)*
June 20	West Virginia Day
July 1	Canada Day
July 4	Independence Day*
July 24	Pioneer Day *(Utah)*
Aug. 1	Colorado Day Civic Holiday *(Canada)*
Aug. 16	Bennington Battle Day *(Vt.)*
Aug. 19	National Aviation Day
Aug. 26	Women's Equality Day
Sept. 5	Labor Day*
Sept. 9	Admission Day *(Calif.)*
Sept. 11	Grandparents Day
Sept. 17	Citizenship Day
Oct. 3	Child Health Day
Oct. 9	Leif Eriksson Day
Oct. 10	Columbus Day *(observed)** Thanksgiving Day *(Canada)* Native Americans Day *(S.Dak.)*
Oct. 18	Alaska Day
Oct. 24	United Nations Day
Oct. 31	Halloween Nevada Day
Nov. 4	Will Rogers Day *(Okla.)*
Nov. 8	Election Day
Nov. 11	Veterans Day* Remembrance Day *(Canada)*
Nov. 19	Discovery Day *(Puerto Rico)*
Nov. 24	Thanksgiving Day*
Nov. 25	Acadian Day *(La.)*
Nov. 27	John F. Kennedy Day *(Mass.)*
Dec. 7	National Pearl Harbor Remembrance Day
Dec. 15	Bill of Rights Day
Dec. 17	Wright Brothers Day
Dec. 25	Christmas Day*
Dec. 26	Boxing Day *(Canada)* First day of Kwanzaa

Get holiday and seasonal advice at www.almanac.com. **2005**

2004

January
S	M	T	W	T	F	S
				1	2	3
4	5	6	7	8	9	10
11	12	13	14	15	16	17
18	19	20	21	22	23	24
25	26	27	28	29	30	31

February
S	M	T	W	T	F	S
1	2	3	4	5	6	7
8	9	10	11	12	13	14
15	16	17	18	19	20	21
22	23	24	25	26	27	28
29						

March
S	M	T	W	T	F	S
	1	2	3	4	5	6
7	8	9	10	11	12	13
14	15	16	17	18	19	20
21	22	23	24	25	26	27
28	29	30	31			

April
S	M	T	W	T	F	S
				1	2	3
4	5	6	7	8	9	10
11	12	13	14	15	16	17
18	19	20	21	22	23	24
25	26	27	28	29	30	

May
S	M	T	W	T	F	S
						1
2	3	4	5	6	7	8
9	10	11	12	13	14	15
16	17	18	19	20	21	22
23	24	25	26	27	28	29
30	31					

June
S	M	T	W	T	F	S
		1	2	3	4	5
6	7	8	9	10	11	12
13	14	15	16	17	18	19
20	21	22	23	24	25	26
27	28	29	30			

July
S	M	T	W	T	F	S
				1	2	3
4	5	6	7	8	9	10
11	12	13	14	15	16	17
18	19	20	21	22	23	24
25	26	27	28	29	30	31

August
S	M	T	W	T	F	S
1	2	3	4	5	6	7
8	9	10	11	12	13	14
15	16	17	18	19	20	21
22	23	24	25	26	27	28
29	30	31				

September
S	M	T	W	T	F	S
			1	2	3	4
5	6	7	8	9	10	11
12	13	14	15	16	17	18
19	20	21	22	23	24	25
26	27	28	29	30		

October
S	M	T	W	T	F	S
					1	2
3	4	5	6	7	8	9
10	11	12	13	14	15	16
17	18	19	20	21	22	23
24	25	26	27	28	29	30
31						

November
S	M	T	W	T	F	S
	1	2	3	4	5	6
7	8	9	10	11	12	13
14	15	16	17	18	19	20
21	22	23	24	25	26	27
28	29	30				

December
S	M	T	W	T	F	S
			1	2	3	4
5	6	7	8	9	10	11
12	13	14	15	16	17	18
19	20	21	22	23	24	25
26	27	28	29	30	31	

2005

January
S	M	T	W	T	F	S
						1
2	3	4	5	6	7	8
9	10	11	12	13	14	15
16	17	18	19	20	21	22
23	24	25	26	27	28	29
30	31					

February
S	M	T	W	T	F	S
		1	2	3	4	5
6	7	8	9	10	11	12
13	14	15	16	17	18	19
20	21	22	23	24	25	26
27	28					

March
S	M	T	W	T	F	S
		1	2	3	4	5
6	7	8	9	10	11	12
13	14	15	16	17	18	19
20	21	22	23	24	25	26
27	28	29	30	31		

April
S	M	T	W	T	F	S
					1	2
3	4	5	6	7	8	9
10	11	12	13	14	15	16
17	18	19	20	21	22	23
24	25	26	27	28	29	30

May
S	M	T	W	T	F	S
1	2	3	4	5	6	7
8	9	10	11	12	13	14
15	16	17	18	19	20	21
22	23	24	25	26	27	28
29	30	31				

June
S	M	T	W	T	F	S
			1	2	3	4
5	6	7	8	9	10	11
12	13	14	15	16	17	18
19	20	21	22	23	24	25
26	27	28	29	30		

July
S	M	T	W	T	F	S
					1	2
3	4	5	6	7	8	9
10	11	12	13	14	15	16
17	18	19	20	21	22	23
24	25	26	27	28	29	30
31						

August
S	M	T	W	T	F	S
	1	2	3	4	5	6
7	8	9	10	11	12	13
14	15	16	17	18	19	20
21	22	23	24	25	26	27
28	29	30	31			

September
S	M	T	W	T	F	S
				1	2	3
4	5	6	7	8	9	10
11	12	13	14	15	16	17
18	19	20	21	22	23	24
25	26	27	28	29	30	

October
S	M	T	W	T	F	S
						1
2	3	4	5	6	7	8
9	10	11	12	13	14	15
16	17	18	19	20	21	22
23	24	25	26	27	28	29
30	31					

November
S	M	T	W	T	F	S
		1	2	3	4	5
6	7	8	9	10	11	12
13	14	15	16	17	18	19
20	21	22	23	24	25	26
27	28	29	30			

December
S	M	T	W	T	F	S
				1	2	3
4	5	6	7	8	9	10
11	12	13	14	15	16	17
18	19	20	21	22	23	24
25	26	27	28	29	30	31

2006

January
S	M	T	W	T	F	S
1	2	3	4	5	6	7
8	9	10	11	12	13	14
15	16	17	18	19	20	21
22	23	24	25	26	27	28
29	30	31				

February
S	M	T	W	T	F	S
			1	2	3	4
5	6	7	8	9	10	11
12	13	14	15	16	17	18
19	20	21	22	23	24	25
26	27	28				

March
S	M	T	W	T	F	S
			1	2	3	4
5	6	7	8	9	10	11
12	13	14	15	16	17	18
19	20	21	22	23	24	25
26	27	28	29	30	31	

April
S	M	T	W	T	F	S
						1
2	3	4	5	6	7	8
9	10	11	12	13	14	15
16	17	18	19	20	21	22
23	24	25	26	27	28	29
30						

May
S	M	T	W	T	F	S
	1	2	3	4	5	6
7	8	9	10	11	12	13
14	15	16	17	18	19	20
21	22	23	24	25	26	27
28	29	30	31			

June
S	M	T	W	T	F	S
				1	2	3
4	5	6	7	8	9	10
11	12	13	14	15	16	17
18	19	20	21	22	23	24
25	26	27	28	29	30	

July
S	M	T	W	T	F	S
						1
2	3	4	5	6	7	8
9	10	11	12	13	14	15
16	17	18	19	20	21	22
23	24	25	26	27	28	29
30	31					

August
S	M	T	W	T	F	S
		1	2	3	4	5
6	7	8	9	10	11	12
13	14	15	16	17	18	19
20	21	22	23	24	25	26
27	28	29	30	31		

September
S	M	T	W	T	F	S
					1	2
3	4	5	6	7	8	9
10	11	12	13	14	15	16
17	18	19	20	21	22	23
24	25	26	27	28	29	30

October
S	M	T	W	T	F	S
1	2	3	4	5	6	7
8	9	10	11	12	13	14
15	16	17	18	19	20	21
22	23	24	25	26	27	28
29	30	31				

November
S	M	T	W	T	F	S
			1	2	3	4
5	6	7	8	9	10	11
12	13	14	15	16	17	18
19	20	21	22	23	24	25
26	27	28	29	30		

December
S	M	T	W	T	F	S
					1	2
3	4	5	6	7	8	9
10	11	12	13	14	15	16
17	18	19	20	21	22	23
24	25	26	27	28	29	30
31						

What on Earth Is Earth Day?

BY CHRISTINE SCHULTZ

"We won't have a society if we destroy the environment."

–Margaret Mead, American anthropologist (1901–1978)

■ IN THE LATE 1960s, water quality had reached such a sorry state that the spark of a passing train set fire to Cleveland's chemical-clogged Cuyahoga River. Overuse of pesticides was killing off America's songbirds, as writer Rachel Carson had warned in *Silent Spring*. Media reports noted the fast decline of Lake Erie, one of the country's largest freshwater sources, and other reports linked noxious factory and car fumes to the death and disease of residents in cities, including New York and Los Angeles.

Despite such startling warnings, the environment did not even rank as a political issue. That bothered both San Francisco activist John McConnell and Gaylord Nelson, who was then a U.S. senator from Wisconsin. "The people were concerned," says Nelson, "but the politicians were not."

In an effort to get the environment on the national agenda, each man challenged Americans to join in a grassroots demonstration in 1970: McConnell chose March 21 (to acknowledge the equinox), and

Nelson, April 22.

Those first Earth Days earned widespread recognition. McConnell's event, which included the tolling of bells around the world, drew the support of the United Nations. Nelson's event "organized itself," he said later. From coast to coast, people of all ages and walks of life attended teach-ins and protested oil spills, eight-lane highways, lead poisoning, DDT, and vanishing forests, among other things.

Today, both days continue to be recognized. The Earth Day Network (EDN), an alliance of about 180 countries, organizes a variety of worldwide events on April 22. Canadians, for instance, celebrate with Edmonton's Earth Day Festival, Victoria's Earth Walk, and Waterways Cleanup in Oakville, Ontario.

Public attitudes have changed, and the environment has benefited from legislation that has been enacted in the past 35 years. But equally significant for Gaylord Nelson is the impact of the movement on the population: "One of the greatest, most important fallouts [of Earth Day] is that sixth-, seventh- and eighth-graders ask much more perceptive, penetrating questions about the environment than college seniors and college graduate students did in 1970."

MEET THE FOUNDERS

To learn more about John McConnell and Gaylord Nelson, go to **www.almanac.com** and click on **Article Links 2005.**

John McConnell   *Gaylord Nelson*

WHAT A DIFFERENCE A DAY MAKES

■ Environmental advocates represented just 1 percent of the U.S. population in May 1969, one year before Earth Day.

■ In 1971, following the second Earth Day, 25 percent of the U.S. population claimed an interest in saving the planet.

■ A Gallup poll from 2000 indicated that 67 percent of the U.S. population would prefer protecting the environment over economic growth, if a choice had to be made.   □□

Christine Schultz, who hates to throw anything away, religiously recycles and participates in hazardous waste pickup days.

Take a few moments
to step back in
time to the
good ol' days of

1955

C ompared with today, life in 1955 seemed idyllic. Those were the days when an average worker with an annual income of about $5,000 felt downright prosperous and had enough disposable income to put a shiny new Ford Thunderbird or Chevrolet Bel Air in the garage. (Safety belts weren't yet much of a concern, two-tone paint jobs were all the rage, and automatic transmissions were a coveted option.) Morality was simple: Adults considered listening to rock 'n' roll on a transistor radio a sure sign of a rebellious teen, and the idea of the married Ricardos of TV's *I Love Lucy* sleeping together in one bed was considered too risqué for prime-time viewers. Back then, a time-saving gadget was an electric stove or a refrigerator with a freezer, and a color television was a luxury. Owning all three signaled the promise of the good life. In 1955, the future of the American family looked very bright, indeed.

by Anastasia Kusterbeck

Everybody, Let's Rock!

Topping the charts were "Ain't That a Shame?" by Fats Domino, "Earth Angel" by the Penguins, and "Rock Around the Clock" by Bill Haley and His Comets. Over 15,000 teenage fans paid two dollars to see acts such as Fats Domino and the Drifters perform at the first Rock 'n' Roll Party in New York City, with girls decked out in appliquéd poodle skirts and neat ponytails and boys wearing a Marlon Brando–inspired outfit of white T-shirt, blue jeans, and leather jacket. Neighbors congregated at TV parties to watch *The $64,000 Question* or *The Lawrence Welk Show,* with the TV owner expected to serve food and drinks.

Bobby-soxers, adolescent girls so named because of their "bobby sox" that reached above the ankle, didn't rock around any clock—despite Bill Haley's encouragement. The girls (and boys as well) had strict curfews.

M'm! M'm! Good!

"Convenience" foods were popular in the kitchen. Mothers cooked Quaker instant oatmeal for kids heading off to school. Dishes concocted with processed ingredients, such as Velveeta cheese, and Lipton and Campbell soups (remember Green Bean Bake?) turned moms into master chefs. Supper staples included tuna noodle casserole, sloppy joes, and hamburger Stroganoff.

continued

–Retrofile.com

Kids' Stuff

Wide-eyed boys and girls scoured the pages of the Sears, Roebuck & Company's Christmas "wishbook" pages. Toy manufacturers saw kids as customers for the first time (although TV ads targeted only parents, the ones with the wallets). The Walt Disney "Davy Crockett" craze led parents to buy 10 million coonskin caps, endangering the nation's raccoon population.

Far Out, Big Daddy

The terms "midlife crisis," "stress management," and "credit card debt" were unknown. "Hip" talk included words such as "threads" (clothing), "go ape" (to get excited), "big daddy" (an authority figure), and "cruisin' for a bruisin'" (making trouble). "Far out," "real gone," or "the most" signified cool, and no one wanted to be called a "square."

The car culture of the 1950s had a lingo all its own:

- **Agitate the gravel:** to leave
- **Burn rubber:** to accelerate quickly and hard, leaving black tire marks on the pavement
- **Drag:** a short race; and, as a verb, to race in one
- **Fire up:** to start your engine (usually loudly)
- **Flip-top, ragtop:** a convertible car
- **Goose it:** to accelerate the car fully
- **Punch it:** to step on the gas
- **Rocket, rod, screamer:** a souped-up car
- **Souped-up:** modified to go fast

—Retrofile.com

Easy Come, Easy Go

Although less than 1 percent of roads were multilane divided highways, the American love affair with the automobile was in full swing. New car sales reached a record 7,915,000, and families took to the nation's newly paved roadways in record numbers. They were greeted by new motor lodges cropping up across the landscape, with blossoming chains such as Holiday Inn, Howard Johnson, and Travelodge introducing

motorists to amenities such as color televisions, in-room phones, and swimming pools. Luxury trains such as the famously sleek, stainless-steel *California Zephyr* proved stiff competition for fledgling jet airliners, which were still not affordable for middle-class Americans.

■

The General Motors "Motorama" auto extravaganza unveiled his-and-hers flying cars, complete with compartments for groceries.

Oops!

- Sam Phillips, owner of Sun Records, sold Elvis Presley's contract for $35,000.

- Chlorophyll (the stuff that makes plants green) was added to toothpaste, deodorant, and chewing gum and promoted as a foolproof way to eliminate bad odors.

- It was commonly believed that filters rendered cigarettes harmless to your health.

Great Expectations

- The Institute for Boiler & Radiator Manufacturers predicted that American homes would soon be heated and cooled by small atomic reactors that would provide unlimited hot water and melt snow from driveways and sidewalks.

- Vacuum cleaner manufacturer Alex Lewyt promised homemakers that nuclear-powered vacuum cleaners would be in stores within the decade.

- President Eisenhower's special assistant, Harold Stassen, predicted that nuclear power would create a world where "hunger is unknown . . . where food never rots and crops never spoil . . . where no one stokes a furnace or curses the smog . . . where the air is everywhere as fresh as on a mountaintop, and the breeze from a factory, as sweet as from a rose."

Timeless Favorites

- The term "cool"
- Bowling alleys
- Backyard barbecues. Sales of outdoor cooking equipment rose to $30 million as dads served up grilled hamburgers and hot dogs in record numbers.

- Baseball. Fans danced and wept for joy in the streets of Brooklyn—and on the field (below)—after the Dodgers beat the Yankees in the 1955 World Series.

–photos left and above: CORBIS

continued

Popular Pastimes

THEN	NOW
Paint-by-number artist kits	Video game consoles
Drive-in movie theaters	DVD home theaters
3-D movies viewed by using special eyewear	Surround-sound at multiplex theaters
One TV per household	One computer (and TV) per room or person
Drive-in restaurants where passengers were served in the car	Drive-up menu boards and take-out windows
One rotary-dial telephone per household	One cell phone per person

–Retrofile.com

By the Numbers

	THEN	NOW
Price of a loaf of bread	$.18	$2.00
Minimum hourly wage	$.75	$5.15
Average size of a new home (sq. ft.)	1,170	2,320
Percent of homes with complete plumbing (hot and cold water, and a flush toilet)	65	99
Percent of mothers working outside the home	27	72

How Time Flew

The typical homemaker made trips to the butcher, the baker, and the grocer to get ingredients to cook three meals a day. She usually found a few free hours for a game of bridge, some socializing, or a Tupperware party. It was customary for her to pay a weekly visit to the hairdresser, and she always had time to "make her face." Businessmen lingered over three-martini lunches and had plenty of time for golf outings. After walking home from school, kids played with other kids in the neighborhood—riding bikes, playing dodgeball or sandlot baseball, skipping rope, or exploring nearby woods or fields until dinnertime, when the family would assemble for a leisurely meal and conversation about the day's events.

–Retrofile.com

Exactly 50 Years Ago

- Disneyland opened in Anaheim, California.

- Johnson & Johnson introduced Baby Shampoo.

- "Walk/Don't Walk" signs appeared on New York City street corners.

- Kentucky Fried Chicken opened its first restaurant.

- Ann Landers' advice column was first published in the *Chicago Sun Times.*

- After a year of clinical trials, Dr. Jonas Salk's polio vaccine was proved to be a success.

- The National Farmer's Organization was founded in Corning, Iowa, with the goal of getting higher prices from food processors.

Anastasia Kusterbeck, who was born too late to experience 1955, writes about history and culture from Long Island, New York.

The Power of One

On December 1, 1955, when Rosa Parks, a 42-year-old African-American woman who worked as a seamstress at a Montgomery, Alabama, department store, was asked to give up her seat on the bus to a white rider, she didn't argue; she just quietly refused to move. The bus driver warned, "Well, I'm going to have you arrested." She replied, "You may go on and do so."

The next morning, 35,000 flyers were handed out to children at all-black schools with a simple message that read in part: "We are asking every Negro to stay off the buses Monday in protest of the arrest and trial." Shortly afterward, a huge crowd assembled at Dexter Avenue Baptist Church to hear the young Dr. Martin Luther King Jr. speak about the incident, which sparked the Montgomery Bus Boycott. Thousands of African-Americans flatly refused to ride the city's buses. Some walked long distances to work each day, and others arranged car pools. Black cab drivers picked

up protesters for ten cents a ride (the same as city bus fare). Some boycotters even rode mules to get to their destinations. Police retaliated by arresting car-pool drivers for picking up hitchhikers and by bringing loitering charges against individuals waiting on street corners for a ride. Dr. King's home was bombed. Three hundred eighty-one days later, the U.S. Supreme Court declared segregation on buses to be illegal. "Our mistreatment was just not right, and I was tired of it," writes Parks in her autobiography, *Quiet Strength.* Today, she still symbolizes the awesome power of one individual to change an unjust system. ▢▢

To mark the 60th anniversary of the end of World War II
and in a salute to armed forces everywhere, we visit

THE TOWN WHERE "TAPS"
NEVER ENDS
by Mel Allen

They come every day: old men walking slowly now
with their wives, often with their children and
grandchildren, to the National D-Day Memorial
in Bedford, Virginia, in the heart of the Blue
Ridge Mountains. They pass the statues of soldiers fighting and soldiers dying; the reflecting
pool where spurting water recreates the effect of
gunfire; and the Memorial Wall, on which are en-
graved the names of soldiers who lost their lives
on June 6, 1944, on a beach in Normandy, France.
Nearly everyone who comes here to the 88-acre
reserve feels the solitude of memory.

"This is a very patriotic place," says April
Cheek, the Memorial's director of education. "It's
for everyone who has been touched by war—any
war. All wars are about sacrifice."

From the Memorial, visitors look out to the
Peaks of Otter and below to the courthouse tower
and church steeples of Bedford—which suffered
more D-Day casualties, per capita, than any other
town in America.

In the 1930s, Bedford had a population of about
3,200. Many of its young men signed up for the
Virginia National Guard. They enlisted out of a
sense of duty and loyalty, yes, but in those days, the
one-dollar-a-day Guard pay was welcome money,
too. The boys all knew each other; they had grown
up together. There were three sets of brothers, including one set of twins, and lots of cousins. While
most were farm boys, others worked in the woods
or the woolen mill, or in construction. Some had just

D-Day's operational code name,
"Overlord," is commemorated
on the Victory Arch at the D-Day
Memorial *(right);* some of
Bedford's comrades-in-arms,
c. 1941 *(below).*

–photo top right, National D-Day Memorial Foundation; right, R. O. Stevens

Twins Ray *(far left)* and Roy Stevens had never really been apart prior to D-Day.

In June 1944, the 29th Division—15,000 strong—received its orders: Along with the battle-seasoned 1st Division, it was to lead the assault on Omaha Beach. In the early-morning darkness of June 6, the men of Company A—each weighted down with a gear- and ammo-filled pack—climbed into boats and huddled in the chill of a storm-swept sea.

graduated from high school; most were in their 20s. They played ball together and hung out together in the movie theater or at Green's Drugstore. They trained in the basement of the courthouse, marched in parades, and mostly had fun together—until February 1941.

With the world at war, Bedford's 98 National Guardsmen were sworn into the regular army at that time, forming Company A, 116th Regiment, 29th Division. After they departed for training at Fort Meade, Maryland, the local newspaper reported, "The town feels strangely empty."

Eighteen months later, Bedford's boys sailed to England, where for nearly two more years they trained to storm a beach. Almost every week, they swam in frigid English lakes and rivers and scaled cliffs while carrying 60-pound packs. Their captain, Taylor Fellers, was a Bedford farm boy who had led them since they started training and was aware of their impending mission. From England, Fellers wrote to his parents: "It is hard to beat a Bedford boy for a soldier. . . . I am truly proud to be commanding my old hometown outfit and just hope I can carry them right on through and bring all of them home."

At 6:35 A.M., the ramps fell away from the landing-craft assault boats as they approached the sand. Captain Fellers, who had crawled out of sick bay earlier, began leading his men in the slog through the surf toward the sector of the beach code-named "Dog Green"—and to their almost certain deaths. From the cliffs, German machine gunners fired thousands of rounds per minute. Mortars exploded. Snipers silenced wounded soldiers as they cried for help. Fellers and 18 other Bedford soldiers died, probably within 15 minutes. Three more died over the next few days.

Nearly six weeks passed before the residents of Bedford learned what had happened to their boys. "It was like waiting for an earthquake," recalled Helen Cundiss, who later married Roy Stevens from Company A. On July 17, Elizabeth Teass, the telegraph operator in Green's Drugstore, turned on the telegraph machine and saw the names of dead Bedford soldiers come clicking out. Teass sent telegrams all over town: to the woolen mill, to farmhouses,

Roy Stevens and his wife Helen embrace in front of their new home just after their marriage on February 2, 1946.

and to the homes of the minister, the doctor, the undertaker, the taxi driver. "It was one quiet, still little town," Teass would remember. "Everybody's heart was broken."

Macie Hoback lost two sons. Her daughter Lucille, who today leads tours at the D-Day Memorial, says that her mother would wake up suddenly in bed and cry out, "Where are my boys? Where are my boys?"

Viola Parker received a telegram that said her husband Earl was missing in action. "I thought, 'Well, I'd better dust.' I dusted the whole house." She then picked

up her infant daughter and began to walk toward the mountains. "We're going to make it," she told her daughter. "We're going to make it."

Two days later, the *Bedford Bulletin* eulogized: "These Bedford men have given their lives in the same cause for which men in all ages have made the supreme sacrifice—the preservation of the ideals of liberty and justice toward which mankind has been struggling since the dawn of time."

Only six Bedford men who landed on D-Day survived and eventually returned home. Roy Stevens (Helen's husband) was one, but his twin, Ray, was not. "We were never separated until June 6, 1944," says Roy. His landing craft had sunk and he had been ferried back to England (only to return to Omaha Beach four days later).

At the dedication of the National D-Day Memorial in 2001, more than 10,000 people pressed together under the Victory Arch to remember every soldier from every town and city who had ever fought in any U.S. war. Bedford had become a place where "Taps" never ends.

NEVER AGAIN

Because so many boys from this one community were lost on D-Day, the U.S. War (now Defense) Department has never again sent into battle a company made up of soldiers all from the same town. □□

Mel Allen, the executive editor of YANKEE Magazine, writes on a variety of topics for *The Old Farmer's Almanac*.

WATCH, READ, REMEMBER. Both D-Day and the soldiers from Bedford, Virginia, have been immortalized in films and books. For lists of recommended titles, as well as more information about the D-Day Memorial, go to **www.almanac.com** and click on **Article Links 2005.**

BURIED ALIVE

Eighty years ago, one man's curiosity led to the most famous rescue drama of the time. by Mel Allen

O n the chilly, windy Friday morning of January 30, 1925, a 37-year-old Kentucky farmer and intrepid cave explorer named Floyd Collins squeezed his lanky, rawboned, 160-pound frame deep into a cave he had discovered a few miles from his Barren County home, just outside of Cave City. He was searching not for adventure but for hope for a new life. Just down the road, Mammoth Cave attracted thousands of tourists. Caves for the new automobile traveler had become a cash crop in Kentucky.

continued

Floyd Collins *(above)* in 1924. Reporter William "Skeets" Miller *(right)* visited the trapped Collins and chronicled the tragedy with stories that captivated the nation *(left)*.

–Wade Highbaugh/courtesy Roger W. Brucker

–newspapers and Miller photo:
The Courier-Journal

Journal.

Largest Morning Circulation
Of Any Kentucky Newspaper

FEBRUARY 5, 1925.   THREE CENTS

COLLINS, REPOR

THIXTON   "Skeets The First"   NEW CAV
NT IN RUM   Is Cave City Ruler   NOW FOUN
KIN HELD!   BY GER

Floyd, who had been caving since boyhood, had experience crawling through narrow places. This picture of him was taken in a Kentucky cavern, about ten days before he entered Sand Cave.

Still, not just any cave would do. Eight years earlier, Floyd had discovered one of Kentucky's most beautiful caves. He had named it Crystal Cave for the gypsum flowers that shined like crystals when his lantern light settled on them. But Crystal was too remote for most tourists. Floyd believed that his latest discovery, an opening he called Sand Cave, might lead into Mammoth, like a tributary feeding into a river. If it did, surely a steady stream of tourists and fame and fortune lay just beyond the darkness.

On this morning, he descended into the shaft as he had done on other days. Crawling homeward, some 120 feet from the entrance and 55 feet underground, he knocked over his oil lamp and was plunged into total darkness. Floyd squirmed headfirst toward the cave's mouth, until, with one thrust, his foot dislodged an overhanging boulder from the cave wall. The boulder fell, pinning his left

ankle in a narrow crevice. The more he fought to free himself, the more rock and debris he tore loose. Soon the cave held him in an ever-tightening vise.

Floyd, who had been crawling into caves since boyhood, had been in tight spots before, but never one in which he felt so helpless. His hands had become scraped and bloody from clawing at rocks. Icy snowmelt dripped through the cave's ceiling onto his face. The damp ground in the 54°F chamber chilled him. Even knowing that it would be hours before family and friends missed him, he yelled for help until he lost his voice. Alone with his thoughts, surely one memory crisscrossed through his mind: A day earlier, he had told his stepmother, Miss Jane, that he'd dreamed about being trapped by a rock in his new cave, and angels had come for him. About his latest discovery, she had warned, "Don't go back in there, Floyd."

On Saturday morning, neighbors found

—Brown Brothers

Floyd's coat hanging just inside the entrance to the cave. They crawled through the narrow passage until they heard him cry out, and then set about gathering a rescue team.

Floyd's younger brother, Homer, was one of the first to reach him. Floyd's body, pinned tightly between the cave's walls, blocked Homer's attempts to reach his foot. The best Homer could do was scrape some dirt away, feed him sausages and coffee, and place an oilcloth over his face to relieve the torture of the incessantly dripping cold water. He watched his brother slip in and out of consciousness and heard him say over and over, "Take me home to bed, Homer." Later, to another neighbor who crawled in, Floyd said, "I'm trapped for life."

On day three of the entrapment, the Louisville *Courier-Journal* dispatched a 21-year-old reporter named William "Skeets" Miller to the scene. When he arrived at the cave, Miller asked Homer for details. Homer, his nerves frayed and body weary, snapped, "If you want information, there's the hole right over there. You can go down and find out for yourself."

The more he fought to free himself, the more rock and debris he tore loose.

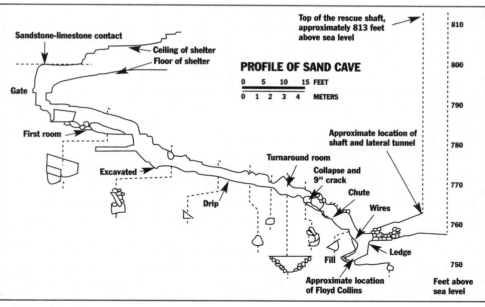

PROFILE OF SAND CAVE

This profile of Sand Cave depicts accurate horizontal and vertical distances. The drop-down cutaways indicate the shape and relative size of the cave shaft in specific places.

–Roger W. Brucker

223

-Russell T. Neville/courtesy Roger W. Brucker

Sand Cave shelter area in the summer of 1925, after Floyd Collins's body was removed.

Later Miller said, "I was ashamed not to go." Terrified, yet spurred by his journalistic duty, Miller entered the cave with Homer, not knowing that soon his life would be inextricably and forever linked to that of the trapped man.

Miller's coverage transformed a local tragedy into a national drama. His descriptions of Floyd's plight riveted the nation:

"Floyd Collins is suffering torture almost beyond description. . . . [He] has been in agony every conscious moment since he was trapped. . . . Before I could see his face, . . . I was forced to raise a small piece of oilcloth covering it.

"'Put it back,' he said. 'Put it back—the water!' . . . I tried to squirm over Collins's body to reach the rock, until he begged me to get off. 'It hurts—hurts awful,' he said. Collins is lying on his back, resting more on the left side. His two arms are held fast in the crevice beside his body, so that he

really is in a natural straightjacket."

Each day's papers brought new stories from Miller, the only reporter to reach Floyd's side. His words went out to more than 1,200 Associated Press–affiliated newspapers and became the historical and emotional witness to the struggle to free Floyd from his tomb.

Readers followed the excruciating rescue attempts. One involved yanking a rope attached to a harness around Floyd's torso—until he screamed, "Stop! It's pulling me in two!" Miller himself tried in vain to rig a jack under a crowbar in a desperate effort to pry loose the rock. Through it all, the reporter gave the trapped man a voice and an uncommon dignity in what has been called the most unusual interview in the history of American journalism—one man talking, one man listening in a dark hole, lit only by a dim light.

"'I prayed as hard as I could. . . . [And] sometimes I would be in a stupor. I could

hear people coming in, but they seemed far away. . . . I dreamed of angels. . . . I have faced death before. It doesn't frighten me. But it is so long. Oh, God, be merciful! I know I am going to get out. I feel it. Something tells me to be brave and I'm going to be. . . . Tell everybody outside that I love every one of them, and tell them I am not going to give up.' "

In the early hours of the fifth day, the cave's walls collapsed, cutting Floyd off from his rescuers, from food, and from hope. The last words rescuers heard from him were, "You're too slow. Too slow."

Yet they didn't give up. In a race against time, engineers concentrated all their efforts into sinking a shaft that would lead to Floyd's chamber. If they could dig two feet an hour, there was a chance—but the muck and rock fought back. Sometimes, they advanced only a few inches per hour. A rift developed between the locals and the outside "experts." Homer insisted that the only way to get Floyd out alive was to continue through the cave's entrance. He became so insistent that state officials barred him from the cave.

On Sunday, February 8, in a tragic and bizarre twist of fate, Floyd himself became the tourist attraction he had sought for so long, as thousands of curious people roamed the area. Everyone seemed to want to be a part of America's most compelling story. Vendors sold balloons, hot dogs, pies, and snake-oil remedies. Traffic was backed up for miles.

The rescue dragged on for another week, finally ending on February 16, when a worker made his way down the shaft and shined a light on Floyd's corpse. A physician estimated that somehow Floyd had stayed alive until only a few days earlier.

The nation's press departed. The curious followed. The state claimed that it was too dangerous to remove the body, but Homer hired miners to bring Floyd home. On April 26, he was laid to rest again in a grave beside the Flint Ridge family homestead—but he would not find peace for more than 60 years.

Floyd's father sold Crystal Cave to a local dentist. The dentist had Floyd's body placed in a glass-topped casket inside the cave on June 13, 1927. In March 1929, the body disappeared, only to be found hours later with the help of bloodhounds, at the edge of the Green River. The remains—one leg was missing—were returned to the cave.

In 1961, Crystal Cave was sold to the federal government, which now inherited the sticky problem of what to do with the body. They let it lie.

Over time, Floyd's relatives pressured the National Park Service to release his body for burial near the ancestral home. On March 24, 1989, the body was buried for the final time at the Mammoth Cave Baptist Church Cemetery on Flint Ridge.

□□

STRANGE BUT TRUE

In 1975, the Louisville *Courier-Journal* conducted a statewide poll to determine the state's top story of the century. The Floyd Collins rescue saga won.

GO DEEPER

To learn more about Floyd Collins and to get some tips on caving today, go to **www.almanac.com** and click on **Article Links 2005**.

Table of Measures

Apothecaries'
1 scruple = 20 grains
1 dram = 3 scruples
1 ounce = 8 drams
1 pound = 12 ounces

Avoirdupois
1 ounce = 16 drams
1 pound = 16 ounces
1 hundredweight = 100 pounds
1 ton = 2,000 pounds
1 long ton = 2,240 pounds

Liquid
4 gills = 1 pint
63 gallons = 1 hogshead
2 hogsheads = 1 pipe or butt
2 pipes = 1 tun

Dry
2 pints = 1 quart
4 quarts = 1 gallon
2 gallons = 1 peck
4 pecks = 1 bushel

Linear
1 hand = 4 inches
1 link = 7.92 inches
1 span = 9 inches
1 foot = 12 inches
1 yard = 3 feet
1 rod = 5½ yards
1 mile = 320 rods = 1,760 yards = 5,280 feet
1 Int. nautical mile = 6,076.1155 feet
1 knot = 1 nautical mile per hour
1 fathom = 2 yards = 6 feet
1 furlong = ⅛ mile = 660 feet = 220 yards
1 league = 3 miles = 24 furlongs
1 chain = 100 links = 22 yards

Square
1 square foot = 144 square inches
1 square yard = 9 square feet
1 square rod = 30¼ square yards = 272¼ square feet
1 acre = 160 square rods = 43,560 square feet
1 square mile = 640 acres = 102,400 square rods
1 square rod = 625 square links
1 square chain = 16 square rods
1 acre = 10 square chains

Cubic
1 cubic foot = 1,728 cubic inches
1 cubic yard = 27 cubic feet
1 cord = 128 cubic feet
1 U.S. liquid gallon = 4 quarts = 231 cubic inches
1 Imperial gallon = 1.20 U.S. gallons = 0.16 cubic foot
1 board foot = 144 cubic inches

Kitchen
3 teaspoons = 1 tablespoon
16 tablespoons = 1 cup
1 cup = 8 ounces
2 cups = 1 pint
2 pints = 1 quart
4 quarts = 1 gallon

Metric Conversions
1 inch = 2.54 centimeters
1 centimeter = 0.39 inch
1 meter = 39.37 inches
1 yard = 0.914 meter
1 mile = 1,609.344 meters = 1.61 kilometers
1 kilometer = 0.62 mile
1 square inch = 6.45 square centimeters
1 square yard = 0.84 square meter
1 square mile = 2.59 square kilometers
1 square kilometer = 0.386 square mile
1 acre = 0.40 hectare
1 hectare = 2.47 acres
1 cubic yard = 0.76 cubic meter
1 cubic meter = 1.31 cubic yards

Household
½ teaspoon = 2 mL
1 teaspoon = 5 mL
1 tablespoon = 15 mL
¼ cup = 60 mL
⅓ cup = 75 mL
½ cup = 125 mL
⅔ cup = 150 mL
¾ cup = 175 mL
1 cup = 250 mL
1 liter = 1.057 U.S. liquid quarts
1 U.S. liquid quart = 0.946 liter
1 U.S. liquid gallon = 3.78 liters
1 gram = 0.035 ounce
1 ounce = 28.349 grams
1 kilogram = 2.2 pounds
1 pound = 0.45 kilogram

Baking Temperature
300°F = 150°C
350°F = 175°C
425°F = 220°C

Astrological Timetable

The following month-by-month chart is based on the Moon's sign and shows the best days each month for certain activities. —*Celeste Longacre*

	JAN.	FEB.	MAR.	APR.	MAY	JUNE	JULY	AUG.	SEPT.	OCT.	NOV.	DEC.
Quit smoking	4, 5, 27	23, 27	8, 27	4, 30	2, 29	25, 29	22, 27	23, 31	1, 19, 29	26, 31	22, 28	20, 25
Begin diet to lose weight	4, 5, 27	23, 27	8, 27	4, 30	2, 29	25, 29	22, 27	23, 31	1, 19, 29	26, 31	22, 28	20, 25
Begin diet to gain weight	12, 16	9, 13	12, 22	9, 19	16, 21	12, 17	9, 14	9, 10	6, 15	4, 13	9, 13	6, 10
Cut hair to discourage growth	3, 4, 30, 31	26, 27	26, 27	5, 6	3, 4, 30, 31	3, 4, 28	1, 2, 28, 29	24, 25	20, 21	30, 31	26, 27	24, 25
Cut hair to encourage growth	18, 19	14, 15	13, 14	10, 11	8, 19, 20	16, 17	13, 14	9, 10	5, 6	14, 15	14, 15	12, 13
Have dental care	1, 28, 29	24, 25	23, 24	19, 20, 21	17, 18	13, 14	10, 11, 12	7, 8	3, 4, 30	1, 27, 28, 29	24, 25	21, 22
End projects	8, 9	6, 7	8, 9	6, 7	6, 7	4, 5	4, 5	3, 4	1, 2	1, 2	1	29, 30
Start projects	11, 12	9, 10	11, 12	9, 10	9, 10	7, 8	7, 8	6, 7	4, 5	4, 5	3, 4	2, 3
Entertain	25, 26	21, 22	20, 21, 22	17, 18	14, 15	11, 12	8, 9	4, 5	1, 2, 28, 29	25, 26	21, 22, 23	19, 20
Go camping	7, 8	3, 4	3, 4, 30, 31	26, 27	24, 25	20, 21	17, 18	14, 15	10, 11	7, 8	4, 5	1, 2, 28, 29
Plant aboveground crops	13, 14, 22, 23	10, 11	18, 19	14, 15, 16	12, 13	8, 9, 18, 19	15, 16	12, 13	8, 9, 17	6, 7, 14, 15	10, 11	7, 8
Plant belowground crops	5, 6, 28, 29	1, 2, 28	1, 2, 28, 29	5, 6, 25	3, 4, 30, 31	26, 27	5, 24	2, 3, 29, 30	25, 26	23, 24	19, 20, 29, 30	26, 27
Destroy pests and weeds	15, 16	12, 13	11, 12	7, 8	5, 6	1, 2, 28, 29	26, 27	22, 23	18, 19	16, 17	12, 13	9, 10
Graft or pollinate	22, 23, 24	19, 20	18, 19	14, 15, 16	12, 13	8, 9	5, 6	2, 3, 29, 30	25, 26	22, 23, 24	19, 20	16, 17
Prune to encourage growth	15, 16	12, 13	11, 12	17, 18	14, 15	11, 12	17, 18	14, 15	10, 11	7, 8	4, 5	9, 10
Prune to discourage growth	7, 8, 26	3, 4	3, 4, 30, 31	7, 26, 27	5, 6, 25	1, 2, 28, 29	26, 27	22, 23, 31	1, 28, 29	25, 26	21, 22	28, 29
Harvest aboveground crops	18, 19	14, 15	13, 14	10, 11	17, 18	13, 14	10, 11	7, 8	4, 12, 13	14, 15	14, 15	12, 13
Harvest belowground crops	1, 28, 29	24, 25	5, 6	1, 2, 29	7, 26, 27	3, 4, 30	1, 2, 28, 29	24, 25	20, 21, 30	18, 19, 28	24, 25	21, 22
Cut hay	15, 16	12, 13	11, 12	7, 8	5, 6	1, 2, 28, 29	26, 27	22, 23	18, 19	16, 17	12, 13	9, 10
Begin logging	9, 10	5, 6	5, 6	1, 2, 28, 29	26, 27	22, 23	19, 20	16, 17	12, 13	9, 10	6, 7	3, 4, 30, 31
Set posts or pour concrete	9, 10	5, 6	5, 6	1, 2, 28, 29	26, 27	22, 23	19, 20	16, 17	12, 13	9, 10	6, 7	3, 4, 30, 31
Breed	5, 6	1, 2, 28	1, 2, 28, 29	24, 25	21, 22	18, 19	15, 16	12, 13	8, 9	5, 6	1, 2, 29, 30	26, 27
Wean	4, 5, 27	23, 27	8, 27	4, 30	2, 29	25, 29	22, 27	23, 31	1, 19, 29	26, 31	22, 28	20, 25
Castrate animals	11, 12	7, 8	7, 8	3, 4, 30	1, 28, 29	24, 25	21, 22	18, 19	14, 15	12, 13	8, 9	5, 6
Slaughter livestock	5, 6	1, 2, 28	1, 2, 28, 29	24, 25	21, 22	18, 19	15, 16	12, 13	8, 9	5, 6	1, 2, 29, 30	26, 27

Secrets of the Zodiac

■ Ancient astrologers believed that each astrological sign influenced a specific part of the body. The first sign of the zodiac—Aries—was attributed to the head, with the rest of the signs moving down the body, ending with Pisces at the feet.

Astrology vs. Astronomy

■ Astrology is a tool we use to time events according to the astrological placements of the Sun, the Moon, and eight planets in the 12 signs of the zodiac. Astronomy, on the other hand, is the study of the actual placement of the known planets and constellations, taking into account the precession of the equinoxes. The placement of the planets in the signs of the zodiac is not the same astrologically and astronomically. The Moon's astrological place is given in **Gardening by the Moon's Sign, page 229;** its astronomical place is given in the **Left-Hand Calendar Pages, 180–202.**

Modern astrology is a study of synchronicities. The planetary movements do not cause events; rather, they explain the path, or "flow," that events tend to follow. Astrologers use the current relationship of the planets and your personal birth chart to determine the best possible times for you to carry out your plans.

The dates in the **Astrological Timetable (page 227)** are based on the astrological passage of the Moon. However, other planets also influence us, so it's best to consider all indicators before making any major decisions.

When Mercury Is Retrograde

■ Sometimes from our perspective here on Earth, the other planets appear to be traveling backward through the zodiac. (All heavenly bodies move forward. An optical illusion makes them seem as if they are moving backward.) We call this *retrograde motion.*

Mercury's retrograde periods, which occur three or four times a year, can cause our

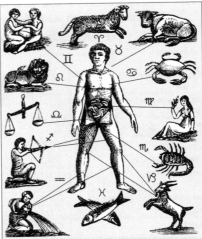

THE MAN OF SIGNS

♈	Aries, head......	**ARI**	*Mar. 21–Apr. 20*
♉	Taurus, neck	**TAU**	*Apr. 21–May 20*
♊	Gemini, arms	**GEM**	*May 21–June 20*
♋	Cancer, breast....	**CAN**	*June 21–July 22*
♌	Leo, heart	**LEO**	*July 23–Aug. 22*
♍	Virgo, belly......	**VIR**	*Aug. 23–Sept. 22*
♎	Libra, reins.......	**LIB**	*Sept. 23–Oct. 22*
♏	Scorpio, secrets...	**SCO**	*Oct. 23–Nov. 22*
♐	Sagittarius, thighs..	**SAG**	*Nov. 23–Dec. 21*
♑	Capricorn, knees..	**CAP**	*Dec. 22–Jan. 19*
♒	Aquarius, legs....	**AQU**	*Jan. 20–Feb. 19*
♓	Pisces, feet	**PSC**	*Feb. 20–Mar. 20*

plans to go awry. However, this is an excellent time to reflect on the past. Intuition is high during these periods and coincidences can be extraordinary.

When Mercury is retrograde, astrologers advise us to be flexible, allow extra time for travel, and avoid signing contracts. It's helpful to review projects and plans because we may see them in a new perspective at these times, but it's best to wait until Mercury is direct again to make any final decisions.

In 2005, Mercury will be retrograde from March 20–April 11, July 23–August 15, and November 14–December 3.

–Celeste Longacre

Gardening by the Moon's Sign

■ The placement of the planets through the signs of the zodiac is not the same in astrology and astronomy. The *astrological* placement of the Moon, by sign, is given in the table below. Its *astronomical*, or actual, placement is given in the **Left-Hand Calendar Pages, 180–202.**

For planting, the most fertile Moon signs are the three water signs: Cancer, Scorpio, and Pisces. Good second choices are Taurus, Virgo, and Capricorn. Weeding and plowing are best done when the Moon occupies Aries, Gemini, Leo, Sagittarius, or Aquarius. Insect pests can also be handled at these times. Transplanting and grafting are best done under a Cancer, Scorpio, or Pisces Moon.

Pruning is best done under an Aries, Leo, or Sagittarius Moon, with growth encouraged during waxing (from the day of new to the day of full Moon) and discouraged during waning (from the day after full to the day before new Moon). For the dates of the Moon's phases, **see pages 180–203.**

Clean out the garden shed when the Moon occupies Virgo. Build or repair fences and permanent garden beds when Capricorn predominates.

Moon's Place in the Astrological Zodiac

	JAN.	FEB.	MAR.	APR.	MAY	JUNE	JULY	AUG.	SEPT.	OCT.	NOV.	DEC.
1	VIR	SCO	SCO	CAP	AQU	ARI	TAU	CAN	LEO	VIR	SCO	SAG
2	LIB	SCO	SCO	CAP	PSC	ARI	TAU	CAN	LEO	VIR	SCO	SAG
3	LIB	SAG	SAG	AQU	PSC	TAU	GEM	CAN	VIR	LIB	SAG	CAP
4	LIB	SAG	SAG	AQU	PSC	TAU	GEM	LEO	VIR	LIB	SAG	CAP
5	SCO	CAP	CAP	PSC	ARI	GEM	CAN	LEO	LIB	SCO	SAG	AQU
6	SCO	CAP	CAP	PSC	ARI	GEM	CAN	VIR	LIB	SCO	CAP	AQU
7	SAG	AQU	AQU	ARI	TAU	GEM	CAN	VIR	LIB	SAG	CAP	PSC
8	SAG	AQU	AQU	ARI	TAU	CAN	LEO	VIR	SCO	SAG	AQU	PSC
9	CAP	PSC	PSC	TAU	GEM	CAN	LEO	LIB	SCO	CAP	AQU	ARI
10	CAP	PSC	PSC	TAU	GEM	LEO	VIR	LIB	SAG	CAP	PSC	ARI
11	AQU	ARI	ARI	TAU	CAN	LEO	VIR	SCO	SAG	AQU	PSC	TAU
12	AQU	ARI	ARI	GEM	CAN	LEO	VIR	SCO	CAP	AQU	ARI	TAU
13	PSC	ARI	TAU	GEM	CAN	VIR	LIB	SCO	CAP	AQU	ARI	TAU
14	PSC	TAU	TAU	CAN	LEO	VIR	LIB	SAG	AQU	PSC	TAU	GEM
15	ARI	TAU	GEM	CAN	LEO	LIB	SCO	SAG	AQU	PSC	TAU	GEM
16	ARI	GEM	GEM	CAN	VIR	LIB	SCO	CAP	PSC	ARI	GEM	CAN
17	TAU	GEM	GEM	LEO	VIR	LIB	SAG	CAP	PSC	ARI	GEM	CAN
18	TAU	CAN	CAN	LEO	VIR	SCO	SAG	AQU	ARI	TAU	GEM	LEO
19	TAU	CAN	CAN	VIR	LIB	SCO	CAP	AQU	ARI	TAU	CAN	LEO
20	GEM	CAN	LEO	VIR	LIB	SAG	CAP	PSC	TAU	GEM	CAN	LEO
21	GEM	LEO	LEO	VIR	SCO	SAG	AQU	PSC	TAU	GEM	LEO	VIR
22	CAN	LEO	LEO	LIB	SCO	CAP	AQU	ARI	GEM	CAN	LEO	VIR
23	CAN	VIR	VIR	LIB	SAG	CAP	PSC	ARI	GEM	CAN	LEO	LIB
24	CAN	VIR	VIR	SCO	SAG	AQU	PSC	TAU	GEM	CAN	VIR	LIB
25	LEO	VIR	LIB	SCO	SAG	AQU	ARI	TAU	CAN	LEO	VIR	LIB
26	LEO	LIB	LIB	SAG	CAP	PSC	ARI	GEM	CAN	LEO	LIB	SCO
27	VIR	LIB	LIB	SAG	CAP	PSC	ARI	GEM	LEO	VIR	LIB	SCO
28	VIR	SCO	SCO	CAP	AQU	ARI	TAU	GEM	LEO	VIR	SCO	SAG
29	VIR	—	SCO	CAP	AQU	ARI	TAU	CAN	LEO	VIR	SCO	SAG
30	LIB	—	SAG	AQU	PSC	TAU	GEM	CAN	VIR	LIB	SCO	CAP
31	LIB	—	SAG	—	PSC	—	GEM	LEO	—	LIB	—	CAP

Outdoor Planting Table

■ The best time to plant flowers and vegetables that bear crops *above ground* is during the *light* of the Moon; that is, from the day the Moon is new to the day it is full. Flowering bulbs and vegetables that bear crops *below ground* should be planted during the *dark* of the Moon; that is, from the day after it is full to the day before it is new again. The Moon Favorable columns at right give these days, which are based on the Moon's phases for 2005 and the safe periods for planting in areas that receive frost. Consult **page 48** for dates of frosts and lengths of growing seasons. See the **Left-Hand Calendar Pages 180–202** for the exact days of the new and full Moons.

■ Aboveground crops are marked *

■ (E) means early   (L) means late

■ Map shades correspond to shades of date columns.

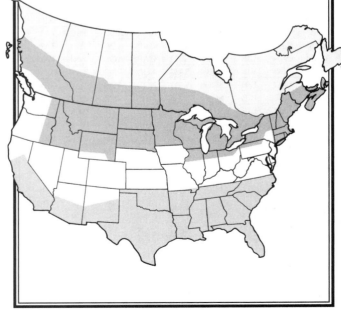

* Barley	
* Beans	(E)
	(L)
Beets	(E)
	(L)
* Broccoli plants	(E)
	(L)
* Brussels sprouts	
* Cabbage plants	
Carrots	(E)
	(L)
* Cauliflower plants	(E)
	(L)
* Celery plants	(E)
	(L)
* Collards	(E)
	(L)
* Corn, sweet	(E)
	(L)
* Cucumbers	
* Eggplant plants	
* Endive	(E)
	(L)
* Flowers	
* Kale	(E)
	(L)
Leek plants	
* Lettuce	
* Muskmelons	
Onion sets	
* Parsley	
Parsnips	
* Peas	(E)
	(L)
* Pepper plants	
Potatoes	
* Pumpkins	
Radishes	(E)
	(L)
* Spinach	(E)
	(L)
* Squashes	
Sweet potatoes	
* Swiss chard	
* Tomato plants	
Turnips	(E)
	(L)
* Watermelons	
* Wheat, spring	
* Wheat, winter	

Planting Dates	Moon Favorable	Planting Dates	Moon Favorable	Planting Dates	Moon Favorable	Planting Dates	Moon Favorable
2/15-3/7	2/15-23	3/15-4/7	3/15-25	5/15-6/21	5/15-23, 6/6-21	6/1-30	6/6-22
3/15-4/7	3/15-25	4/15-30	4/15-24	5/7-6/21	5/8-23, 6/6-21	5/30-6/15	6/6-15
8/7-31	8/7-19	7/1-21	7/6-21	6/15-7/15	6/15-22, 7/6-15	—	—
2/7-28	2/7, 2/24-28	3/15-4/3	3/26-4/3	5/1-15	5/1-7	5/25-6/10	5/25-6/5
9/1-30	9/1-2, 9/18-30	8/15-31	8/20-31	7/15-8/15	7/22-8/3	6/15-7/8	6/23-7/5
2/15-3/15	2/15-23, 3/10-15	3/7-31	3/10-25	5/15-31	5/15-23	6/1-25	6/6-22
9/7-30	9/7-17	8/1-20	8/4-19	6/15-7/7	6/15-22, 7/6-7	—	—
2/11-3/20	2/11-23, 3/10-20	3/7-4/15	3/10-25, 4/8-15	5/15-31	5/15-23	6/1-25	6/6-22
2/11-3/20	2/11-23, 3/10-20	3/7-4/15	3/10-25, 4/8-15	5/15-31	5/15-23	6/1-25	6/6-22
2/15-3/7	2/24-3/7	3/7-31	3/7-9, 3/26-31	5/15-31	5/24-31	5/25-6/10	5/25-6/5
8/1-9/7	8/1-3, 8/20-9/2	7/7-31	7/22-31	6/15-7/21	6/23-7/5	6/15-7/8	6/23-7/5
2/15-3/7	2/15-23	3/15-4/7	3/15-25	5/15-31	5/15-23	6/1-25	6/6-22
8/7-31	8/7-19	7/1-8/7	7/6-21, 8/4-7	6/15-7/21	6/15-22, 7/6-21	—	—
2/15-28	2/15-23	3/7-31	3/10-25	5/15-6/30	5/15-23, 6/6-22	6/1-30	6/6-22
9/15-30	9/15-17	8/15-9/7	8/15-19, 9/3-7	7/15-8/15	7/15-21, 8/4-15	—	—
2/11-3/20	2/11-23, 3/10-20	3/7-4/7	3/10-25	5/15-31	5/15-23	6/1-25	6/6-22
9/7-30	9/7-17	8/15-31	8/15-19	7/1-8/7	7/6-21, 8/4-7	—	—
3/15-31	3/15-25	4/1-17	4/8-17	5/10-6/15	5/10-23, 6/6-15	5/30-6/20	6/6-20
8/7-31	8/7-19	7/7-21	7/7-21	6/15-30	6/15-22	—	—
3/7-4/15	3/10-25, 4/8-15	4/7-5/15	4/8-24, 5/8-15	5/7-6/20	5/8-23, 6/6-20	5/30-6/15	6/6-15
3/7-4/15	3/10-25, 4/8-15	4/7-5/15	4/8-24, 5/8-15	6/1-30	6/6-22	6/15-30	6/15-22
2/15-3/20	2/15-23, 3/10-20	4/7-5/15	4/8-24, 5/8-15	5/15-31	5/15-23	6/1-25	6/6-22
8/15-9/7	8/15-19, 9/3-7	7/15-8/15	7/15-21, 8/4-15	6/7-30	6/7-22	—	—
3/15-4/7	3/15-25	4/15-30	4/15-24	5/7-6/21	5/8-23, 6/6-21	6/1-30	6/6-22
2/11-3/20	2/11-23, 3/10-20	3/7-4/7	3/10-25	5/15-31	5/15-23	6/1-15	6/6-15
9/7-30	9/7-17	8/15-31	8/15-19	7/1-8/7	7/6-21, 8/4-7	6/25-7/15	7/6-15
2/15-4/15	2/24-3/9, 3/26-4/7	3/7-4/7	3/7-9, 3/26-4/7	5/15-31	5/24-31	6/1-25	6/1-5, 6/23-25
2/15-3/7	2/15-23	3/1-31	3/10-25	5/15-6/30	5/15-23, 6/6-22	6/1-30	6/6-22
3/15-4/7	3/15-25	4/15-5/7	4/15-24	5/15-6/30	5/15-23, 6/6-22	6/1-30	6/6-22
2/1-28	2/1-7, 2/24-28	3/1-31	3/1-9, 3/26-31	5/15-6/7	5/24-6/5	6/1-25	6/1-5, 6/23-25
2/20-3/15	2/20-23, 3/10-15	3/1-31	3/10-25	5/15-31	5/15-23	6/1-15	6/6-15
1/15-2/4	1/26-2/4	3/7-31	3/7-9, 3/26-31	4/1-30	4/1-7, 4/25-30	5/10-31	5/24-31
1/15-2/7	1/15-25	3/7-31	3/10-25	4/15-5/7	4/15-24	5/15-31	5/15-23
9/15-30	9/15-17	8/7-31	8/7-19	7/15-31	7/15-21	7/10-25	7/10-21
3/1-20	3/10-20	4/1-30	4/8-24	5/15-6/30	5/15-23, 6/6-22	6/1-30	6/6-22
2/10-28	2/24-28	4/1-30	4/1-7, 4/25-30	5/1-31	5/1-7, 5/24-31	6/1-25	6/1-5, 6/23-25
3/7-20	3/10-20	4/23-5/15	4/23-24, 5/8-15	5/15-31	5/15-23	6/1-30	6/6-22
1/21-3/1	1/26-2/7, 2/24-3/1	3/7-31	3/7-9, 3/26-31	4/15-30	4/25-30	5/15-6/5	5/24-6/5
10/1-21	10/1-2, 10/18-21	9/7-30	9/18-30	8/15-31	8/20-31	7/10-31	7/22-31
2/7-3/15	2/8-23, 3/10-15	3/15-4/20	3/15-25, 4/8-20	5/15-31	5/15-23	6/1-25	6/6-22
10/1-21	10/3-17	8/1-9/15	8/4-19, 9/3-15	7/17-9/7	7/17-21, 8/4-19, 9/3-7	7/20-8/5	7/20-21, 8/4-5
3/15-4/15	3/15-25, 4/8-15	4/15-30	4/15-24	5/15-6/15	5/15-23, 6/6-15	6/1-30	6/6-22
3/23-4/6	3/26-4/6	4/21-5/9	4/25-5/7	5/15-6/15	5/24-6/5	6/1-30	6/1-5, 6/23-30
2/7-3/15	2/8-23, 3/10-15	3/15-4/15	3/15-25, 4/8-15	5/1-31	5/8-23	5/15-31	5/15-23
3/7-20	3/10-20	4/7-30	4/8-24	5/15-31	5/15-23	6/1-15	6/6-15
1/20-2/15	1/26-2/7	3/15-31	3/26-31	4/7-30	4/7, 4/25-30	5/10-31	5/24-31
9/1-10/15	9/1-2, 9/18-10/2	8/1-20	8/1-3, 8/20	7/1-8/15	7/1-5, 7/22-8/3	—	—
3/15-4/7	3/15-25	4/15-5/7	4/15-24	5/15-6/30	5/15-23, 6/6-22	6/1-30	6/6-22
2/15-28	2/15-23	3/1-20	3/10-20	4/7-30	4/8-24	5/15-6/10	5/15-23, 6/6-10
10/15-12/7	10/15-17, 11/1-15, 12/1-7	9/15-10/20	9/15-17, 10/3-17	8/11-9/15	8/11-19, 9/3-15	8/5-30	8/5-19

Tide Corrections

■ Many factors affect the times and heights of the tides: the coastal configuration, the time of the Moon's southing (crossing the meridian), and the Moon's phase. The High Tide column on the **Left-Hand Calendar Pages 180–202** lists the times of high tide at Commonwealth Pier in Boston Harbor. The heights of some of these tides, reckoned from Mean Lower Low Water, are given on the **Right-Hand Calendar Pages 181–203.** Use this table to calculate the approximate times and heights of high water at the places shown. Apply the time difference to the times of high tide at Boston **(pages 180–202)** and the height difference to the heights at Boston **(pages 181–203).**

E X A M P L E :

■ The conversion of the times and heights of the tides at Boston to those at Cape Fear, North Carolina, is given below:

High tide at Boston	2:30 P.M.
Correction for Cape Fear	−3:55 hrs.
High tide at Cape Fear	10:35 A.M.
Tide height at Boston	10.3 ft.
Correction for Cape Fear	−5.0 ft.
Tide height at Cape Fear	5.3 ft.

Estimations derived from this table are *not* meant to be used for navigation. *The Old Farmer's Almanac* accepts no responsibility for errors or any consequences ensuing from the use of this table.

Coastal Site	Difference: Time (h. m.)	Height (ft.)
Canada		
Alberton, PE	*−5 45	−7.5
Charlottetown, PE.	*−0 45	−3.5
Halifax, NS.	−3 23	−4.5
North Sydney, NS.	−3 15	−6.5
Saint John, NB	+0 30	+15.0
St. John's, NL	−4 00	−6.5
Yarmouth, NS	−0 40	+3.0
Maine		
Bar Harbor	−0 34	+0.9
Belfast	−0 20	+0.4
Boothbay Harbor	−0 18	−0.8
Chebeague Island	−0 16	−0.6
Eastport	−0 28	+8.4
Kennebunkport	+0 04	−1.0
Machias	−0 28	+2.8
Monhegan Island	−0 25	−0.8
Old Orchard	0 00	−0.8
Portland	−0 12	−0.6
Rockland	−0 28	+0.1
Stonington	−0 30	+0.1
York	−0 09	−1.0
New Hampshire		
Hampton	+0 02	−1.3
Portsmouth	+0 11	−1.5
Rye Beach	−0 09	−0.9
Massachusetts		
Annisquam	−0 02	−1.1
Beverly Farms.	0 00	−0.5
Boston	0 00	0.0

Coastal Site	Difference: Time (h. m.)	Height (ft.)
Cape Cod Canal		
East Entrance	−0 01	−0.8
West Entrance	−2 16	−5.9
Chatham Outer Coast . . .	+0 30	−2.8
Inside	+1 54	**0.4
Cohasset	+0 02	−0.07
Cotuit Highlands.	+1 15	**0.3
Dennis Port	+1 01	**0.4
Duxbury–Gurnet Point. .	+0 02	−0.3
Fall River	−3 03	−5.0
Gloucester	−0 03	−0.8
Hingham	+0 07	0.0
Hull	+0 03	−0.2
Hyannis Port	+1 01	**0.3
Magnolia–Manchester . .	−0 02	−0.7
Marblehead	−0 02	−0.4
Marion.	−3 22	−5.4
Monument Beach	−3 08	−5.4
Nahant	−0 01	−0.5
Nantasket.	+0 04	−0.1
Nantucket	+0 56	**0.3
Nauset Beach	+0 30	**0.6
New Bedford.	−3 24	−5.7
Newburyport.	+0 19	−1.8
Oak Bluffs.	+0 30	**0.2
Onset–R.R. Bridge	−2 16	−5.9
Plymouth	+0 05	0.0
Provincetown	+0 14	−0.4
Revere Beach	−0 01	−0.3
Rockport	−0 08	−1.0
Salem.	0 00	−0.5

Coastal Site	Difference:	Time (h. m.)	Height (ft.)
Scituate		−0 05	−0.7
Wareham.		−3 09	−5.3
Wellfleet		+0 12	+0.5
West Falmouth		−3 10	−5.4
Westport Harbor		−3 22	−6.4
Woods Hole			
Little Harbor.		−2 50	**0.2
Oceanographic Institute		−3 07	**0.2
Rhode Island			
Bristol		−3 24	−5.3
Narragansett Pier		−3 42	−6.2
Newport.		−3 34	−5.9
Point Judith		−3 41	−6.3
Providence		−3 20	−4.8
Sakonnet		−3 44	−5.6
Watch Hill.		−2 50	−6.8
Connecticut			
Bridgeport		+0 01	−2.6
Madison.		−0 22	−2.3
New Haven		−0 11	−3.2
New London		−1 54	−6.7
Norwalk.		+0 01	−2.2
Old Lyme			
Highway Bridge.		−0 30	−6.2
Stamford		+0 01	−2.2
Stonington.		−2 27	−6.6
New York			
Coney Island		−3 33	−4.9
Fire Island Light		−2 43	**0.1
Long Beach.		−3 11	−5.7
Montauk Harbor		−2 19	−7.4
New York City–Battery. .		−2 43	−5.0
Oyster Bay		+0 04	−1.8
Port Chester.		−0 09	−2.2
Port Washington		−0 01	−2.1
Sag Harbor		−0 55	−6.8
Southampton			
Shinnecock Inlet		−4 20	**0.2
Willets Point		0 00	−2.3
New Jersey			
Asbury Park		−4 04	−5.3
Atlantic City		−3 56	−5.5
Bay Head–Sea Girt		−4 04	−5.3
Beach Haven.		−1 43	**0.24
Cape May		−3 28	−5.3
Ocean City		−3 06	−5.9
Sandy Hook.		−3 30	−5.0
Seaside Park		−4 03	−5.4
Pennsylvania			
Philadelphia		+2 40	−3.5
Delaware			
Cape Henlopen		−2 48	−5.3

Coastal Site	Difference:	Time (h. m.)	Height (ft.)
Rehoboth Beach		−3 37	−5.7
Wilmington.		+1 56	−3.8
Maryland			
Annapolis		+6 23	−8.5
Baltimore.		+7 59	−8.3
Cambridge.		+5 05	−7.8
Havre de Grace		+11 21	−7.7
Point No Point.		+2 28	−8.1
Prince Frederick			
Plum Point		+4 25	−8.5
Virginia			
Cape Charles.		−2 20	−7.0
Hampton Roads		−2 02	−6.9
Norfolk		−2 06	−6.6
Virginia Beach		−4 00	−6.0
Yorktown		−2 13	−7.0
North Carolina			
Cape Fear		−3 55	−5.0
Cape Lookout		−4 28	−5.7
Currituck		−4 10	−5.8
Hatteras			
Inlet.		−4 03	−7.4
Kitty Hawk.		−4 14	−6.2
Ocean		−4 26	−6.0
South Carolina			
Charleston		−3 22	−4.3
Georgetown.		−1 48	**0.36
Hilton Head.		−3 22	−2.9
Myrtle Beach.		−3 49	−4.4
St. Helena			
Harbor Entrance.		−3 15	−3.4
Georgia			
Jekyll Island		−3 46	−2.9
St. Simon's Island.		−2 50	−2.9
Savannah Beach			
River Entrance		−3 14	−5.5
Tybee Light		−3 22	−2.7
Florida			
Cape Canaveral.		−3 59	−6.0
Daytona Beach		−3 28	−5.3
Fort Lauderdale.		−2 50	−7.2
Fort Pierce Inlet		−3 32	−6.9
Jacksonville			
Railroad Bridge		−6 55	**0.1
Miami Harbor Entrance. .		−3 18	−7.0
St. Augustine.		−2 55	−4.9

*Varies widely; accurate within only 1½ hours. Consult local tide tables for precise times and heights.

**Where the difference in the Height column is so marked, height at Boston should be multiplied by this ratio.

Tidal Glossary

Apogean Tide: A monthly tide of decreased range that occurs when the Moon is at apogee (farthest from Earth).

Diurnal Tide: A tide with one high water and one low water in a tidal day of approximately 24 hours.

Mean Lower Low Water: The arithmetic mean of the lesser of a daily pair of low waters, observed over a specific 19-year cycle called the National Tidal Datum Epoch.

Neap Tide: A tide of decreased range that occurs twice a month, when the Moon is in quadrature (during its first and last quarters, when the Sun and the Moon are at right angles to each other relative to Earth).

Perigean Tide: A monthly tide of increased range that occurs when the Moon is at perigee (closest to Earth).

Semidiurnal Tide: A tide with one high water and one low water every half day. East Coast tides, for example, are semidiurnal, with two highs and two lows during a tidal day of approximately 24 hours.

Spring Tide: A tide of increased range that occurs at times of syzygy each month. Named not for the season of spring but from the German *springen* ("to leap up"), a spring tide also brings a lower low water.

Syzygy: The nearly straight-line configuration that occurs twice a month, when the Sun and the Moon are in conjunction (on the same side of Earth at the new Moon) and when they are in opposition (on opposite sides of Earth at the full Moon). In both cases, the gravitational effects of the Sun and the Moon reinforce each other, and tidal range is increased.

Vanishing Tide: A mixed tide of considerable inequality in the two highs and two lows, so that the lower high (or higher low) may become indistinct or appear to vanish.

Time Corrections

■ Times for Sun and Moon rise and set, bright star transits, and planetary observations are given for Boston on **pages 180–202, 173,** and **170–171.** Use the Key Letter shown to the right of each time on those pages with this table to find the number of minutes (adjusted for location and time zone) that you must add to or subtract from Boston time to get the correct time for your city. (Because of complex calculations for different locales, times may not be precise to the minute.) If your city is not listed, use the figures for the city closest to you in latitude and longitude. Boston's latitude is 42° 22' and its longitude is 71° 03'. Canadian cities are at the end of the table. For more information on the use of Key Letters and this table, see **How to Use This Almanac, page 176.**

TIME ZONES: Codes represent *standard time.* Atlantic is –1, Eastern is 0, Central is 1, Mountain is 2, Pacific is 3, Alaska is 4, and Hawaii-Aleutian is 5.

City	North Latitude ° '	West Longitude ° '	Time Zone Code	A (min.)	B (min.)	C (min.)	D (min.)	E (min.)
Aberdeen, SD..............	45 28	98 29	1	+37	+44	+49	+54	+59
Akron, OH	41 5	81 31	0	+46	+43	+41	+39	+37
Albany, NY	42 39	73 45	0	+ 9	+10	+10	+11	+11
Albert Lea, MN	43 39	93 22	1	+24	+26	+28	+31	+33
Albuquerque, NM	35 5	106 39	2	+45	+32	+22	+11	+ 2
Alexandria, LA............	31 18	92 27	1	+58	+40	+26	+ 9	– 3
Allentown–Bethlehem, PA..	40 36	75 28	0	+23	+20	+17	+14	+12
Amarillo, TX	35 12	101 50	1	+85	+73	+63	+52	+43
Anchorage, AK	61 10	149 59	4	–46	+27	+71	+122	+171
Asheville, NC	35 36	82 33	0	+67	+55	+46	+35	+27
Atlanta, GA	33 45	84 24	0	+79	+65	+53	+40	+30
Atlantic City, NJ	39 22	74 26	0	+23	+17	+13	+ 8	+ 4
Augusta, GA	33 28	81 58	0	+70	+55	+44	+30	+19
Augusta, ME	44 19	69 46	0	–12	– 8	– 5	– 1	0
Austin, TX	30 16	97 45	1	+82	+62	+47	+29	+15
Bakersfield, CA...........	35 23	119 1	3	+33	+21	+12	+ 1	– 7
Baltimore, MD............	39 17	76 37	0	+32	+26	+22	+17	+13
Bangor, ME	44 48	68 46	0	–18	–13	– 9	– 5	– 1
Barstow, CA..............	34 54	117 1	3	+27	+14	+ 4	– 7	–16
Baton Rouge, LA..........	30 27	91 11	1	+55	+36	+21	+ 3	–10
Beaumont, TX	30 5	94 6	1	+67	+48	+32	+14	0
Bellingham, WA	48 45	122 29	3	0	+13	+24	+37	+47
Bemidji, MN	47 28	94 53	1	+14	+26	+34	+44	+52
Berlin, NH	44 28	71 11	0	– 7	– 3	0	+ 3	+ 7
Billings, MT..............	45 47	108 30	2	+16	+23	+29	+35	+40
Biloxi, MS	30 24	88 53	1	+46	+27	+11	– 5	–19
Binghamton, NY	42 6	75 55	0	+20	+19	+19	+18	+18
Birmingham, AL..........	33 31	86 49	1	+30	+15	+ 3	–10	–20
Bismarck, ND	46 48	100 47	1	+41	+50	+58	+66	+73
Boise, ID	43 37	116 12	2	+55	+58	+60	+62	+64
Brattleboro, VT...........	42 51	72 34	0	+ 4	+ 5	+ 5	+ 6	+ 7
Bridgeport, CT............	41 11	73 11	0	+12	+10	+ 8	+ 6	+ 4
Brockton, MA	42 5	71 1	0	0	0	0	0	– 1
Brownsville, TX	25 54	97 30	1	+91	+66	+46	+23	+ 5
Buffalo, NY	42 53	78 52	0	+29	+30	+30	+31	+32
Burlington, VT............	44 29	73 13	0	0	+ 4	+ 8	+12	+15
Butte, MT.................	46 1	112 32	2	+31	+39	+45	+52	+57
Cairo, IL.................	37 0	89 11	1	+29	+20	+12	+ 4	– 2
Camden, NJ	39 57	75 7	0	+24	+19	+16	+12	+ 9
Canton, OH	40 48	81 23	0	+46	+43	+41	+38	+36
Cape May, NJ	38 56	74 56	0	+26	+20	+15	+ 9	+ 5
Carson City–Reno, NV	39 10	119 46	3	+25	+19	+14	+ 9	+ 5

City	North Latitude ° '		West Longitude ° '		Time Zone Code	A (min.)	B (min.)	Key Letters C (min.)	D (min.)	E (min.)
Casper, WY	42	51	106	19	2	+19	+19	+20	+21	+22
Charleston, SC	32	47	79	56	0	+64	+48	+36	+21	+10
Charleston, WV	38	21	81	38	0	+55	+48	+42	+35	+30
Charlotte, NC	35	14	80	51	0	+61	+49	+39	+28	+19
Charlottesville, VA	38	2	78	30	0	+43	+35	+29	+22	+17
Chattanooga, TN	35	3	85	19	0	+79	+67	+57	+45	+36
Cheboygan, MI	45	39	84	29	0	+40	+47	+53	+59	+64
Cheyenne, WY	41	8	104	49	2	+19	+16	+14	+12	+11
Chicago–Oak Park, IL	41	52	87	38	1	+ 7	+ 6	+ 6	+ 5	+ 4
Cincinnati–Hamilton, OH	39	6	84	31	0	+64	+58	+53	+48	+44
Cleveland–Lakewood, OH	41	30	81	42	0	+45	+43	+42	+40	+39
Columbia, SC	34	0	81	2	0	+65	+51	+40	+27	+17
Columbus, OH	39	57	83	1	0	+55	+51	+47	+43	+40
Cordova, AK	60	33	145	45	4	−55	+13	+55	+103	+149
Corpus Christi, TX	27	48	97	24	1	+86	+64	+46	+25	+ 9
Craig, CO	40	31	107	33	2	+32	+28	+25	+22	+20
Dallas–Fort Worth, TX	32	47	96	48	1	+71	+55	+43	+28	+17
Danville, IL	40	8	87	37	1	+13	+ 9	+ 6	+ 2	0
Danville, VA	36	36	79	23	0	+51	+41	+33	+24	+17
Davenport, IA	41	32	90	35	1	+20	+19	+17	+16	+15
Dayton, OH	39	45	84	10	0	+61	+56	+52	+48	+44
Decatur, AL	34	36	86	59	1	+27	+14	+ 4	− 7	−17
Decatur, IL	39	51	88	57	1	+19	+15	+11	+ 7	+ 4
Denver–Boulder, CO	39	44	104	59	2	+24	+19	+15	+11	+ 7
Des Moines, IA	41	35	93	37	1	+32	+31	+30	+28	+27
Detroit–Dearborn, MI	42	20	83	3	0	+47	+47	+47	+47	+47
Dubuque, IA	42	30	90	41	1	+17	+18	+18	+18	+18
Duluth, MN	46	47	92	6	1	+ 6	+16	+23	+31	+38
Durham, NC	36	0	78	55	0	+51	+40	+31	+21	+13
Eastport, ME	44	54	67	0	0	−26	−20	−16	−11	− 8
Eau Claire, WI	44	49	91	30	1	+12	+17	+21	+25	+29
Elko, NV	40	50	115	46	3	+ 3	0	− 1	− 3	− 5
Ellsworth, ME	44	33	68	25	0	−18	−14	−10	− 6	− 3
El Paso, TX	31	45	106	29	2	+53	+35	+22	+ 6	− 6
Erie, PA	42	7	80	5	0	+36	+36	+35	+35	+35
Eugene, OR	44	3	123	6	3	+21	+24	+27	+30	+33
Fairbanks, AK	64	48	147	51	4	−127	+ 2	+61	+131	+205
Fall River– New Bedford, MA	41	42	71	9	0	+ 2	+ 1	0	0	− 1
Fargo, ND	46	53	96	47	1	+24	+34	+42	+50	+57
Flagstaff, AZ	35	12	111	39	2	+64	+52	+42	+31	+22
Flint, MI	43	1	83	41	0	+47	+49	+50	+51	+52
Fort Myers, FL	26	38	81	52	0	+87	+63	+44	+21	+ 4
Fort Scott, KS	37	50	94	42	1	+49	+41	+34	+27	+21
Fort Smith, AR	35	23	94	25	1	+55	+43	+33	+22	+14
Fort Wayne, IN	41	4	85	9	0	+60	+58	+56	+54	+52
Fresno, CA	36	44	119	47	3	+32	+22	+15	+ 6	0
Gallup, NM	35	32	108	45	2	+52	+40	+31	+20	+11
Galveston, TX	29	18	94	48	1	+72	+52	+35	+16	+ 1
Gary, IN	41	36	87	20	1	+ 7	+ 6	+ 4	+ 3	+ 2
Glasgow, MT	48	12	106	38	2	− 1	+11	+21	+32	+42
Grand Forks, ND	47	55	97	3	1	+21	+33	+43	+53	+62
Grand Island, NE	40	55	98	21	1	+53	+51	+49	+46	+44
Grand Junction, CO	39	4	108	33	2	+40	+34	+29	+24	+20
Great Falls, MT	47	30	111	17	2	+20	+31	+39	+49	+58
Green Bay, WI	44	31	88	0	1	0	+ 3	+ 7	+11	+14
Greensboro, NC	36	4	79	47	0	+54	+43	+35	+25	+17

City	North Latitude ° '		West Longitude ° '		Time Zone Code	A (min.)	B (min.)	Key Letters C (min.)	D (min.)	E (min.)
Hagerstown, MD 39	39	77	43	0	+35	+30	+26	+22	+18
Harrisburg, PA 40	16	76	53	0	+30	+26	+23	+19	+16
Hartford–New Britain, CT... 41	46	72	41	0	+ 8	+ 7	+ 6	+ 5	+ 4
Helena, MT............... 46	36	112	2	2	+27	+36	+43	+51	+57
Hilo, HI................. 19	44	155	5	5	+94	+62	+37	+ 7	−15
Honolulu, HI............. 21	18	157	52	5	+102	+72	+48	+19	− 1
Houston, TX............. 29	45	95	22	1	+73	+53	+37	+19	+ 5
Indianapolis, IN 39	46	86	10	0	+69	+64	+60	+56	+52
Ironwood, MI............. 46	27	90	9	1	0	+ 9	+15	+23	+29
Jackson, MI.............. 42	15	84	24	0	+53	+53	+53	+52	+52
Jackson, MS 32	18	90	11	1	+46	+30	+17	+ 1	−10
Jacksonville, FL......... 30	20	81	40	0	+77	+58	+43	+25	+11
Jefferson City, MO........ 38	34	92	10	1	+36	+29	+24	+18	+13
Joplin, MO 37	6	94	30	1	+50	+41	+33	+25	+18
Juneau, AK.............. 58	18	134	25	4	−76	−23	+10	+49	+86
Kalamazoo, MI............ 42	17	85	35	0	+58	+57	+57	+57	+57
Kanab, UT 37	3	112	32	2	+62	+53	+46	+37	+30
Kansas City, MO 39	1	94	20	1	+44	+37	+33	+27	+23
Keene, NH 42	56	72	17	0	+ 2	+ 3	+ 4	+ 5	+ 6
Ketchikan, AK 55	21	131	39	4	−62	−25	0	+29	+56
Knoxville, TN............ 35	58	83	55	0	+71	+60	+51	+41	+33
Kodiak, AK.............. 57	47	152	24	4	0	+49	+82	+120	+154
LaCrosse, WI 43	48	91	15	1	+15	+18	+20	+22	+25
Lake Charles, LA 30	14	93	13	1	+64	+44	+29	+11	− 2
Lanai City, HI............ 20	50	156	55	5	+99	+69	+44	+15	− 6
Lancaster, PA 40	2	76	18	0	+28	+24	+20	+17	+13
Lansing, MI 42	44	84	33	0	+52	+53	+53	+54	+54
Las Cruces, NM 32	19	106	47	2	+53	+36	+23	+ 8	− 3
Las Vegas, NV 36	10	115	9	3	+16	+ 4	− 3	−13	−20
Lawrence–Lowell, MA 42	42	71	10	0	0	0	0	0	+ 1
Lewiston, ID............. 46	25	117	1	3	−12	− 3	+ 2	+10	+17
Lexington–Frankfort, KY ... 38	3	84	30	0	+67	+59	+53	+46	+41
Liberal, KS 37	3	100	55	1	+76	+66	+59	+51	+44
Lihue, HI................ 21	59	159	23	5	+107	+77	+54	+26	+ 5
Lincoln, NE 40	49	96	41	1	+47	+44	+42	+39	+37
Little Rock, AR 34	45	92	17	1	+48	+35	+25	+13	+ 4
Los Angeles–Pasadena– Santa Monica, CA........ 34	3	118	14	3	+34	+20	+ 9	− 3	−13
Louisville, KY 38	15	85	46	0	+72	+64	+58	+52	+46
Macon, GA.............. 32	50	83	38	0	+79	+63	+50	+36	+24
Madison, WI............. 43	4	89	23	1	+10	+11	+12	+14	+15
Manchester–Concord, NH... 42	59	71	28	0	0	0	+ 1	+ 2	+ 3
McAllen, TX 26	12	98	14	1	+93	+69	+49	+26	+ 9
Memphis, TN............ 35	9	90	3	1	+38	+26	+16	+ 5	− 3
Meridian, MS 32	22	88	42	1	+40	+24	+11	− 4	−15
Miami, FL............... 25	47	80	12	0	+88	+57	+37	+14	− 3
Miles City, MT........... 46	25	105	51	2	+ 3	+11	+18	+26	+32
Milwaukee, WI........... 43	2	87	54	1	+ 4	+ 6	+ 7	+ 8	+ 9
Minneapolis–St. Paul, MN .. 44	59	93	16	1	+18	+24	+28	+33	+37
Minot, ND............... 48	14	101	18	1	+36	+50	+59	+71	+81
Moab, UT 38	35	109	33	2	+46	+39	+33	+27	+22
Mobile, AL.............. 30	42	88	3	1	+42	+23	+ 8	− 8	−22
Monroe, LA 32	30	92	7	1	+53	+37	+24	+ 9	− 1
Montgomery, AL.......... 32	23	86	19	1	+31	+14	+ 1	−13	−25
Muncie, IN 40	12	85	23	0	+64	+60	+57	+53	+50
Nashville, TN 36	10	86	47	1	+22	+11	+ 3	− 6	−14
Newark–East Orange, NJ.... 40	44	74	10	0	+17	+14	+12	+ 9	+ 7

City	North Latitude ° '		West Longitude ° '		Time Zone Code	Key Letters				
						A (min.)	B (min.)	C (min.)	D (min.)	E (min.)
New Haven, CT	41	18	72	56	0	+11	+ 8	+ 7	+ 5	+ 4
New London, CT	41	22	72	6	0	+ 7	+ 5	+ 4	+ 2	+ 1
New Orleans, LA	29	57	90	4	1	+52	+32	+16	− 1	−15
New York, NY	40	45	74	0	0	+17	+14	+11	+ 9	+ 6
Norfolk, VA	36	51	76	17	0	+38	+28	+21	+12	+ 5
North Platte, NE	41	8	100	46	1	+62	+60	+58	+56	+54
Norwalk–Stamford, CT	41	7	73	22	0	+13	+10	+ 9	+ 7	+ 5
Oakley, KS	39	8	100	51	1	+69	+63	+59	+53	+49
Ogden, UT	41	13	111	58	2	+47	+45	+43	+41	+40
Ogdensburg, NY	44	42	75	30	0	+ 8	+13	+17	+21	+25
Oklahoma City, OK	35	28	97	31	1	+67	+55	+46	+35	+26
Omaha, NE	41	16	95	56	1	+43	+40	+39	+37	+36
Orlando, FL	28	32	81	22	0	+80	+59	+42	+22	+ 6
Ortonville, MN	45	19	96	27	1	+30	+36	+40	+46	+51
Oshkosh, WI	44	1	88	33	1	+ 3	+ 6	+ 9	+12	+15
Palm Springs, CA	33	49	116	32	3	+28	+13	+ 1	−12	−22
Parkersburg, WV	39	16	81	34	0	+52	+46	+42	+36	+32
Paterson, NJ	40	55	74	10	0	+17	+14	+12	+ 9	+ 7
Pendleton, OR	45	40	118	47	3	− 1	+ 4	+10	+16	+21
Pensacola, FL	30	25	87	13	1	+39	+20	+ 5	−12	−26
Peoria, IL	40	42	89	36	1	+19	+16	+14	+11	+ 9
Philadelphia–Chester, PA	39	57	75	9	0	+24	+19	+16	+12	+ 9
Phoenix, AZ	33	27	112	4	2	+71	+56	+44	+30	+20
Pierre, SD	44	22	100	21	1	+49	+53	+56	+60	+63
Pittsburgh–McKeesport, PA	40	26	80	0	0	+42	+38	+35	+32	+29
Pittsfield, MA	42	27	73	15	0	+ 8	+ 8	+ 8	+ 8	+ 8
Pocatello, ID	42	52	112	27	2	+43	+44	+45	+46	+46
Poplar Bluff, MO	36	46	90	24	1	+35	+25	+17	+ 8	+ 1
Portland, ME	43	40	70	15	0	− 8	− 5	− 3	− 1	0
Portland, OR	45	31	122	41	3	+14	+20	+25	+31	+36
Portsmouth, NH	43	5	70	45	0	− 4	− 2	− 1	0	0
Presque Isle, ME	46	41	68	1	0	−29	−19	−12	− 4	+ 2
Providence, RI	41	50	71	25	0	+ 3	+ 2	+ 1	0	0
Pueblo, CO	38	16	104	37	2	+27	+20	+14	+ 7	+ 2
Raleigh, NC	35	47	78	38	0	+51	+39	+30	+20	+12
Rapid City, SD	44	5	103	14	2	+ 2	+ 5	+ 8	+11	+13
Reading, PA	40	20	75	56	0	+26	+22	+19	+16	+13
Redding, CA	40	35	122	24	3	+31	+27	+25	+22	+19
Richmond, VA	37	32	77	26	0	+41	+32	+25	+17	+11
Roanoke, VA	37	16	79	57	0	+51	+42	+35	+27	+21
Roswell, NM	33	24	104	32	2	+41	+26	+14	0	−10
Rutland, VT	43	37	72	58	0	+ 2	+ 5	+ 7	+ 9	+11
Sacramento, CA	38	35	121	30	3	+34	+27	+21	+15	+10
St. Johnsbury, VT	44	25	72	1	0	− 4	0	+ 3	+ 7	+10
St. Joseph, MI	42	5	86	26	0	+61	+61	+60	+60	+59
St. Joseph, MO	39	46	94	50	1	+43	+38	+35	+30	+27
St. Louis, MO	38	37	90	12	1	+28	+21	+16	+10	+ 5
St. Petersburg, FL	27	46	82	39	0	+87	+65	+47	+26	+10
Salem, OR	44	57	123	1	3	+17	+23	+27	+31	+35
Salina, KS	38	50	97	37	1	+57	+51	+46	+40	+35
Salisbury, MD	38	22	75	36	0	+31	+23	+18	+11	+ 6
Salt Lake City, UT	40	45	111	53	2	+48	+45	+43	+40	+38
San Antonio, TX	29	25	98	30	1	+87	+66	+50	+31	+16
San Diego, CA	32	43	117	9	3	+33	+17	+ 4	− 9	−21
San Francisco–Oakland–San Jose, CA	37	47	122	25	3	+40	+31	+25	+18	+12
Santa Fe, NM	35	41	105	56	2	+40	+28	+19	+ 9	0

City	North Latitude ° '		West Longitude ° '		Time Zone Code	A (min.)	B (min.)	Key Letters C (min.)	D (min.)	E (min.)
Savannah, GA	32	5	81	6	0	+70	+54	+40	+25	+13
Scranton–Wilkes-Barre, PA..	41	25	75	40	0	+21	+19	+18	+16	+15
Seattle–Tacoma– Olympia, WA	47	37	122	20	3	+ 3	+15	+24	+34	+42
Sheridan, WY	44	48	106	58	2	+14	+19	+23	+27	+31
Shreveport, LA	32	31	93	45	1	+60	+44	+31	+16	+ 4
Sioux Falls, SD	43	33	96	44	1	+38	+40	+42	+44	+46
South Bend, IN	41	41	86	15	0	+62	+61	+60	+59	+58
Spartanburg, SC	34	56	81	57	0	+66	+53	+43	+32	+23
Spokane, WA	47	40	117	24	3	−16	− 4	+ 4	+14	+23
Springfield, IL	39	48	89	39	1	+22	+18	+14	+10	+ 6
Springfield–Holyoke, MA...	42	6	72	36	0	+ 6	+ 6	+ 6	+ 5	+ 5
Springfield, MO	37	13	93	18	1	+45	+36	+29	+20	+14
Syracuse, NY	43	3	76	9	0	+17	+19	+20	+21	+22
Tallahassee, FL	30	27	84	17	0	+87	+68	+53	+35	+22
Tampa, FL	27	57	82	27	0	+86	+64	+46	+25	+ 9
Terre Haute, IN	39	28	87	24	0	+74	+69	+65	+60	+56
Texarkana, AR	33	26	94	3	1	+59	+44	+32	+18	+ 8
Toledo, OH	41	39	83	33	0	+52	+50	+49	+48	+47
Topeka, KS	39	3	95	40	1	+49	+43	+38	+32	+28
Traverse City, MI	44	46	85	38	0	+49	+54	+57	+62	+65
Trenton, NJ	40	13	74	46	0	+21	+17	+14	+11	+ 8
Trinidad, CO	37	10	104	31	2	+30	+21	+13	+ 5	0
Tucson, AZ	32	13	110	58	2	+70	+53	+40	+24	+12
Tulsa, OK	36	9	95	60	1	+59	+48	+40	+30	+22
Tupelo, MS	34	16	88	34	1	+35	+21	+10	− 2	−11
Vernal, UT	40	27	109	32	2	+40	+36	+33	+30	+28
Walla Walla, WA	46	4	118	20	3	− 5	+ 2	+ 8	+15	+21
Washington, DC	38	54	77	1	0	+35	+28	+23	+18	+13
Waterbury–Meriden, CT	41	33	73	3	0	+10	+ 9	+ 7	+ 6	+ 5
Waterloo, IA	42	30	92	20	1	+24	+24	+24	+25	+25
Wausau, WI	44	58	89	38	1	+ 4	+ 9	+13	+18	+22
West Palm Beach, FL	26	43	80	3	0	+79	+55	+36	+14	− 2
Wichita, KS	37	42	97	20	1	+60	+51	+45	+37	+31
Williston, ND	48	9	103	37	1	+46	+59	+69	+80	+90
Wilmington, DE	39	45	75	33	0	+26	+21	+18	+13	+10
Wilmington, NC	34	14	77	55	0	+52	+38	+27	+15	+ 5
Winchester, VA	39	11	78	10	0	+38	+33	+28	+23	+19
Worcester, MA	42	16	71	48	0	+ 3	+ 2	+ 2	+ 2	+ 2
York, PA	39	58	76	43	0	+30	+26	+22	+18	+15
Youngstown, OH	41	6	80	39	0	+42	40	+38	+36	+34
Yuma, AZ	32	43	114	37	2	+83	+67	+54	+40	+28
CANADA										
Calgary, AB	51	5	114	5	2	+13	+35	+50	+68	+84
Edmonton, AB	53	34	113	25	2	− 3	+26	+47	+72	+93
Halifax, NS	44	38	63	35	−1	+21	+26	+29	+33	+37
Montreal, QC	45	28	73	39	0	− 1	+ 4	+ 9	+15	+20
Ottawa, ON	45	25	75	43	0	+ 6	+13	+18	+23	+28
Peterborough, ON	44	18	78	19	0	+21	+25	+28	+32	+35
Saint John, NB	45	16	66	3	−1	+28	+34	+39	+44	+49
Saskatoon, SK	52	10	106	40	1	+37	+63	+80	+101	+119
Sydney, NS	46	10	60	10	−1	+ 1	+ 9	+15	+23	+28
Thunder Bay, ON	48	27	89	12	0	+47	+61	+71	+83	+93
Toronto, ON	43	39	79	23	0	+28	+30	+32	+35	+37
Vancouver, BC	49	13	123	6	3	0	+15	+26	+40	+52
Winnipeg, MB	49	53	97	10	1	+12	+30	+43	+58	+71

MADDENING
Mind-Manglers

Answers appear on page 251.

Math Challenges

1. DIAMOND DILEMMA
■ In a series of spring training games, the Yankees scored 35 runs. The Dodgers and Tigers, respectively, tallied half and a third as many as the Reds. The Reds' scores were as much below the Yankees' as the Dodgers' were above the Tigers'. How many runs did each team score?

2. STICKY PROBLEM
■ On her bookshelf, Mary has a ten-volume set of books, numbered 1 through 10, in order, from left to right. Each volume has 100 pages. She took the books off the shelf, and on the front of the first page of volume 1, she attached a sticky note. On the back of the last page of volume 10, she attached another sticky note. Then she put the books back, in order, as they were. Ignoring the covers, how many pages lie between the two sticky notes?

3. ANIMAL INVENTORY
■ The proprietor of a menagerie was asked how many parrots and how many elephants it included. He replied, "Well, the lot have 32 heads and 100 feet." How many of each kind were there?

–The Old Farmer's Almanac, 1905

Word Play

■ Use the numbers and letters as clues to fill in the answers, which are facts about familiar phenomena (plus one song lyric).

1. There are 32 T _ _ _ H in an adult
H _ _ _ N.

2. There are 3 T _ _ _ _ _ _ _ S in a
T _ _ _ _ _ _ _ _ N.

3. 3 S _ _ _ S form the B _ _ T of the
O _ _ _ N C _ _ _ _ E L L _ _ _ _ N.

4. There are 10 P _ _ _ _ N _ E S in
C _ _ _ _ A.

5. There are 5 L _ _ _ S on a
M _ _ _ C A L S _ _ _ F.

6. There are 2 H _ _ _ _ _ _ N
M _ L E _ _ _ E S in W _ _ _ R.

7. There are 50 S _ _ _ S on the
A _ _ _ _ _ _ N F _ _ G.

8. There are 360 D _ _ _ _ E S in a
C _ _ _ _ E.

9. There are 225 S _ _ _ R E S on a
S _ _ _ _ _ L E B _ _ _ D.

10. "76 T _ _ _ _ _ _ _ S led the
B _ _ P _ _ _ _ _."

–Heidi Stonehill

☐☐

2005   THE OLD FARMER'S ALMANAC

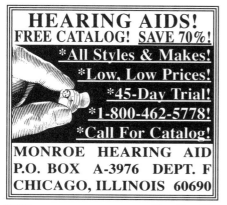

Classified Advertising

ALTERNATIVE ENERGY

YOUR OWN ELECTRIC COMPANY! Diesel generators. Free brochures. Imperial-OFA, 507 Kinsman, Greenville PA 16125. 800-830-0498.

ART

NORMAN ROCKWELL prints, posters, collectibles, calendar. Annual Christmas tree ball and ornament, etc. Rockwell Gallery Collection. 215-969-5619. www.rockwellsite.com

ASTROLOGY/OCCULT

ASTROLOGY: FREE CATALOG. Books, tapes, tarot, spirituality. 800-500-0453 or 714-255-9218. Church of Light, www.light.org

OCCULT CATALOG: complete needs. Herbs, oils, books, incense, etc. $3. Power Products, PO Box 442, Mars Hill NC 28754.

FREE MINI-READINGS. Psychic Diana has the ability to solve all problems. Removes spells and reunites loved ones. Toronto, Ontario; 416-226-5418.

SPIRITUAL ADVISOR. Help for all problems: relationships, nature, money, jobs. See results in 3 days. Call Dewberry, 800-989-1059 or 912-264-3259.

SISTER ROGERS, psychic reader and advisor. Can help you with problems, love, business, marriage, and health. 903-454-4406.

FREE! ONE PERSONALIZED MAGIC SPELL! Tell us exactly what you need! EKSES, PO Box 9315(B), San Bernardino CA. 92427-9315. Phone: 909-880-7971. www.ekses.com

MRS. KING, spiritual reader, advisor, helps in matters of life where others have failed. Call 912-283-0635.

MISS LISA, astrology reader and advisor. Extraordinary powers. Call for help with all problems. Waycross GA. 912-283-3206.

FREE OCCULT CATALOG! Books, bumper stickers, jewelry, ritual items. AzureGreen, PO Box 48-OFA, Middlefield MA 01243. 413-623-2155. Retail/wholesale. www.azuregreen.com

EXPERIENCE A QUALITY PSYCHIC READING with the insights you want and integrity you deserve! Privacy and satisfaction guaranteed. Entertainment only, 18+. Call 866-268-6544 or visit our Web site, www.psychicsource.com

GOD-GIFTED LOVE SPIRITUALIST restores impossible cases. Reunites lovers immediately and permanently. 100% accurate. Phone: Rachel Green, 877-994-2387.

MALEENA, GOD-GIFTED. Can reunite lovers. Guaranteed results with all situations. FREE mini-reading. 757-549-1177.

ATTENTION: SISTER LIGHT, Spartanburg, South Carolina. One free reading when you call. I will help in all problems. 864-576-9397.

EUROPEAN PSYCHIC READER and advisor guarantees help with all problems. Call Sylvia for one free reading. 864-583-5776.

POWERFUL SPELLS performed by Gabriella. Specializing in reuniting lovers. Guaranteed in two hours. 504-628-1260.

DIAL YOUR HOROSCOPE. Reveals future! Specialty love, career, marriage. Removes negativity. Amazing! Free reading. 817-461-9211.

SISTER MOSES can remove bad luck, sickness, suffering. Restores love, luck, happiness. Guarantees help in 3 days. One free reading. 601-425-5211.

FREE LUCKY NUMBERS. Send birth date, self-addressed, stamped envelope. Mystic, Box 2009-R, Jamestown NC 27282.

PSYCHIC READINGS by Miss Day. Tells past, present, future on love, marriage, business. Reuniting lovers in days. 877-952-1234. www.thepsychicshop.com

POWERFUL SPELLS PERFORMED. Alexandria reunites lovers immediately. Reveals future love, finance. One free reading. 423-593-4563.

NEED A MIRACLE? Licensed PhD psychics Caroline Hudson and Natalie Morgan. God-gifted, nominated by Astrological Association for their amazing abilities and accuracy. Never-fail advice on love, marriage, business, health. Reunites lovers guaranteed. 800-790-5044 or 800-657-5608.

BEEKEEPING EQUIPMENT

ROSSMAN APIARIES. Established 1936 and family-owned. Manufacturers of cypress beehives, protective clothing, honey extracting equipment, honey containers. 800-333-7677. www.gabees.com

BEER & WINE MAKING

FREE ILLUSTRATED CATALOG. Fast service. Since 1967. Kraus, PO Box 7850-YB, Independence MO 64054. Phone: 800-841-7404. Web site: www.eckraus.com/offers/fd.asp

BOOKS/PUBLICATIONS/CATALOGS

WORRIED ABOUT YOUR JOB in any capacity? Scared, confused? Then you need this! Visit www.self-protection.info or call 219-765-5019. "Better" health information also available.

GRACE LIVINGSTON HILL BOOKS! Free list. We have great L. Walker Arnold books! Call 800-854-8571.

FREE CATALOG of Classics Illustrated comics. 1940s–1970s. Philip Gaudino, 49 Park Ave., Port Washington NY 11050.

FREE BOOKLETS: Life, death, soul, resurrection, pollution crisis, hell, Judgment Day, restitution. Bible Standard (OF), 1156 St. Matthews Rd., Chester Springs PA 19425. www.biblestandard.com

FAMILY FUN. 100-year-old book of children's manners: "Goops and How to Be Them." Web site: www.TheGoops.net

ANGRY? Turn anger's energy into powers for happiness, success, security. Order today. Powerful booklet by Vernon Howard: "Conquer Harmful Anger 100 Ways." $3.00. Newlife, PO Box 2230-TB, Pine AZ 85544. www.anewlife.org

BUSINESS OPPORTUNITIES

MAILERS WANTED! $500 weekly possible mailing our free list circulars from home! Send stamped envelope: Primesource (#148), Box 700, Worth IL 60482.

CELLULAR TOWER LEASES. Leases earn $2,000 monthly. Already have or want a lease? Visit: www.walkertowers.com

$400 WEEKLY ASSEMBLING PRODUCTS from home. For free information, send SASE to Home Assembly-FA, PO Box 216, New Britain CT 06050-0216.

LET GOVERNMENT GRANTS AND LOANS FINANCE your business, to $2,200,000.00. Free recorded message: 707-448-0270. (KE1) Web site: www.usgovernmentinformation.com

$1,000's WEEKLY mailing burglar alarm advertisements! Free supplies/postage! SASE: RBM-FA, PO Box 759, Lake Zurich IL 60047.

DOUBLE YOUR MONEY in 3 years with stock options. Reply James Detmer, 600 East 5th St. #B-9, Fulton MO 65251.

RECORD VIDEOTAPES, BURN DVDs! Easy $1,800.00 weekly income. Free start-up information kit. 205-663-9888. Dept. 174, 210 Lorna Square, Birmingham AL 35416-5439. www.CMSVideo.net

TURN YOUR LOVE OF FRAGRANCES into a home business. Read "Creating Your Own Perfume With a 1700% Markup!" Details plus free perfume developer's resources at www.Bio-Byte.com

WATKINS PRODUCTS. Buy retail or wholesale or start your own Watkins business, 800-215-2743 or www.cbbirch.com

GET PAID TO SHOP! Shoppers wanted nationwide to evaluate customer service. Free details. Phone: 800-242-0363, ext. 1793.

EARN $400 TO $700 for 5 to 6 hours' work. Free information. Send stamped envelope to "Off Air DJ," Box 332, Big Bend WI 53103.

BUY! SELL! FULLER BRUSH PRODUCTS. Extra Money. Learn How. Independent Distributor. 910-582-8757. www.fullersuccess.com

CLOTHING

FREE CARHARTT clothing catalog! Shrock-OFA, 507 Kinsman, Greenville PA 16125. 866-655-2467. "Saving you money … every day!"

EDUCATION/INSTRUCTION

BRITISH INSTITUTE OF HOMEOPATHY. Home-study courses in herbology, clinical nutrition, homeopathy, Bach Flower Remedies, and more. Free prospectus. Call 607-927-5660.

FARM & GARDEN

NEPTUNE'S HARVEST ORGANIC FERTILIZERS: Extremely effective. Commercially proven. Out-perform chemicals. Wholesale/retail/farm. Catalog. 800-259-4769. www.neptunesharvest.com

GET MORE FROM YOUR LAND! "Metrofarm: The guide to growing for big profit on a small parcel of land." Learn how the AVERAGE acre of farmland near one city earns $123,000 per year! Web site: www.metrofarm.com

FERTILIZER

ALFALFA AND BERMUDA GRASS hay producers! Use the fertilizer that top producers use for higher yields and higher-quality hay. 479-531-4642.

FINANCIAL/LOANS BY MAIL

FREE GRANT MONEY! Immediate approval. No repayment. Debts, personal needs, business. Rush SASE: Grants-FA, PO Box 458, New Britain CT 06050-0458.

IT'S SCOT-FREE! Wealthy families unload millions in grants! Any purpose! Everyone eligible! Never repay! $1.00 application fee to: Hope, PO Box 647, Poway CA 92064.

$750/WEEK working through the Government. Free grants. 800-306-0873. 800-306-0990. 888-3849608. www.capitalpublications.com

FOOD & RECIPES

TOTALLY NUTS brand peanuts and cashews. Call us at 888-489-6887 or visit our Web site, www.totallynuts.biz

SAN FRANCISCO HERB CO. Since 1973. High-quality culinary herbs, spices, teas, essential oils. Free catalog. Phone: 800-227-4530. Web site: www.sfherb.com

YOU-MAKE-IT. Supplies for cheese to wine, beer to bubblegum, hot sauce and more! Web site: www.leeners.com

COUNTRY SPIRIT

Beautiful photography, country musings, proverbs, and more! Best days to plant, set eggs, fish, etc.

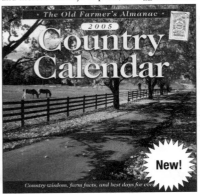

New!

$9.99 plus $2.95 shipping and handling each.
MA tax: $0.50

To order:
Call 800-223-3166

Order online at www.almanac.com/
countryspirit   A94C03

GLORIOUS HERBS!

Exquisite illustrations, in-depth profiles and growing information. Plus ... recipes and other uses for each month's featured herb!

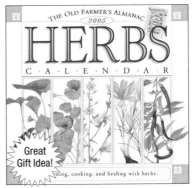

Great Gift Idea!

$9.99 plus $2.95 shipping and handling each.
MA tax: $0.50

To order:
Call 800-223-3166

Order online at www.almanac.com/2005Cal
A94503

C l a s s i f i e d s

HEALTH & FITNESS

AMAZING DIABETES TEA used internationally, contains natural insulin, stimulates and detoxifies pancreas. Guaranteed. Toll-free 877-832-9369. www.diabetestea.com

VISUALIZE DESIRED RESULTS and create a successful future. Write for instructions. Farrar's, Box 210526, Normandy MO 63121.

HELP WANTED

100 WORKERS NEEDED. Assemble crafts, wood items. Materials provided. Earn $480+ per week. Free information package. Call 24 hours, 801-428-4635.

HOME PRODUCTS

LESS/NO DETERGENT using Earth Friendly Laundry Ball. Brochure, FREE sample of New Wonder Balm. Phone: 888-452-4968. Web site: www.mysticwondersinc.com

INVENTORS/INVENTIONS/PATENTS

INVENTIONS/NEW PRODUCTS. ISC, America's leading invention firm, helps submit to companies. Patent services. 1-888-439-IDEA.

MAINE RESORTS

ATLANTIC EYRIE INN, Bar Harbor, Maine. Acadia National Park. Oceanview rooms. Call 800-HabaVue. E-mail: atlanticeyrie@acadia.net. Fax: 207-288-8500. www.barharbor.com/eyrie

INTIMATE OCEANFRONT HOTEL townhomes and house. The Bayview, 111 Eden Street, Bar Harbor, Maine. Phone: 800-356-3585. Web site: www.barharbor.com/bayview

BAR HARBOR AND ACADIA National Park. 153 oceanview rooms. Atlantic-Oakes-by-the-Sea. Open year-round. 800-33-MAINE (62463). Web site: www.barharbor.com

MISCELLANEOUS

CASH FOR 78-RPM RECORDS! Send $2 (refundable) for illustrated booklet identifying collectible labels, numbers, with actual prices I pay. Docks, Box 691035(FA), San Antonio TX 78269-1035.

NURSERY STOCK

TREE/SHRUB SEEDLINGS direct from grower. Plants for landscaping, wildlife food and cover, timber, and Christmas tree production. Free color catalog. Carino Nurseries, PO Box 538AL, Indiana PA 15701. 800-223-7075. www.carinonurseries.com

OF INTEREST TO ALL

AMAZING DIET! All you have to lose is the weight. Send $2 and SASE: 3900 Augusta Rd., W. Columbia SC 29170.

ORGANIZATIONS

H.E.L.P. ANIMALS, INC. 501 (c)3 Tax Deductible. Health-educate-love-protect! Help us help them. 386-775-4966. www.HelpAnimalsInc.org

PERSONALS

MEET BEAUTIFUL Latin women seeking marriage. All ages singles vacations. FREE brochure! TLC, 713-896-9993 or www.tlcworldwide.com

ASIAN BRIDES! WORLDWIDE! Friendship, romance, lifemates! Color photos/details: P.I.C., PO Box 4601-FA, Thousand Oaks CA 91362. 805-492-8040. Web: www.pacisl.com

IT'S FREE! Ladies talk to local guys. It's new, fun, and exciting! Call 800-485-4047. 18+.

FREE INFORMATION! Unmarried Catholics. Established 1980. Sparks Service, Box 872-F11, Troy NY 12181.

DIAL-A-MATE LIVE TALK and voice personals. 10,000 singles call every day! Try it Free! Phone: 800-234-5558. 18+.

POND SUPPLIES

CERTIFIED ORGANIC barley straw and other natural pond and water garden supplies. Wholesale/retail. Phone: 315-531-8803. Web site: www.naturalsolutionsetc.com

POND RESTORATION NATURE'S WAY. Naturalclean Pond Clarifier. Environmentally friendly. Natural, nonchemical. FREE brochure. 800-599-9980. www.pro-agdirect.com

POULTRY

FREE CATALOG. Baby chicks, ducks, geese, turkeys, game birds, Canadian honkers, wood ducks. Eggs to incubators. Books and supplies. Stromberg's, Pine River 45, MN 56474-0400. Visit our Web site: www.strombergschickens.com

GOSLINGS, DUCKLINGS, GUINEAS, chicks, turkeys, bantams, quails, pheasants. Books, medications, equipment. Hoffman Hatchery, PO Box 129P, Gratz PA 17030.

REAL ESTATE

CLAIM GOVERNMENT LAND. 320 acres/person now available. www.usgovernmentinformation.com Free recorded message: 707-448-1887. (4KE1)

LET THE GOVERNMENT PAY for your new or existing home. 100+ programs. Call for free information: 707-448-3210. (8KE1) Web site: www.usgovernmentinformation.com

RELIGION

FREE BOOKLET. What Is This World Coming To? Clearwater Bible Students, PO Box 8216, Clearwater FL 33758.

RELIGION (CONTINUED)

DISCOVER how extraordinary you really are. www.rosicrucian.org/seeker

SEEDS & PLANTS

THE ORIGINAL "Grow Your Own" seed company. Tobacco, medicinal plants, tropicals, and more. Free catalog. E.O.N.S., Dept./FA, PO Box 4604, Hallandale FL 33008. Phone: 954-455-0229. www.eonseed.com

HERBS AND BIRD BOXES. Herb plants, 100+ varieties. Bluebird and wren houses. 724-735-4700. www.alwayssummerherbs.com

PUTTING DOWN ROOTS? Plant blueberries! Northern and southern highbush blueberry plants. Free catalog. Highlander Nursery, PO Box 177, Pettigrew AR 72752. 888-282-3705.

SEPTIC SUPPLIES

SEPTIC SYSTEM PREVENTATIVE MAINTE-NANCE: 8 cents per day. Natural, nonchemical. Free information package. 800-599-9980. Web site: www.pro-agdirect.com

SPIRITUAL ADVICE

LADY OF MIRACLES. Experiencing bad luck, suffering? Stop struggling. Guaranteed results now. FREE reading. 770-222-4977.

REVEREND MITCHELL. Are you sick? Suffering? This spiritual healer will remove all evil, bad luck. I succeed where others have failed in love, business, nature problems. Guaranteed! Call for lucky numbers and help today. FREE reading, 228-547-8823.

SISTER CHRISTIAN. God-gifted spiritual woman helps in love, money, health, nature. Removes evil, bad luck. Guaranteed results. Free reading. Phone: 678-516-9153.

READINGS BY ANGELA. Reunites lovers. Solves all problems. 100% guaranteed. One FREE reading. 940-612-4757.

REMOVES EVIL SPELLS, court cases. Where others fail, I guarantee results in 24 hours. Mrs. Anderson, 334-281-1116.

GOD-GIFTED PSYCHIC. Sister Celine solves all problems, reunites lovers, turns dreams/wishes into reality. 512-845-2053.

MARGIE HAS ANSWERS. Provides lifetime protection. Fast results on love, money, court cases. Removes bad luck and curses. 321-239-6089.

READINGS BY NORA. Specializing in reuniting lovers, helps in all problems. Free reading. Phone: 817-461-2683.

PSYCHIC SHEILA helps in all matters of life. Call now for Free sample reading. 512-383-1650.

WORLD-RENOWNED READER. Are you unhappy? Unlucky? Health, love, business. Removes bad luck. Free reading. 731-589-4450.

MRS. GRAHAM, PSYCHIC, spiritualist, solves all problems, reunites loved ones. One free reading by phone. 706-733-7358 or 561-496-0700.

SPIRITUAL READER AND ADVISOR can solve your problems, remove evil influences, bad luck, money. Guaranteed returned loved ones in 4 days. Call 609-332-2985.

WORLD-RENOWNED SPIRITUALIST reader and advisor, Mrs. Moreno, can help you with all problems. 888-737-1258.

REV. MONTGOMERY, through prayer, can help you with all problems, bad luck, evil influences. Call 706-790-7509.

MYSTIC CRYSTAL helps with all troubles. Results in hours. Tells past, present, and future. Phone: 404-325-7336.

ANDREA SOLVES ALL PROBLEMS. Specializes in returning lovers. Results within hours. Free reading. 214-366-2738.

WARRIOR NANCY destroys negativity. Reunites lovers. Immediate results. Help in all matters of life. 904-669-7585.

MADAM LINDA guarantees magical results reuniting lovers. Removes negative energy. Helps love, money, health. 904-669-5488.

REVEREND HOPE guarantees the power to remove bad luck, restores good health, happiness, loved ones. Call for blessing and peace of mind. Her voice will convince you! Experience the true one! Phone: 704-494-4896.

CHRISTINA specializes in reuniting lovers, helps with all problems. Guaranteed immediate results. Free reading. 423-614-0902.

NEED HELP DESPERATELY? Rev. Samuel solves impossible problems. Evil, lost nature, love, sickness, luck. 843-681-8118.

PSYCHIC OF CHARLESTON, South Carolina, solves all problems of life. Call today, tomorrow may be too late. 843-766-9097.

MISS ANGEL, specializing in Spiritual cleansing, removing evil influences. Guaranteed results. One Free reading. 706-335-4323.

SPIRITUAL HEALER and advisor. Guaranteed help in all problems. Call for your Free reading. Phone: 817-613-0509.

SISTER ANN. Having bad luck? Been touched by evil hands? Need help in love, luck, financial, or unnatural sickness? Guaranteed results. Call now, tomorrow may be too late. One free reading. Phone: 770-614-9998.

MOTHER CHRISTIAN, holy reader, specializes in relationships. Depressed? Need answers? Removes evil and bad luck. Responds instantly! 954-822-5506.

SPIRITUAL HEALERS

SPIRITUAL HEALER. Guaranteed help in all problems. FREE reading. Phone: 940-642-2439 or 817-599-5532.

REVEREND GINGER—Indian healer—works miracles, guaranteed in hours. Specializing in reuniting the separated. Call 504-463-3358.

SPIRITUAL HEALER SOPHIA helps all problems: love, luck, money, health, marriage, and happiness. Free reading. 334-688-1709.

NEFERTITI. Specializing: Egyptians, Tarot, past, present, future. Guaranteed results. Immediately solves all problems. 866-375-3518.

MS. LOVE SPIRITUAL HEALER guarantees to remove all bad luck and evil around you. Will protect from enemies and help in love. Fast results. Free reading. 770-333-9622.

EVANGELIST ADAMS, spiritual healer for all problems. Suffering with unhappiness, sickness, nature? A holy religious healer woman can change your life. One call away from happiness. Immediate results! Call now! 404-603-9443.

SPIRITUAL HEALER. $25 guaranteed to resolve bad luck. Evil controls you! Call today for more information. 770-650-7171 or 877-650-7177.

SOUTHERN HEALER resolves all problems in life, love, business, marriage, nature, bad luck, and evil influences. Guaranteed results! 678-455-0107.

SPIRITUALISTS

FREE SAMPLE READING! Mrs. Ruth, southern-born spiritualist, removes evil, bad luck. Helps with all problems. 334-616-6363.

REVEREND MOTHER MILLIE helps remove bad luck, evil. Reunites loved ones. Spiritual cleansing, healing. Do you want help? Call 803-796-8974.

EUROPEAN PSYCHIC READER reunites loved ones within 24 hours. In business 45 years. Call 903-655-6355.

MRS. GAIL HELPS IN LOVE, money, health. Removes Evil influences. Guaranteed results. Free reading. 601-342-1201.

LYN GOODMAN, Master God-gifted Ph.D. Love worker, 49 years' experience. 100% successful. No disappointments, no matter how severe. Results in hours. Complimentary consultation. 800-996-3052.

MADELINE HAYES STOPS DIVORCE, cheating, depression. Reunites lovers permanently. Results in 35 minutes. Complimentary reading. Flat rate, no hidden costs. 24 hours. 800-228-8914.

MRS. RAINBOW. Spiritual psychic and advisor. Reunites lovers in 24 hours. Removes bad luck, helps in all problems. 626-339-8606.

GUARANTEED OR MONEY BACK. Love Psychic Kate! Soul mate specialist. Helps all problems. 8491 W. Sunset Blvd. #362, Los Angeles CA 90069. 800-275-0030.

TREES & SHRUBS

CATALOG FREE! Tree seedlings. Wholesale prices. Flickinger's Nursery, Box 245, Sagamore PA 16250. 800-368-7381.

ANTIQUE APPLE TREES. 90+ varieties! Catalog $3.00. Urban Homestead, 818-B Cumberland St., Bristol VA 24201.

The Old Farmer's Almanac classified rates: $18.50 per word (15-word minimum per insertion). Payment required with order: MasterCard, Visa, AmEx, and Discover/NOVUS accepted. For *Gardener's Companion* rates, Web classifieds, or information, contact Marie Knopp: 203-263-7171; fax 203-263-7174; or E-mail to OFAads@aol.com. Write to: Marie Knopp, Gallagher Group, PO Box 959, Woodbury, CT 06798. **The 2006 Old Farmer's Almanac closing date is May 13, 2005.**

Index to Advertisers

ANSWERS TO

MADDENING MIND-MANGLERS
from page 240

MATH CHALLENGES
1. Diamond Dilemma

Reds 30, Dodgers 15, Tigers 10.
$Y = 35$, $D = R/2$, $T = R/3$; $Y - R = D - T$; $35 - R = R/2 - R/3$; $35 = R/2 - R/3 + R$. Using the common denominator 6, $35 = 3R/6 - 2R/6 + 6R/6$; $35 = 7R/6$; $7R = 210$; $R = 210/7 = 30$; $D = R/2 = 30/2 = 15$; $T = R/3 = 30/3 = 10$.

2. Sticky Problem

800 pages. Page 1 lies at the right-hand side of volume 1 as you view its spine. Similarly, the last page of volume 10 lies at the left-hand side of the book with its spine facing you. No pages in volume 1 or volume 10 lie between the sticky notes.

3. Animal Inventory

14 parrots, 18 elephants. $P + E = 32$; $E = 32 - P$. With a parrot having two feet and an elephant four, $2P + 4E = 100$; $2P + 4(32 - P) = 100$; $2P + 128 - 4P = 100$; $-2P = -28$; $P = 14$; $14 + E = 32$; $E = 32 - 14 = 18$.

WORD PLAY

1. There are 32 teeth in an adult human. **2.** There are 3 teaspoons in a tablespoon. **3.** 3 stars form the belt of the Orion constellation. **4.** There are 10 provinces in Canada. **5.** There are 5 lines on a musical staff. **6.** There are 2 hydrogen molecules in water. **7.** There are 50 stars on the American flag. **8.** There are 360 degrees in a circle. **9.** There are 225 squares on a Scrabble board. **10.** "76 trombones led the big parade." [Editor's Note: from *The Music Man*] □□

MANGLE OUR MINDS

Got a mind-bending math or word puzzle that will challenge even the nimblest number crunchers? Send it to us! We may use it in the Almanac. E-mail your puzzle to almanac@yankeepub.com (subject: Mind-Manglers) or send via regular mail to The Old Farmer's Almanac, P.O. Box 520, Dublin, NH 03444. Include the solution clearly stated. All submissions become the property of Yankee Publishing Inc., which reserves the rights to the material.

Amusement

A sampling from the hundreds of letters, clippings, and e-mails sent to us by Almanac readers from all over the United States and Canada during the past year.

How Your Favorite Sleeping Position May Reveal Your True Personality

Courtesy of M. J., Hancock, New Hampshire, who credits www.thewmurchannel.com

Professor Chris Idzikowski, director of the Sleep Assessment and Advisory Service in Great Britain, claims that how you sleep can tell a lot about who you are:

■ According to his survey of sleep positions and associated character traits, those who sleep in the soldier position—flat on their back with arms at their sides—are quiet and reserved.

■ Those who drift off on their sides with legs outstretched and arms down are easygoing and very sociable.

■ If arms are outstretched, in what is called the yearner position, the person

tends to be more skeptical and suspicious.

■ People tend to be brash and gregarious if they sleep in the free-fall position, i.e., flat on their stomach with hands beside their head.

■ Those who sleep in the starfish position (flat on their back with arms and legs spread out) usually have an unassuming personality and are very good listeners, according to the study.

■ Finally, those who sleep in the fetal position, which was favored by more than half of those in the study, tend to be quite shy and sensitive.

At Last We Know the Way the Cookie Crumbles
(and we now know why, too!)

Courtesy of R.T.M., Oklahoma City, Oklahoma, who credits the online edition of the journal Measurement Science and Technology

It seems that about a year ago, a doctoral student at Loughborough University in the United Kingdom, one Qasim Saleem, used a sophisticated digital-image processing system to "study" some freshly baked cookies while they were cooling. He and his colleagues observed cracks

appearing on them only a few minutes after they were removed from the oven.

After an additional observation period, they concluded that during this cooling process, moisture drifts from the center of the cookie, building stress toward the outside while, indeed, the center actually shrinks. This results in the formation of tiny cracks, which often cause cookies to crumble during handling and shipment.

Low-fat, low-sugar cookies fared the worst, they reported, while the sugary, high-fat (and more delicious) varieties were far less likely to crumble.

So . . . well . . . that seems to be the way the cookie crumbles.

What's Wrong With This Title

Courtesy of H. B., Manalapan, New Jersey

So you're an expert in English, eh? Guess again.

1. What is the longest one-syllable word in the English language?

2. Can you think of words that rhyme with "month," "orange," "silver," and "purple"?

3. What is the longest English word that is typed with only the left hand?

4. The one word in the English language that ends with the letters "mt" is . . .?

Answers: 1. Screeched. 2. There are none. 3. Stewardesses. 4. Dreamt. [Editor's Note: OK, OK. We'll also allow "undreamt" and "adreamt" for this one.] Title: Needs a question mark!

Before You Go Fishing, Look for a Cow

Courtesy of D.R.H., Mount Olive, North Carolina

Doesn't seem possible but, yes, there's apparently some mysterious connection between fish and cows . . .

I used to bass-fish with an older gentleman, and when we were riding along, he would note that the fish would bite "good" that day. When I would ask how he knew that the fish would bite better that day, he would tell me that the percentage of cows standing would indicate how well the fish would bite. For example, if nearly all were lying down, it would be a poor day; if nearly all were standing, it would be a good day. If eating and standing, an even better day.

The first time he said this, I thought he was teasing me. Over the years, I've found that I can defend his view as being more than 80 percent correct.

CONTINUED

253

How Close Can You Get to a Hog Barn Before Smelling It?

Courtesy of B.S.P., Winnipeg, Manitoba, who credits CBC News Online

Scientists at the University of Manitoba, Canada, have been using 15 expert sniffers to determine the all-important answer to that question.

"We actually use a GPS [global positioning system] to put our 15 volunteer sniffers in the exact positions we want," says Qiang Zhang, a biosystems engineer at the University of Manitoba. He and his volunteers, all with extremely keen noses, have been working in fields surrounding various hog barns. Last year, similar tests were conducted by the University of Saskatchewan, using hog barns located around Good Spirit Lake. Their goal, of course, was to learn how far away houses must be to avoid having to put up with the smell of pig manure.

One of the problems has to do with, as Zhang puts it, "the saturation of the nose." In other words, if a sniffer's nose is exposed to the odor of pig manure for a long time, the nose becomes saturated and the smell seems to disappear or change intensity.

"So we ask our sniffers to wear a mask to keep their noses fresh," says Zhang. "When they're ready to sniff, they take the mask off, take a good long sniff, record the degree of offensiveness or intensity, time, and location, and then put the mask back on." Smelling sessions last about an hour, and readings are taken anywhere from 100 meters to one kilometer from a hog barn.

Incidentally, not every person is a good hog sniffer. Volunteers must undergo a chemical calibration process, and only worthy noses are elevated to the coveted level of pig manure sniffer.

The Day It Rained Frogs

Courtesy of S. T., Albany, New York

It actually happened—in Berlin, Connecticut, on September 19, 2003.

■ As many remember, Hurricane Isabel brought high winds and lashing rains to the East Coast in September 2003. When the remnants of the hurricane moved through his area, one Primo D'Agata was startled by what he thought was hail smacking down onto his porch. When he went out to investigate, though, he

discovered tiny, gelatinous eggs with dark spots in the middle. He assumed that the dark spots were frog eggs, a presumption eventually confirmed by Nicolas Diaz, a naturalist and teacher at the New Britain Youth Museum at Hungerford Park.

Later, after putting some of the eggs in a large bowl of water for a few days, D'Agata observed a few sprouting tails—the beginnings of pollywogs. For sure, it had rained frogs on his porch.

There was one more mystery to unravel, however. No frogs in Connecticut lay eggs so late in the year. So it was surmised that D'Agata's frog eggs must have been picked up in North Carolina or thereabouts and then carried north on the fierce winds of Isabel.

Best Not to Underestimate a Grandmother

Courtesy of F. P., West Caldwell, New Jersey

Of all the great jokes submitted to us by readers during this past year, this was our favorite.

■ Standing on the shore, a Jewish lady watches her grandson playing in the water. She is thunderstruck when she sees a huge wave crash over him, because when it recedes, the boy is no longer there—vanished!

Screaming, she holds her hands to the sky and cries, "Lord, how could you? Have I not been a wonderful mother and grandmother? Have I not scrimped and saved so that I could tithe to the temple and contribute to B'nai Brith? Have I not always put others before myself? Have I not always turned my other cheek and loved my neighbors? Have I not . . ."

A deep voice from the sky booms down: "Enough already, give me a break!"

Immediately, another huge wave appears and crashes on the beach. When it recedes, the boy is standing there, smiling and splashing around as if nothing had ever happened.

The voice continues: "I have returned your grandson. Are you satisfied now?"

Grandmother responds, "He had a hat."

□□

Share Your Anecdotes and Pleasantries

Send your contribution for the 2006 edition of *The Old Farmer's Almanac* by January 28, 2005, to "A & P," The Old Farmer's Almanac, P.O. Box 520, Dublin, NH 03444; or send e-mail to almanac@yankeepub.com (subject: A & P).

Are you over 55?
"It's All Free for Seniors"

Washington DC (Special) An amazing new book reveals thousands of little-known Government giveaways for people over 55.

Each year, lots of these benefits are NOT given away simply because people don't know they're available... and the government doesn't advertise them.

Many of these fabulous freebies can be yours regardless of your income or assets. Entitled "Free for Seniors," the book tells you all about such goodies as how you can:

▶ Get free prescription drugs. (This one alone could save you thousands of dollars!)

▶ Get free dental care... for yourself AND for your grandkids.

▶ Get up to $800 for food.

▶ How you can get free legal help.

▶ How to get some help in paying your rent, wherever you live.

▶ How to get up to $15,000 free money to spruce up your home!

▶ Here's where to get $1,800 to keep you warm this winter.

▶ Access the very best research on our planet on how you can live longer.

▶ Are you becoming more forgetful? Here's valuable free information you should get now.

▶ Stop high blood pressure and cholesterol worries from ruling your life.

▶ Free help if you have arthritis of any type.

▶ Incontinence is not inevitable. These free facts could help you.

▶ Free eye treatment.

▶ Depression: Being down in the dumps is common, but it doesn't have to be a normal part of growing old.

▶ Free medical care from some of the very best doctors in the world for Alzheimer's, cataracts, or heart disease.

▶ New Cancer Cure? Maybe! Here's how to find out what's known about it to this point.

▶ Promising new developments for prostate cancer.

▶ Get paid $100 a day plus expenses to travel overseas!

▶ Up to $5,000 free to help you pay your bills.

▶ Free and confidential help with your sex life.

▶ Impotence? Get confidential help... Free therapies, treatments, implants, and much more.

▶ Hot Flashes? This new research could help you now!

▶ Find out if a medicine you're taking could be affecting your sex life.

There's more! Much, much more, and "Free for Seniors" comes with a solid no-nonsense guarantee. Send for your copy today and examine it at your leisure. Unless it makes or saves you AT LEAST ten times its cost, simply return it for a full refund within 90 days.

Although certain of these benefits are only available to persons of modest means, many of them are available regardless of age, income or assets! Some services may have restrictions or require pre-qualification.

To get your copy of "Free for Seniors," send your name and address along with a check or money-order for only $12.95 plus $3.98 postage and handling (total of $16.93) to: FREE FOR SENIORS, Dept. FS3833, 718-12th Street N.W., Box 24500, Canton, Ohio 44701.

To charge to your VISA or MasterCard, include your card number, expiration date, and signature. For even faster service, have your credit card handy and call toll-free 1-800-772-7285, Ext. FS3833.

Want to save even more? Do a favor for a friend or relative and order 2 books for only $20 postpaid.   ©2004 TCO FS0311S10

http://www.trescocorp.com

A Reference Compendium

compiled by Mare-Anne Jarvela

R
E
F
E
R
E
N
C
E

A Table Foretelling the Weather Through All the Lunations of Each Year, or Forever

This table is the result of many years of actual observation and shows what sort of weather will probably follow the Moon's entrance into any of its quarters. For example, the table shows that the week following January 3, 2005, will be snowy or rainy, because the Moon enters the last quarter that day at 12:46 P.M. EST. (See the **Left-Hand Calendar Pages 180–202** for 2005 Moon phases.)

EDITOR'S NOTE: *Although the data in this table is taken into consideration in the yearlong process of compiling the annual long-range weather forecasts for* The Old Farmer's Almanac, *we rely far more on our projections of solar activity.*

Time of Change	Summer	Winter
Midnight to 2 A.M.	Fair	Hard frost, unless wind is south or west
2 A.M. to 4 A.M.	Cold, with frequent showers	Snow and stormy
4 A.M. to 6 A.M.	Rain	Rain
6 A.M. to 8 A.M.	Wind and rain	Stormy
8 A.M. to 10 A.M.	Changeable	Cold rain if wind is west; snow if east
10 A.M. to noon	Frequent showers	Cold with high winds
Noon to 2 P.M.	Very rainy	Snow or rain
2 P.M. to 4 P.M.	Changeable	Fair and mild
4 P.M. to 6 P.M.	Fair	Fair
6 P.M. to 10 P.M.	Fair if wind is northwest; rain if wind is south or southwest	Fair and frosty if wind is north or northeast; rain or snow if wind is south or southwest
10 P.M. to midnight	Fair	Fair and frosty

This table was created about 170 years ago by Dr. Herschell for the Boston Courier; *it first appeared in* The Old Farmer's Almanac *in 1834.*

Safe Ice Thickness*

Ice Thickness	Permissible Load	Ice Thickness	Permissible Load
3 inches	Single person on foot	12 inches	Heavy truck (8-ton gross)
4 inches	Group in single file	15 inches	10 tons
7½ inches	Passenger car (2-ton gross)	20 inches	25 tons
8 inches	Light truck (2½-ton gross)	30 inches	70 tons
10 inches	Medium truck (3½-ton gross)	36 inches	110 tons

*Solid, clear, blue/black pond and lake ice

■ Slush ice has only half the strength of blue ice.
■ The strength value of river ice is 15 percent less.

Winter Weather Terms

Winter Storm Outlook
■ Issued prior to a winter storm watch. An outlook is issued when forecasters believe that storm conditions are possible, usually 48 to 60 hours before the beginning of a storm.

Winter Storm Watch
■ Indicates the possibility of a winter storm and is issued to provide 12 to 36 hours' notice. A watch is announced when the specific timing, location, and path of a storm are undetermined. Be alert to changing weather conditions, and avoid unnecessary travel.

Winter Storm Warning
■ Indicates that a severe winter storm has started or is about to begin. A warning is issued when more than six inches of snow, a significant ice accumulation, a dangerous windchill, or a combination of the three is expected. Anticipated snow accumulation during a winter storm is six or more inches in 24 hours. You should stay indoors during the storm.

Heavy Snow Warning
■ Issued when snow accumulations are expected to approach or exceed six inches in 12 hours but will not be accompanied by significant wind. The warning could also be issued if eight or more inches of snow accumulation is expected in a 24-hour period. During a heavy snow warning, freezing rain and sleet are not expected.

Blizzard Warning
■ Indicates that sustained winds or frequent gusts of 35 miles per hour or greater will occur in combination with considerable falling and/or blowing snow for at least three hours. Visibility will often be reduced to less than one-quarter mile.

Whiteout
■ Caused by falling and/or blowing snow that reduces visibility to zero miles—typically only a few feet. Whiteouts are most frequent during blizzards and can occur rapidly, often blinding motorists and creating chain-reaction crashes involving multiple vehicles.

Northeaster
■ Usually produces heavy snow and rain and creates tremendous waves in Atlantic coastal regions, often causing beach erosion and structural damage. Wind gusts associated with these storms can exceed hurricane force in intensity. A northeaster gets its name from the strong, continuous, northeasterly ocean winds that blow in over coastal areas ahead of the storm.

Sleet
■ Frozen or partially frozen rain in the form of ice pellets that hit the ground so fast that they bounce and do not stick to it. However, the pellets can accumulate like snow and cause hazardous conditions for pedestrians and motorists.

Freezing Rain
■ Liquid precipitation that turns to ice on contact with a frozen surface to form a smooth ice coating called a glaze.

Ice Storm Warning
■ Issued when freezing rain results in ice accumulations measuring one-half inch thick or more. This can cause trees and utility lines to fall down, causing power outages.

Windchill Advisory
■ Issued when windchill temperatures are expected to be between –20° and –34°F.

Windchill Warning
■ Issued when windchill temperatures are expected to be below –34°F.

Windchill

As wind speed increases, the air temperature against your body falls. The combination of cold temperature and high wind can create a cooling effect so severe that exposed flesh can freeze. (Inanimate objects, such as cars, do not experience windchill.)

To gauge wind speed: At 10 miles per hour, you can feel wind on your face; at 20, small branches move, and dust or snow is raised; at 30, large branches move and wires whistle; at 40, whole trees bend.

TEMPERATURE (°F)

Calm	35	30	25	20	15	10	5	0	−5	−10	−15	−20	−25	−30	−35
5	31	25	19	13	7	1	−5	−11	−16	−22	−28	−34	−40	−46	−52
10	27	21	15	9	3	−4	−10	−16	−22	−28	−35	−41	−47	−53	−59
15	25	19	13	6	0	−7	−13	−19	−26	−32	−39	−45	−51	−58	−64
20	24	17	11	4	−2	−9	−15	−22	−29	−35	−42	−48	−55	−61	−68
25	23	16	9	3	−4	−11	−17	−24	−31	−37	−44	−51	−58	−64	−71
30	22	15	8	1	−5	−12	−19	−26	−33	−39	−46	−53	−60	−67	−73
35	21	14	7	0	−7	−14	−21	−27	−34	−41	−48	−55	−62	−69	−76
40	20	13	6	−1	−8	−15	−22	−29	−36	−43	−50	−57	−64	−71	−78
45	19	12	5	−2	−9	−16	−23	−30	−37	−44	−51	−58	−65	−72	−79
50	19	12	4	−3	−10	−17	−24	−31	−38	−45	−52	−60	−67	−74	−81
55	18	11	4	−3	−11	−18	−25	−32	−39	−46	−54	−61	−68	−75	−82
60	17	10	3	−4	−11	−19	−26	−33	−40	−48	−55	−62	−69	−76	−84

WIND SPEED (mph)

Frostbite occurs in 15 minutes or less.

EXAMPLE: When the temperature is 15°F and the wind speed is 30 miles per hour, the windchill, or how cold it feels, is −5°F. For a Celsius version of the Windchill table, visit **www.almanac.com/weathercenter.** *–courtesy National Weather Service*

Is It Raining, Drizzling, or Misting?

	NUMBER OF DROPS (per sq. ft. per sec.)	DIAMETER OF DROPS (mm)	INTENSITY (in. per hr.)
Cloudburst	113	2.85	4.0
Excessive rain	76	2.4	1.6
Heavy rain	46	2.05	0.6
Moderate rain	46	1.6	0.15
Light rain	26	1.24	0.04
Drizzle	14	0.96	0.01
Mist	2,510	0.1	0.002
Fog	6,264,000	0.01	0.005

R E F E R E N C E

Saffir-Simpson Hurricane Scale

This scale assigns a rating from 1 to 5 based on a hurricane's intensity. It is used to give an estimate of the potential property damage and flooding expected along the coast from a hurricane landfall. Wind speed is the determining factor in the scale, as storm surge values are highly dependent on the slope of the continental shelf in the landfall region. Wind speeds are measured using a 1-minute average.

CATEGORY ONE. Average wind: 74–95 mph. No real damage to building structures. Damage primarily to unanchored mobile homes, shrubbery, and trees. Also, some coastal road flooding and minor pier damage.

CATEGORY TWO. Average wind: 96–110 mph. Some roofing material, door, and window damage to buildings. Considerable damage to vegetation, mobile homes, and piers. Coastal and low-lying escape routes flood 2 to 4 hours before arrival of center. Small craft in unprotected anchorages break moorings.

CATEGORY THREE. Average wind: 111–130 mph. Some structural damage to small residences and utility buildings; minor amount of curtainwall failures. Mobile homes destroyed. Flooding near coast destroys smaller structures; larger structures damaged by floating debris.

CATEGORY FOUR. Average wind: 131–155 mph. More extensive curtainwall failures with some complete roof failure on small residences. Major beach erosion. Major damage to lower floors near the shore.

CATEGORY FIVE. Average wind: 156+ mph. Complete roof failure on many residences and industrial buildings. Some complete building failures; small buildings blown over or away. Major damage to lower floors located less than 15 feet above sea level (ASL) and within 500 yards of the shoreline.

Atlantic Tropical (and Subtropical) Storm Names for 2005

Arlene	Gert	Maria	Tammy
Bret	Harvey	Nate	Vince
Cindy	Irene	Ophelia	Wilma
Dennis	Jose	Philippe	
Emily	Katrina	Rita	
Franklin	Lee	Stan	

Eastern North-Pacific Tropical (and Subtropical) Storm Names for 2005

Adrian	Greg	Max	Todd
Beatriz	Hilary	Norma	Veronica
Calvin	Irwin	Otis	Wiley
Dora	Jova	Pilar	Xina
Eugene	Kenneth	Ramon	York
Fernanda	Lidia	Selma	Zelda

Retired Atlantic Hurricane Names

These storms have been some of the most destructive and costly; as a result, their names have been retired from the six-year rotating list of names.

NAME	YEAR RETIRED	NAME	YEAR RETIRED	NAME	YEAR RETIRED
Agnes	1972	Elena	1985	Andrew	1992
Carmen	1974	Gloria	1985	Opal	1995
Eloise	1975	Gilbert	1988	Roxanne	1995
Anita	1977	Joan	1988	Fran	1996
David	1979	Hugo	1989	Mitch	1998
Frederic	1979	Diana	1990	Floyd	1999
Allen	1980	Klaus	1990	Keith	2000
Alicia	1983	Bob	1991	Lily	2002

REFERENCE

Heat Index °F (°C)

	RELATIVE HUMIDITY (%)								
TEMPERATURE °F (°C)	**40**	**45**	**50**	**55**	**60**	**65**	**70**	**75**	**80**
100 (38)	109 (43)	114 (46)	118 (48)	124 (51)	129 (54)	136 (58)			
98 (37)	105 (41)	109 (43)	113 (45)	117 (47)	123 (51)	128 (53)	134 (57)		
96 (36)	101 (38)	104 (40)	108 (42)	112 (44)	116 (47)	121 (49)	126 (52)	132 (56)	
94 (34)	97 (36)	100 (38)	103 (39)	106 (41)	110 (43)	114 (46)	119 (48)	124 (51)	129 (54)
92 (33)	94 (34)	96 (36)	99 (37)	101 (38)	105 (41)	108 (42)	112 (44)	116 (47)	121 (49)
90 (32)	91 (33)	93 (34)	95 (35)	97 (36)	100 (38)	103 (39)	106 (41)	109 (43)	113 (45)
88 (31)	88 (31)	89 (32)	91 (33)	93 (34)	95 (35)	98 (37)	100 (38)	103 (39)	106 (41)
86 (30)	85 (29)	87 (31)	88 (31)	89 (32)	91 (33)	93 (34)	95 (35)	97 (36)	100 (38)
84 (29)	83 (28)	84 (29)	85 (29)	86 (30)	88 (31)	89 (32)	90 (32)	92 (33)	94 (34)
82 (28)	81 (27)	82 (28)	83 (28)	84 (29)	84 (29)	85 (29)	86 (30)	88 (31)	89 (32)
80 (27)	80 (27)	80 (27)	81 (27)	81 (27)	82 (28)	82 (28)	83 (28)	84 (29)	84 (29)

EXAMPLE: When the temperature is 88°F (31°C) and the relative humidity is 60 percent, the heat index, or how hot it feels, is 95°F (35°C).

The UV Index for Measuring Ultraviolet Radiation Risk

The U.S. National Weather Service daily forecasts of ultraviolet levels use these numbers for various exposure levels:

UV Index Number	Exposure Level	Time to Burn	Actions to Take
0, 1, 2	Minimal	60 minutes	Apply SPF 15 sunscreen
3, 4	Low	45 minutes	Apply SPF 15 sunscreen; wear a hat
5, 6	Moderate	30 minutes	Apply SPF 15 sunscreen; wear a hat
7, 8, 9	High	15–25 minutes	Apply SPF 15 to 30 sunscreen; wear a hat and sunglasses
10 or higher	Very high	10 minutes	Apply SPF 30 sunscreen; wear a hat, sunglasses, and protective clothing

"Time to Burn" and "Actions to Take" apply to people with fair skin that sometimes tans but usually burns. People with lighter skin need to be more cautious. People with darker skin may be able to tolerate more exposure.

85	90	95	100
135 (57)			
126 (52)	131 (55)		
117 (47)	122 (50)	127 (53)	132 (56)
110 (43)	113 (45)	117 (47)	121 (49)
102 (39)	105 (41)	108 (42)	112 (44)
96 (36)	98 (37)	100 (38)	103 (39)
90 (32)	91 (33)	93 (34)	95 (35)
85 (29)	86 (30)	86 (30)	87 (31)

Richter Scale for Measuring Earthquakes

Magnitude	Possible Effects
1	Detectable only by instruments
2	Barely detectable, even near the epicenter
3	Felt indoors
4	Felt by most people; slight damage
5	Felt by all; minor to moderate damage
6	Moderate destruction
7	Major damage
8	Total and major damage

–devised by American geologist Charles W. Richter in 1935 to measure the magnitude of an earthquake

Temperature Conversion Scale

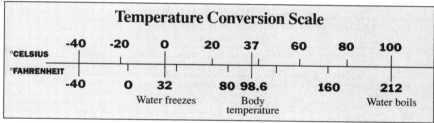

°CELSIUS: -40 -20 0 20 37 60 80 100

°FAHRENHEIT: -40 0 32 80 98.6 160 212

Water freezes · Body temperature · Water boils

The Volcanic Explosivity Index (VEI) for Measuring Volcanic Eruptions

VEI	Description	Plume Height	Volume	Classification	Frequency
0	Nonexplosive	<100 m	1,000 m^3	Hawaiian	Daily
1	Gentle	100–1,000 m	10,000 m^3	Hawaiian/Strombolian	Daily
2	Explosive	1–5 km	1,000,000 m^3	Strombolian/Vulcanian	Weekly
3	Severe	3–15 km	10,000,000 m^3	Vulcanian	Yearly
4	Cataclysmic	10–25 km	100,000,000 m^3	Vulcanian/Plinian	10 years
5	Paroxysmal	>25 km	1 km^3	Plinian	100 years
6	Colossal	>25 km	10 km^3	Plinian/Ultra-Plinian	100 years
7	Supercolossal	>25 km	100 km^3	Ultra-Plinian	1,000 years
8	Megacolossal	>25 km	1,000 km^3	Ultra-Plinian	10,000 years

REFERENCE

Beaufort Wind Force Scale

"Used Mostly at Sea but of Help to All Who Are Interested in the Weather"

Admiral Beaufort arranged the numbers 0 to 12 to indicate the strength of the wind from calm, force 0, to hurricane, force 12. Here's a scale adapted to land.

Beaufort Force	Description	When You See or Feel This Effect	Wind (mph)	(km/h)
0	Calm	Smoke goes straight up	less than 1	less than 2
1	Light air	Wind direction is shown by smoke drift but not by wind vane	1–3	2–5
2	Light breeze	Wind is felt on the face; leaves rustle; wind vanes move	4–7	6–11
3	Gentle breeze	Leaves and small twigs move steadily; wind extends small flags straight out	8–12	12–19
4	Moderate breeze	Wind raises dust and loose paper; small branches move	13–18	20–29
5	Fresh breeze	Small trees sway; waves form on lakes	19–24	30–39
6	Strong breeze	Large branches move; wires whistle; umbrellas are difficult to use	25–31	40–50
7	Moderate gale	Whole trees are in motion; walking against the wind is difficult	32–38	51–61
8	Fresh gale	Twigs break from trees; walking against the wind is very difficult	39–46	62–74
9	Strong gale	Buildings suffer minimal damage; roof shingles are removed	47–54	75–87
10	Whole gale	Trees are uprooted	55–63	88–101
11	Violent storm	Widespread damage	64–72	102–116
12	Hurricane	Widespread destruction	73+	117+

Fujita Scale (or F Scale) for Measuring Tornadoes

■ This is a system developed by Dr. Theodore Fujita to classify tornadoes based on wind damage. All tornadoes, and most other severe local windstorms, are assigned a single number from this scale according to the most intense damage caused by the storm.

F0 (weak)	40–72 mph, light damage
F1 (weak)	73–112 mph, moderate damage
F2 (strong)	113–157 mph, considerable damage
F3 (strong)	158–206 mph, severe damage
F4 (violent)	207–260 mph, devastating damage
F5 (violent)	261–318 mph (rare), incredible damage

Torro Hailstorm Intensity Scale

INTENSITY	DESCRIPTION OF DAMAGE
H0	True hail of pea size causes no damage
H1	Leaves and flower petals are punctured and torn
H2	Leaves are stripped from trees and plants
H3	Panes of glass are broken; auto bodies are dented
H4	Some house windows are broken; small tree branches are broken off; birds are killed
H5	Many windows are smashed; small animals are injured; large tree branches are broken off
H6	Shingle roofs are breached; metal roofs are scored; wooden window frames are broken away
H7	Roofs are shattered to expose rafters; cars are seriously damaged
H8	Shingle and tiled roofs are destroyed; small tree trunks are split; people are seriously injured
H9	Concrete roofs are broken; large tree trunks are split and knocked down; people are at risk of fatal injuries
H10	Brick houses are damaged; people are at risk of fatal injuries

Cloud Definitions

—Weatherstock

High Clouds
(bases starting at an average of 20,000 feet)

CIRRUS: Thin, featherlike crystal clouds.

CIRROCUMULUS: Thin clouds that appear as small "cotton patches."

CIRROSTRATUS: Thin white clouds that resemble veils.

Middle Clouds
(bases starting at about 10,000 feet)

ALTOCUMULUS: Gray or white layer or patches of solid clouds with rounded shapes.

ALTOSTRATUS: Grayish or bluish layer of clouds that can obscure the Sun.

Low Clouds
(bases starting near Earth's surface to 6,500 feet)

STRATUS: Thin, gray, sheetlike clouds with low bases; may bring drizzle and snow.

STRATOCUMULUS: Rounded cloud masses that form on top of a layer.

NIMBOSTRATUS: Dark, gray, shapeless cloud layers containing rain, snow, and ice pellets.

Clouds With Vertical Development
(high clouds that form at almost any altitude and reach up to 14,000 feet)

CUMULUS: Fair-weather clouds with flat bases and dome-shape tops.

CUMULONIMBUS: Large, dark, vertical clouds with bulging tops that bring showers, thunder, and lightning.

R E F E R E N C E

PHASES OF THE MOON

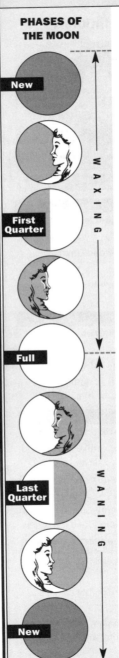

New

WAXING

First Quarter

Full

Last Quarter

WANING

New

Origin of Full-Moon Names

Historically, the Native Americans who lived in the area that is now the northern and eastern United States kept track of the seasons by giving a distinctive name to each recurring full Moon. This name was applied to the entire month in which it occurred. These names, and some variations, were used by the Algonquin tribes from New England to Lake Superior.

Name	Month	Variations
Full Wolf Moon	**January**	Full Old Moon
Full Snow Moon	**February**	Full Hunger Moon
Full Worm Moon	**March**	Full Crow Moon Full Crust Moon Full Sugar Moon Full Sap Moon
Full Pink Moon	**April**	Full Sprouting Grass Moon Full Egg Moon Full Fish Moon
Full Flower Moon	**May**	Full Corn Planting Moon Full Milk Moon
Full Strawberry Moon	**June**	Full Rose Moon Full Hot Moon
Full Buck Moon	**July**	Full Thunder Moon Full Hay Moon
Full Sturgeon Moon	**August**	Full Red Moon Full Green Corn Moon
Full Harvest Moon*	**September**	Full Corn Moon Full Barley Moon
Full Hunter's Moon	**October**	Full Travel Moon Full Dying Grass Moon
Full Beaver Moon	**November**	Full Frost Moon
Full Cold Moon	**December**	Full Long Nights Moon

The Harvest Moon is always the full Moon closest to the autumnal equinox. If the Harvest Moon occurs in October, the September full Moon is usually called the Corn Moon.

REFERENCE

When Will the Moon Rise Today?

A lunar puzzle involves the timing of moonrise. If you enjoy the out-of-doors and the wonders of nature, you may wish to commit to memory the following gem:

 The new Moon always rises at sunrise

 And the first quarter at noon.

 The full Moon always rises at sunset

 And the last quarter at midnight.

■ Moonrise occurs about 50 minutes later each day.

■ The new Moon is invisible because its illuminated side faces away from Earth, which occurs when the Moon lines up between Earth and the Sun.

■ One or two days after the date of the new Moon, you can see a thin crescent setting just after sunset in the western sky as the lunar cycle continues. (See pages 180–202 for exact moonrise times.)

Origin of Month Names

January Named for the Roman god Janus, protector of gates and doorways. Janus is depicted with two faces, one looking into the past, the other into the future.

February From the Latin word *februa,* "to cleanse." The Roman Februalia was a month of purification and atonement.

March Named for the Roman god of war, Mars. This was the time of year to resume military campaigns that had been interrupted by winter.

April From the Latin word *aperio,* "to open (bud)," because plants begin to grow in this month.

May Named for the Roman goddess Maia, who oversaw the growth of plants. Also from the Latin word *maiores,* "elders," who were celebrated during this month.

June Named for the Roman goddess Juno, patroness of marriage and the well-being of women. Also from the Latin word *juvenis,* "young people."

July Named to honor Roman dictator Julius Caesar (100 B.C.–44 B.C.). In 46 B.C., Julius Caesar made one of his greatest contributions to history: With the help of Sosigenes, he developed the Julian calendar, the precursor to the Gregorian calendar we use today.

August Named to honor the first Roman emperor (and grandnephew of Julius Caesar), Augustus Caesar (63 B.C.–A.D. 14).

September From the Latin word *septem,* "seven," because this had been the seventh month of the early Roman calendar.

October From the Latin word *octo,* "eight," because this had been the eighth month of the early Roman calendar.

November From the Latin word *novem,* "nine," because this had been the ninth month of the early Roman calendar.

December From the Latin word *decem,* "ten," because this had been the tenth month of the early Roman calendar.

R
E
F
E
R
E
N
C
E

Origin of Day Names

The days of the week were named by the Romans with the Latin words for the Sun, the Moon, and the five known planets. These names have survived in European languages, but English names also reflect an Anglo-Saxon influence.

English	Latin	French	Italian	Spanish	Saxon
SUNDAY	Solis (Sun)	dimanche	domenica	domingo	Sun
MONDAY	Lunae (Moon)	lundi	lunedì	lunes	Moon
TUESDAY	Martis (Mars)	mardi	martedì	martes	Tiw (the Anglo-Saxon god of war, the equivalent of the Norse Tyr or the Roman Mars)
WEDNESDAY	Mercurii (Mercury)	mercredi	mercoledì	miércoles	Woden (the Anglo-Saxon equivalent of the Norse Odin or the Roman Mercury)
THURSDAY	Jovis (Jupiter)	jeudi	giovedì	jueves	Thor (the Norse god of thunder, the equivalent of the Roman Jupiter)
FRIDAY	Veneris (Venus)	vendredi	venerdì	viernes	Frigg (the Norse god of love and fertility, the equivalent of the Roman Venus)
SATURDAY	Saturni (Saturn)	samedi	sabato	sábado	Saterne (Saturn, the Roman god of agriculture)

Best Planetary Encounters of the 21st Century

Me = Mercury   V = Venus   Mn = Moon   Ma = Mars   J = Jupiter   S = Saturn

In all these cases, face west between twilight and 10 P.M. to see the conjunction.

DATE	OBJECTS	DATE	OBJECTS	DATE	OBJECTS
June 30, 2007	V, S	March 7, 2047	V, J	November 15, 2080	Ma, J, S
December 1, 2008	V, Mn, J	May 13, 2066	V, Ma	November 17, 2080	Mn, Ma, J, S
February 20, 2015	V, Mn, Ma	July 1, 2066	V, S	December 24, 2080	V, J
June 30–July 1, 2015	V, J	March 14, 2071	V, J	March 6, 2082	V, J
July 18, 2015	V, Mn, J	June 21, 2074	V, J	April 28, 2085	Mn, Ma, J
December 20, 2020	J, S	June 27, 2074	V, Mn, J	June 13, 2085	Me, V, J
March 1, 2023	V, J	June 28, 2076	Ma, J	May 15, 2098	V, Ma
December 1–2, 2033	Ma, J	October 31, 2076	Mn, Ma, S	June 29, 2098	V, J
February 23, 2047	V, Ma	November 7, 2080	Ma, J, S		

R
E
F
E
R
E
N
C
E

How to Find the Day of the Week for Any Given Date

To compute the day of the week for any given date as far back as the mid-18th century, proceed as follows:

■ Add the last two digits of the year to one-quarter of the last two digits (discard any remainder), the day of the month, and the month key from the key box below. Divide the sum by 7; the remainder is the day of the week (1 is Sunday, 2 is Monday, and so on). If there is no remainder, the day is Saturday. If you're searching for a weekday prior to 1900, add 2 to the sum before dividing; prior to 1800, add 4. The formula doesn't work for days prior to 1753. From 2000 to 2099, subtract 1 from the sum before dividing.

Example:
The Dayton Flood was on March 25, 1913.

Last two digits of year:	13
One-quarter of these two digits:	3
Given day of month:	25
Key number for March:	4
Sum:	**45**

45 ÷ 7 = 6, with a remainder of 3. The flood took place on Tuesday, the third day of the week.

KEY	
January	1
leap year	0
February	4
leap year	3
March	4
April	0
May	2
June	5
July	0
August	3
September	6
October	1
November	4
December	6

Easter Dates (2005–2009)

■ Christian churches that follow the Gregorian calendar celebrate Easter on the first Sunday after the full Moon that occurs on or just after the vernal equinox.

YEAR	EASTER
2005	March 27
2006	April 16
2007	April 8
2008	March 23
2009	April 12

■ Eastern Orthodox churches follow the Julian calendar.

YEAR	EASTER
2005	May 1
2006	April 23
2007	April 8
2008	April 27
2009	April 19

Triskaidekaphobia Trivia

Here are a few facts about Friday the 13th:

■ Of the 14 possible configurations for the annual calendar (see any perpetual calendar), the occurrence of Friday the 13th is this:

6 of 14 years have one Friday the 13th.

6 of 14 years have two Fridays the 13th.

2 of 14 years have three Fridays the 13th.

■ There is no year without one Friday the 13th, and no year with more than three.

■ There is one Friday the 13th in 2005. The next year to have three Fridays the 13th is 2009.

■ The reason we say "Fridays the 13th" is that no one can pronounce "Friday the 13ths."

The Animal Signs of the Chinese Zodiac

The animal designations of the Chinese zodiac follow a 12-year cycle and are always used in the same sequence. The Chinese year of 354 days begins three to seven weeks into the western 365-day year, so the animal designation changes at that time, rather than on January 1. See page 179 for the exact date.

RAT
Ambitious and sincere, you can be generous with your money. Compatible with the dragon and the monkey. Your opposite is the horse.

1900	1936	1996
1912	1948	1984
1924	1960	2008
1972		

OX OR BUFFALO
A leader, you are bright, patient, and cheerful. Compatible with the snake and the rooster. Your opposite is the sheep.

1901	1937	1985
1913	1949	1997
1925	1961	2009
1973		

TIGER
Forthright and sensitive, you possess great courage. Compatible with the horse and the dog. Your opposite is the monkey.

1902	1938	1986
1914	1950	1998
1926	1962	2010
1974		

RABBIT OR HARE
Talented and affectionate, you are a seeker of tranquility. Compatible with the sheep and the pig. Your opposite is the rooster.

1903	1939	1987
1915	1951	1999
1927	1963	2011
1975		

DRAGON
Robust and passionate, your life is filled with complexity. Compatible with the monkey and the rat. Your opposite is the dog.

1904	1940	1988
1916	1952	2000
1928	1964	2012
1976		

SNAKE
Strong-willed and intense, you display great wisdom. Compatible with the rooster and the ox. Your opposite is the pig.

1905	1941	1989
1917	1953	2001
1929	1965	2013
1977		

HORSE
Physically attractive and popular, you like the company of others. Compatible with the tiger and the dog. Your opposite is the rat.

1906	1942	1990
1918	1954	2002
1930	1966	2014
1978		

SHEEP OR GOAT
Aesthetic and stylish, you enjoy being a private person. Compatible with the pig and the rabbit. Your opposite is the ox.

1907	1943	1991
1919	1955	2003
1931	1967	2015
1979		

MONKEY
Persuasive, skillful, and intelligent, you strive to excel. Compatible with the dragon and the rat. Your opposite is the tiger.

1908	1944	1992
1920	1956	2004
1932	1968	2016
1980		

ROOSTER OR COCK
Seeking wisdom and truth, you have a pioneering spirit. Compatible with the snake and the ox. Your opposite is the rabbit.

1909	1945	1993
1921	1957	2005
1933	1969	2017
1981		

DOG
Generous and loyal, you have the ability to work well with others. Compatible with the horse and the tiger. Your opposite is the dragon.

1910	1946	1994
1922	1958	2006
1934	1970	2018
1982		

PIG OR BOAR
Gallant and noble, your friends will remain at your side. Compatible with the rabbit and the sheep. Your opposite is the snake.

1911	1947	1995
1923	1959	2007
1935	1971	2019
1983		

Sowing Vegetable Seeds

Sow or plant in cool weather	Beets, broccoli, Brussels sprouts, cabbage, lettuce, onions, parsley, peas, radishes, spinach, Swiss chard, turnips
Sow or plant in warm weather	Beans, carrots, corn, cucumbers, eggplant, melons, okra, peppers, squash, tomatoes
Sow or plant for one crop per season	Corn, eggplant, leeks, melons, peppers, potatoes, spinach (New Zealand), squash, tomatoes
Resow for additional crops	Beans, beets, cabbage, carrots, kohlrabi, lettuce, radishes, rutabagas, spinach, turnips

A Beginner's Vegetable Garden

A good size for a beginner's vegetable garden is 10x16 feet. It should have crops that are easy to grow. A plot this size, planted as suggested below, can feed a family of four for one summer, with a little extra for canning and freezing (or giving away).

Make 11 rows, 10 feet long, with 6 inches between them. Ideally, the rows should run north and south to take full advantage of the Sun. Plant the following:

ROW
1 Zucchini (4 plants)
2 Tomatoes (5 plants, staked)
3 Peppers (6 plants)
4 Cabbage

ROW
5 Bush beans
6 Lettuce
7 Beets
8 Carrots
9 Chard
10 Radishes
11 Marigolds (to discourage rabbits!)

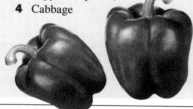

Traditional Planting Times

■ Plant **corn** when elm leaves are the size of a squirrel's ear, when oak leaves are the size of a mouse's ear, when apple blossoms begin to fall, or when the dogwoods are in full bloom.

■ Plant **lettuce, spinach, peas,** and other cool-weather vegetables when the lilacs show their first leaves or when daffodils begin to bloom.

■ Plant **tomatoes, early corn,** and **peppers** when dogwoods are in peak bloom or when daylilies start to bloom.

■ Plant **cucumbers** and **squashes** when lilac flowers fade.

■ Plant **perennials** when maple leaves begin to unfurl.

■ Plant **morning glories** when maple trees have full-size leaves.

■ Plant **pansies, snapdragons,** and other hardy annuals after the aspen and chokecherry trees leaf out.

■ Plant **beets** and **carrots** when dandelions are blooming.

Growing Vegetables

Vegetable	Start Seeds Indoors (weeks before last spring frost)	Start Seeds Outdoors (weeks before or after last spring frost)	Minimum Soil Temperature to Germinate (°F)	Cold Hardiness
Beans		Anytime after	48–50	Tender
Beets		4 before to 4 after	39–41	Half-hardy
Broccoli	6–8	4 before	55–75	Hardy
Brussels sprouts	6–8		55–75	Hardy
Cabbage	6–8	Anytime after	38–40	Hardy
Carrots		4–6 before	39–41	Half-hardy
Cauliflower	6–8	4 before	65–75	Half-hardy
Celery	6–8		60–70	Tender
Corn		2 after	46–50	Tender
Cucumbers	3–4	1–2 after	65–70	Very tender
Lettuce	4–6	2–3 after	40–75	Half-hardy
Melons	3–4	2 after	55–60	Very tender
Onion sets		4 before	34–36	Hardy
Parsnips		2–4 before	55–70	Hardy
Peas		4–6 before	34–36	Hardy
Peppers	8–10		70–80	Very tender
Potato tubers		2–4 before	55–70	Half-hardy
Pumpkins	3–4	1 after	55–60	Tender
Radishes		4–6 before	39–41	Hardy
Spinach		4–6 before	55–65	Hardy
Squash, summer	3–4	1 after	55–60	Very tender
Squash, winter	3–4	1 after	55–60	Tender
Tomatoes	6–8		50–55	Tender

When to Fertilize	When to Water
After heavy bloom and set of pods	Regularly, from start of pod to set
At time of planting	Only during drought conditions
Three weeks after transplanting	Only during drought conditions
Three weeks after transplanting	At transplanting
Three weeks after transplanting	Two to three weeks before harvest
Preferably in the fall for the following spring	Only during drought conditions
Three weeks after transplanting	Once, three weeks before harvest
At time of transplanting	Once a week
When eight to ten inches tall, and again when first silk appears	When tassels appear and cobs start to swell
One week after bloom, and again three weeks later	Frequently, especially when fruits form
Two to three weeks after transplanting	Once a week
One week after bloom, and again three weeks later	Once a week
When bulbs begin to swell, and again when plants are one foot tall	Only during drought conditions
One year before planting	Only during drought conditions
After heavy bloom and set of pods	Regularly, from start of pod to set
After first fruit-set	Once a week
At bloom time or time of second hilling	Regularly, when tubers start to form
Just before vines start to run, when plants are about one foot tall	Only during drought conditions
Before spring planting	Once a week
When plants are one-third grown	Once a week
Just before vines start to run, when plants are about one foot tall	Only during drought conditions
Just before vines start to run, when plants are about one foot tall	Only during drought conditions
Two weeks before, and after first picking	Twice a week

R
E
F
E
R
E
N
C
E

Vegetable Gardening in Containers

Lack of yard space is no excuse for not gardening, because many vegetables can be readily grown in containers. In addition to providing five hours or more of full sun, you must give attention to choosing the proper container, using a good soil mix, observing planting and spacing requirements, fertilizing, watering, and selecting appropriate varieties. Here are some suggestions:

Vegetable	Type of Container	Recommended Varieties
Beans, snap	5-gallon window box	Bush 'Blue Lake', Bush 'Romano', 'Tender Crop'
Broccoli	1 plant/5-gallon pot 3 plants/15-gallon tub	'DeCicco', 'Green Comet'
Carrots	5-gallon window box at least 12 inches deep	'Danvers Half Long', 'Short 'n Sweet', 'Tiny Sweet'
Cucumbers	1 plant/1-gallon pot	'Patio Pik', 'Pot Luck', 'Spacemaster'
Eggplant	5-gallon pot	'Black Beauty', 'Ichiban', 'Slim Jim'
Lettuce	5-gallon window box	'Ruby', 'Salad Bowl'
Onions	5-gallon window box	'White Sweet Spanish', 'Yellow Sweet Spanish'
Peppers	1 plant/2-gallon pot 5 plants/15-gallon tub	'Cayenne', 'Long Red', 'Sweet Banana', 'Wonder', 'Yolo'
Radishes	5-gallon window box	'Cherry Belle', 'Icicle'
Tomatoes	Bushel basket	'Early Girl', 'Patio', 'Small Fry', 'Sweet 100', 'Tiny Tim'

TIPS

■ Clay pots are usually more attractive than plastic ones, but plastic pots retain moisture better. To get the best of both, slip a plastic pot into a slightly larger clay pot.

■ Avoid small containers. They often can't store enough water to get through hot days.

■ Add about one inch of coarse gravel in the bottom of the container to improve drainage.

■ Vegetables that can be easily transplanted are best suited for containers. Transplants can be purchased from local nurseries or started at home.

■ Feed container plants at least twice a month with liquid fertilizer, following the instructions on the label.

■ An occasional application of fish emulsion or compost will add trace elements to container soil.

■ Place containers where they will receive maximum sunlight and good ventilation. Watch for and control insect pests.

Fertilizer Formulas

Fertilizers are labeled to show the percentages by weight of nitrogen (N), phosphorus (P), and potassium (K). Nitrogen is needed for leaf growth. Phosphorus is associated with root growth and fruit production. Potassium helps the plant fight off diseases. A 100-pound bag of 10-5-10 contains 10 pounds of nitrogen, 5 pounds of phosphorus, and 10 pounds of potassium. The rest is filler.

Manure Guide

PRIMARY NUTRIENTS (pounds per ton)

Type of Manure	Water Content	Nitrogen	Phosphorus	Potassium
Cow, horse	60%–80%	12–14	5–9	9–12
Sheep, pig, goat	65%–75%	10–21	7	13–19
Chicken:				
Wet, sticky, and caked	75%	30	20	10
Moist, crumbly to sticky	50%	40	40	20
Crumbly	30%	60	55	30
Dry	15%	90	70	40
Ashed	None	None	135	100

TYPE OF GARDEN	BEST TYPE OF MANURE	BEST TIME TO APPLY
Flowers	Cow, horse	Early spring
Vegetables	Chicken, cow, horse	Fall, spring
Potatoes or root crops	Cow, horse	Fall
Acid-loving plants (blueberries, azaleas, mountain laurels, rhododendrons)	Cow, horse	Early fall or not at all

Soil Fixes

If you have . . .

CLAY SOIL: Add coarse sand (not beach sand) and compost.

SILT SOIL: Add coarse sand (not beach sand) or gravel and compost, or well-rotted horse manure mixed with fresh straw.

SANDY SOIL: Add humus or aged manure, or sawdust with some extra nitrogen. Heavy, clay-rich soil can also be added.

Soil Amendments

To improve soil, add . . .

BARK, GROUND: Made from various tree barks; improves soil structure.

COMPOST: Excellent conditioner.

LEAF MOLD: Decomposed leaves; adds nutrients and structure to soil.

LIME: Raises the pH of acidic soil; helps loosen clay soil.

MANURE: Best if composted; a good conditioner.

SAND: Improves drainage in clay soil.

TOPSOIL: Usually used with another amendment; replaces existing soil.

pH Preferences of Trees, Shrubs, Vegetables, and Flowers

An accurate soil test will tell you where your pH currently stands and will specify the amount of lime or sulfur that is needed to bring it up or down to the appropriate level. A pH of 6.5 is just about right for most home gardens, since most plants thrive in the 6.0 to 7.0 (slightly acidic to neutral) range. Some plants (blueberries, azaleas) prefer more strongly acidic soil, while a few (ferns, asparagus) do best in soil that is neutral to slightly alkaline. Acidic (sour) soil is counteracted by applying finely ground limestone, and alkaline (sweet) soil is treated with gypsum (calcium sulfate) or ground sulfur.

Common Name	Optimum pH Range	Common Name	Optimum pH Range	Common Name	Optimum pH Range
TREES AND SHRUBS		Spruce	5.0–6.0	Canna	6.0–8.0
Apple	5.0–6.5	Walnut, black	6.0–8.0	Carnation	6.0–7.0
Ash	6.0–7.5	Willow	6.0–8.0	Chrysanthemum	6.0–7.5
Azalea	4.5–6.0			Clematis	5.5–7.0
Basswood	6.0–7.5	**VEGETABLES**		Coleus	6.0–7.0
Beautybush	6.0–7.5	Asparagus	6.0–8.0	Coneflower, purple	5.0–7.5
Birch	5.0–6.5	Bean, pole	6.0–7.5	Cosmos	5.0–8.0
Blackberry	5.0–6.0	Beet	6.0–7.5	Crocus	6.0–8.0
Blueberry	4.0–6.0	Broccoli	6.0–7.0	Daffodil	6.0–6.5
Boxwood	6.0–7.5	Brussels sprout	6.0–7.5	Dahlia	6.0–7.5
Cherry, sour	6.0–7.0	Carrot	5.5–7.0	Daisy, Shasta	6.0–8.0
Chestnut	5.0–6.5	Cauliflower	5.5–7.5	Daylily	6.0–8.0
Crab apple	6.0–7.5	Celery	5.8–7.0	Delphinium	6.0–7.5
Dogwood	5.0–7.0	Chive	6.0–7.0	Foxglove	6.0–7.5
Elder, box	6.0–8.0	Cucumber	5.5–7.0	Geranium	6.0–8.0
Fir, balsam	5.0–6.0	Garlic	5.5–8.0	Gladiolus	5.0–7.0
Fir, Douglas	6.0–7.0	Kale	6.0–7.5	Hibiscus	6.0–8.0
Hemlock	5.0–6.0	Lettuce	6.0–7.0	Hollyhock	6.0–8.0
Hydrangea, blue-flowered	4.0–5.0	Pea, sweet	6.0–7.5	Hyacinth	6.5–7.5
Hydrangea, pink-flowered	6.0–7.0	Pepper, sweet	5.5–7.0	Iris, blue flag	5.0–7.5
Juniper	5.0–6.0	Potato	4.8–6.5	Lily-of-the-valley	4.5–6.0
Laurel, mountain	4.5–6.0	Pumpkin	5.5–7.5	Lupine	5.0–6.5
Lemon	6.0–7.5	Radish	6.0–7.0	Marigold	5.5–7.5
Lilac	6.0–7.5	Spinach	6.0–7.5	Morning glory	6.0–7.5
Maple, sugar	6.0–7.5	Squash, crookneck	6.0–7.5	Narcissus, trumpet	5.5–6.5
Oak, white	5.0–6.5	Squash, Hubbard	5.5–7.0	Nasturtium	5.5–7.5
Orange	6.0–7.5	Tomato	5.5–7.5	Pansy	5.5–6.5
Peach	6.0–7.0			Peony	6.0–7.5
Pear	6.0–7.5	**FLOWERS**		Petunia	6.0–7.5
Pecan	6.4–8.0	Alyssum	6.0–7.5	Phlox, summer	6.0–8.0
Pine, red	5.0–6.0	Aster, New England	6.0–8.0	Poppy, oriental	6.0–7.5
Pine, white	4.5–6.0	Baby's breath	6.0–7.0	Rose, hybrid tea	5.5–7.0
Plum	6.0–8.0	Bachelor's button	6.0–7.5	Rose, rugosa	6.0–7.0
Raspberry, red	5.5–7.0	Bee balm	6.0–7.5	Snapdragon	5.5–7.0
Rhododendron	4.5–6.0	Begonia	5.5–7.0	Sunflower	6.0–7.5
		Black-eyed Susan	5.5–7.0	Tulip	6.0–7.0
		Bleeding heart	6.0–7.5	Zinnia	5.5–7.0

Get more gardening advice at www.almanac.com.

Lawn-Growing Tips

■ Test your soil: The pH balance should be 7.0 or more; 6.2 to 6.7 puts your lawn at risk for fungal diseases. If the pH is too low, correct it with liming, best done in the fall.

■ The best time to apply fertilizer is just before it rains.

■ If you put lime and fertilizer on your lawn, spread half of it as you walk north to south, the other half as you walk east to west to cut down on missed areas.

■ Any feeding of lawns in the fall should be done with a low-nitrogen, slow-acting fertilizer.

■ In areas of your lawn where tree roots compete with the grass, apply some extra fertilizer to benefit both.

■ Moss and sorrel in lawns usually means poor soil, poor aeration or drainage, or excessive acidity.

■ Control weeds by promoting healthy lawn growth with natural fertilizers in spring and early fall.

■ Raise the level of your lawn-mower blades during the hot summer days. Taller grass resists drought better than short.

■ You can reduce mowing time by redesigning your lawn, reducing sharp corners and adding sweeping curves.

■ During a drought, let the grass grow longer between mowings, and reduce fertilizer.

■ Water your lawn early in the morning or in the evening.

Herbs to Plant in Lawns

Choose plants that suit your soil and your climate. All these can withstand mowing and considerable foot traffic.

Ajuga or bugleweed *(Ajuga reptans)*

Corsican mint *(Mentha requienii)*

Dwarf cinquefoil *(Potentilla tabernaemontani)*

English pennyroyal *(Mentha pulegium)*

Green Irish moss *(Sagina subulata)*

Pearly everlasting *(Anaphalis margaritacea)*

Roman chamomile *(Chamaemelum nobile)*

Rupturewort *(Herniaria glabra)*

Speedwell *(Veronica officinalis)*

Stonecrop *(Sedum ternatum)*

Sweet violets *(Viola odorata* or *V. tricolor)*

Thyme *(Thymus serpyllum)*

White clover *(Trifolium repens)*

Wild strawberries *(Fragaria virginiana)*

Wintergreen or partridgeberry *(Mitchella repens)*

A Gardener's Worst Phobias

Name of Fear	Object Feared
Alliumphobia	Garlic
Anthophobia	Flowers
Apiphobia	Bees
Arachnophobia	Spiders
Batonophobia	Plants
Bufonophobia	Toads
Dendrophobia	Trees
Entomophobia	Insects
Lachanophobia	Vegetables
Melissophobia	Bees
Mottephobia	Moths
Myrmecophobia	Ants
Ornithophobia	Birds
Ranidaphobia	Frogs
Rupophobia	Dirt
Scoleciphobia	Worms
Spheksophobia	Wasps

REFERENCE

Growing Herbs

Herb	Propagation Method	Start Seeds Indoors (weeks before last spring frost)	Start Seeds Outdoors (weeks before or after last spring frost)	Minimum Soil Temperature to Germinate (°F)	Height (inches)
Basil	Seeds, transplants	6–8	Anytime after	70	12–24
Borage	Seeds, division, cuttings	Not recommended	Anytime after	70	12–36
Chervil	Seeds	Not recommended	3–4 before	55	12–24
Chives	Seeds, division	8–10	3–4 before	60–70	12–18
Cilantro/ coriander	Seeds	Not recommended	Anytime after	60	12–36
Dill	Seeds	Not recommended	4–5 before	60–70	36–48
Fennel	Seeds	4–6	Anytime after	60–70	48–80
Lavender, English	Seeds, cuttings	8–12	1–2 before	70–75	18–36
Lavender, French	Transplants	Not recommended	Not recommended	—	18–36
Lemon balm	Seeds, division, cuttings	6–10	2–3 before	70	12–24
Lovage	Seeds, division	6–8	2–3 before	70	36–72
Oregano	Seeds, division, cuttings	6–10	Anytime after	70	12–24
Parsley	Seeds	10–12	3–4 before	70	18–24
Rosemary	Seeds, division, cuttings	8–10	Anytime after	70	48–72
Sage	Seeds, division, cuttings	6–10	1–2 before	60–70	12–48
Sorrel	Seeds, division	6–10	2–3 after	60–70	20–48
Spearmint	Division, cuttings	Not recommended	Not recommended	—	12–24
Summer savory	Seeds	4–6	Anytime after	60–70	4–15
Sweet cicely	Seeds, division	6–8	2–3 after	60–70	36–72
Tarragon, French	Cuttings, transplants	Not recommended	Not recommended	—	24–36
Thyme, common	Seeds, division, cuttings	6–10	2–3 before	70	2–12

R
E
F
E
R
E
N
C
E

Spread (inches)	Blooming Season	Uses	Soil	Light*	Growth Type
12	Midsummer	Culinary	Rich, moist	○	Annual
12	Early to midsummer	Culinary	Rich, well-drained, dry	○	Annual, biennial
8	Early to midsummer	Culinary	Rich, moist	◑	Annual, biennial
18	Early summer	Culinary	Rich, moist	○	Perennial
4	Midsummer	Culinary	Light	○◑	Annual
12	Early summer	Culinary	Rich	○	Annual
18	Mid- to late summer	Culinary	Rich	○	Annual
24	Early to late summer	Ornamental, medicinal	Moderately fertile, well-drained	○	Perennial
24	Early to late summer	Ornamental, medicinal	Moderately fertile, well-drained	○	Tender perennial
18	Midsummer to early fall	Culinary, ornamental	Rich, well-drained	○◑	Perennial
36	Early to late summer	Culinary	Fertile, sandy	○◑	Perennial
18	Mid- to late summer	Culinary	Poor	○	Tender perennial
6–8	Mid- to late summer	Culinary	Medium-rich	◑	Biennial
48	Early summer	Culinary	Not too acid	○	Tender perennial
30	Early to late summer	Culinary, ornamental	Well-drained	○	Perennial
12–14	Late spring to early summer	Culinary, medicinal	Rich, organic	○	Perennial
18	Early to midsummer	Culinary, medicinal, ornamental	Rich, moist	◑	Perennial
6	Early summer	Culinary	Medium rich	○	Annual
36	Late spring	Culinary	Moderately fertile, well-drained	○◑	Perennial
12	Late summer	Culinary, medicinal	Well-drained	○◑	Perennial
7–12	Early to midsummer	Culinary	Fertile, well-drained	○◑	Perennial

*○ = full sun   ◑ = partial shade

R
E
F
E
R
E
N
C
E

Flowers and Herbs That Attract Butterflies

Allium............................ *Allium*
Aster .... *Aster*
Bee balm.................... *Monarda*
Butterfly bush............. *Buddleia*
Catmint....................... *Nepeta*
Clove pink .... *Dianthus*
Cornflower.............. *Centaurea*
Creeping thyme ..... *Thymus serpyllum*
Daylily................ *Hemerocallis*
Dill .... *Anethum graveolens*
False indigo .... *Baptisia*
Fleabane .... *Erigeron*
Floss flower.............. *Ageratum*
Globe thistle.............. *Echinops*
Goldenrod .... *Solidago*
Helen's flower .... *Helenium*
Hollyhock..................... *Alcea*
Honeysuckle................ *Lonicera*
Lavender.................. *Lavendula*
Lilac .... *Syringa*
Lupine............................ *Lupinus*
Lychnis .... *Lychnis*

Mallow .... *Malva*
Mealycup sage........ *Salvia farinacea*
Milkweed.................. *Asclepias*
Mint .... *Mentha*
Oregano .... *Origanum vulgare*
Pansy........................... *Viola*
Parsley .... *Petroselinum crispum*
Phlox .... *Phlox*
Privet...................... *Ligustrum*
Purple coneflower.. *Echinacea purpurea*
Purple loosestrife .... *Lythrum*
Rock cress................... *Arabis*
Sea holly .... *Eryngium*
Shasta daisy .... *Chrysanthemum*
Snapdragon .... *Antirrhinum*
Stonecrop .... *Sedum*
Sweet alyssum .... *Lobularia*
Sweet marjoram ... *Origanum majorana*
Sweet rocket .... *Hesperis*
Tickseed .... *Coreopsis*
Zinnia .... *Zinnia*

Flowers* That Attract Hummingbirds

Beard tongue .... *Penstemon*
Bee balm................... *Monarda*
Butterfly bush .... *Buddleia*
Catmint....................... *Nepeta*
Clove pink................. *Dianthus*
Columbine .... *Aquilegia*
Coral bells .... *Heuchera*
Daylily .... *Hemerocallis*
Desert candle .... *Yucca*
Flag iris....................... *Iris*
Flowering tobacco ..... *Nicotiana alata*
Foxglove .... *Digitalis*
Larkspur .... *Delphinium*
Lily .... *Lilium*
Lupine...................... *Lupinus*
Petunia...................... *Petunia*
Pincushion flower.......... *Scabiosa*
Red-hot poker .... *Kniphofia*
Scarlet sage.......... *Salvia splendens*
Soapwort.................. *Saponaria*
Summer phlox .... *Phlox paniculata*

Trumpet honeysuckle........ *Lonicera sempervirens*
Verbena .... *Verbena*
Weigela.................... *Weigela*

* Note: Choose varieties in red and orange shades.

Plant Resources

Bulbs

American Daffodil Society
4126 Winfield Rd., Columbus, OH 43220
www.daffodilusa.org

American Dahlia Society
1 Rock Falls Ct., Rockville, MD 20854
www.dahlia.org

American Iris Society
www.irises.org

International Bulb Society (IBS)
www.bulbsociety.org

Netherlands Flower Bulb Information Center
30 Midwood St., Brooklyn, NY 11225
718-693-5400 • www.bulb.com

Ferns

American Fern Society
326 West St. NW, Vienna, VA 22180
http://amerfernsoc.org

The Hardy Fern Foundation
P.O. Box 166, Medina, WA 98039
www.hardyferns.org

Flowers

American Peony Society
www.americanpeonysociety.org

American Rhododendron Society
11 Pinecrest Dr., Fortuna, CA 95540
707-725-3043 • www.rhododendron.org

American Rose Society
P.O. Box 30,000, Shreveport, LA 71130
318-938-5402 • www.ars.org

Hardy Plant Society
Mid-Atlantic Group
1380 Warner Rd., Meadowbrook, PA 19046

International Waterlily and Water Gardening Society
6828 26th St. W., Bradenton, FL 34207
941-756-0880 • www.iwgs.org

Lady Bird Johnson Wildflower Center
4801 La Crosse Ave., Austin, TX 78739
512-292-4200 • www.wildflower.org

Perennial Plant Association
3383 Schirtzinger Rd., Hilliard, OH 43026
614-771-8431 • www.perennialplant.org

Fruits

California Rare Fruit Growers
The Fullerton Arboretum-CSUF
P.O. Box 6850, Fullerton, CA 92834
www.crfg.org

Home Orchard Society
P.O. Box 230192, Tigard, OR 97281
www.wvi.com/~dough/hos/hos1.html

North American Fruit Explorers
1716 Apples Rd., Chapin, IL 62628
www.nafex.org

Herbs

American Herb Association
P.O. Box 1673, Nevada City, CA 95959
530-265-9552 • www.ahaherb.com

The Flower and Herb Exchange
3076 North Winn Rd., Decorah, IA 52101
319-382-5990 • www.seedsavers.org

Herb Research Foundation
1007 Pearl St., Ste. 200, Boulder, CO 80302
800-748-2617 • www.herbs.org

Herb Society of America
9019 Kirtland Chardon Rd., Kirtland, OH 44094
440-256-0514 • www.herbsociety.org

REFERENCE

Cooperative Extension Services

Contact your local state cooperative extension Web site to get help with tricky insect problems, best varieties to plant in your area, or general maintenance of your garden.

Alabama
www.aces.edu

Alaska
www.uaf.edu/coop-ext

Arizona
www.ag.arizona.edu/
extension

Arkansas
www.uaex.edu

California
www.ucanr.org

Colorado
www.ext.colostate.edu

Connecticut
www.canr.uconn.edu/ces/
index.html

Delaware
http://ag.udel.edu/
extension

Florida
www.ifas.ufl.edu/
extension/ces.htm

Georgia
http://extension.caes.uga.edu

Hawaii
www2.ctahr.hawaii.edu/
extout/extout.asp

Idaho
www.uidaho.edu/ag/
extension

Illinois
www.extension.uiuc.edu/
welcome.html

Indiana
www.ces.purdue.edu

Iowa
www.exnet.iastate.edu

Kansas
www.oznet.ksu.edu

Kentucky
www.ca.uky.edu

Louisiana
www.lsuagcenter.com/nav/
extension/extension.asp

Maine
www.umext.maine.edu

Maryland
www.agnr.umd.edu/MCE/
index.cfm

Massachusetts
www.umassextension.org

Michigan
www.msue.msu.edu/msue

Minnesota
www.extension.umn.edu

Mississippi
www.msucares.com

Missouri
www.extension.missouri
.edu

Montana
http://extn.msu.montana.edu

Nebraska
www.extension.unl.edu

Nevada
www.unce.unr.edu

New Hampshire
www.ceinfo.unh.edu

New Jersey
www.rce.rutgers.edu

New Mexico
www.cahe.nmsu.edu/ces

New York
www.cce.cornell.edu

North Carolina
www.ces.ncsu.edu

North Dakota
www.ext.nodak.edu

Ohio
www.ag.ohio-state.edu

Oklahoma
www.dasnr.okstate.edu/oces

Oregon
http://osu.orst.edu/extension

Pennsylvania
www.extension.psu.edu

Rhode Island
www.edc.uri.edu

South Carolina
www.clemson.edu/
extension

South Dakota
http://sdces.sdstate.edu

Tennessee
www.utextension.utk.edu

Texas
http://agextension.tamu.edu

Utah
www.extension.usu.edu

Vermont
www.uvm.edu/~uvmext

Virginia
www.ext.vt.edu

Washington
http://ext.wsu.edu

West Virginia
www.wvu.edu/~exten

Wisconsin
www.uwex.edu/ces

Wyoming
www.uwyo.edu/ces/
ceshome.htm

Makeshift Measurers

When you don't have a measuring stick or tape, use what is at hand. To this list, add other items that you always (or nearly always) have handy.

Credit card. . . . . 3⅜" x 2⅛"
Business card (standard) . . . . . . 3½" x 2"
Floor tile . . . . 12" square
Dollar bill . . . . 6⅛" x 2⅝"
Quarter (diameter) . . . . 1"
Penny (diameter) . . . . ¾"
Sheet of paper . . . . 8½" x 11"
    (legal size: 8½" x 14")

Your foot/shoe: _____
Your outstretched arms, fingertip
    to fingertip: _____
Your shoelace: _____
Your necktie: _____
Your belt: _____

If you don't have a scale or a measuring spoon handy, try these for size:
A piece of meat the size of your hand or a deck of cards = 3 to 4 ounces.
A piece of meat or cheese the size of a golf ball = about 1 ounce.
From the tip of your smallest finger to the first joint = about 1 teaspoon.
The tip of your thumb = about 1 tablespoon.

The idea of using available materials to measure is not new.
1 foot = the length of a person's foot.
1 yard = the distance from a person's nose to the fingertip of an outstretched arm.
1 acre = the amount of land an ox can plow in a day.

Hand Thermometer for Outdoor Cooking

■ Hold your palm close to where the food will be cooking: over the coals or in front of a reflector oven. Count "one-and-one, two-and-two," and so on (each pair is roughly equivalent to one second), for as many seconds as you can hold your hand still.

Seconds Counted	Heat	Temperature
6–8	Slow	250°–350°F
4–5	Moderate	350°–400°F
2–3	Hot	400°–450°F
1 or less	Very hot	450°–500°F

Miscellaneous Length Measures

ASTRONOMICAL UNIT (A.U.): 93,000,000 miles; the average distance from Earth to the Sun

BOLT: 40 yards; used for measuring cloth

CHAIN: 66 feet; one mile is equal to 80 chains; used in surveying

CUBIT: 18 inches; derived from distance between elbow and tip of middle finger

HAND: 4 inches; derived from the width of the hand

LEAGUE: usually estimated at 3 miles

LIGHT-YEAR: 5,880,000,000,000 miles; the distance light travels in a vacuum in a year at the rate of 186,281.7 miles per second

PICA: about ⅙ inch; used in printing for measuring column width, etc.

SPAN: 9 inches; derived from the distance between the end of the thumb and the end of the little finger when both are outstretched

R E F E R E N C E

Body Mass Index (BMI) Formula

Here's an easy formula to figure your Body Mass Index (BMI), thought to be a fairly accurate indicator of relative body size. **W** is your weight in pounds and **H** is your height in inches.

$$\text{BMI} = \left(\frac{W}{H^2}\right) \times 703$$

■ If the result is 18.5 to 24.9, you are within a healthy weight range.

■ If it's below 18.5, you are too thin.

■ From 25 to 29.9, you are overweight and at increased risk for health problems.

■ At 30 and above, you are considered obese and at a dramatically increased risk for serious health problems.

There are exceptions to the above, including children, expectant mothers, and the elderly. Very muscular people with a high BMI generally have nothing to worry about, and extreme skinniness is generally a symptom of some other health problem, not the cause.

Tape-Measure Method

■ Here's another way to see if you are dangerously overweight. Measure your waistline. A waist measurement of more than 35 inches in women and more than 40 inches in men, regardless of height, suggests a serious risk of weight-related health problems.

Calorie-Burning Comparisons

If you hustle through your chores to get to the fitness center, relax. You're getting a great workout already. The left-hand column lists "chore" exercises, the middle column shows the number of calories burned per minute per pound of body weight, and the right-hand column lists comparable "recreational" exercises. For example, a 150-pound person forking straw bales burns 9.45 calories per minute, the same workout he or she would get playing basketball.

Chore	Calories	Recreational
Chopping with an ax, fast	**0.135**	Skiing, cross country, uphill
Climbing hills, with 44-pound load	**0.066**	Swimming, crawl, fast
Digging trenches	**0.065**	Skiing, cross country, steady walk
Forking straw bales	**0.063**	Basketball
Chopping down trees	**0.060**	Football
Climbing hills, with 9-pound load	**0.058**	Swimming, crawl, slow
Sawing by hand	**0.055**	Skiing, cross country, moderate
Mowing lawns	**0.051**	Horseback riding, trotting
Scrubbing floors	**0.049**	Tennis
Shoveling coal	**0.049**	Aerobic dance, medium
Hoeing	**0.041**	Weight training, circuit training
Stacking firewood	**0.040**	Weight lifting, free weights
Shoveling grain	**0.038**	Golf
Painting houses	**0.035**	Walking, normal pace, asphalt road
Weeding	**0.033**	Table tennis
Shopping for food	**0.028**	Cycling, 5.5 mph
Mopping floors	**0.028**	Fishing
Washing windows	**0.026**	Croquet
Raking	**0.025**	Dancing, ballroom
Driving a tractor	**0.016**	Drawing, standing position

HOW MUCH DO YOU NEED?
Tile and Vinyl Flooring

Make a scale drawing of your room with all measurements clearly marked, and take it with you when you shop for tile flooring. Ask the salespeople to help you calculate your needs if you have rooms that feature bay windows, unusual jogs, or turns, or if you plan to use special floor patterns or tiles with designs.

Ceramic Tile

■ Ceramic tiles for floors and walls come in a range of sizes, from 1x1-inch mosaics up to 12x12-inch (or larger) squares. The most popular size is the 4¼-inch-square tile, but there is a trend toward larger tiles (8x8s, 10x10s, 12x12s). Installing these larger tiles can be a challenge because the underlayment must be absolutely even and level.

■ Small, one-inch mosaic tiles are usually joined together in 12x12-inch or 12x24-inch sheets to make them easier to install. You can have a custom pattern made, or you can mix different-color tiles to create your own mosaic borders, patterns, and pictures.

Sheet Vinyl

■ Sheet vinyl typically comes in 6- and 12-foot widths. If your floor requires two or more pieces, your estimate must include enough overlap to allow you to match the pattern.

Vinyl Tile

■ Vinyl tiles generally come in 9- and 12-inch squares. To find the number of 12-inch tiles you need, just multiply the length of the room (in feet) by the width (rounding fractions up to the next foot) to get the number of tiles you need. Add 5 percent extra for cutting and waste. Measure any obstructions on the floor that you will be tiling around (such as appliances and cabinets), and subtract that square-footage from the total. To calculate the number of 9-inch tiles, divide the room's length (in inches) by 9, then divide the room's width by 9. Multiply those two numbers together to get the number of tiles you need, and then add 5 percent extra for cutting and waste.

HOW MUCH DO YOU NEED?
Wallpaper

Before choosing your wallpaper, keep in mind that wallpaper with little or no pattern to match at the seams and the ceiling will be the easiest to apply, thus resulting in the least amount of wasted wallpaper. If you choose a patterned wallpaper, a small repeating pattern will result in less waste than a large repeating pattern. And a pattern that is aligned horizontally (matching on each column of paper) will waste less than one that drops or alternates its pattern (matching on every other column).

To determine the amount of wall space you're covering:

■ Measure the length of each wall, add these figures together, and multiply by the height of the walls to get the area (square footage) of the room's walls.

■ Calculate the square footage of each door, window, and other opening in the room. Add these figures together and subtract the total from the area of the room's walls.

■ Take that figure and multiply by 1.15, to account for a waste rate of about 15 percent in your wallpaper project. You'll end up with a target amount to purchase when you shop.

■ Wallpaper is sold in single, double, and triple rolls. Coverage can vary, so be sure to refer to the roll's label for the proper square footage. (The average coverage for a double roll, for example, is 56 square feet.) After choosing a paper, divide the coverage figure (from the label) into the total square footage of the walls of the room you're papering. Round the answer up to the nearest whole number. This is the number of rolls you need to buy.

■ Save leftover wallpaper rolls, carefully wrapped to keep clean.

HOW MUCH DO YOU NEED?
Interior Paint

Estimate your room size and paint needs before you go to the store. Running out of a custom color halfway through the job could mean disaster. For the sake of the following exercise, assume that you have a 10x15-foot room with an 8-foot ceiling. The room has two doors and two windows.

For Walls
■ Measure the total distance (perimeter) around the room:
(10 ft. + 15 ft.) x 2 = 50 ft.

■ Multiply the perimeter by the ceiling height to get the total wall area:
50 ft. x 8 ft. = 400 sq. ft.

■ Doors are usually 21 square feet (there are two in this exercise):
21 sq. ft. x 2 = 42 sq. ft.

■ Windows average 15 square feet (there are two in this exercise):
15 sq. ft. x 2 = 30 sq. ft.

■ Take the total wall area and subtract the area for the doors and windows to get the wall surface to be painted:

```
 400 sq. ft.  (wall area)
– 42 sq. ft.  (doors)
– 30 sq. ft.  (windows)
 328 sq. ft.
```

■ As a rule of thumb, one gallon of quality paint will usually cover 400 square feet. One quart will cover 100 square feet. Because you need to cover 328 square feet in this example, one gallon will be adequate to give one coat of paint to the walls. (Coverage will be affected by the porosity and texture of the surface. In addition, bright colors may require a minimum of two coats.)

For Ceilings
■ Using the rule of thumb for coverage above, you can calculate the quantity of paint needed for the ceiling by multiplying the width by the length:
10 ft. x 15 ft. = 150 sq. ft.
This ceiling will require approximately two quarts of paint. (A flat finish is recommended to minimize surface imperfections.)

For Doors, Windows, and Trim
■ The area for the doors and windows has been calculated above. (The windowpane area that does not get painted should allow for enough paint for any trim around doors and windows.) Determine the baseboard trim by taking the perimeter of the room, less 3 feet per door (3 ft. x 2 = 6 ft.), and multiplying this by the average trim width of your baseboard, which in this example is 6 inches (or 0.5 feet).
50 ft. (perimeter) – 6 ft. = 44 ft.
44 ft. x 0.5 ft. = 22 sq. ft.

■ Add the area for doors, windows, and baseboard trim.

```
 42 sq. ft.  (doors)
+30 sq. ft.  (windows)
+22 sq. ft.  (baseboard trim)
 94 sq. ft.
```

One quart will be sufficient to cover the doors, windows, and trim in this example.

–courtesy M.A.B. Paints

HOW MUCH DO YOU NEED?
Lumber and Nails

The amount of lumber and nails you need will depend on your project, but these guidelines will help you determine quantities of each.

Lumber Width and Thickness (in inches)

Nominal Size	Actual Size DRY OR SEASONED	Nominal Size	Actual Size DRY OR SEASONED
1 x 3	¾ x 2½	2 x 3	1½ x 2½
1 x 4	¾ x 3½	2 x 4	1½ x 3½
1 x 6	¾ x 5½	2 x 6	1½ x 5½
1 x 8	¾ x 7¼	2 x 8	1½ x 7¼
1 x 10	¾ x 9¼	2 x 10	1½ x 9¼
1 x 12	¾ x 11¼	2 x 12	1½ x 11¼

Nail Sizes

The nail on the left is a 5d (penny) finish nail; on the right, 20d common. The numerals below the nail sizes indicate the approximate number of nails per pound.

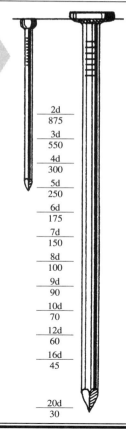

Lumber Measure in Board Feet

Size in inches	12 ft.	14 ft.	16 ft.	18 ft.	20 ft.
1 x 4	4	4⅔	5⅓	6	6⅔
1 x 6	6	7	8	9	10
1 x 8	8	9⅓	10⅔	12	13⅓
1 x 10	10	11⅔	13⅓	15	16⅔
1 x 12	12	14	16	18	20
2 x 3	6	7	8	9	10
2 x 4	8	9⅓	10⅔	12	13⅓
2 x 6	12	14	16	18	20
2 x 8	16	18⅔	21⅓	24	26⅔
2 x 10	20	23⅓	26⅔	30	33⅓
2 x 12	24	28	32	36	40
4 x 4	16	18⅔	21⅓	24	26⅔
6 x 6	36	42	48	54	60
8 x 8	64	74⅔	85⅓	96	106⅔
10 x 10	100	116⅔	133⅓	150	166⅔
12 x 12	144	168	192	216	240

Nail sizes (number per pound):

2d	875
3d	550
4d	300
5d	250
6d	175
7d	150
8d	100
9d	90
10d	70
12d	60
16d	45
20d	30

The Golden Rule

(It's true in all faiths.)

Brahmanism:
This is the sum of duty: Do naught unto others which would cause you pain if done to you.
Mahabharata 5:1517

Buddhism:
Hurt not others in ways that you yourself would find hurtful.
Udana-Varga 5:18

Christianity:
All things whatsoever ye would that men should do to you, do ye even so to them; for this is the law and the prophets.
Matthew 7:12

Confucianism:
Surely it is the maxim of loving-kindness: Do not unto others what you would not have them do unto you. *Analects 15:23*

Islam:
No one of you is a believer until he desires for his brother that which he desires for himself.
Sunnah

Judaism:
What is hateful to you, do not to your fellowman. That is the entire Law; all the rest is commentary. *Talmud, Shabbat 31a*

Taoism:
Regard your neighbor's gain as your own gain and your neighbor's loss as your own loss.
T'ai Shang Kan Ying P'ien

Zoroastrianism:
That nature alone is good which refrains from doing unto another whatsoever is not good for itself.
Dadistan-i-dinik 94:5

—courtesy Elizabeth Pool

Famous Last Words

■ **Waiting, are they? Waiting, are they? Well—let 'em wait.**
(In response to an attending doctor who attempted to comfort him by saying, "General, I fear the angels are waiting for you.")
—Ethan Allen, American Revolutionary general, d. February 12, 1789

■ **A dying man can do nothing easy.**
—Benjamin Franklin, American statesman, d. April 17, 1790

■ **Now I shall go to sleep. Good night.**
—Lord George Byron, British writer, d. April 19, 1824

■ **Is it the Fourth?**
—Thomas Jefferson, 3rd U.S. president, d. July 4, 1826

■ **Thomas Jefferson—still survives . . .**
(Actually, Jefferson had died earlier that same day.)
—John Adams, 2nd U.S. president, d. July 4, 1826

■ **Friends, applaud. The comedy is finished.**
—Ludwig van Beethoven, German-Austrian composer, d. March 26, 1827

■ **Moose . . . Indian . . .**
—Henry David Thoreau, American writer, d. May 6, 1862

■ **Go on, get out—last words are for fools who haven't said enough.**
(To his housekeeper, who urged him to tell her his last words so she could write them down for posterity.)
—Karl Marx, German political philosopher, d. March 14, 1883

■ **Is it not meningitis?**
—Louisa M. Alcott, American writer, d. March 6, 1888

■ **How were the receipts today at Madison Square Garden?**
—P. T. Barnum, American entrepreneur, d. April 7, 1891

■ **Turn up the lights, I don't want to go home in the dark.**
—O. Henry (William Sidney Porter), American writer, d. June 4, 1910

■ **Get my swan costume ready.**
—Anna Pavlova, Russian ballerina, d. January 23, 1931

■ **I should never have switched from Scotch to martinis.**
—Humphrey Bogart, American actor, d. January 14, 1957

■ **Is everybody happy? I want everybody to be happy. I know I'm happy.**
—Ethel Barrymore, American actress, d. June 18, 1959

■ **I'm bored with it all.**
(Before slipping into a coma. He died nine days later.)
—Winston Churchill, British statesman, d. January 24, 1965